Social Work Policy Practice

Social Work Policy Practice

Changing Our Community, Nation, and the World

Third Edition

JESSICA A. RITTER

Metropolitan State University of Denver

cognella® ACADEMIC PUBLISHING

Bassim Hamadeh, CEO and Publisher

Amy Smith, Senior Project Editor

Jeanine Rees, Production Editor

Emely Villavicencio, Senior Graphic Designer

Alexa Lucido, Licensing Manager

Jennifer Redding, Interior Designer

Natalie Piccotti, Director of Marketing

Kassie Graves, Senior Vice President of Editorial

Jamie Giganti, Director of Academic Publishing

This book was previously published by: Pearson Education, Inc.

Printed in the United States of America.

Dedication

This book is dedicated to my family, who provide me with immeasurable levels of love, support, and groundedness. My heartfelt thanks goes to: My father, Clint Ritter, for reading all of my chapters and giving me invaluable feedback. You helped inspire my passion for politics and the importance of fighting for the underdog; my mother, Christina Ritter, for sharing my interest in politics and teaching me how women can be compassionate, strong, and fierce; and my sister, Alissa Ritter, for your constant focus and dedication to righting what is wrong in this world and for being my best friend in this life.

And to all of the social justice advocates, who work tirelessly, without fame, accolades, or recognition, to change the world for the better, every day, one small and sometimes large, step at a time.

Brief Contents

Detailed Contents

ACTIVE LEARNING

This book has interactive activities available to complement your reading.

Your instructor may have customized the selection of activities available for your unique course. Please check with your professor to verify whether your class will access this content through the Cognella Active Learning portal (http://active.cognella.com) or through your home learning management system.

Preface

Some social work majors are not exactly overjoyed when they learn that they will be required to take one, and sometimes two, courses focused on social work policy practice. They find it perplexing because they want to work directly with individuals, families, and communities; if they wanted to learn about political advocacy, the political process, and how laws are enacted, they would have majored in political science after all! The purpose of this book is to demystify the world of policy-making and demonstrate why this is an exciting and critical dimension of social work practice. After all, social work's mission of social justice and person-in-environment perspective sets it apart from almost all other helping professions in the United States. This book argues that all social work is political.

Vision of Book

The vision of this book, and what sets it apart from other policy practice texts, is that it reads as an extremely engaging and accessible policy practice text for social work students who are often not very excited about policy practice, despite its importance in fulfilling the profession's mission of social justice, currently and historically. Students are provided with an extensive introductory overview that will allow them to begin doing work in the legislative and/or political arena. The ultimate aim is to inspire students to engage in political advocacy as a social worker (no matter what field of practice they want to work in).

The **key to bringing this material to life** is the inclusion of multiple stories of groups of people who set out to work for an important policy change (in Chapters 7–12). By reading these stories, students (1) learn *how* social workers effect change in the political arena; (2) see that it is not as intimidating as they might think to be a change agent in this environment; and (3) are inspired by stories of advocates making a real difference on behalf of various vulnerable groups in our society by engaging in the policy-making process at the local, state, federal, and even international levels.

New to This Edition

This book is a third edition that has been fully updated to be as current as possible with regard to policy issues in child welfare, aging, health care, mental health, poverty and income inequality, rights for racial minorities, and immigration. A new chapter titled "Advocacy for Gender Equality and LGBTQ rights" was added to the second edition to capture important policy issues with regard to gender, sexual orientation, and gender identity. Fresh material was added on social movements that have recently emerged such as #MeToo and #BlackLivesMatter. Finally, new material regarding the Trump presidency, 2020 presidential election, and coronavirus pandemic was added.

Part I includes four chapters that provide an introduction to social work policy practice in the United States. Chapter 1 sets the stage by exploring the social work profession's mission of social justice and how policy practice helps fulfill that mission. It highlights the tensions that exist within the profession, which have led some social work scholars to argue that social work has largely neglected the policy realm. It defines social work policy practice and social welfare policy. Chapter 2 provides a brief history of social welfare legislation in the United States and the role of social workers in the development of policies that have advanced human rights and the well-being of vulnerable, underserved populations. Chapter 3 explores the critical role of values and ideology that are inherent in political debate surrounding social welfare policy. Finally, Chapter 4 is a chapter on economic literacy, which shows very clearly the connection between economics and politics, and how in many cases economic issues are the most political of all.

Part II of this book includes Chapters 5 and 6. The purpose of these two chapters is to provide concrete information about how policies get enacted into law and *how* to engage in policy practice. Chapter 5 contains content on civics 101, an overview of the levels and branches of government as well as the U.S. judicial system. A thorough description of the six stages of the policy change process is also included. Chapter 6 outlines and describes the various strategies that are used when advocates are working for policy change, such as coalition building, lobbying, creating advocacy materials, using social media, and testifying at a legislative hearing.

Part III has six chapters that include compelling stories of advocates and advocacy organizations in their efforts to make changes in the political and/or legal arenas on behalf of vulnerable populations in the United States. The topical areas covered include healthcare, mental healthcare, child welfare and children's rights, advocacy for aging adults, end-of-life policies, advocacy for racial justice, immigrant rights, and advocacy for gender equality and LGBTQ rights. By critically evaluating these stories, students can learn from the tactics and strategies used by these change agents.

The **final chapter of the book**, Chapter 13, summarizes the major themes of the book and provides a look towards the future by discussing hot-button policy issues on the horizon that are of interest to the social work profession. Chapter 13 also provides an important discussion of needed advocacy efforts on behalf of the social work profession itself. After reading this book, students will have a thorough understanding of why social work practice includes policy practice and why this must be one of the tools in our toolbox for creating needed social and political change at the macro level.

Part I

CHAPTER 1

Policy Practice

The Hidden Side of Social Work

"Action indeed is the sole medium of expression for ethics."

~Jane Addams (1860–1935), early social worker, founder of Hull House, Chicago

Figure 1.1   Social workers at a political rally

CHAPTER SUMMARY

Chapter 1 explores the social work profession's mission of social justice and how social work policy practice helps fulfill that mission. Most are aware of social workers' activities at the individual level, but do not realize that social workers have a rich history of working in a political context on behalf of various social causes and client populations. Since the profession's beginning, social workers have engaged in political advocacy in efforts to achieve social justice for the poor and disenfranchised in society. Evidence of the social work profession's commitment to social change and political action on behalf of marginalized populations can be seen in various sections of the National Association of Social Worker's Code of Ethics (2017), particularly in section 6, which outlines social workers' ethical obligation to engage in social and political action in order to advocate for policies and legislation that promote social justice and improve individuals' capacity to develop and meet their basic human needs.

Chapter 1 highlights the tensions and criticisms that exist within the profession, which have led some social work scholars to argue that social work has largely neglected the macro realm and that social workers are not adequately prepared for work in the legislative or political arena. Despite this, some social work scholars argue that policy practice is as integral to the social work profession as is the study of human behavior. For social workers, *policy practice* is defined as "efforts to change policies in legislative, agency, and community settings, whether by establishing new policies, improving existing ones or defeating the policy initiatives of other people" (Jansson, 2008, p. 14), which are undertaken by social workers as an integral part of their professional activity with the aim of contributing to the well-being of service users (Gal & Weiss-Gal, 2013). There are many levels of policy change that social workers may try to impact, such as laws and policies at the local, state, federal, and international levels, as well as administrative policies where social workers are employed.

Despite the fact that social workers often find politics to be corrupt and distasteful, and the legislative process to be intimidating, it is important that they share their expertise with elected officials in order to help shape crucial policies that benefit the individuals and families whom they serve. To be effective change agents in the legislative arena, social workers must understand the policy process and the political arena and develop the advocacy skills that are needed to be effective in this exciting, yet often challenging, environment. When social workers are not involved with political advocacy, they are neglecting to use an important tool in their toolbox. Perhaps the most powerful reason to be engaged in political action is that it is an opportunity for social workers to be advocates—to be the voice of those who have little political power.

STUDENT LEARNING OBJECTIVES

- Students will be able to explain the social work profession's commitment to social justice and summarize the criticisms that have been leveled against the profession.

- Students will be able to define policy practice and differentiate the three levels of social welfare policy.

- Students will be able to identify the reasons why policies are powerful and should be in every social worker's toolbox.

- Students will be able to describe social workers' ethical obligation to engage in social and political action.

- Students will be able to critically examine whether "all social work is political."

M ost people have no idea that there is a political dimension to social work practice in the United States and around the world. That is why the title of this chapter is "Policy Practice: The Hidden Side of Social Work." When most people think about social workers, the most common image that springs to mind is a professional who works directly with individuals and families experiencing a range of problems such as poverty, child abuse, family violence, substance abuse, illness, and other problems of daily living. They envision trained professionals who work in a range of settings such as government agencies, hospitals, domestic violence programs, homeless shelters, schools, residential settings for older adults, and various nonprofit and community organizations. Even college students who enter social work programs in universities across the country are often surprised, and later delighted, to learn that social work includes **macro practice** and that one of the core values of the social work profession is **social justice**. In the policy arena, social workers work to support social policies that advance social justice. Social justice can be conceptualized or defined in a number of ways:

- Justice in terms of distribution of wealth, opportunities, and privileges within a society
- The ability people have to realize their potential in the society in which they live
- Promoting a just society by challenging injustice
- Promotion of human rights and a fair allocation of community resources
- Equal opportunity in society
- Justice as fairness

Using Social Policy to Advance Social Justice

The social work profession has long recognized that to help people change efforts must be directed at both the individual, or **micro-level**, and at the **macro-level**, which can include the neighborhood, community, or broader society where one resides. Thus, one of the defining features of the profession is a dual focus on individuals and their social environment, what we refer to as the **person-in-environment perspective** (see Figure 1.2). A basic tenet of social work is that when helping individuals sometimes the appropriate target of intervention is the individual (e.g., when someone needs assistance with various problems of daily living), whereas at other times it is necessary to target social systems, societal structures, and social injustices within the individual's social environment (e.g., discrimination, social stratification, violence, poverty, income inequality).

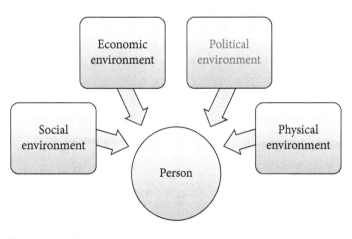

Figure 1.2   Person-in-environment perspective

This dual commitment to individuals and their social environment is clearly articulated in the Preamble of the **Code of Ethics** of the National Association of Social Workers (2017).

Most are aware of social workers' activities at the individual level, but do not realize that social workers have a rich history of working in a political context on behalf of various social causes and client populations. Since the profession's beginning, social workers have engaged in political advocacy in efforts to achieve social justice for the poor and disenfranchised in society. Some of the most politically active social workers were the **settlement house workers** during the late 1800s and early 1900s. In their efforts to improve living conditions for immigrants and those living in poverty, they influenced state and federal legislation on issues such as child labor, women's suffrage, occupational safety, and immigrant rights. During the Great Depression, social workers were involved in the development of humane federal policies for the millions thrown into poverty, and during the 1960s many social workers engaged in **community organizing** and worked to support the developing fight for welfare rights and civil rights (see Chapter 2 for a more detailed history). Today, you can find social workers working in an array of settings (e.g., advocacy organizations, legislators' offices) that are focused on advocacy and policy change efforts.

Evidence of the social work profession's commitment to social change and political action on behalf of the poor and disenfranchised can be seen in various sections of the National Association of Social Worker's Code of Ethics (2017), particularly in section 6, which outlines social workers' ethical obligation to engage in social and political action (see below).

6.04 Social and Political Action (a) Social workers should engage in social and political action that seeks to ensure that all people have equal access to the resources, employment, services, and opportunities they require to meet their basic human needs and to develop fully. Social workers should be aware of the impact of the political arena on practice and should advocate for changes in policy and legislation to improve social conditions to meet basic human needs and promote social justice

Source: National Association of Social Workers. (2017). Code of Ethics. Approved by the 1996 NASW Delegate Assembly and revised by the 2017 NASW Delegate Assembly. Retrieved from https://www.socialworkers.org/About/Ethics/Code-of-Ethics/Code-of-Ethics-English

---

Additionally, the Council on Social Work Education's 2015 Educational Policy and Accreditation Standards require accredited social work programs to prepare students for policy practice and help them understand the impact of policies and legislation on service delivery in the United States.

The Debate Between the "Micro-Changers" and the "Macro-Changers"

Despite social work's history of political advocacy and the language that is included in a few of the most important documents of the social work profession, some social work academics have argued that this commitment to social justice and political action is not carried out in practice (Byers & Stone, 1999; Figueira-McDonough, 1993; Harding, 2004; Haynes & Mickelson, 2009; Ritter, 2007, 2008; Shamai & Boehm, 2001; Specht & Courtney, 1994). The social work profession has historically had a love–hate relationship with politics, and depending on the decade, has alternated between being very active in advocacy and legislative efforts and being relatively absent from the political arena. Figueira-McDonough (1993) and Harding (2004) discuss the consequences of social workers' absence from the legislative process at home and abroad:

> Most often, the decision makers who define the contexts within which social workers practice their profession tend to have backgrounds in economics, law, management, and politics. This fact raises two problems. First, it subordinates the exercise of the social work profession to purposes and regulations that are not informed by and often not consistent with the goals and values of social work. Second, decisions that are likely to have enormous impact on the lives of the recipients are made by people who have little or no direct knowledge of that constituency or contact with their circumstances. Policy decisions are predominantly made from the top down without input from the ground up. In sum, the absence of social workers from social policy practice is damaging to the identity of the profession and to the clients whose interest they should represent and defend.

> (Figueira-McDonough, 1993, p. 180)

> Silence on global problems, especially those dealing with overtly political issues, reinforces the false notion that politics—especially on the international stage—has little bearing on the social work profession, education, and research. Given the numerous social problems that transcend national borders and impact human well-being. . . . the task of engagement with such issues is vital to creating policies worldwide that reflect the values of the profession.

> (Harding, 2004, pp. 180–181)

So, while some social workers are uncomfortable with the profession taking political stands and would prefer to operate above the political fray, others argue that social work is inherently political due to its emphasis on social change and quest for social justice. Others assert that social workers must often advocate for individuals, such as children, who cannot advocate for themselves in the political and/or legislative arena (Andrews, 1998).

Has Social Work Abandoned Its Mission of Social Justice?

Since the beginning, the profession has grappled with tensions between social workers who prefer radical political approaches versus moderates who believe in the adaptability of the American political system and are uneasy with radical thoughts and behaviors. The social work profession has been accused of neglecting its commitment to social problems such as racism, poverty, and income inequality and of being more committed to private practice and efforts to enhance the status of the profession. Epstein (1992) argued that social work disengaged from the economically disadvantaged as a result of being tempted into a "Faustian bargain"—professional gain at the expense of its obligation to marginal populations (p. 154). Specht and Courtney's controversial book *Unfaithful Angels* (1994) claimed that social work has abandoned its historic mission to the poor in favor of popular psychotherapies with the middle class. They argued that social work is at risk of being undifferentiated from other mental health or counseling professions. Social work has also been criticized by those outside of the profession. In 1945, the famous community organizer Saul Alinsky made his views about social workers abundantly clear:

> They come to the people of the slums not to help them rebel and fight their way out of the muck … most social work does not even reach the submerged masses. Social work is largely a middle class activity and guided by a middle class psychology. In the rare instances where it reaches the slum dwellers it seeks to get them adjusted to their environment so they will live in hell and like it. A higher form of treason would be difficult to conceive.

> (cited in Homan, 2016, p. 5)

Thus, a fundamental criticism that the social work profession has long grappled with is whether it has been more committed to improving people's lives via individual interventions at the expense of working to create needed social and political change at the local, state, national, and international levels. It appears that the person-in-environment perspective that defines the social work profession, and sets it apart from other helping professions, has also created tensions between clinical-oriented social workers and those with a macro-change focus. Some have characterized this conflict as a profession "at war with itself" (Thompson, 1994, p. 457), whereas others have described it as a healthy debate between the "micro-changers" and the "macro-changers," which only becomes destructive when one declares itself to be "the profession" (Abramovitz & Bardill, 1993, p. 14).

This debate has been argued on a number of levels: What is the appropriate role of a profession in political activity and social change? Should social work have a political ideology, or does it require professional impartiality? Because most social workers come from the middle-class or majority culture, do the values of the social work profession lean toward preservation of the status quo rather than social change? Is social work a dissenting profession or an acquiescing profession? Should the profession have a special commitment to serve those who are low income and marginalized? In short, how political should the social work profession be?

Is All Social Work Political?

Some social work scholars, such as Haynes and Mickelson (2009), have argued that "all social work is political" and that political advocacy is central to the mission of the profession. However, social services are provided through a political process over which social workers seem to have little influence. As Epstein (1992) observed, "Physicians are in charge of medical care; lawyers of legal practice; but social workers are not in charge of social service agencies" (p. 160). Ortiz, Wirz, Semion, and Rodriguez (2004) further argue, "As a profession wholly dependent on social policy for practice, the profession needs to continue to find ways to increase its presence in the policy arena" (p. 67).

However, despite the many criticisms that have been leveled at the social work profession, there is evidence of the profession's dedication to political action and there has been a resurgent focus on social work policy practice in recent years, which has been a very exciting development. All social work programs accredited by the Council on Social Work Education are required to prepare students to engage in policy practice; of the nine social work competencies included in the 2015 Educational Policy and Accreditation Standards, number 5 is "Engage in policy practice." Additionally, there are a small number of social work programs in the United States that offer concentrations in macro-level social work, which includes policy change. In 1997, Influencing Social Policy (www.influencingsocial-policy.org) was formed by 30 social work practitioners and educators. The mission of this organization is to assist faculty and students in learning how to influence effectively the formation, implementation, and evaluation of state-level policy and legislation. They accomplish this by organizing a yearly conference that is focused on social work policy practice, sending information to their member database via email, and by giving monetary awards to recognize the political action activities undertaken by social work students and faculty.

The Social Welfare Action Alliance (SWAA; www.socialwelfareactionalliance.org) is a "national organization of progressive workers in social welfare" that works primarily on issues of peace and social justice. Furthermore, a significant number of social workers feel committed to macro-level change efforts. Dickinson (2007) found that 83% of social workers strongly agreed with or agreed with the statement, "Actions for improving social conditions should be a primary responsibility for all social workers."

Indeed, the National Association of Social Workers (NASW) has embraced the view that the profession should be involved in both the legislative and electoral processes. NASW, and many of its state chapters, employ professional lobbyists who work on legislation that impacts professional practice and various social welfare policy initiatives. In 1976, NASW established a political action committee called PACE (Political Action for Candidate Election), which endorses and financially contributes to candidates (from any party) who support NASW's legislative agenda. Many NASW state chapters also have formally organized political action committees (PACs), which is the legal designation for groups that want to be involved in activities to elect candidates to political office. NASW publishes a book titled *Social Work Speaks* that includes policy positions on various political issues such as capital punishment, end-of-life care, health care, immigration, human trafficking, environmental policy, economic justice, and family planning and reproductive choice, just to name a few. And a significant portion of the NASW website is dedicated to advocacy and includes information on current legislation, includes tips on communicating with elected officials, and enables members to sign up for legislative action alerts.

In 2011, the Congressional Social Work Congress (http://socialworkcaucus-lee.house.gov) was formed to represent the interests of the over 600,000 social workers in the United States and the individuals and communities they serve. Members of this caucus consist of those in Congress who are social workers and those who share the values and commitment of the social work profession. They do this by organizing briefings on Capitol Hill, facilitating social work internships on the Hill, and sponsoring legislation that enables social workers to respond to the country's most pressing social problems. The caucus is currently chaired by Congresswoman Barbara Lee from the state of California.

The Congressional Research Institute for Social Work and Policy (CRISP) is a 501(c)(4) organization that was formed in 2012 to support and complement the work that is being done by the Congressional Social Work Congress. CRISP is "committed to expanding the participation of social workers in federal legislative and policy processes" (http://crispinc.org). CRISP works to facilitate communication between social work researchers and the federal government to ensure that their research is known to federal policymakers, and they also work to expand internship or practicum opportunities for social work students. They organize congressional briefings on Capitol Hill on a range of topics, most recently focused on racism and policing and the role of social workers in addressing these problems. They organize lobby days at the nation's Capitol for social work students and professional social workers.

Finally, in recent years a Special Commission to Advance Macro Practice in Social Work was established by leaders of the Association for Community Organization and Social Administration (ACOSA). The focus of this group is to enhance macro-level social work and to give it the same emphasis as micro-level social work in social work education and practice.

What Exactly Is "Policy Practice"?

Some social work leaders and scholars argue that policy practice is as integral to the social work profession as is the study of human behavior. Social workers recognize that most social problems require interventions at both the micro level and the macro level, and sometimes they demand a policy solution. For example, many social workers work with parents to help them address problems that are occurring within their family, such as substance abuse or harmful discipline practices that are placing their children at risk of child abuse and/or neglect. These adults may receive a range of services such as individual counseling, parenting classes, and substance abuse treatment. However, there are times when social workers must enter the legislative arena to propose legislation, or advocate for legislation, that addresses the social problem of child abuse and neglect at the local, state, or federal level. Examples of legislation might include requesting increased funding for parent education, substance abuse programs, or other prevention programs; improved training and support for child welfare workers; harsher penalties for those who seriously harm children; incentives for people who foster or adopt children in the foster care system; or assistance to foster youth who age out of the foster care system after graduating from high school.

According to Weiss-Gal (2017), there are two primary routes for social workers to be engaged in policy work: (1) voluntary civic engagement and (2) professional policy practice.

Many social workers get involved politically as private citizens, for example. These are activities that occur outside of their professional work, such as voting, attending a political rally or protest, volunteering for a political campaign, and even running for political office. Policy practice, in contrast, includes activities that occur in social workers' work settings when it is part of their job responsibilities. For example, this would include social workers who work as lobbyists, are employed by an advocacy organization or legislator's office, or social workers who use their skills and knowledge to influence policy in some way. **Policy practice** is defined as "efforts to change policies in legislative, agency, and community settings, whether by establishing new policies, improving existing ones or defeating the policy initiatives of other people" (Jansson, 2008, p. 14), which are undertaken by social workers as an integral part of their professional activity with the aim of contributing to the well-being of service users (Gal & Weiss-Gal, 2013).

This realm of work is also sometimes referred to as **political advocacy**. Advocacy should not be a new concept for social workers because this is a role that we often take on in our professional work. However, it may be helpful to think about the difference between case advocacy and cause advocacy. **Case advocacy** occurs when a social worker represents the interests of or defends the rights of an individual or family. For example, social workers may serve as an advocate for a victim of domestic violence or child abuse within the court system. This book is more about cause advocacy, however. **Cause advocacy** occurs when a social worker is representing the interests of or defending the rights of groups of people. In the political arena, for example, social workers might work to pass legislation that protects the rights of LGBTQ Americans from job discrimination in the workplace or legislation that protects older adults from financial exploitation.

Social workers may try to impact policy change at three levels: micro, mezzo, and micro. At the **macro level**, social workers work to pass legislation or policies at the international, federal, state, or local level. At the **mezzo level,** social workers try to influence policies within the organizations where they are employed. At the **micro level**, social workers are often charged with implementing policies that were passed at the macro and mezzo levels (see Figure 1.3). Policy practice also includes working to elect legislators with similar values, concerns, and priorities who are likely to support legislative efforts benefitting the various vulnerable populations that social workers serve. Finally, it should be noted that in order to be a successful change agent in this area of social work practice, many skills are necessary, such

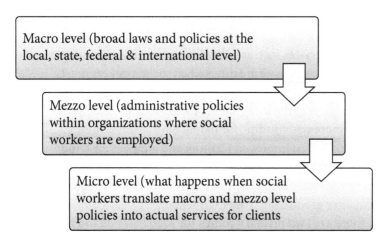

Macro level (broad laws and policies at the local, state, federal & international level)

Mezzo level (administrative policies within organizations where social workers are employed)

Micro level (what happens when social workers translate macro and mezzo level policies into actual services for clients

Figure 1.3   Three levels of policy change process

as organizing people, using the media, building a compelling argument, artfully framing an issue, building coalitions, conducting research, and producing professional written communication and/or campaign tools (see Chapters 5 and 6 for more on this).

This book focuses on how social workers can use public policy to advance social justice. In the simplest terms, **public policy** is what government (local, state, national, or international) does or does not do about a problem that comes before them for consideration and possible action. In this book, the word *policy* is used interchangeably with *legislation*, *bills*, and *laws*. Legislators consider proposed legislation, in the form of bills and resolutions, and once a bill has been passed by a legislative body it becomes law. And in some states, new laws can come about due to state ballot measures passed by the voters. The legislative branch of our government makes laws, and the judicial branch of our government interprets laws according to the U.S. Constitution.

Social work students often wonder why they have to learn about politics in their social policy courses. Is it not enough to learn about our systems of government, how laws are enacted, and how to logically navigate through that process? **Politics**, at its most basic definition, is the process by which groups make decisions. In 1936, a political scientist named Harold Lasswell wrote a book titled, *Politics: Who Gets What, When, How,* and this later became the standard lay definition of politics. Politics can be found in all kinds of groups, organizations, and institutions—even in families! We often see politics playing out in the workplace or any environment where there are power dynamics at play. People who are good at politics are skilled at using their power to get what they want. *Merriam-Webster's Dictionary* (n.d.) defines politics as "the art or science concerned with guiding or influencing government policy" or "with winning and holding control over a government."

Some may like the idea of legislators using some sort of objective or rational problem-solving model when they are making policy decisions. They would learn about the problem, discuss various alternatives that could be used to address the problem, and choose the best option based on the available research and evidence. However, for good or bad, the legislative process is embedded in a larger political process that involves personal values, political ideology, political parties vying for power, compromise, and powerful special interests who have a great deal of influence with legislators.

It is understandable that many Americans are turned off by politics since our political system often does not operate the way that we wish it did. It is an imperfect system that is sometimes corrupt and often operates in the interests of powerful special interests rather than the interests of ordinary people. The unfortunate outcome is that large numbers of citizens feel alienated from the political process and do not participate in the civic and political affairs of their community or government. Despite the fact that social workers often find politics to be corrupt and distasteful, and the legislative process to be intimidating, it is important that they share their expertise with elected officials in order to help shape crucial policies that benefit the individuals and families whom they serve. To be effective change agents in the legislative arena, social workers must understand the policy process and the political arena and develop the advocacy skills that are needed to be effective in this exciting, yet often challenging, environment.

Practice Activity 1.1

You are a social worker working in a community counseling center that serves individuals from the surrounding community, most of whom are Latinx. You work with them on a range of issues, including depression and other mental health disorders, family problems, and other challenges of daily living. You see your role as working directly with individuals and families in a micro context because this is where you feel most skilled and passionate.

However, a new law is being proposed in your border state to address some of the public's concerns about illegal immigration. This issue has been heating up in the last couple of years and has divided people living in various communities across the state. Racial tensions are at an all-time high. A new law proposed by the state legislature would do the following: To address the perceived problem of "anchor babies," children who were born in the United States but whose parents do not have legal status will be denied social services from many state programs.

Questions

1. Think about your own values and the values of the social work profession. How does this proposed law fit within those values? *Personally*, do you agree or disagree with this law? *Professionally*, do you agree or disagree with this law?

2. Google the term *anchor babies* to see what this phrase refers to and the various opinions out there regarding this loaded terminology.

3. According to the NASW Code of Ethics, what is your responsibility if you believe that this new law would be harmful to the clients you serve?

4. If you believe this new law causes harm, what actions would you take, if any? Brainstorm some possibilities.

5. How do you feel about taking this on? Does it seem scary or intimidating? Or, does this kind of work feel thrilling and energizing?

6. Should this be part of your job even though your work is primarily clinical? Why or why not?

Social Welfare Policy

There are many different types or categories of legislation: tax policy, transportation policy, environmental policy, education policy, energy policy, agriculture policy, labor policy, and foreign policy, just to name a few. However, this text will focus primarily on *social welfare* policy. The **social welfare system** in the United States refers to our nation's complex set of programs and services that address the health, social, economic, and educational needs of its citizens. A vast array of social welfare programs are offered at the local, state, and federal levels such as Social Security, Head Start, SNAP (formerly known as the Food Stamp

Program), unemployment compensation, Medicare, Medicaid, public education, college financial aid, TANF, public housing, the U.S. Department of Veterans Affairs, and many more. Though many people only think about government-funded social welfare programs, there are also many private organizations that receive government funding to assist people with these needs as well (e.g., faith-based organizations, nonprofit organizations, and for-profit organizations). Thus, **social welfare policy** specifically refers to legislation, laws, rules, and regulations that govern the vast social welfare system in the United States (please refer to Figure 1.4 for a sample of social welfare programs in the United States).

DiNitto and Johnson (2016) define *social welfare policy* as "anything a government chooses to do, or not to do, which affects the quality of life of its people" (p. 2). This is an interesting definition because it points out that there are some services that government may choose *not* to offer to its citizens and/or some social problems that they choose to ignore. One of the biggest political debates in the United States concerns what the role of government should be in regard to providing for the general welfare of its citizens. According to DiNitto and Johnson (2016), "The boundaries of social welfare policy are indeed fuzzy" but they define it as those policies that "directly affect the income, services, and opportunities available to people who are aged, poor, disabled, ill, or otherwise vulnerable" (p. 3). Social welfare policy includes many topics that are of interest to social workers, such as health; mental health; poverty and homelessness;

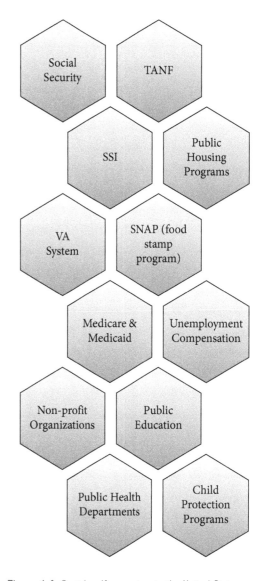

Figure 1.4. Social welfare system in the United States

criminal justice; family violence; education; civil rights; child welfare; and issues that affect women, older adults, those who are LGBTQ, and people with disabilities (see Figure 1.5).

When social workers are not involved with political advocacy, they are neglecting to use an important tool in their toolbox. Policies are powerful for the following reasons:

- Legislation can *create new social programs* or improve existing ones.
- Policies *determine funding levels* for many social welfare programs; many legislative efforts by social workers involve asking the government to preserve funding or appropriate additional resources for various programs and/or initiatives.

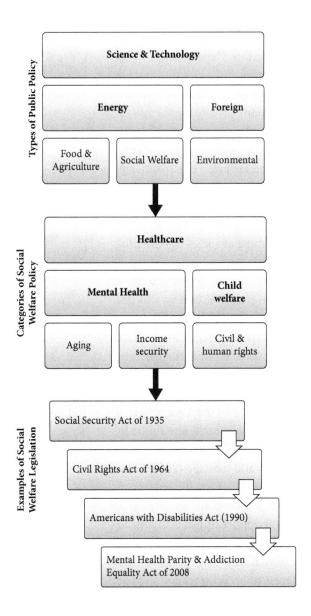

Figure 1.5 (a) Types of public policy, (b) Categories of social welfare policy, (c) Select examples of social welfare legislation

- Policies often *determine the goals* of social welfare programs, how they operate, and who is eligible to receive services.
- Legislation can be designed to *provide protections to vulnerable populations* and advance human rights.
- Policies can cause harm.

Though policies have the capacity to improve people's lives for the better, it is important to keep in mind that throughout U.S. history there are many examples of policies that have been harmful to groups of people, such as laws that legalized slavery; President Franklin Delano Roosevelt's executive order that forced thousands of Japanese Americans into internment camps during World War II; laws that forced Native Americans to give up their land and resettle (e.g., Indian Removal Act); Jim Crow laws that restricted the civil rights of African Americans and legally mandated racial segregation; stop-and-frisk policies used by police officers; laws that barred women from voting and made birth control illegal; and the "Don't Ask, Don't Tell" policy used in the military as well as state laws that barred same-sex couples from getting married or adopting children.

Are Social Workers Active Enough Politically?

A common critique from prominent academics in the field has been that there are low levels of political participation by practicing social work professionals. However, this should be put into context because Americans in general are criticized for their lack of civic and political engagement. Though many social work academics have written about the importance of social workers' engagement in the political process, surprisingly few empirical studies have examined this topic. The social work literature is full of studies and evaluations of clinical interventions, but strikingly few have assessed how well social workers are faring in the policy arena. This has only been examined in a handful of studies (see below).

Findings from Studies of Social Workers' Political Participation

- Social workers are more politically active than the general population and as active as other professional groups (Andrews, 1998; Ezell, 1993; Hamilton & Fauri, 2001; Parker & Sherraden, 1992; Ritter, 2007, 2008; Wolk, 1981).
- Most common political activities are voting, communicating directly with legislators, belonging to an organization that takes public stands, and attending political meetings or rallies (Andrews, 1998; Ezell, 1993; Hamilton & Fauri, 2001; Harris Rome & Hoechstetter, 2010; Ritter, 2007, 2008; Wolk, 1981).
- Least common political activities are volunteering for a political campaign, contributing financially to a campaign, voicing opinions through the media, attending a march or demonstration, and testifying before a legislative committee (Andrews, 1998; Ezell, 1993; Harris Rome & Hoechstetter, 2010; Ritter, 2007, 2008; Wolk, 1981).
- The most active social workers tend to be macro practitioners, older, more experienced, African American, belong to NASW or other professional association, high degree of political interest and efficacy, and have higher incomes and educational levels (Andrews, 1998; Ezell, 1993; Hamilton & Fauri, 2001; Harris Rome & Hoechstetter, 2010; Parker & Sherraden, 1992; Ritter, 2007, 2008; Wolk, 1981).

These studies show that social workers are more politically active than the general public, although there are a number of political activities where their participation is quite low (e.g., volunteering for a political campaign, contributing money to a campaign, testifying before a legislative committee, attending a march or demonstration, voicing one's opinion in the media). One analysis of social workers' political participation was a national study that surveyed licensed social workers from 11 states. This study found that approximately 46% of survey respondents can be characterized as "active" or "very active," while 54% can be considered "inactive" or "somewhat active" (Ritter, 2007). This study also found that social workers are twice as active as the public when it comes to advertising for a party or candidate during an election year, three times as active in contributing financially to a candidate or party, and four times as active when it comes to attending political meetings or rallies and volunteering for political campaigns. Harris Rome and Hoechstetter (2010) surveyed 1,274 professional social workers and found that 47% exhibited high levels of political activity while 53% ranked low. They reported that "many social workers continue to harbor ambivalent feelings toward participation in the political process" (p. 121). Sixty-five percent of the social workers in their sample agreed that every social worker has an obligation to promote policies that benefit his or her clients, while more than 30% disagreed that it is "part of my mission to empower my clients politically as well as personally" (p. 115).

It has been suggested that social workers do not receive sufficient preparation for work in the political arena. In other words, they must acquire the knowledge and skills necessary so they feel competent performing this role. One national study that surveyed licensed social workers from 11 states found that roughly half of social workers (47%) do not feel that they were adequately prepared by their social work program for work in the legislative arena (Ritter, 2007).

Practice Activity 1.2

Assess your own level of political participation by completing the following survey:

1. Did you happen to vote in the last presidential election?

   ○ Yes
   ○ No

2. During the last presidential campaign, did you volunteer to work for any candidate who was running for political office or for a political party (local, state, or national)?

   ○ Yes
   ○ No

3. During the last presidential campaign, did you talk to any people and try to persuade them why they should vote for or against one of the parties or candidates running for political office (local, state, or national)?

○ Yes
○ No

4. During the last presidential campaign, did you wear a campaign button or T-shirt, put a campaign sticker on your car, or place a sign in your window or in front of your residence?

    ○ Yes
    ○ No

5. During the last presidential campaign, did you attend any political meetings, rallies, speeches, dinners, or things like that in support of a particular candidate that was running?

    ○ Yes
    ○ No

6. During the last presidential campaign, did you make a financial contribution to a candidate, a political party, or any organization that was supporting candidates?

    ○ Yes
    ○ No

7. Are you currently a member of a political party or an organization that tries to influence public policy (e.g., NASW)?

    ○ Yes
    ○ No

8. In the last year, did you contact any local or federal officials about an issue you were concerned about—either in person, by phone, letter, or email?

    ○ Yes
    ○ No

9. In the past 2 years, have you taken part in a protest, consumer boycott, march, or demonstration on some national or local issue?

    ○ Yes
    ○ No

10. In the last 2 years, did you testify at a local, state, or federal legislative hearing?

    ○ Yes
    ○ No

11. In the last 2 years, did you voice your opinion on policy issues to a media outlet?

    ○ Yes
    ○ No

12. In the past year, did you lobby legislators or work to get legislation passed *as part of* your job?

   ○ Yes
   ○ No

Now count the number of "yes" answers that you marked. My score:
   0–4: Not Very Active
   5–8: Active
   9–12: Very Active

Being the Voice of the Voiceless

This book will demonstrate how social workers can impact the lives of many vulnerable populations by being advocates and working for policy change. Perhaps the biggest strength of the social work profession is the opportunity to effect change with individuals, families, groups, organizations, communities—and even at the national and international levels. There is no doubt that many social workers are motivated by the idea that you can change the world by changing the lives of individuals and families at the micro level. However, other social workers are motivated by the idea of changing the world by using policies and legislation for large-scale social and/or political change. Most social workers will end up doing both micro- and macro-level work over the course of their careers because the two are so intertwined.

Many social workers who want to work in direct services or clinical practice often wonder why they need to learn about the legislative process because their main desire is to help people one-on-one. This is a good question with multiple answers. First, all social workers are ethically bound to engage in social and political action as outlined in the NASW Code of Ethics. Furthermore, policies and laws impact the programs where social workers are employed and the clients they serve. For example, in recent years, federal legislators have made significant changes to the U.S. welfare system and the child welfare system. The **Personal Responsibility and Work Opportunity Act of 1996** created a new 5-year time limit for families receiving welfare, and the **Adoption and Safe Families Act of 1997** required states to follow a much shorter timeline when filing for the termination of parental rights. These were significant changes that dramatically impacted the work of social workers in these agencies as well as the lives of many vulnerable children and families. However, we should ask, "How many social workers were at the table, sharing their expertise with lawmakers, when these policies were being debated and considered?"

Because social workers have firsthand experience working with individuals, families, and communities, they should weigh in on whether proposed policies are sound. In other words, will the policy be effective in solving the identified problem? Is the policy supported by research and people with expertise? Does the policy operate in the best interests of the individuals that we serve? Does it promote the dignity and worth of individuals and their self-determination? How will the policy impact populations-at-risk? Does the policy support social justice, or does it seek to oppress?

Perhaps the most powerful reason to be engaged in political action is that it is an opportunity for social workers to be advocates—to be the voice of those who often have no voice on the political stage. Legislation can be extremely powerful and can create dramatic changes in our society, and there are numerous examples of this: The **Social Security Act of 1935**, which created the Social Security program in the United States, lifting millions of older adults out of poverty; the **Civil Rights Act of 1964** that outlawed racial segregation; legislation in the 1960s that created the **Medicare** and **Medicaid** programs; the **Americans with Disabilities Act**, which outlawed discrimination against people with disabilities and required buildings to be accessible; the **Mental Health Parity and Addiction Equity Act**, which required that health insurers provide coverage for mental illness and substance abuse treatment that is comparable to that provided for physical illnesses; and the **Matthew Shepard and James Byrd, Jr. Hate Crimes Prevention Act** that expanded federal hate crimes laws to include cases where a perpetrator targets a victim based on his or her perceived gender, sexual orientation, gender identity, or disability (named after Matthew Shepard and James Byrd, Jr. who were both killed in violent hate crime incidents).

Can All Problems Be Solved with Legislation?

This chapter has provided numerous examples where policies have been instrumental in improving conditions for various groups of people. However, it is important to keep in mind that not all problems can be solved via legislation. Social work programs prepare students to be **generalist social work practitioners,** which means that they are prepared to effect change with individuals, families, groups, organizations, and communities using a **planned change process** whereby the most appropriate intervention method(s) is determined. Sometimes policies that have little chance of success are proposed to solve the problem at hand. A skilled social worker has the knowledge and experience to understand when a problem requires a policy solution and when there is a more appropriate alternative.

For example, in recent years a number of cities and states have proposed legislation to ban smoking in cars when children are present, and it is believed that Bangor, Maine, was the first state to outlaw this practice in 2007. Parents who are caught are typically fined. Now, some believe that this is an example of a brilliant piece of legislation that has the power to protect children from harmful secondhand smoke. Others disagree and believe that there are better alternatives to punishing parents for this type of behavior. They argue that it would be more effective for cities or states to create effective public education campaigns to raise awareness about this issue (similar to campaigns that aimed to educate parents about shaken baby syndrome or the dangers of leaving children in a hot car). Perhaps there are other options that experts have determined to be most effective to address this problem. There are no easy answers, but social workers are trained to weigh the alternatives and select the method with the best possible outcome.

Work Settings for Social Workers Engaged in Social and Political Action

Social workers engaged in policy practice are interested in creating **social change** and **political change**. Social and political action often go hand in hand, and both are critical to advancing the health and welfare of oppressed groups. **Social action** involves promoting social change by advocating for the rights of marginalized or oppressed groups. A strong component of this work involves educating the public, raising awareness about important social problems, and working to change societal attitudes. **Political action** typically involves a range of activities that are designed to (1) pass legislation on behalf of a particular group and (2) elect legislators who support an organization's mission and political agenda. One question that may arise is, "Which one comes first—social change or political change?" Is it necessary to change attitudes before making progress politically on a particular issue, or will political change lead to social change? There is no easy answer to this question, and there are many examples throughout history to support both of these scenarios. For example, when the Civil Rights Act of 1964 was passed into law, policy change occurred before widespread social change (i.e., before hearts were changed with regard to racial equality), whereas same-sex marriage was legalized in the United States as a result of rapidly changing societal attitudes with regard to LGBTQ Americans. Social workers who wish to engage in policy practice can find employment working in an advocacy organization at the local, state, national, or international level. Examples of prominent advocacy organizations include the following:

- American Association of Retired Persons (AARP)
- American Cancer Society
- American Civil Liberties Union (ACLU)
- American Public Health Association
- Amnesty International
- Campaign to End the Death Penalty
- Child Welfare League of America
- Children's Defense Fund
- Children's Rights
- Coalition on Human Needs
- Death with Dignity National Center
- Disability Rights Advocates
- Dream Activist
- Every Child Matters
- Gray Panthers
- Human Rights Campaign (HRC)
- Human Rights Watch
- Innocence Project
- Mothers Against Drunk Driving
- NAACP

- National Alliance on Mental Illness (NAMI)
- National Association of Social Workers
- National Center for Victims of Crime
- National Coalition Against Domestic Violence
- National Coalition for the Homeless
- National Council of La Raza
- National Network for Immigrant and Refugee Rights
- National Organization for Women (NOW)
- National Urban League
- Physicians for a National Health Program
- Planned Parenthood
- Save the Children
- Service Employees International Union
- Stand for Children
- Transgender Law Center
- United Farmworkers

Note: this list is not exhaustive

Every day social workers and advocates in the United States, and around the world, fight for laws and policies that advance social and economic justice for many vulnerable groups, such as children, older adults, women, ethnic and sexual minorities, those with disabilities, and people living in poverty. In this book, a number of their stories will be told. However, first it is important to revisit three critical periods in U.S. history where significant efforts were made to radically improve the social welfare of its citizens.

REFERENCES

Abramovitz, M., & Bardill, D. R. (1993). Should all social work students be educated for social change? *Journal of Social Work Education, 29*(1), 6–18.

Andrews, A. B. (1998). An exploratory study of political attitudes and acts among child and family services workers. *Children and Youth Services Review, 20*, 435–461.

Byers, K., & Stone, G. (1999). Roots of activism: A qualitative study of BSW students. *Journal of Baccalaureate Social Work, 5*(1), 1–14.

Council on Social Work Education (2015). 2015 educational policy and accreditation standards. Retrieved from https://www.cswe.org/getattachment/Accreditation/Accreditation-Process/2015-EPAS/2015EPAS_Web_FINAL.pdf.aspx

Dickinson, J. C. (2007). A survey of social policy placements in BSW education. *Journal of Policy Practice, 6*(1), 47–63.

DiNitto, D. M., & Johnson, D. H. (2016). *Social welfare: Politics and public policy* (8th ed.). Boston, MA: Pearson.

Epstein, W. M. (1992) Professionalization of social work: The American experience. *Social Science Journal, 29*(2), 153–166.

Ezell, M. (1993). The political activities of social workers: A post-Reagan update. *Journal of Sociology and Social Welfare, 20*(4), 81–98.

Figueira-McDonough, J. (1993). Policy practice: The neglected side of social work intervention. *Social Work, 38*(2), 179–188.

Gal, J., & Weiss-Gal, I. (2013). *Social workers affecting social policy: An international perspective.* Bristol, UK: Policy Press.

Hamilton D., & Fauri, D. (2001). Social workers' political participation: Strengthening the political confidence of social work students. *Journal of Social Work Education, 37*(2), 321–332.

Harding, S. (2004). The sound of silence: Social work, the academy, and Iraq. *Journal of Sociology and Social Welfare, 31,* 179–197.

Harris Rome, S., & Hoechstetter, S. (2010). Social work and civic engagement: The political participation of professional social workers. *Journal of Sociology and Social Welfare, 37*(3), 107–129.

Haynes, K., & Mickelson, J. (2009). *Affecting change: Social workers in the political arena* (7th ed.). Boston, MA: Pearson.

Homan, M. (2016). *Promoting community change: Making it happen in the real world* (6th ed.). Boston: Cenage Learning.

Jansson, B. S. (2008). *Becoming an effective policy advocate: From policy practice to social justice* (5th ed.). Belmont, CA: Brooks/Cole.

Lasswell, H. (1936). *Politics: Who gets what, when, how.* McGraw-Hill, New York.

Merriam-Webster's Dictionary. (n.d.). Politics. Retrieved from https://www.merriam-webster.com/dictionary/politics

National Association of Social Workers. (2017). Code of Ethics. Approved by the 1996 NASW Delegate Assembly and revised by the 2017 NASW Delegate Assembly. Retrieved from https://www.socialworkers.org/About/Ethics/Code-of-Ethics/Code-of-Ethics-English

Ortiz, L. P., Wirz, C., Semion, K., & Rodriguez, C. (2004). Legislative casework: Where policy and practice intersect. *Journal of Sociology and Social Welfare, 31,* 49–68.

Parker, M., & Sherraden, M. (1992). Electoral participation of social workers. *New England Journal of Human Services, 11,* 23–28.

Ritter, J. A. (2006). An empirical study evaluating the political participation of licensed social workers in the United States: A multi-state study. Retrieved from https://repositories.lib.utexas.edu/bitstream/handle/2152/2629/ritterd28699.pdf

Ritter, J. A. (2007). Evaluating the political participation of licensed social workers in the new millennium. *Policy Practice Journal, 6*(4), 61–78.

Ritter, J. A. (2008). A national study predicting social workers' levels of political participation: The role of resources, psychological engagement, and recruitment networks. *Social Work, 53*(4), 347–357.

Shamai, M., & Boehm, A. (2001). Politically oriented social work intervention. *International Social Work, 44,* 343–360.

Specht, H., & Courtney, M. E. (1994). *Unfaithful angels: How social work has abandoned its mission.* New York, NY: The Free Press.

Thompson, J. J. (1994). Social workers and politics: Beyond the Hatch Act. *Social Work*, *39*(4), 457–465.

Weiss-Gal, E. (2017). What options do we have? Exploring routes for social workers' policy engagement. *Journal of Policy Practice*, *16*(3), 247–260.

Wolk, J. (1981). Are social workers politically active? *Social Work*, *26*, 283–288.

CHAPTER 2

Social Workers and Political Action

Three Relevant Historical Periods

"In these days of difficulty, we Americans everywhere must and shall choose the path of social justice, the path of faith, the path of hope and the path of love toward our fellow men."

~President Franklin Delano Roosevelt, campaign address, Detroit, Michigan, October 2, 1932

CHAPTER SUMMARY

Chapter 2 provides a brief history of social welfare legislation in the United States and the role of social workers in the development of policies that have advanced human rights and the well-being of vulnerable, underserved populations. Countries around the world have been faced with the dilemma of how to best assist citizens in need or in times of crisis. Some countries, such as many in Western Europe and Scandinavia, are known for having very generous social welfare systems, whereas others, such as many developing countries, cannot afford the luxury of having a social safety net for their citizens. The United States has been called "the reluctant welfare state" because the government and the American public have been ambivalent when it comes to answering the question, "Is it the role of the government to help provide for the general welfare of its citizens, and if so, to what extent?"

In fact, the United States did not have large-scale, federal social welfare programs until the presidency of Franklin Delano Roosevelt (FDR), when his administration was faced with a country reeling from the devastation caused by the Great Depression in the 1930s. Entire books have been written on the history of social welfare policies in the United States; this chapter provides an overview and highlights three very significant time periods in U.S. history when major advancements were made regarding how the U.S. government responded to the needs of vulnerable and struggling people by enacting historic, landmark social welfare legislation: the settlement house movement during the Progressive Era; the Great Depression and FDR's presidency; and President Johnson's Great Society during the 1960s. These time periods are also noteworthy because they mark a time when social workers were highly politically active and made efforts to push policymakers toward needed social change. The chapter ends by documenting the rise of conservatism in the 1980s through the present day in the United States and covers the presidential elections of Barack Obama, Donald Trump, and Joseph Biden. Some social work researchers and academics have observed that despite a number of policy issues and social problems that are of concern to the social work profession, such as rising income inequality and poverty rates, police brutality and systemic racism, healthcare reform, climate change, and efforts to dismantle the social safety net, social workers have largely retreated to their micro roles in recent decades.

Student Learning Objectives

- Students will be able to cite the individuals responsible for working to enact historic, landmark social welfare legislation in the United States.

- Students will be able to identify and describe important social welfare policies and programs that were passed into law since the Progressive Era in the United States.

- Students will be able to analyze how the early efforts of social workers and government leaders influenced current social welfare policies and programs.

- Students will critically examine where we are today with regard to the enactment of social welfare legislation to meet the needs of marginalized and vulnerable populations.

Countries around the world have been faced with the dilemma of how to best assist citizens in need or in times of crisis. Some countries, such as many in Western Europe and Scandinavia, are known for having very generous social welfare systems, while others, such as many developing countries, cannot afford the luxury of having a social safety net for their citizens. The United States has been called "the reluctant welfare state" by one scholar (Jansson, 2008) because the government and the American public have been quite ambivalent when it comes to answering the question, "Is it the role of the government to help provide for the general welfare of its citizens, and if so, to what extent?" In fact, the United States did not have large-scale, federal social welfare programs until the presidency of Franklin Delano Roosevelt (FDR) when his administration was faced with a country reeling from the devastation caused by the Great Depression. Entire books have been written on the history of social welfare policies in the United States; however, this chapter provides an overview and highlights three very significant time periods in recent U.S. history where major advancements were made regarding how the U.S. government responded to the needs of vulnerable and struggling people by enacting historic, landmark social welfare legislation. These time periods are also noteworthy because they mark a time when social workers were highly politically active and made efforts to push policymakers toward needed social change. The following box provides a list of important social welfare policies and court decisions that social workers should be familiar with.

Important Social Welfare Legislation and Court Decisions

1930s to 1950s: FDR's New Deal and Beyond
- Social Security Act of 1935 (created public assistance; unemployment compensation; Social Security; aid to the blind and disabled)
- National Labor Relations Act (1935)
- Fair Labor Standards Act (1938)
- GI Bill of Rights (1944)
- UN Declaration of Human Rights (1948)
- *Brown v. Board of Education* (1954)

1960s: LBJ's Great Society
- Equal Pay Act of 1963
- Civil Rights Act of 1964
- Economic Opportunity Act of 1964
- Food Stamp Act of 1964
- Voting Rights Act of 1965
- Elementary and Secondary Education Act of 1965
- Higher Education Act of 1965
- Older Americans Act (1965)
- Creation of Medicare and Medicaid programs (1965)
- Age Discrimination in Employment Act of 1967

1970s: Policies Affecting Women and Children
- *Roe v. Wade* (1973)
- Child Abuse Prevention and Treatment Act (1974)
- Individuals with Disabilities Education Act (1975)
- UN Convention on the Elimination of All Forms of Discrimination Against Women (1979)

1990s: A Mix of Progressive and Conservative Policies Passed into Law
- UN Convention on the Rights of the Child (1990)
- Americans with Disabilities Act (1990)
- Ryan White Care Act (1990)
- Family and Medical Leave Act (1993)
- Violence Against Women Act (1994)
- Defense of Marriage Act (1996)
- Personal Responsibility and Work Opportunity Reconciliation Act of 1996
- Adoption and Safe Families Act (1997)
- State Children's Health Insurance Program (1997)
- Oregon's Death with Dignity Act (1997)

Notable Policies and Court Decisions in the New Millennium

- No Child Left Behind (2001)
- *Atkins v. Virginia* (2002) (U.S. Supreme Court ruling that it is unconstitutional to execute those with intellectual disabilities)
- Medicare Prescription Drug Modernization Act (2003)
- Massachusetts becomes first U.S. state to issue same-sex marriage licenses (2004)
- *Roper v. Simmons* (2005) (U.S. Supreme Court ruling that the death penalty for those who committed crimes as juveniles is cruel and unusual punishment and a violation of the U.S. Constitution)
- Paul Wellstone and Pete Domenici Mental Health Parity and Addiction Equality Act of 2008
- Lilly Ledbetter Fair Pay Act (2009)
- Matthew Shepard and James Byrd, Jr. Hate Crimes Prevention Act (2009)
- Repeal of "Don't Ask, Don't Tell" (2010)
- Patient Protection and Affordable Care Act (2010) (i.e., "Obamacare")
- *Obergefell v. Hodges* (2015) (U.S. Supreme Court ruling legalizing same-sex marriage)
- First Step Act (2018) (criminal justice reform bill)
- Family First Prevention Services Act (2018) (focused on child maltreatment prevention)
- *Bostock v. Clayton County, Georgia* (2020) (U.S. Supreme Court ruling that Americans who are gay or transgender are protected from workplace discrimination)
- Coronavirus Aid, Relief, and Economic Security (CARES) (2020) (Act passed by Congress to protect Americans from the health and economic impacts of the COVID-19 pandemic)

For most of our early history, the U.S. federal government did not play a significant role in assisting Americans in need. Help was provided by one's relatives. If this was not an option, it was the role of the community to step in, and churches or private philanthropic organizations helped those deemed "worthy" of assistance. The able-bodied poor who needed relief were often punished and treated as criminals and were considered to be going against God's law (Day, 2008). Common approaches to dealing with the poor included the practice of indentured servitude, being forced to leave town, being auctioned off, flogging, branding, and jailing (Day, 2008). Children were often apprenticed out and were forced to labor.

When cities began to be overwhelmed with those in need, the United States saw the rise of institutions such as asylums, orphanages, correctional facilities, and **workhouses/poorhouses/almshouses** where the poor and destitute were warehoused. When a poor person was required to enter an institution such as a poorhouse, they were provided with **indoor relief**. The conditions of poorhouses were wretched and included people of all ages with all kinds of problems who were often mistreated by staff. Residents were poorly clothed and fed, had no privacy, and were not afforded proper medical care; many died from malnutrition and neglect. The almshouse was a popular option at this time because residents were forced to work; thus, it was seen as an economical option that would promote better morals among the poor. However, **outdoor relief** (providing alms to people in their own homes) was also used in many cities. The first time in U.S. history when federal funds were used to help people in need occurred in 1865 when the Freedman's Bureau was established to help freed slaves make the transition from slavery to freedom.

The Settlement House Movement (Late 1800s)

The **Progressive Era** in the United States (1890–1920) was characterized by rapid economic growth due to the move from an agrarian economy to one increasingly reliant on machine-based manufacturing. During this period, millions of people moved to large urban cities in the North to take jobs in factories where goods and services were manufactured. Cities such as Boston, Chicago, and New York were suddenly overwhelmed with these new inhabitants from Eastern and Western Europe and rural areas of the U.S. South, many of whom were African American, who were seeking work and opportunity. This period is called the *Progressive Era* because of the work of progressive social reformers who rejected the idea of social Darwinism and instead worked toward resolving the social and economic problems of the day that were brought on by corporate greed, government corruption, rapid industrialization, and social inequality. **Social Darwinism** was an idea that was popular during this time and espoused by some prominent thinkers of the day who took Darwin's ideas of natural selection and applied them to sociology in efforts to develop a theory of social evolution. The basic idea was that life is a struggle and only the fittest or strongest people will survive. Social Darwinism provided a moral justification for the vast inequalities between rich and poor and was used as an argument for not providing people with public assistance given the belief that it would lead to dependency and interfere with the notion of "survival of the fittest." During this same time, a whole host of new social problems emerged in large urban areas:

- Housing structures called **tenement buildings** that were unsafe, unsanitary, and overcrowded;
- The development of **sweatshops** (characterized by low wages, long hours, and exploitation) where people labored under poor and often dangerous working conditions;
- **Child labor**, whereby many young children and adolescents worked in factories, agriculture, and coal mines instead of going to school;
- An abundance of orphaned, abandoned, and homeless children on the streets (prompting the founding of **orphan trains** by Charles Loring Brace of the Children's Aid Society, whereby thousands of children from large cities such as Boston and New York City were transported to other states to live with rural, Christian families);
- Millions of immigrants moving to large urban U.S. cities, unfamiliar with local customs, who experienced serious hardships and discrimination;
- Congested **city slums** that were riddled with garbage, crime, violence, and prostitution;
- Illness and death caused by poor sanitation, communicable diseases, malnutrition, and industrial hazards;
- A range of barriers affecting women who were treated as second-class citizens (lack of child care for working women; job discrimination; little information about birth control; legally barred from voting or joining trade unions).

Progressives of the day included the settlement house workers. In the United States, **settlement houses** were patterned after Toynbee Hall, a settlement house in London. The purpose of settlement houses was to provide a less patronizing form of charity whereby middle- to upper-class volunteers would live alongside newly arriving, and often poor, immigrants as equal participants as they delivered a range of recreation, education, and health programs to its inhabitants. By 1910, there were more than 400 settlement houses in the United States.

The settlement house movement differed in practice and philosophy from the **Charity Organization Societies (COS)**, which focused more on an individualized approach to aid that was prominent during this period. The COS model was also borrowed from England and embraced the common ideas and values of the time, including social Darwinism, Christian charity, worries that relief promoted dependency, and the belief that poverty was due to a moral flaw in the individual. Paid COS workers conducted an investigation to determine whether the individual was "worthy" of being provided services. COS were against providing direct relief (i.e., money). Instead, they believed that individuals could be cured by being in contact with middle- and upper-class "friendly visitors" who could uplift the poor by teaching values of hard work and thrift. Although it is easy to be critical of these early social workers, it is important to note that the views of COS leaders did evolve over time as they came to have a more sophisticated understanding of the causes of poverty. COS workers such as **Mary Richmond** helped to further professionalize social work in the United States by calling on schools to train professional social workers and by the publication of her book *Social Diagnosis* (1917), which laid the groundwork for casework in social work practice.

Settlement house workers strived to change neighborhoods and expand opportunities for all people. The women who founded the settlement houses in the United States were from privileged backgrounds and were among the first women in the United States to attend college. Many earned advanced degrees in academic fields such as medicine, sociology, and economics (this was before there were formal social work programs). They sought to live and work in settlement homes in order to participate in social reform, seek solutions to the social problems of the day, and escape the rigid gender roles that were common during this time. The settlement house movement provided many women the opportunity to participate in local and national politics. Today's social workers look back on the work of these early social workers in the settlement house movement with pride, and their accomplishments as social reformers are quite remarkable. However, it is important to note that they likely imposed their own white middle-class values onto those they were seeking to help, and this may have been experienced as paternalistic or condescending. Another important criticism is that the major settlement houses excluded African Americans, and settlement houses were segregated by race. The major settlement houses of the day chose to serve white immigrant communities from Europe and excluded African Americans who were also moving to these large urban cities in the North seeking job opportunities.

The most famous settlement house in the United States was Chicago's Hull House, founded by **Jane Addams** and her friend **Ellen Gates Starr** in 1889. Jane Addams relied on several principles that guided the work of Hull House: it was important to live in the community alongside those they were assisting; individuals should be treated with dignity and respect,

Figure 2.1 Famous social worker and activist, Jane Addams
Photograph shows British and American delegates to the International Congress of Women, which was held at the Hague, the Netherlands in 1915. Jane Addams, second from left.

and their culture and customs should be honored; the goal would be to help people to help themselves; and finally, there was a strong belief that poverty, lack of opportunity, and economic desperation were the cause of people's problems, not some moral flaw in one's character. Hull House was decorated in Victorian style, and art from the European masters was displayed. It greatly expanded over the years due to financial contributions from wealthy women, and eventually the Hull House compound covered an entire city block.

Hull House offered an impressive array of programs and services to the people of the surrounding neighborhood, including art classes; day nurseries, day care, and kindergarten; social clubs; cooking, sewing, and housekeeping classes; citizenship and literacy classes; lending libraries and reading rooms; theater and dance programs; political discussion groups; health clinics; and a visiting nurse program.

The hallmark of the settlement house movement was the recognition that macro-level change efforts were needed to improve conditions for women, children, and the newly arriving immigrants. A large part of the Hull House volunteers' work involved conducting investigations (i.e., survey research) of various social problems and then working to change laws that would improve life for many in the urban slums. The settlement house workers lobbied on behalf of legislation that guaranteed protections that today are taken for granted, such as the eight-hour work day, the minimum wage, worker's compensation, old age pensions, health insurance, outlawing child labor and sweat shops, safe housing, and laws protecting the public's health from industrial hazards such as lead poisoning. They established the world's first juvenile court and improved neighborhood conditions by adding public baths, gyms, and playgrounds and improving sanitation and garbage removal. Their work led to the establishment of clinics to diagnose and treat venereal disease and efforts to provide birth control information to women.

Many of the settlement house workers picketed in various labor strikes and marched for women's suffrage and peace. Some were offered important positions in government. The governor of Illinois appointed **Florence Kelley** as Chicago's first chief factory inspector with a staff of 12. She also served as head of the National Consumers League. Jane Addams served as a garbage inspector, one of the only salaried positions she held. **Julia Lathrop** was the first person to head the U.S. Children's Bureau, and she was later succeeded by **Grace Abbott**. Ms. Abbott had an important role in ensuring that children's services were included in the

Social Security program and helping to get the Social Security Act through Congress in 1935. **Dr. Alice Hamilton** worked for the U.S. Bureau of Labor studying industrial diseases and was a pioneer in the field of toxicology and industrial poisons.

Jane Addams became a well-known peace activist and traveled the world espousing pacifist ideals. In 1919, she helped found the Women's International League for Peace and Freedom. In 1931, Jane Addams became the first U.S. woman to be awarded the Nobel Peace Prize. In 2010, *Time Magazine* included Jane Addams on its list of "The 25 Most Powerful Women of the Past Century." Many social workers today cite the settlement house period as the birth of policy practice and community practice in social work, and some critics believe that social work's commitment to these areas of practice has waned in recent years (Specht & Courtney, 1994).

Franklin Delano Roosevelt's New Deal

Prior to 1935, the U.S. federal government played a very limited role in protecting its most vulnerable citizens from poverty and the uncertainties of the market. This was left largely to local communities and the states. The strong value of individualism in the United States goes back to the country's founding, and citizens who were poor or struggling were often blamed for their circumstances and personal failings. This stood in contrast to European countries that had some form of social insurance by the 1900s. However, this all changed with the Stock Market Crash of 1929, and the ensuing **Great Depression**. The Great Depression left millions of Americans destitute and disillusioned; at its height, one in four American workers was unemployed. However, when the American economy collapsed, there was a new focus on the structural causes of poverty, and the idea took root that sometimes bad things happen to people that are beyond their control. Social workers saw firsthand the desperation and hardship caused when millions of Americans were thrown into poverty. They began lobbying the government for reform and action, including an unemployment program. They also gathered data on the effects of the Great Depression on communities.

Franklin Delano Roosevelt (FDR) was a member of the Democratic Party and took office in 1933 at a time when Americans were desperate for help from their government. Roosevelt's optimism, charisma, and ability to take action stood in stark contrast to his predecessor, Hebert Hoover, who believed that government aid to the people went against the principle of self-sufficiency. FDR was known for his skill in communicating with the American public through his speeches and radio fireside chats. Americans elected FDR president four times—clear evidence of his popularity and the public's confidence in his leadership during this turbulent time.

The theme of Roosevelt's administration was the **New Deal**, and the focus would be on providing immediate relief to the suffering, reforming the financial system to prevent future economic catastrophes, and passing legislation that would create a social safety net for all Americans. Work relief programs, such as the **Works Progress Administration (WPA)** and the **Civilian Conservation Corps (CCC)**, were created to give the unemployed a job until the economy recovered. Workers were paid by the government to work on a variety of public works projects, including the construction of roads, schools, hospitals, libraries, bridges, state parks, public buildings, and public utilities. These New Deal jobs programs also included cultural projects for unemployed artists, sewing projects for women, as well as jobs for teachers, doctors, and nurses. WPA wages were higher than poor relief, and by 1936 the WPA employed one-third of all unemployed Americans (Day, 2006). In its eight years of operation, the WPA spent almost $11 billion employing approximately 8.5 million jobless Americans. One unfortunate aspect of these work programs, however, was the discrimination faced by women and ethnic minorities who sought equal participation. Perhaps one of Roosevelt's greatest failings was not fighting harder for civil rights for African Americans. Historians note that he needed the support of southern White Democrats to get his New Deal legislation passed, and so he chose not to antagonize them when it came to civil rights. As a result, some New Deal programs discriminated against Blacks by excluding them from certain benefits or paying them lower wages than Whites. Although he privately supported anti-lynching legislation and opposed the poll tax, Roosevelt did not spend his political capital on these issues for risk of losing the political support that he needed in the South. Other historians argue that some New Deal programs, such as the WPA, were especially helpful to African Americans in providing jobs.

I see one-third of a nation ill-housed, ill-clad, and ill-nourished. The test of our progress is not whether we add more to the abundance of those who have much; it is whether we provide enough for those who have too little.

~President Franklin Delano, Roosevelt, second inaugural address, Washington, D.C., January 20, 1937

In response to the suffering and economic hardships being experienced by millions of Americans, FDR worked with the Congress to pass the **Social Security Act of 1935**, which was landmark social welfare legislation. At the signing of the Social Security Act on August 14, 1935, FDR stated,

> We can never insure one hundred percent of the population against one hundred percent of the hazards and vicissitudes of life, but we have tried to frame a law which will give some measure of protection to the average citizen and to his family against the loss of a job and against poverty-ridden old age.

The Social Security Act of 1935 attempted to protect those most vulnerable in society, including older adults, the unemployed, the poor, the disabled, widows, and children. The act would create a combination of social insurance (for those participating in the workforce) and public assistance programs (for nonworking and dependent individuals). The key program would be social security, a program that would insure people against poverty in old age. The Social Security Act included the following:

- Grants to states for old age assistance (Title I)
- Federal old age benefits (Title II)
- Unemployment compensation (Title III)
- Aid to dependent children (Title IV)
- Maternal and child welfare (Title V)
- Public health work (Title VI)
- Aid to the blind (Title X)

FDR also passed legislation to protect the rights of workers, which is referred to as labor rights. In 1935, the National Labor Relations Act gave workers the right to join unions and engage in collective bargaining to fight for fair wages and working conditions. And in 1938, FDR signed the Fair Labor Standards Act, which abolished child labor and established a minimum wage and a maximum work week of 44 hours. Finally, he worked to restore trust in the banking system by creating the FDIC to give Americans the assurance that their bank deposits would be safe and guaranteed by the government.

Figure 2.2   FDR and Frances Perkins

Roosevelt signing the Social Security Act of 1983, with social worker Frances Perkins in attendance.

Two key figures in FDR's administration were **Frances Perkins** and **Harry Hopkins**, both of whom were social workers in their early careers. Hopkins was one of FDR's closest advisors and was hired to oversee the Federal Emergency Relief Administration (FERA), the Civil Works Administration (CWA), and the Works Progress Administration, all of which were focused on creating work relief programs for the unemployed. Perkins was a remarkable woman. Early in her career, she volunteered her time in the settlement house movement and soon became a passionate advocate for the rights of laborers. As head of the New York Consumers League, she focused on improved work conditions and was successful in lobbying for a bill that limited the number of hours women and children could work per week in that state. An event that had great impact on her life, and further enhanced her advocacy efforts, was watching 146 people (mostly young immigrant women) jump to their death in the Triangle Shirtwaist fire of 1911.

Frances Perkins served as the secretary of labor under FDR, the first woman to hold a U.S. cabinet post. FDR appointed her chairman of the Committee on Economic Security, which was tasked with conducting an investigation of social insurance. Although FDR is credited in the history books with passing the Social Security Act, in reality Ms. Perkins was one of the chief architects of the Social Security Act and championed the legislation until its passage in 1935. After the passage of the Social Security Act, she spoke about the capacity of this policy to provide economic security for the individual as well as the nation, because it is better for the economy when low-income people have purchasing power. In addition to her work on the Social Security Act, she is known for working on behalf of other important New Deal reform legislation such as the abolition of child labor, the minimum wage, and a maximum workweek. It is a shame that most Americans do not know much about her and her incredible contributions.

The passage of the Social Security Act of 1935 is considered the **birth of the welfare state** in the United States. FDR was opposed by some conservatives of the day who viewed it as government intervention that was overly intrusive; it was their hope that the programs created by this act would end once the economy recovered. Throughout U.S. history, many have agreed with the philosophy that "the dole" would lead to idleness, dependency, and reduce people's incentive to work. However, to the delight of many happy beneficiaries of these popular social programs, almost all of the federal social welfare programs created by the Social Security Act were expanded over time and are still in existence today.

The Social Security Act was not a perfect piece of legislation. The benefits were very low and did not include health insurance (due to heavy resistance from the American Medical Association) or disability coverage. Some were excluded from coverage, such as farmworkers, domestic workers, and many people of color who were discriminated against. Finally, it continued the notions of worthy and unworthy poor because the public assistance programs created by the act included means testing and gave welfare staff much discretion in deciding who would be given aid. However, many of these problems were addressed and improved upon in subsequent years through the policymaking process. For more on Social Security, see Chapter 10, Aging Policy and Advocacy.

Whether the United States would have passed a social security act without a Great Depression is an interesting question. Frances Perkins did not believe so, as she explained in a speech to the Social Security Administration titled "The Roots of Social Security" when she was 80 years old. In her view, despite the fact that many brilliant thinkers had studied and written about the need for such a policy, only something as terrifying as the Great Depression could have led the U.S. Congress to pass the Social Security Act (Perkins, 1962).

The philosophical differences between liberals and conservatives over what role, if any, the government should play in protecting the general welfare of its people are still with us today. In 1944, President Roosevelt laid out an **Economic Bill of Rights** in his State of the Union speech in which he stated that people cannot be free without economic security. Among the rights he felt should be included in this second Bill of Rights were the right to a job, an adequate salary, a good education, adequate medical care, and a good home. FDR proposed a constitutional amendment to guarantee Americans these fundamental economic rights, but his proposal was never adopted by the lawmakers of the day. An excerpt of this speech is provided in the following box. It cannot be overstated how important the FDR period of U.S. history was in shaping public opinion about the need for the federal government to play a more expansive role in assisting those in need via social safety net programs.

FDR's Bill of Economic Rights from the 1944 State of the Union Address

It is our duty now to begin to lay the plans and determine the strategy for the winning of a lasting peace and the establishment of an American standard of living higher than ever before known. We cannot be content, no matter how high that general standard of living may be, if some fraction of our people—whether it be one-third or one-fifth or one-tenth—is ill-fed, ill-clothed, ill housed, and insecure.

This Republic had its beginning, and grew to its present strength, under the protection of certain inalienable political rights—among them the right of free speech, free press, free worship, trial by jury, freedom from unreasonable searches and seizures. They were our rights to life and liberty.

As our Nation has grown in size and stature, however—as our industrial economy expanded—these political rights proved inadequate to assure us equality in the pursuit of happiness.

We have come to a clear realization of the fact that true individual freedom cannot exist without economic security and independence. Necessitous men are not free men. People who are hungry and out of a job are the stuff of which dictatorships are made.

In our day these economic truths have become accepted as self-evident. We have accepted, so to speak, a second Bill of Rights under which a new basis of security and prosperity can be established for all regardless of station, race, or creed.

Among these are:

> The right to a useful and remunerative job in the industries or shops or farms or mines of the Nation;
> The right to earn enough to provide adequate food and clothing and recreation;
> The right of every farmer to raise and sell his products at a return which will give him and his family a decent living;
> The right of every businessman, large and small, to trade in an atmosphere of freedom from unfair competition and domination by monopolies at home or abroad;
> The right of every family to a decent home;
> The right to adequate medical care and the opportunity to achieve and enjoy good health;
> The right to adequate protection from the economic fears of old age, sickness, accident, and unemployment;
> The right to a good education.

All of these rights spell security. And after this war is won we must be prepared to move forward, in the implementation of these rights, to new goals of human happiness and well-being.

America's own rightful place in the world depends in large part upon how fully these and similar rights have been carried into practice for our citizens. For unless there is security here at home there cannot be lasting peace in the world.

One of the great American industrialists of our day—a man who has rendered yeoman service to his country in this crisis—recently emphasized the grave dangers of "rightist reaction" in this Nation. All clear-thinking businessmen share his concern. Indeed, if such reaction should develop—if history were to repeat itself and we were to return to the so-called "normalcy" of the 1920s—then it is certain that even though we shall have conquered our enemies on the battlefields abroad, we shall have yielded to the spirit of Fascism here at home.

Franklin D. Roosevelt, State of the Union Message to Congress. 1944.

I ask the Congress to explore the means for implementing this economic bill of rights—for it is definitely the responsibility of the Congress so to do. Many of these problems are already before committees of the Congress in the form of proposed legislation. I shall from time to time communicate with the Congress with respect to these and further proposals. In the event that no adequate program of progress is evolved, I am certain that the Nation will be conscious of the fact.

Our fighting men abroad—and their families at home—expect such a program and have the right to insist upon it. It is to their demands that this Government should pay heed rather than to the whining demands of selfish pressure groups who seek to feather their nests while young Americans are dying.

Source: Roosevelt, F. D. (1944, January 11). State of the Union Message to Congress. Retrieved from http://www.presidency.ucsb.edu/ws/index.php?pid=16518

Lyndon B. Johnson's Great Society and War on Poverty

Another very significant time period when the country moved forward in the way it responded to the needs of those on the margins of society was in the 1960s under the leadership of Democratic president **Lyndon B. Johnson (LBJ)**. The social upheaval of the 1960s led to many social workers' involvement in social movements along with a renewed commitment to the need for social change in order to achieve social and economic justice. This was an interesting time for social workers, because the Great Society programs created by the Johnson administration created thousands of new community-based programs across the country that sought to create a more just society for those who have been left out. Many social workers began to view the community, rather than just the individual, as their client. Social work programs also responded to the changing landscape by offering more courses and concentrations in community practice and community organizing.

Lyndon Johnson was John. F. Kennedy's vice president and was sworn in as president after Kennedy's assassination. Johnson hailed from Texas and often felt out of place among President Kennedy and his advisors, who had been educated in Ivy League universities and grew up among great wealth and privilege. President Johnson served in office during an extremely turbulent time in the United States that was marked by race riots, the civil rights movement, the women's movement, the gay liberation movement, the Vietnam War and the resulting antiwar movement, the publication of Michael Harrington's book *The Other America (1962)* (which exposed high rates of poverty in the United States), and the assassinations of President Kennedy, his brother Bobby who was running for president, and Dr. Martin Luther King, Jr.

LBJ lived and breathed politics and is one of only a few U.S. presidents who held office as a congressman, senator, vice president, and president. Some point to his more than 20 years of experience in the U.S. Congress as critical to his success in getting a voluminous amount of legislation passed as president. Johnson was a skilled politician and was not above using intimidation, bribing, or shaming others to vote his way. FDR was his political hero, but unlike Roosevelt, LBJ was not privileged. He grew up in rural Texas and saw poverty around him. Early in his career he was a teacher in a public elementary school in Cotulla, Texas, where he taught Mexican American children, most of whom were from very poor families. As the quote below shows, this experience seemed to make a large impression on him and how he viewed the importance of education in order to rise above poverty.

I shall never forget the faces of the boys and the girls in that little Welhausen Mexican School, and I remember even yet the pain of realizing and knowing then that college was closed to practically every one of those children because they were too poor. And I think it was then that I made up my mind that this Nation could never rest while the door to knowledge remained closed to any American. So here, today, back on the campus of my youth, that door is swinging open far wider than it ever did before.

~President Johnson's Remarks at Southwest Texas State College upon signing the Higher Education Act of 1965, November 8, 1965

The theme of his administration would be the **Great Society,** and the focus would be on the elimination of poverty and racial injustice. Johnson would also declare a **War on Poverty** with the goal of eliminating poverty in the United States. This was the first and last time that a sitting U.S. president devoted such a focus to addressing poverty in this country. In terms of passing progressive social welfare legislation, few U.S. presidents have surpassed Johnson; the number of bills passed by the Johnson administration is truly astounding by any measure. The focus of the Great Society was to remove barriers for the disadvantaged and to create a plethora of social programs that would provide them with the opportunity to rise out of poverty and into the middle class.

Johnson supported and signed two of the most famous pieces of civil rights legislation: the Civil Rights Act of 1964 and the Voting Rights Act of 1965. The **Civil Rights Act of 1964** made discrimination based on race, color, religion, sex, or national origin illegal and included the following:

- Voting rights (Title I);
- Banned segregation and discrimination in places of public accommodation (e.g., hotels; restaurants; theaters) (Title II);
- The Attorney General was empowered to undertake civil action on behalf of anyone being denied equal protection of the laws (Title III);

Figure 2.3   President Lyndon Johnson with civil rights leaders
LBJ in a civil rights meeting; Dr. Martin Luther King, Jr., on his right; social worker Whitney Young on his left.

- Called for the desegregation of public schools (Title IV);
- Expanded the powers and rules of the Commission on Civil Rights (Title V);
- Nondiscrimination in federally assisted programs (Title VI); and
- Equal Employment Opportunity (Discrimination in employment was prohibited) (Title VII).

The **Voting Rights Act of 1965** outlawed discriminatory voting practices used in many states to prevent African Americans from voting such as poll taxes, literacy tests, harassment, intimidation, and violence and empowered the federal government to oversee voter registration and elections. This law had an immediate impact as hundreds of thousands of African Americans were registered to vote over the next couple of years following passage.

Freedom is the right to share, share fully and equally, in American society: to vote, to hold a job, to enter a public place, to go to school. It is the right to be treated in every part of our national life as a person equal in dignity and promise to all others.

But freedom is not enough. You do not wipe away the scars of centuries by saying, "Now you are free to go where you want, and do as you desire, and choose the leaders you please."

You do not take a person who, for years, has been hobbled by chains and liberate him, bring him up to the starting line of a race and then say, "You are free to compete with all the others," and still justly believe that you have been completely fair.

Thus it is not enough just to open the gates of opportunity. All our citizens must have the ability to walk through those gates."

~President Johnson, commencement address at Howard University, June 4, 1965

Johnson relished using the power of the federal government to create programs that would help people in need. His administration focused on the structural causes of poverty and the idea that people needed access to resources and opportunity in order to be successful. The legislation that he signed into law focused on health care, job training programs, education, food programs, and housing. Perhaps his greatest legacy is creating social programs for the poor, the vulnerable, and the disadvantaged, many of which are still in existence today such as Medicare, Medicaid, VISTA (today named AmeriCorps), federal aid to public schools to equalize funding to less affluent schools, federal money given to universities to provide financial assistance to students, and Head Start.

This was an extremely interesting time for the social work profession in the United States because many of these new and expanded social welfare programs needed the expertise of social workers. Prominent social workers during this time included **Whitney Young** and **Dorothy Height**. Whitney Young was the executive director of the National Urban League and president of NASW; he was ultimately awarded the Presidential Medal of Freedom by

President Johnson for his civil rights accomplishments. Dorothy Height was a civil rights leader, a champion of women's rights, and served as president of the National Council of Negro Women. She passed away in April 2010, and President Obama delivered a eulogy at her funeral service.

> I want to be the president who educated young children to the wonders of their world. I want to be the president who helped to feed the hungry and to prepare them to be taxpayers instead of tax eaters. I want to be the president who helped the poor to find their own way and who protected the right of every citizen to vote in every election.
>
> ~President Johnson, voting rights address to Congress, March 15, 1965

The **Economic Opportunity Act of 1964** was one of the cornerstones of LBJ's War on Poverty. It established the Office of Economic Opportunity (OEO), which was charged with directing and coordinating antipoverty programs that were focused on education, job training, and employment for the poor and people of color. The act had many components and included the following:

- Training people for better jobs (e.g., **Job Corps** training centers);
- Adult education;
- Providing incentives to encourage industries to move to depressed areas with high unemployment;
- **Work study programs** to enable young people to go to college;
- Providing small business loans to African American entrepreneurs to increase African American owned businesses;
- Providing incentives to employers to hire low-income and minority individuals, including those on welfare;
- The **VISTA program**, a domestic version of the Peace Corps where VISTA volunteers were assigned to work in community programs designed to assist communities in need;
- The creation of thousands of **community action agencies** across the country; these were grassroots public or nonprofit community organizations that offered an array of programs that were designed to address the causes of poverty, such as job training and employment services, **Head Start**, **Upward Bound**, preparing young people for college, day care centers for working parents, recreation centers for children, and health and family planning centers. An important principle of community action agencies was termed **maximum feasible participation**, meaning that programs were developed, conducted, and administered by the actual residents of the areas served.

Great Society Legislation/Programs During the LBJ Administration Aimed at Eliminating Poverty and Racial Injustice

- Civil Rights Act of 1964
- Voting Rights Act of 1965
- Law banning housing discrimination (fair housing)
- Establishment of the Department of Housing and Urban Development (HUD)
- Economic Opportunity Act of 1964
- Medicare
- Medicaid
- VISTA Program (domestic version of the Peace Corps)
- Vocational and job training programs (e.g., Job Corps)
- Community Action Programs
- Economic Opportunity Act of 1964
- Food Stamp Act of 1964
- Minimum wage increase
- Age Discrimination in Employment Act of 1967
- Older Americans Act
- Public Broadcasting Act of 1967 (allowed creation of PBS and NPR)
- School breakfast program
- National Endowment for the Arts
- National Product Safety Commission
- Air Quality Act
- Wilderness Act
- Land and Water Conservation Fund Act
- Wild and Scenic Rivers Act
- National Trails Systems Act
- Immigration and Nationality Services Act of 1965 (abolished strict immigration quotas)
- Education (60 bills to improve schools and access to education)
- Head Start
- Upward Bound program (helps low income high school students go to college)
- Elementary and Secondary Education Act of 1965
- Higher Education Act of 1965
- College Work Study Program
- Bilingual Education Act of 1968

The creation of the **Medicare** and **Medicaid** programs created by legislation during this time was a major achievement in health care. The Medicare program was a social insurance program that would provide healthcare coverage for those older than 65 years and for those with disabilities on Social Security. In contrast, the Medicaid program was created as a means-tested, public assistance healthcare program for the poor. This was a major achievement, as previous U.S. presidents, most notably Franklin Roosevelt and Harry Truman, were unsuccessful in their efforts to expand healthcare coverage to the poor and aged. LBJ signed Medicare into law at the Truman Library on July 30, 1965, with Truman and his wife in attendance. President Johnson enrolled Truman as the first Medicare beneficiary and issued him the first Medicare card.

On March 31, 1968, LBJ announced to the nation that he would not be running for reelection. His presidency and beloved Great Society were done in by the Vietnam War. Many scholars have debated whether Johnson's War on Poverty was a success or a failure, and the data are somewhat mixed. Of course, he was not successful in eradicating poverty in America, but the poverty rate was greatly decreased. The overall poverty rate was almost cut in half from 1959 (before the War on Poverty) to 1970 (from 22% to 12%). The poverty rate for African Americans and older adults also decreased significantly during this time period (from 55% to 33% for African Americans, and from 35% to 25% for those over 65). This has been attributed to the combination of rapid economic growth and concerted government efforts. One downside was that although living standards for the poor were greatly improved, many now found themselves on the welfare rolls. This was not LBJ's vision; he wanted to see people rising out of poverty and earning a decent salary as a result of new skills and education provided by Great Society programs.

LBJ's Great Society slowly became overshadowed by the war in Vietnam. It seems that the War on Poverty could not compete with the attention, time, and resources that were devoted to this war. However, many of the programs that his administration created are still with us today (e.g., Head Start, Medicaid, Medicare, Food Stamp Program [now called the Supplemental Nutrition Assistance Program, or SNAP], federal funding for public and higher education, AmeriCorps). It is unfortunate that Johnson's commitment to ending poverty and historic achievement of shepherding through an impressive array of domestic social welfare legislation is often overshadowed by his failure during Vietnam.

The Rise of Conservatism and the Decline of Social Responsibility

In many respects, the heyday of progressive social welfare legislation ended with the LBJ administration. The rise of conservatism in the 1980s through the present day has coincided with decreasing levels of social and political action by social workers in the United States. Despite a number of issues and social problems that are of concern to the social work profession, such as rising income inequality and poverty rates, the wars in Iraq and Afghanistan, healthcare reform, and efforts to dismantle the social safety net, social workers largely retreated to their micro roles.

The conservative backlash in the United States began with the election of **Ronald Reagan** as president, as Republican lawmakers began arguing that large-scale, federal social welfare programs were incapable of solving the problems of the poor. President Reagan championed low taxes, government deregulation, and small government. His opinion of government's ability to operate effectively and efficiently was clear when he famously stated that "government is not the solution to our problems, it is the problem." He also advocated **supply-side** or **trickle-down economics**, the idea that giving tax cuts and other benefits to the wealthy is good for the middle class and those living in poverty because it leads to job creation, lower prices, and other societal benefits. He angered liberals by making significant cuts to government spending in the area of social welfare, and during his administration the federal government began devolving responsibility for social welfare to the states and the private sector. During the 1980s and 1990s, Americans saw the rise of the **Christian right** and their increasing influence in the Republican Party. Leaders and organizations in this movement emerged, such as Focus on the Family and the Moral Majority, and gained increasing prominence as they contributed conservative positions to the national discourse on issues such as prayer in the schools, abstinence-only sex education, abortion, and same-sex marriage.

During this same time, the Democratic Party was also moving to the right as evidenced by the founding of the **Democratic Leadership Council (DLC)** in 1985 and increasing numbers of Democrats who began embracing an ideology of **neoliberalism** (see Chapter 3). These new, more centrist Democrats, such as Bill Clinton, embraced a more conservative view of economics and began aligning themselves more with U.S. corporate interests, in part, to be able to compete with Republicans for political fundraising. Some were glad to see the Democratic Party moving away from its "bleeding heart," leftist policies of the past, whereas others referred to these centrists as "corporatist Democrats" who were now indistinguishable from their Republican colleagues on the Hill. Many on the left were dismayed to see **Bill Clinton**, a Democratic president, sign policies into law that had been passionately promoted by conservatives, such as the **Defense of Marriage Act (DOMA)**, the **1996 welfare reform law**, government deregulation of private industry, and the **North American Free Trade Agreement (NAFTA)**. When Clinton made good on his promise to "end welfare as we knew it" by signing the 1996 welfare reform into law, three high-ranking officials at the Department of Health and Human Services resigned in protest. The middle class flourished under Clinton, but many liberals were disappointed that the plight of the poor was not a major policy focus of his administration.

Political progressives were further dismayed to witness the election of **George W. Bush**, an unabashed conservative who espoused government funding of faith-based social services and led the country to war against Iraq and Afghanistan in the aftermath of the September 11 attacks. President George W. Bush shared the same philosophy as his father, George Bush Sr. and President Reagan—that government should have a limited role in ensuring the

Figure 2.4   President Obama

Barack Obama was sworn in as 44th President of United States on Tuesday, January 20, 2009, at the U.S. Capitol.

social welfare of its citizens. However, despite this conservative era of U.S. politics, some notable progressive social policies were passed into law, such as the Americans with Disabilities Act, the Violence Against Women Act, the creation of the State Children's Health Insurance Program (S-CHIP), the Mental Health Parity Act of 2008, and the Matthew Shepard and James Byrd, Jr. Hate Crimes Prevention Act of 2009.

The Election of Barack Obama

The pendulum swung back the other way for the 2008 presidential election when Americans chose between Senator John McCain, the Republican nominee, and Senator **Barack Obama,** the Democratic nominee. Senator McCain was an established Republican candidate who wanted to continue the Republicans' reign of the presidency. He selected Sarah Palin to be his running mate, a controversial pick. The theme of Senator Obama's campaign was "change," the importance of bipartisanship in order to solve the country's most pressing problems, and putting the United States on a very different path from the previous eight years under George W. Bush. He made many campaign promises, including passage of healthcare reform, ending the "Don't ask, don't tell" policy in the military, getting U.S. troops out of Iraq, repairing our tarnished reputation in the international community, passing an immigration bill, and closing Guantanamo Bay. Many social workers around the country were hopeful that this would be a new era in U.S. politics that would tackle issues of social justice and economic inequality.

The 2008 presidential election between Senators Barack Obama and John McCain was the most expensive campaign in history up to that time, and voter turnout was high as record numbers of young people and independents turned out. The election was historic, as Americans witnessed the election of the first African American president in Barack Obama. President Obama came into office facing immense challenges, including the biggest economic recession since the Great Depression and the continuing wars in Iraq and Afghanistan. Democrats have been split when it comes to grading President Obama. Many point to his legislative achievements, such as saving the U.S. economy from a great depression, appointing two women to the Supreme Court, withdrawing troops from Iraq, and signing a number of bills into law that cover topics ranging from economic stimulus, healthcare reform, hate crimes, financial reform, and gender pay discrimination. Others on the left have been disappointed that some of the dramatic changes that President Obama promised did not materialize (e.g., immigration bill, closing Guantanamo Bay) and that some of the legislation passed was too compromised and incremental (see Chapter 7 for an overview of the Affordable Care Act). President Obama himself has admitted that he underestimated how hard Republicans would work against him in efforts to prevent him from having any legislative accomplishments. Other political observers have noted the role that racism played in many conservatives who opposed the first Black president.

The 2016 and 2020 Presidential Elections of Donald Trump and Joe Biden

Americans witnessed another historic election in the 2016 presidential election between Hillary Clinton and Donald Trump, as it was the first time in U.S. history that a female was on the ticket to run for president of the United States. Hillary Clinton defeated Senator Bernie Sanders, a popular liberal Democrat, to clinch the Democratic nomination. It was an extremely contentious election between a political candidate with a lifetime of experience in politics (former First Lady, U.S. senator, and secretary of state) against a controversial wealthy businessman/political outsider/reality TV star. Donald Trump won the election in a major upset when he won the Electoral College despite losing the national popular vote by around 3 million votes. Democrats and many mainstream Republicans were shocked to see Americans elect a divisive "outsider" candidate who ran on building a wall between the United States and Mexico, nationalism ("America First," "Make America Great Again"), fighting terrorism and restricting immigration from Muslim countries, strengthening the economy by creating jobs and lowering taxes, and ending Obamacare, which he viewed as a failure.

It is hard to put into words the political strife and divisiveness that came to define the Trump presidency. The first indication of this was the Women's March on January 21, 2017, that was held in cities around the world the day after President Trump's inauguration as a way to protest his election. It was reportedly the largest single-day protest in U.S. history. More than any other president in recent U.S. history, Trump's presidency divided Americans into two passionately opposing camps where there appeared to be little common ground.

President Trump's supporters backed him for different reasons. For some, it was his pro-life stance. For others, it was his status as an outsider who thumbed his nose at the political establishment and used the office of the presidency to bully his detractors with scathing insults in direct opposition to conventional standards of temperament and professionalism for a U.S. president. Still others supported him for his economic policies that focused on government deregulation of corporations and reducing taxes on the wealthy. Finally, some of his most ardent supporters seemed to respond to his inflammatory rhetoric with regard to issues of race, gender, and immigration. Trump supporters were delighted that he was able to appoint three justices to the U.S. Supreme Court and more than 200 judges to the federal bench, thereby shaping the federal judiciary in profound ways for decades to come. One rare issue where he gets credit from those on both sides of the aisle is his support of the First Step Act, a bipartisan piece of legislation that addressed much needed criminal justice reform at the federal level.

President Trump's adversaries included Democrats, those on the left, as well as some Republicans who decided to break from the Republican Party when Trump was elected. Some of these prominent Republicans started an organization called The Lincoln Project, which raised money and organized around defeating Trump in the 2020 election, because in their view he violated traditional Republican values and norms for a U.S. president. President Trump's detractors were disheartened to witness a president behave in ways that were historically unprecedented. Criticism of President Trump fell into two main categories:

(1) his personal temperament, which many felt made him unfit for being president, and (2) his policies.

In terms of his personal leadership style, opponents of the President Trump pointed to his constant lying, personal attacks and bullying behavior (much of it via daily tweets on Twitter), nepotism by appointing his own family members as advisors, and abuse of power of the office by commingling his personal business interests with his elected position. Multiple lawsuits were filed against Trump for fraudulent activities by his charitable foundation, tax evasion, profiting from the presidency, and payoffs to a pornographic film actress. Trump had an extremely high turnover rate among those who worked for him, as he was quick to fire people who he perceived as not being loyal to him. Many others resigned. Many point to how Trump cultivated a cult of personality among his followers and how much he appeared to relish attacking his adversaries at his MAGA rallies throughout his presidency. In December 2019, Trump was impeached by the U.S. House of Representatives for abuse of power and obstruction of Congress related to allegations that he pressured Ukraine to investigate his political rival Joe Biden by withholding military aid to them. However, he was acquitted in the U.S. Senate and was not removed from office. Support and opposition to the president during his impeachment trial was extremely partisan, and Senator Mitt Romney was the only Republican lawmaker in Congress who voted to convict him.

Opponents of President Trump were also critical of his policy positions such as his family separation policy at the U.S.–Mexico border, which had catastrophic outcomes for many children and families; his tax cuts that disproportionately benefitted the wealthiest Americans and corporations; his dismantling of climate policies and environmental protections (e.g., his withdrawal from the Paris Agreement on climate change), and how he aligned with dictators who had previously been enemies of the United States (e.g., Russian president Vladimir Putin and North Korean leader Kim Jong Un) while alienating many of our traditional allies. When race relations were strained due to police brutality against Black Americans, and the Black Lives Matter movement became a mainstream movement, Trump continually refused to renounce White supremacy—even after a protester was killed and 35 others were injured in Charlottesville, Virginia by a neo-Nazi who drove his car into a crowd of antiracist protesters. And perhaps the biggest failure of leadership was how the Trump administration mismanaged the coronavirus pandemic and resulting economic recession that resulted in millions of Americans becoming unemployed and the closing of thousands of small businesses. President Trump and many in his administration contracted the virus and did not support the messaging and public policy recommendations of leading scientists and public health experts in the country. As a result, the United States suffered the highest coronavirus cases and deaths rate of any nation in the world.

Many have written about how the Trump presidency started to feel like a true threat to American democracy, particularly when he began to argue that the 2020 election results were fraudulent and that the election was stolen from him. The results of the 2020 presidential election are perhaps the best evidence for how divided Americans are when it comes to grading President Trump. Joe Biden received the most votes ever for a person running for president, and Donald Trump received the second highest votes ever. The never-ending 2020 presidential campaign was stressful for Americans on both sides, those who desired a change in leadership and those who were committed to supporting the incumbent president. After a tough Democratic primary, former vice president Joe Biden emerged as the winner to run on the Democratic ticket, beating out early front-runners such as Senator Kamala Harris, Senator Bernie Sanders, and Senator Elizabeth Warren. Biden chose Senator Kamala Harris to be his running mate, and he ran on traditional Democratic values and policies, including a message that he would bring the country together and would be the president of all Americans, even those who did not vote for him.

Many predicted that the election would likely be close, and Americans would not know the results on election night, November 3, 2020. That turned out to be the case. Americans would have to wait until Saturday, November 7th to learn that Joe Biden was declared the winner. He won the popular vote by more than seven million votes and handily won the Electoral College. It was striking (and unprecedented) to see video footage of people dancing in the streets and celebrating Biden's win in major cities in the United States and around the world. Democrats were ecstatic to win the presidency but were disillusioned to learn that the blue wave they predicted did not materialize in the U.S. Congress. They retained control of the House, but lost some seats. And they did not gain as much traction in the Senate as they thought they would. Americans would have to wait two more months to see which party would control the U.S. Senate after both of the Senate races in Georgia were ruled too close to call. The run-off election in January 2021 for the two Senate seats in Georgia would determine which party would win control of the Senate, and the Democrats needed to win both to gain control. Democrats were thrilled to see Democrats Raphael Warnock and Jon Ossoff win their races. The U.S. Senate is now 50–50, Democrat–Republican, but Democratic vice president Kamala Harris will serve as the tie-breaking vote, giving Democrats a very slight edge.

It was remarkable that a record number of Americans came out to vote in a presidential election, and during a pandemic no less. And the United States for the first time elected Senator Kamala Harris, a woman and biracial person (i.e., Black and South Asian descent) as vice president of the United States. Joe Biden was sworn in as president on January 20, 2021. President Trump did not attend the inauguration, which broke with a long history of tradition.

The Violent Insurrectionist Mob at the Capitol on January 6, 2021

It was unprecedented to see a U.S. president failing to concede and attempting to change the outcome of the election. And it was unprecedented to witness Republican lawmakers in Congress fail to congratulate the winner of the election. In the weeks after the election, President Trump and other Republicans filed more than 50 lawsuits contesting the results of the election, yet no court found any evidence of election fraud. In fact, 126 party members and 18 state attorneys general supported a case before the U.S. Supreme Court that legal experts agreed had no merit. The Supreme Court later rejected the case. President Trump continued to state that the election included widespread voter fraud and was stolen from him by the Democratic Party.

However, Americans and the rest of the world were completely unprepared for what unfolded at the U.S. Capitol on January 6, 2021. On this date, lawmakers on Capitol Hill were scheduled to certify the results of the Electoral College that would designate Joe Biden to be the next president of the United States, a procedure that is conducted every time a new president is elected. On this same date, President Trump and some of his most zealous supporters organized a protest in the nation's capital. On December 19, 2020, Trump tweeted, "Big protest in DC on January 6th. Be there, will be wild!" Those who traveled across the country to attend this protest were among Trump's most passionate supporters, and many were members of organized groups such as White nationalists (e.g., the Proud Boys), conspiracy theorists (QAnon), antigovernment militias, and other far-right extremist groups. At the protest, many believe that President Trump and his attorney Rudy Giuliani incited the mob by using inflammatory language to entice the crowd to storm the Capitol. Later evidence also revealed that many protesters planned the attack at the Capitol because they came prepared with guns, weapons (e.g., pipe bombs, Molotov cocktails), and other implements to help them break into the Capitol.

Americans watched their televisions in shock as the protest turned into a violent mob. They overpowered the Capitol Police and entered the Capitol while federal lawmakers were meeting to certify the results of the 2020 presidential election. It was hours until large numbers of National Guard and law enforcement were able to arrive and get this mob out of the Capitol and under control. In the meantime, the mob stole and destroyed property at the Capitol; waved Trump flags, as well as Confederate flags; injured police officers; and attempted to gain entry into various offices and meetings spaces where federal lawmakers were scared and hiding. Some rioters had intentions of harming Vice President Pence, Speaker of the House Nancy Pelosi, and other Democratic lawmakers. President Trump was criticized for waiting too long to get help for these lawmakers and asking his supporters to stop their actions. In his first video statement, he asked them to go home but also restated that the election was stolen and told them he loved them. Five people died during this horrific event—one police officer and four people who were part of the mob. Many law enforcement officers suffered injuries as well. In a show of unity and strength, lawmakers in the U.S. House and Senate reconvened later that evening to finish their job of certifying the presidential election results. Shockingly, even after the terrifying event that had just transpired, 147 Republicans (8 U.S. senators and 139 U.S. representatives) still voted to overturn the election results based on false claims that the election included widespread voter fraud.

The consequences for those who participated in the insurrection, including Republicans who appeared to support and/or incite them, were swift and immediate. The FBI made over 100 arrests of those who participated in the mob at the Capitol, and they continue to investigate and track people down. Luckily their job was made easier due to widespread footage posted on social media by those who participated. Many Republican lawmakers who voted "no" on certifying the election results faced a serious backlash by voters and various media outlets, including calls for them to resign (particularly, Senator Josh Hawley of Missouri and Senator Ted Cruz of Texas, who were among the most vocal supporters of overturning the election results in favor of President Trump). Both Hawley and Cruz are facing ethics complaints in the U.S. Congress for their role in this event. A number of high-ranking officials working in the Trump administration, who found this event disturbing, resigned their positions. And President Trump, who failed to take any responsibility for his role in this episode, was banned from social media by Facebook, Twitter, and Instagram.

On January 13, 2021, Trump was impeached by the House of Representatives for incitement of insurrection. This marked the first time in U.S. history that a U.S. president was impeached twice. The next step was to hold a trial in the U.S. Senate to convict him of these charges. Democratic lawmakers who led the trial in the Senate showed previously disturbing, previously unseen video footage of the rioters that revealed how well armed many of the rioters were, how they attacked and injured police officers, and their desire to seriously harm lawmakers, particularly Speaker of the House Nancy Pelosi and Vice President Mike Pence. They also showed a lot of video footage of Trump and argued that his actions and speech inciting the mob began with his constant assertions that the election was stolen from him. However, the Democrats were not able to persuade two-thirds of the Senate to convict the former president of these charges. However, the trial was historic trial given that seven Republican senators voted to convict Trump, the most bipartisan impeachment trial verdict ever. Because Trump was not convicted, nothing prevents him from holding public office again in the future. On his last day in office, Trump pardoned and/or commuted the sentences of 143 people, a combination of former business and political associates, business leaders, rappers, and others. The events of January 6, 2021, led to a disturbing realization that a small segment of the American population made a serious attempt to seriously harm and undermine American democracy. Only time will tell whether these deep divisions will heal under the Biden–Harris administration and how law enforcement officials will deal with the increasing threat of domestic terrorism in the United States.

Biden's First 100 Days in Office

President-elect Joe Biden came into office facing staggering challenges that he vowed to address—the coronavirus pandemic, an economic recession caused by the pandemic, climate change, systemic racism, the need to repair relationships with allied nations, and an American populace that was incredibly divided politically. He was lauded for appointing one of the most diverse presidential administrations in U.S. history, including the first Native American cabinet secretary (Deb Haaland), the first female national intelligence director (Avril Haines), the first Latino homeland security chief (Alejandro Mayorkas), the first African American to head the Pentagon (General Lloyd Austin), and the first openly gay cabinet member (Pete Buttigieg).

In his first month in office, President Biden used the power of executive action, issuing more than 40 executive orders, to overturn many of the executive orders of his predecessor, President Trump, as well as to create new policies via this power. Examples include the following:

- **Coronavirus:** A lengthy list of executive orders focused on the nation's ability to combat COVID-19, including travel restrictions from some nations, a mask mandate for federal workers, and ending Trump's withdrawal from the World Health Organization (WHO)
- **Health care:** Strengthened the Medicaid program and the Affordable Care Act and rescinded a Trump administration rule that blocked healthcare providers in the Title X family planning program from referring patients for abortions
- **Equity:** Lifted the ban on transgender people serving in the military, directed federal agencies to review their actions to ensure racial equity, prevented workplace discrimination on the basis of sexual orientation or gender identity, issued a memorandum on "Condemning and Combating Racism, Xenophobia, and Intolerance Against Asian Americans and Pacific Islanders in the United States," directed the Attorney General not to renew federal contracts with private prisons, and issued a memorandum on "Redressing Our Nation's and the Federal Government's History of Discriminatory Housing Practices and Policies"
- **Immigration:** Ended many of Trump's draconian immigration policies that focused heavily on deporting all undocumented immigrants; proposed a comprehensive immigration reform bill that would provide a path to citizenship for undocumented immigrants, including DACA recipients; protected the DACA program for undocumented youth; halted construction of the border wall with Mexico; ended the Muslim travel ban; and required noncitizens to be counted in the U.S. Census
- **Environment:** Rejoined the Paris Agreement, cancelled the Keystone XL Pipeline, established a National Climate Task Force, paused new oil and natural gas leases on public lands or offshore waters, instructed the Director of National Intelligence to prepare a national intelligence estimate on the security implications of the climate crisis, and reestablished the President's Council of Advisors on Science and Technology
- **Economy:** Issued a host of executive orders focused on helping those impacted by the recession, such as a focus on Buy American products; work protections for federal workers, including Biden's priority for increasing the minimum wage; and extending the pause on student loan payments and eviction and foreclosure moratoriums
- **Ethics:** Required executive branch appointees to sign an ethics pledge barring them from acting in their own personal interests; issued an executive order upholding the independence of the Department of Justice

Similar to President Franklin Delano Roosevelt's leadership style (who became president during the Great Depression), President Biden took swift and immediate action upon taking office. He vowed to make combatting the coronavirus one of his very highest priorities by focusing on significantly increasing the number of Americans getting vaccinated and passing a $1.9 trillion coronavirus relief bill (dubbed the "American Rescue Plan") that included $1,400 checks for Americans earning less than $75,000; an extension of unemployment benefits; an expansion of the child tax credit; an expansion of the Affordable Care Act; and billions of dollars in finding to reopen schools, provide assistance to small businesses, landlords, and their tenants, aid to state and local governments; and to expand coronavirus vaccine testing and distribution. This legislation was one of the largest economic relief measures in U.S. history (for more details on this stimulus package, see Chapter 4). Biden's covid relief bill was passed in the U.S. Congress along party lines and did not receive a single Republican vote. President Biden has earned a very high approval rating from Americans on his handling of the pandemic. He reached his goal of delivering 100 million vaccine shots in his first 100 days in office early, and then increased the goal to 200 million. Biden's next ambitious goal is to pass a $2 trillion bill to rebuild the nation's infrastructure (e.g., roads; bridges), and which would also create new jobs and address climate change. Biden's supporters are hoping that his lifetime of experience in political office (including eight years serving as vice president under President Barack Obama) will pay off and that he will be able to bring some much needed healing and unity to the country.

REFERENCES

Day, P. J. (2008). *New history of social welfare* (6th ed.). Boston, MA: Pearson.

Jansson, B. S. (2008). *The reluctant welfare state: Engaging history to advance social welfare practice in contemporary society*. Belmont, CA: Brooks/Cole.

Perkins, F. (1962, October). The roots of Social Security. Retrieved from http://www.ssa.gov/history/perkins5.html

Roosevelt, F. D. (1944, January 11). State of the Union address to Congress. Retrieved from http://www.presidency.ucsb.edu/ws/index.php?pid=16518

Specht, H., & Courtney, M. E. (1994). *Unfaithful angels: How social work has abandoned its mission*. New York, NY: The Free Press.

The 25 most powerful women of the past century. (2010, November 18). *Time Magazine*. Retrieved from www.time.com/time/specials/packages/article/0,28804,2029774_2029776,00.html?iid=moreontime

Credits

CHAPTER 3

The Role of Values in the Political Arena

"If you're not a liberal at 20 you have no heart, if you're not a conservative at 40 you have no brain."

~*Winston Churchill*

"Your beliefs become your thoughts. Your thoughts become your words. Your words become your actions. Your actions become your habits. Your habits become your values. Your values become your destiny."

~*Mahatma Gandhi*

Figure 3.1   Planned Parenthood supporters

CHAPTER SUMMARY

Some have argued that values constitute the most important dimension for understanding social welfare policy. Many astute observers of the political process will tell you that social policies are based heavily on values, and that the development of these policies is often not a rational process based on evidence or the careful consideration of alternative policies. In social work education, values are discussed quite frequently. Students learn about important social work values such as service, social justice, the dignity and worth of individuals, and self-determination, and are encouraged to explore their own personal values. "The personal is political" is a famous saying that came out of the women's movement in the 1960s, though this is true for many people.

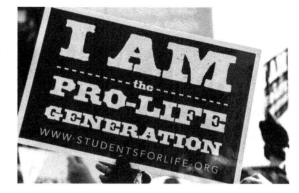

Figure 3.2   Pro-life supporters

The idea behind this phrase is that people tend to be politically active about issues that affect their lives directly (e.g., discrimination, gun ownership, sexual violence, lack of health insurance, funding for public education). Our personal values are influenced by family members; the community in which we were raised; people we admire, such as teachers and mentors; dominant societal values; and our spiritual or religious beliefs. It should not be a surprise then that our personal value system affects our political beliefs. For example, our personal values shape our thinking about how our country should help people, especially the more vulnerable members of our society; what kinds of problems we should be addressing in our country; and where the government should intervene and when it should stay out of our lives. They also affect our opinions on hot-button social issues such as abortion rights, the death penalty, and same-sex marriage. Politics is personal, and our positions on many political issues are rooted in personal values that we hold very dear. This might explain why Americans are so divided politically and why the national discourse around politics has gotten so toxic over the past few decades. Chapter 3 provides an overview of political ideology, political parties, new political movements, and the intersection of religion and politics.

STUDENT LEARNING OBJECTIVES

- Students will be able to explain the vital role of values in political debates surrounding social welfare policy.

- Students will be able to differentiate between the dominant political ideologies and political parties in the United States.

- Students will learn about new social movements in the United States.

- Students will be able to examine the intersection of religion and politics.

- Students will be able to come to their own assessment of how social work values intersect with the values of the dominant political ideologies in the United States.

Since the 1990s, U.S. politics has become increasingly divisive, and the chasm between conservatives and progressives has continued to widen. Political discourse in the United States is often ugly, heated, and toxic, and it seems that citizens with opposing political ideologies are living in completely different worlds or realities. During the eight years of the George W. Bush presidency, progressives were disillusioned and believed the country was on the wrong track as they witnessed U.S. troops being sent to Iraq and Afghanistan in the aftermath of 9/11; approval of the use of torture, termed "enhanced interrogation techniques"; the erosion of civil liberties after the passage of the USA PATRIOT Act; further deregulation of the private sector; and the diminished reputation of the United States on the world stage.

In 2008, Barack Obama became the 44th president of the United States after a record number of Americans went to the polls, and conservatives were similarly inconsolable. While the new president and his administration went into action to deal with the biggest economic recession since the Great Depression, Americans witnessed the birth of two new and wildly opposing social movements, the **Tea Party movement** and the **Occupy Wall Street movement**. The country seemed as polarized as ever as those on opposite sides of the political spectrum continued to disagree about the best way to move the country forward and address the country's most pressing social and economic challenges. Tea Party activists overwhelmed town hall meetings around the country and took to the streets to express their outrage at "out-of-control" government spending and the ballooning deficit due to the passage of the stimulus package, the bailout of the U.S. financial system, and President Obama's plans to reform the healthcare system. A few years later another protest movement emerged called Occupy Wall Street with the rallying call, "We are the 99%!" On the 24-hour cable news cycle, political pundits reduced Americans to either "red state" salt-of-the-earth Americans who tune into Fox News to watch news commentators call President Obama a socialist, or "blue state" latte-drinking intellectuals whose favorite pastime was watching Jon Stewart chiding conservatives on his "fake" news show, *The Daily Show.*

In 2016, Donald Trump defeated Hillary Clinton in a contentious election to become the 45th president of the United States, and Americans once again found themselves living in a country with stark political divisions. In the view of the vast majority of social workers, this new president expressed views and supported policy positions that are at odds with the mission and values of the social work profession. The 2016 election exposed many values debates between progressives and conservatives in the electorate on issues such as women's rights, racism, immigrant rights, access to health care, and economic issues such as government regulation and taxation. The 2020 presidential election between Donald Trump and Joe Biden was equally contentious, and voters would choose between two candidates with vastly different political values and visions for the country. A record number of Americans came out to vote in the midst of a pandemic, and both candidates received a historic number of votes. After Biden was declared the winner, President Trump and many of his supporters refused to accept the results of the election, and Trump supporters turned out to protest the results in some states where the results were close. Only time will tell whether

Americans will be able to find a way to move beyond their stark ideological differences in order to work together to solve the country's most pressing challenges.

It's All About Values

In social work education, **values** are discussed quite frequently. Students learn about important social work values such as service, social justice, the dignity and worth of individuals, and self-determination, and are encouraged to explore their own personal values. At times personal values and professional values conflict, and social workers must find a way to sort this out. "The personal is political" is a famous saying that came out of the women's movement in the 1960s, though this is true for many people. The idea behind this phrase is that people tend to be politically active about issues that affect their lives directly (e.g., discrimination, gun ownership, sexual violence, lack of health insurance, funding for public education). Our personal values can be informed by family members; the communities in which we were raised; people we admire, such as teachers and mentors; dominant societal values; and spiritual or religious beliefs.

It should not be a surprise then that our personal value system affects our political beliefs. For example, our personal values shape our thinking about how our country should help people, particularly the more vulnerable members of our society; what kinds of problems we should be addressing in our country; and where the government should intervene and when it should stay out of our lives. They also affect our opinions on hot-button social issues such as abortion rights, the death penalty, and same-sex marriage. Many of us can recall occasions when we found ourselves in heated political arguments with others. Why is this? Politics is personal, and our positions on many political issues are rooted in personal values that we hold very dear.

Many astute observers of the political process will tell you that social policies are based primarily on values, and that the development of these policies is often not a "rational" process based on evidence or the careful consideration of alternative policies. Many of us may prefer that our legislators use a logical problem-solving model when making policy. It would look something like the following: (1) examine the problem, (2) identify various courses of action to solve the problem, (3) consult experts and available research on the topic, (4) select the best option based on available information, and (5) evaluate the outcome and revise as needed. Sometimes policies are made in this manner. However, much of the time legislators make decisions based on their values and what is moral or right, in their view. For example, based on their religious convictions, some conservative lawmakers advocate the use of abstinence-based sex education in the public schools. Many of these lawmakers would not be persuaded by research showing that comprehensive sex education is far more effective in preventing teen pregnancy. On the other side, some liberals might hesitate to eliminate a social program they have supported for decades even if they were presented with evidence that it was ineffective. Time and again, values and ideology trump rationality when it comes to making public policy.

American Values

Some have argued that values constitute the most important dimension for understanding social welfare policy. According to Prigmore and Atherton (1986), the following 15 American values influence our social policies:

- Achievement and success
- Activity and work
- Public morality
- Humanitarian concerns
- Efficiency and practicality
- Progress
- Material comfort
- Marketplace capitalism
- Equality
- Freedom
- Conformity versus individualism
- Science and rationality
- Nationalism and patriotism
- Democracy
- Racism and group superiority

When a particular policy embraces some of the above values, it is more likely to pass. Policies that violate these cherished American values will face strong opposition. Some are surprised to see the last "value" on the list; however, Prigmore and Atherton (1986) argue that many of our policies historically have been based on the belief that some groups are superior to other groups.

Sometimes American values and social work values are at odds with each other, which can be challenging when social workers are trying to get certain types of legislation passed. Social work values include:

- Service
- Social justice
- Importance of human relationships
- Dignity and worth of the person
- Integrity
- Competence

For example, legislation to expand funding for social programs that serve those living in poverty, such as early childhood education programs, Medicaid, housing programs, or food stamps, are often not popular with the public because they are perceived as going against American values of individualism, hard work, and success. Policy work from a social work perspective often involves asking the public to be willing support public policies and social programs (via taxation) that are investments in human and social capital. The definitions of human capital and social capital are provided below.

Defining Terms

Capital: The stock of capacity to do something.

Human capital: Skills and talents that increase one's value in the marketplace; public investments in human capital can include programs that provide individuals with education, job training, and employment experience.

Social capital: The concept of social capital is applied to communities. Communities with a substantial stock of social capital are healthy communities; you will see established social networks, social connectedness, high levels of civic engagement, collaboration, reciprocity, social trust, and a value of less "I" and more "We." Investments to enhance the social capital of communities can include community revitalization projects, community development projects, and programs that bring people together to improve their community. Robert Putnam is one of the gurus of social capital and has written best-selling books on the topic including *Bowling Alone: The Collapse and Revival of the American Community* (2001) and *Better Together: Restoring the American Community* (2004).

Political Ideology

In the political arena, people often refer to *ideology*. **Ideology**, in a general sense, means a way of looking at things, or one's worldview. It may include beliefs through which we view the world, how the world works, what has value, what is worth living and dying for, what is good and true, and what is right. **Political ideology** largely concerns itself with how society should work and the best way to achieve this ideal arrangement. Political ideology includes ideas on what is considered to be the best form of government, the best economic system, and often identifies where someone falls on the political spectrum (e.g., left, center, or right). Even though there are a number of political ideologies, the two dominant ideologies in the United States are **liberalism** and **conservatism**. In recent years, fewer people identify as belonging to a particular political party and are more likely to use one of the following terms to describe themselves politically: conservative, liberal, progressive, or moderate. As Self-Reflection Exercise 3.1 indicates, political ideology can be conceptualized as a continuum from extremely liberal to extremely conservative.

Why Can't Liberals and Conservatives Get Along?

A number of recent books and articles (e.g., *Why We're Polarized* (2020) by Ezra Klein) explore why Americans are so divided politically and why the national discourse around politics has gotten so toxic over the past few decades. Earlier in the chapter the phrase "the personal is political" was discussed; thus, it is not surprising that political disagreements often become heated. For many, one's political beliefs are rooted in cherished and deeply held personal values. Many longstanding political observers note there was a time when Americans and American lawmakers could be friendly with those on the other side of the political spectrum and could more easily "agree to disagree." However, today Americans often live in their "political bubbles" by living around people who think like them politically, selecting romantic partners who share their political views, and only consuming news media from sources that confirm their view of politics (e.g., Fox News versus MSNBC; the *Wall Street Journal* versus the *New York Times*). And today it is rare to see federal lawmakers in Washington, D.C., who are friends with those on the other side of the aisle.

You may have heard the term *identity politics*, which refers to the idea that some individuals, particularly those who have experienced oppression in our society, support the party or candidates that advocate for their interests or concerns based on one or more of their social identities. Ezra Klein (2020) argues that for many people, political identity overlaps with other intersecting identities (e.g., religious, gender, race/ethnicity, sexual orientation, socioeconomic status, etc.), making political identity all the more powerful. A popular term to describe this phenomenon is *tribalism*—that perhaps it is in our DNA or psychological makeup to join with like-minded people and view others as the enemy. It may be natural and healthy to fight for issues that we care deeply about and to spend time with people we connect with on important values and worldviews. It is also incredibly difficult to be friendly to those who support policies that are hateful and/or harmful to one's community. But these stark divisions might also be limiting our ability to listen openly to alternative viewpoints and compromise. Politics is frequently called the art of compromise after all (particularly in a democracy).

A study by the Center for Media Engagement at the University of Texas at Austin (Duchovnay, Moore, & Masullo, 2020) identified five main approaches to use when talking to people whom you disagree with politically:

1. Focus on the people, not the politics.

    o Build a relationship before talking politics.
    o Don't take comments personally.
    o Share your own relevant experiences.
    o Give a relatable hypothetical situation.

2. Find common ground.

    o Bond over less-polarized issues.
    o Be open to listening and understanding.
    o Ask questions to understand a different viewpoint.
    o Focus on shared beliefs.

3. Stick to the facts and avoid confrontation.

    o Stick to information that can be verified.
    o Back up your opinions with evidence.
    o Limit emotion in discussion.
    o Avoid confrontational language.

4. Be an advocate rather than an opponent.

    o Adapt conversational style to audience.
    o Avoid words that might upset people.

5. Pick your battles.

- Talk about local politics instead of national politics.
- Focus on policy instead of party.
- Avoid hot-button issues.

Americans frequently state their desire for legislators to work together on various issues and to find areas of compromise. Often, the desire for more **bipartisanship** is voiced. However, this is a fairly large challenge to overcome in light of the fact that conservatives and liberals have starkly different worldviews and ideologies. Perhaps the biggest difference between **conservatives** and **liberals** concerns what the role of government should be and where we should spend our federal resources (see Table 3.1). Conservatives value tradition, individual responsibility, minimal government intervention into the lives of individuals and corporations, privatization, competition, and low taxes. President Ronald Reagan, a conservative icon in the Republican Party, is a good example of a politician espousing conservative ideology in that he championed supply-side economics and small government.

Liberals, in contrast, value social change; social justice; progress; social responsibility; and strong government intervention via taxation, regulation, and government programs to address social and economic inequality and to bring about a more level playing field. President Franklin Delano Roosevelt is a hero to many liberals because he was responsible for the creation of large-scale social programs such as Social Security, workers' compensation, unemployment compensation, and public assistance in the aftermath of the Great Depression. Some on the left prefer to describe themselves as *progressives* because the term *liberal* has been tainted by conservatives (e.g., "tax-and-spend liberal," "bleeding-heart liberal," the "liberal elite").

In recent years, Americans having been hearing more about **democratic socialism**, or **social democracy**, because this is how Senator Bernie Sanders describes his political leanings. The word *socialism* raises fear in many Americans, and people often confuse the terms *communism* and *socialism*, which is unfortunate. Social democracy is more familiar to people in Scandinavia and Western Europe, where they have long-standing Democratic Socialist political parties. You can visit the website of the Democratic Socialists of America to learn more about their political values, but they are rooted in transforming our economy and government so that it works for all citizens, not just the wealthy and the corporate elite. The ultimate aim is to make our society and economy as democratic and fair as possible. Social democrats accept capitalism but argue that it is profoundly undemocratic, run by a small, elite group of corporate interests, and that this results in vast income inequalities. They advocate for an economic system where workers have equal decision-making power and where all workers share in the benefits of the larger economy. In sum, the government needs to play an active role in tempering the greed and excesses of capitalism. Finally, in a social democracy, there is support for a generous "cradle-to-grave" social welfare system, like those in the Scandinavian nations. Poverty rates in these nations are among the lowest in the world due to social benefits such as free universal healthcare, government subsidized daycare, free college tuition, and social security benefits for the aged. The word *socialism* is scary for many Americans but the United States and many other nations around the world have parts of their system that can be described as socialism. In the United States, the best examples of this are Social Security, Medicare, the Veterans Administration, the U.S. Postal Service, and the public education system, because Americans pay for and receive benefits from these programs and social institutions.

Radicalism is another political ideology that sometimes gets confused with liberalism; however, there are important philosophical differences between the two. Liberals strive to improve society by changing the social order, but they strive to make the system more fair, not change the system altogether. In other words, liberals want to bring people into the system who have traditionally been left out. Radicals, in contrast, believe that the system itself is flawed and thus seek more fundamental changes in society. Radicals are critical of free-market economies and believe that they result in the exploitation of labor and those who are poor. Socialist economic systems often are advocated by people with a radical worldview. Note a couple of interesting points in the last two rows of Table 3.1. During the last 20 to 30 years, the United States has witnessed the growth and development of new factions within both conservative and liberal camps, as described in the following sections.

Table 3.1.   Conservatism Versus Liberalism

	Conservatism	**Liberalism**
Change	Change is generally not desirable; it is better to keep things as they are. Preserving the status quo is more important than social change.	Change is generally good; it brings progress. Supports social change and institutional reform (but not structural change, as espoused by *radicalism*).
View of society	Society is inherently fair and functions well on its own.	Society needs regulation to ensure fair competition between various interests.
Responsibility	*Individual responsibility*: Individuals have free will and are responsible for their own lives and problems. They have the right and responsibility to pursue their own self-interest and to receive a fair share of societal resources based on merit and hard work.	*Social responsibility*: Individuals are not entirely autonomous because the larger social environment plays a significant role in the problems that people face. We have a *collective responsibility* to ensure the social welfare of our citizens; individuals need to be afforded a fair chance to secure societal resources.
Role of government	Freedom means freedom from government coercion; government should not interfere with the free market; strong focus on state's rights: • Government should have a minimal role in ensuring the social welfare of its citizens. • "Government is not the solution to our problems, it is the problem" (President Ronald Reagan). • Prefer private-sector approaches over government welfare.	Government is needed to bring about a more level playing field and to compensate for the market's inability to meet basic needs; strong federal government: • Government programs are needed to ensure a minimum standard of living below which no one should fall. • The state protects people from the following risks: loss of income due to illness, old age, death, disability, economic downturns, and globalization. • Social welfare expenditures are investments in human capital, which increase the nation's wealth.

Table 3.1.   Continued

	Conservatism	Liberalism
Size of government	Small government: • Reduce the size and power of government programs. • Focus on privatization of social services. • "Starve the beast" through high deficits.	Large, active government through expanded government programs: • Social Security • Unemployment insurance • Public assistance programs • Universal health care
View of the free market	Free market economy is the best mechanism for distributing a fair share of societal resources; strongly value competition. Opposed to the rights of unions to bargain collectively and government regulation of corporations and industries.	Market is not equipped to meet basic needs; produces an unequal distribution of income, resources, and life chances; and fails to account for discriminatory barriers that stand in people's way. Government regulation and labor unions are needed to protect workers and average citizens (e.g., Food and Drug Administration, environmental protections, consumer protections).
Taxes	Lower taxes for corporations and the rich; Reagan's notion of "trickledown economics."	Tax the wealthy and corporations to fund programs for the middle class and the poor; redistribution of wealth.
View of inequality	Historically, have been opposed to extending civil rights legislation (e.g., women; nonwhites; gays and lesbians) and supporting worker's right to unionize. Inequality is inevitable and even necessary. Equality, or leveling the playing field, rewards a lack of initiative, reduces work effort, and leads to economic stagnation.	Strong focus on social/economic justice and equality, or leveling the playing field. Too much inequality is problematic. Large gap between haves and have-nots creates tensions that undermines individual life chances, economic productivity, and social harmony.
Church	Separation of church and state.	Separation of church and state.
New factions	Social/religious conservatives.	Neoliberalism.

Self-Reflection Exercise 3.1

Where would you place yourself on the following scale?

☐   Extremely liberal

☐   Liberal

☐   Slightly liberal

☐   Moderate

☐   Slightly conservative

☐   Conservative

☐   Extremely conservative

Do one of these labels accurately describe your political ideology? Why or why not?

Religion and Politics

Historically, conservatives have strongly valued the separation of church and state because this supports the idea of limited government intrusion into the lives of individuals. However, the 1980s saw the birth of the **religious right** in the United States and a new kind of conservative—the **social** or **religious conservative**. The religious right was a grassroots movement that included groups such as Jerry Falwell's Moral Majority, Pat Robertson's Christian Coalition, Phyllis Schlafly's Eagle Forum, and James Dobson's Focus on the Family, all which embrace traditional conservatives' laissez-faire approach to economics yet argue for government intervention into citizens' private lives when it comes to issues such as same-sex marriage, abortion, prayer in the schools, and end-of-life decisions.

The Christian Coalition is a political organization that seeks to mobilize pro-family Christians for political action. The mission of Focus on the Family is to spread the gospel of Jesus Christ, and the organization is based on the following six pillars: the preeminence of evangelism, the permanence of marriage, the value of children, the sanctity of human life, the importance of social responsibility, and the value of male and female (Focus on the Family, n.d.). Social conservatives are a very powerful force within the Republican Party and today outnumber traditional conservatives.

A good example to illustrate the difference between traditional conservatives and religious conservatives is the famous case of Terri Schiavo. In 1990, Ms. Schiavo suffered from severe brain damage after collapsing in her home and experiencing respiratory and cardiac arrest. She lived in a persistent vegetative state and required institutionalized care for 15 years until her feeding tube was removed at the request of her husband Michael Schiavo, her legal guardian. But this was only after a lengthy legal battle between Michael and Terri's parents, Robert and Mary Schindler, who fought against the removal of the feeding tube. The nation soon became spectators to one of the most fascinating, yet heart-wrenching, right-to-die battles in recent U.S. history that included vigorous protests by various right-to-life groups and the involvement of the Florida state legislature, the U.S. Congress, Governor Jeb Bush, President George W. Bush, and the U.S. Supreme Court. A timeline of the events that unfolded in this case is provided below.

Timeline of the Terri Schiavo Case

- **February 11, 2000**: Circuit Judge George W. Greer approves Michael Schiavo's request to have Terri's feeding tube removed, agreeing that she had told her husband that she would not want to be kept alive artificially.
- **April 2001**: Terri's feeding tube is removed but another judge orders it reinserted two days later.
- **November 2002**: Judge Greer finds no evidence that Terri has any hope of recovery and again orders tube removed.
- **October 15, 2003**: Feeding tube removed for second time.

- **October 21, 2003**: Republican governor Jeb Bush signs a bill called Terri's Law, allowing him to intervene, then orders that the tube be reinserted.
- **September 23, 2004**: Florida supreme court rules that Terri's Law is unconstitutional.
- **February 25, 2005**: Judge Greer gives permission for tube removal at 1 p.m. March 18, 2005.
- **March 18, 2005**: Feeding tube is removed. Judge Greer rules against congressional Republicans who had tried to put off tube removal by seeking her appearance at hearings.
- **March 20–21, 2005**: U.S. Congress passes a bill that would allow a federal court to review the case. President Bush signs the bill. Terri's parents file an emergency request with a federal judge to have the tube reconnected.
- **March 22, 2005**: U.S. District Judge James Whittemore refuses to order the reinsertion of the tube. Terri's parents appeal to the 11th U.S. Circuit Court of Appeals.
- **March 23, 2005**: The 11th Circuit declines to order the reinsertion of the tube. Terri's parents then appeal to the U.S. Supreme Court.
- **March 24, 2005**: U.S. Supreme Court denies the appeal.
- **March 31, 2005**: Terri Schiavo dies at age 41.

American public opinion on the Terri Schiavo case varied widely. Some, because of their religious beliefs, which include a right-to-life philosophy, sided with Terri's parents. Others believed that Terri had no quality of life and that Terri's husband was upholding her wishes and right to die. Many liberals and traditional conservatives were horrified as they watched lawmakers at the state and federal level intervene in a family's private life, which in their view, should have been left to the family to battle it out in the courts. Religious conservatives have also fought against same-sex marriage laws and have been successful rolling back women's access to seek abortion services in many states across the country.

Secularism is freedom from government imposition of religion on its citizens. Many Americans are uncomfortable with the idea of religion and politics mixing, especially when it is perceived as a particular religion pushing its beliefs onto others and codifying these beliefs into law. However, it is hard to imagine not relying on one's spiritual or religious convictions when entering the political arena when so many of our stances on political issues are informed by our personal value systems. For some, the way we want the world to be stems from beliefs that are secular in nature, while for others they are strongly rooted in spiritual or religious beliefs. It is not unusual for churches in the United States to enter the political fray. For example, the Catholic Church takes political stands on issues such as abortion, capital punishment, and end-of-life legislation, and urges the government to do more to assist those living in poverty. The U.S. civil rights movement was led by the Reverend Dr. Martin Luther King, Jr. and other church leaders in the South.

Even though conservative religious groups tend to get a lot of attention in this country, liberal religious organizations, such as Red-Letter Christians and the Interfaith Alliance, have a liberal and nonfundamentalist interpretation of Christianity and advocate addressing poverty, caring for the environment, and advancing peace and religious freedom. Finally, several prominent secular organizations such as the American Civil Liberties (ACLU) and the Texas Freedom Network fight against religious extremism and promote the separation of church and state. The mission of the Texas Freedom Network, for example, is to defeat initiatives backed by the religious right such as textbook censorship, abstinence-only sex education, defining marriage as between a man and a woman, and using tax dollars to fund religious schools and faith-based organizations. To learn more about these organizations where religion and politics intersect, complete Practice Exercise 3.1.

Practice Exercise 3.1: Religion and Politics

Visit the websites for the following groups and organizations to learn more about these organizations, their mission statement, and their message:

Christian Coalition: www.cc.org

Eagle Forum: www.eagleforum.org

Focus on the Family: www.focusonthefamily.com

Red Letter Christians: www.redletterchristians.org

Interfaith Alliance: www.interfaithalliance.org

Texas Freedom Network: www.tfn.org

ACLU: www.aclu.org

Neoliberalism

After the defeat of Democratic President Jimmy Carter in 1980, Democrats began a process of reevaluating their party's traditional stances, particularly in relation to domestic policy. This was the beginning of the party's "move to the middle" and a new political philosophy that was more cautious of large-scale federal government programs for those who are poor and vulnerable and more embracing of big business and government deregulation. In 1985, the **Democratic Leadership Council (DLC)** was founded by these new centrist Democrats who were focused on issues such as welfare reform, fiscal responsibility, expanding trade, and catering to the middle class; they called themselves "New Democrats." The DLC espouses the idea that economic growth generated in the private sector is the prerequisite for opportunity, and that government's role is to promote growth and equip Americans with the tools they need to prosper in the New Economy. They also argue that government programs should be grounded in the values most Americans share: work, family, personal responsibility, individual liberty, faith, tolerance, and inclusion. Some Democrats embraced this new strategy, whereas others derided this new group of "corporate" Democrats for abandoning some of the core values of the Democratic Party.

President Bill Clinton is a good example of a politician who embraced the goals and philosophy of **neoliberalism**. Despite the fact that conservatives branded Clinton a liberal, many progressives were greatly disillusioned by many policy decisions of the Clinton administration, including its support for the North American Free Trade Agreement (NAFTA), deregulation of the private sector, the military's "Don't ask, don't tell" policy, and the Defense of Marriage Act (DOMA) that defined marriage as a union between a man and a woman. But perhaps the decision that was most upsetting to some liberals was Clinton's support for welfare reform and his goal to "end welfare as we know it." The **Personal Responsibility and Work Opportunity Reconciliation Act of 1996** ended the 60-year federal entitlement to welfare in this country and was an effort by conservatives to reduce dependence on government assistance. The new law replaced the **Aid to Families with Dependent Children (AFDC)** program with the **Temporary Assistance for Needy Families (TANF)** program and included the following features:

- States would now receive federal block grants and would have much more discretion in designing and operating their welfare and work programs.
- Instituted a **5-year lifetime limit** on cash assistance, though states can set shorter time limits.
- Included new work requirements for parents receiving cash benefits. Adults are required to participate in work activities two years after they start receiving assistance.
- Permitted states to impose a family cap, denying cash benefits to children born into families already receiving assistance.
- Required unmarried parents under age 18 to live with an adult and stay in school in order to receive benefits.
- Prohibited parents who have been convicted of felony drug offenses from receiving benefits under TANF or the Food Stamp Program for life.
- Denied benefits to most legal immigrants entering the country for five years, with states having the option of extending the ban for a longer time period.

Think Tanks

Thinks tanks, or policy institutes, are extremely influential when it comes to shaping social policy in the United States. **Think tanks** are policy-oriented research organizations that engage in advocacy and provide expertise to politicians, including U.S. presidents. They employ experts and researchers who write policy briefs on a range of social issues and provide advice and ideas about how to solve social, political, or economic problems. In the United States, think tanks are privately funded, and they are often criticized for being biased because a number of them are aligned with a particular political party or ideology. It is fairly common for legislators to cite a report from one of these think tanks when they are working toward the passage or defeat of a particular piece of legislation.

Examples of prominent right-of-center think tanks are: the American Enterprise Institute, the Heritage Foundation, the Hoover Institution, the National Policy Institute, and the

Cato Institute. The mission of the Heritage Foundation (n.d.) is to "formulate and promote conservative public policies based on principles of free enterprise, limited government, individual freedom, traditional American values, and a strong national defense." Examples of prominent left-leaning think tanks are: the Center on Budget and Policy Priorities, the Center for American Progress, the Progressive Policy Institute, the Brookings Institution, the Urban Institute, the Institute for Policy Studies, and the Economic Policy Institute. The mission of the Center on Budget and Policy Priorities is to develop policy options to alleviate poverty and to focus lawmakers' attention on the needs of low-income individuals and families.

Political Parties in the United States

Throughout American history, Americans have vacillated between supporting Democratic candidates who embrace liberal or progressive policies and Republican candidates who advocate for policies rooted in conservative philosophy. **Partisanship**, or identifying as a member of a particular political party, has waned significantly in recent years as more and more people identify themselves as **independents**. The United States is dominated by two political parties, the Democratic and Republican parties. In recent times, the **Democratic Party** has been the home of liberal or progressive politics, while the **Republican Party** has been the home base of conservatives. Some Americans see obvious differences between these two political parties, whereas others feel that neither of the two major parties represent their interests.

During election time, each party works hard to convince voters why they are the party to best represent voters' interests and needs at the local, state, and national levels. Democrats often embrace policies where the government takes a more active role in providing social welfare benefits, protecting consumers, and regulating the economy. They embrace high taxation on wealthy Americans and corporations in order to be able to fund social benefits and government programs for all Americans. Recently, they have been active in calling on government leaders to address climate change. Republicans, on the other hand, strongly advocate for small and weak government, particularly when it comes to regulating the economy and providing social welfare benefits. They argue for lower taxes, especially for wealthier Americans and corporations, because they believe this creates a stronger economy. They have a strong pro-life stance and argue that military funding should be a significant part of the federal budget.

Although Democrats and Republicans are often seen fighting with each other, both parties have their own internal struggles as they argue over what their party should stand for. The Democratic Party is made up of those on the continuum from the far left (e.g., Senator Bernie Sanders and Congresswoman Alexandria Ocasio-Cortez) to more moderate Democrats who currently are in control of the party. The Republican Party includes a small minority of moderate Republicans (e.g., Senators Mitt Romney and Susan Collins) who work alongside those on the far right who have taken over the party in recent years.

On the Democratic side, Americans have elected presidents who were very liberal (e.g., Franklin Delano Roosevelt, Lyndon B. Johnson) and more moderate (e.g., Bill Clinton). On the Republican side, Americans have elected presidents who were very conservative (e.g., Ronald Reagan, Donald Trump) and more moderate (e.g., George H. W. Bush). With the increase of religious conservatives in the Republican Party and those embracing neoliberalism in the Democratic Party, it can be argued that both political parties have moved to the right over the last 30 to 40 years. Self-Reflection Exercise 3.2 asks you to reflect on your own level of partisanship.

Social workers who are involved in policy-change efforts must understand the two dominant political parties, what they stand for, and how they differ. One way to do this is to examine each party's political platform, a lengthy document that lays out each party's priorities and concerns. It is important to note not only what is emphasized, but also what is not emphasized in these party platforms. These party platforms change over time and are not static.

Many would like to see the development of third parties as a way to challenge the two-party system in the United States. In some other advanced nations, it is common to see multiple political parties. The only two political parties that have gained some traction in the United States in recent years are the **Green Party** on the left and the **Libertarian Party**. Libertarians believe in extremely limited government intervention in all areas of human and social life. According to the Libertarian Party's website (https://www.lp.org/about/):

> We seek to substantially reduce the size and intrusiveness of government and cut and eliminate taxes at every opportunity. We believe that peaceful, honest people should be able to offer their goods and services to willing consumers without inappropriate interference from government. We believe that peaceful, honest people should decide for themselves how to live their lives, without fear of criminal or civil penalties. We believe that government's only responsibility, if any, should be protecting people from force and fraud.

Because Libertarians emphasize individual freedom and personal responsibility, they advocate for minimal taxation (only for police and military defense), the legalization of drugs, the right to bear arms, minimal involvement in foreign policy, and the right of immigrants to come to the United States as long as they are peaceful. They believe the government should not interfere in education and health care (e.g., keep in free market) and who people can marry (e.g., same-sex marriage).

The Green Party includes many Americans who are disillusioned with the Democratic Party, which they believe has abandoned its commitment to poor and working families. Famous activist and consumer advocate Ralph Nader ran for president as a Green Party candidate in 1996 and 2000. The Green Party website (www.gp.org) lists the following 10 core values of the Green Party: grassroots democracy; social justice and equal opportunity; ecological wisdom; nonviolence; decentralization (of wealth and power); community-based economics and economic justice; feminism and gender equity; respect for diversity; personal and global responsibility; and future focus and sustainability.

Self-Reflection Exercise 3.2

Where would you place yourself on the following scale?

- ☐ Strong Democrat
- ☐ Weak Democrat
- ☐ Independent leaning to the Democrats
- ☐ Pure independent
- ☐ Independent leaning to the Republicans
- ☐ Weak Republican
- ☐ Strong Republican
- ☐ Other political party (e.g., Green Party; Libertarian Party, etc.)

Why do you think that people are less partisan today than in previous decades? (Partisanship means that you identify with a particular political party.)

New Political Movements in the United States

The Tea Party Movement

A recent development in U.S. politics is the birth of the **Tea Party**, a conservative movement that developed as a reaction to the presidency of Barack Obama and his administration's policies, in particular legislation that allocated a huge amount of federal dollars to bailout the financial system and stimulate the economy, as well as healthcare reform. Their name is a reference to the Boston Tea Party of 1773, a protest of the ruling British government by disenfranchised American colonists. The Tea Party is a decentralized movement, though it is supported by wealthy donors; a number of prominent individuals inside the Republican Party, such as former Speaker of the House Newt Gingrich; and conservative organizations such as FreedomWorks and Americans for Prosperity.

The Tea Party Patriots call themselves the official home of the Tea Party movement and their mission is to fight against excessive government spending and taxation, which is in line with their three guiding principles of personal freedom, economic freedom, and a debt-free future. In 2010 leaders within this movement developed a "Contract From America" that included 10 agenda items that they asked candidates to sign (e.g., demand a balanced federal budget; limit growth in federal spending; repeal Obamacare; simplify the tax system; and reduce taxes). There was a lot of activity across the country at the local and national levels, including local protests, a national Tea Party convention hosted by Tea Party Nation where Sarah Palin was the keynote speaker, and a Taxpayer March on Washington in September 2009. In the 2010 midterm elections, a number of Tea Party candidates were elected to political office at the state and national levels. The power and influence of the Tea Party within the Republican Party has declined over the past 10 years, and the ideas that were once passionately embraced by the Republican Party waned under President Trump. It will be interesting to see whether this faction will be reinvigorated under President Biden.

Occupy Wall Street

The Tea Party movement was not the only new movement to emerge during the Obama administration. In September 2011, the United States witnessed the emergence of the Occupy Wall Street movement on the left. The first protest was in Manhattan's financial district, but protests soon spread to other major cities in the United States and around the globe. Many media pundits criticized the movement for not having a clear agenda with a list of specific goals or demands. But the protesters resisted doing this. Instead, they communicated a broad message of fighting against the immense power amassed by banks, the financial industry, and multinational corporations, which they believe has distorted the democratic process in the United States and led to rising levels of economic inequality and injustice. According to the Occupy Wall Street website, this movement was inspired by the popular uprisings in Egypt and Tunisia.

The slogan they embraced is, "We are the 99%" to make the point that it is the 1% of the richest Americans who have enjoyed most of the financial gains in recent years at the expense of average working Americans as well as those at the bottom of the economic ladder. This movement was in large part a reaction to the 2008 financial collapse of Wall Street and the resulting economic recession that threw millions of Americans out of work and out of their homes. Many Americans were outraged when the government decided that the banks would be bailed out by the American taxpayer. Soon it appeared that the financial industry was back to business as usual with no serious reforms of the system to prevent something like this from happening again. Feelings of helplessness and anger helped to fuel this movement for those who felt that the rich and powerful collude with politicians to bend the rules in their favor with no one looking out for the interests of average Americans.

The Occupy Wall Street movement used nonviolent civil disobedience tactics, such as peaceful assembly, and tent cities were seen in many major cities where protesters organized and carried out their work. The decision-making process used by Occupy Wall Street was called a People's Assembly, a nonhierarchical consensus-building model that encourages dialogue and where all opinions are heard. Even though the protests were nonviolent, there were a number of incidents of police brutality where protesters were pepper-sprayed and beaten and arrested by police when mayors grew impatient. The protests spread to some U.S. college campuses, and one incident made national news when police in riot gear pepper-sprayed students at the University of California, Davis. For the most part, the Occupy Wall Street movement has fizzled out, but they were extremely successful in gaining extensive media coverage and branding phrases such as "the 1%" and "We are the 99%" into the American national consciousness.

Black Lives Matter (#BlackLivesMatter)

The Black Lives Matter movement (**#BlackLivesMatter**) began somewhat organically as a result of a number of high-profile shootings of primarily unarmed black men in various U.S. cities. The hashtag was first coined and popularized by activists Alicia Garza, Opal Tometi, and Patrisse Cullors in 2013 after the acquittal of private citizen George Zimmerman who shot and killed Trayvon Martin. However, the movement really took off in 2014 after the police shooting of Michael Brown in Ferguson, Missouri, and the death of Eric Garner in Staten Island, New York, after police used a chokehold that resulted in his death. The movement gained more momentum with additional high-profile shootings of unarmed black Americans by police, almost all of whom were later acquitted in court. But the Black Lives Matter movement was elevated to a whole new level and became a mainstream social movement after the horrific murder of George Floyd in Minneapolis by a police officer who pinned Mr. Floyd to the ground and kept his knee on his neck for over 8 minutes as bystanders looked on helplessly and three other police officers failed to intervene. The Black Lives Matter movement has been incredibly successful in focusing national attention on the issue of police brutality against populations of color and has propelled a number of activists onto the national stage who have successfully raised awareness of the unequal treatment of people of color by the U.S. criminal justice system. For more on this new and thriving social movement, see Chapter 11, "Advocacy for Racial Justice and Immigrant Rights."

A Revived Women's Movement (#MeToo/#Time'sUp)

In 2018, a new women's movement emerged on the national scene in response to a number of high profile cases of sexual misconduct (e.g., Bill Cosby; Harvey Weinstein; President Trump; Matt Lauer). On social media, it became known as #MeToo and #Time'sUp as women across the country began to share their personal stories of sexual harassment and sexual violence. The movement gained even more momentum after allegations of sexual assault were made against Supreme Court nominee Brett Kavanaugh by Dr. Christine Blasey Ford and other women from his high school and college years. See Chapter 12 for a fuller exploration of this social movement.

Antigun Youth Movement (#NeverAgain)

In February 2018, a new social movement, led by youth, emerged on the national scene after the mass school shooting at Marjory Stoneman Douglas High School in Parkland, Florida, which resulted in 17 casualties. Some have questioned why this incident galvanized young people in a way that seems different from previous school shootings such as Sandy Hook and Virginia Tech, and the answer seems to be that these young people have grown up in a time saturated by social media—and they are very adept at knowing how to use it as a tool for social change. Youth activists organized a national school walkout on March 14, 2018, followed by a March for Our Lives protest on March 24. The largest March for Our Lives protests were held in Washington, D.C., and New York City, where they were joined by prominent lawmakers and celebrities. However, protests were held in every U.S. state, and some observed that this was the largest youth protest since the Vietnam War. It is too soon to know how long this movement will sustain itself and what impact the movement will have on state and federal policy, but youth activists are calling on state and federal lawmakers to pass gun control legislation or be faced with being voted out of office.

Are All Social Workers Liberal?

In 2007 conservative journalist George Will published a scathing indictment of the social work profession in the *Washington Post* and referred to social work programs as schools of indoctrination with a sign on the door proclaiming "conservatives need not apply." He cited the social work profession's mission of social and economic justice and many of the constructs that are commonly examined in social work courses such as "diversity," "classism," "white privilege," "inclusion," and "racism" as evidence of the profession's liberal bias and opposition to conservative thought.

Then executive director of the NASW, Elizabeth J. Clark, responded in her piece to the *Washington Post*, "Social work students learn to use advocacy for the benefit of individuals, families, and populations that are most vulnerable to the unresolved problems of the day." She went on to say:

> Members of NASW hold a diverse array of opinions on many social issues, including abortion and homosexuality as mentioned in Will's column. However, professional social workers are united in their commitment to respecting the rights of clients to access services and expand options available to them. Social workers do not apologize for caring about people who are marginalized by society, nor do we apologize for holding members of our profession to high standards.

The social work profession certainly has a reputation for being associated with liberal causes and of embracing a progressive political ideology. Many social work scholars argue that social work's mission of working for social and economic justice makes it impossible to be neutral politically. A 2007 national study that surveyed 396 licensed social workers from 11 states found that almost half of respondents affiliated themselves with the Democratic Party, 22% described themselves as "Independents leaning to the Democratic Party," a little over 6% identified as Independents, almost 6% described themselves as "Independents leaning to the Republican party," and 13% affiliated themselves with the Republican party (Ritter, 2007). According to this study's findings, when compared to the general public, social workers identify more with the Democratic Party and less with the Republican Party.

Respondents were also asked to place themselves on a scale from extremely liberal to extremely conservative. The majority of respondents (60%) described themselves as liberal,

16% as moderate, and roughly 20% as conservative (Ritter, 2007). When compared to the general public at that time, more social workers rated themselves as liberal (60% versus 23%) (National Election Studies, 2004). A study of 294 licensed social workers in Maryland found that 55% ranked their political ideology from liberal to radical left, 34% as moderate, and 10% as right of center (Rosenwald, 2006).

As described in Chapter 1, the social work profession has a long history of being active in progressive political causes and embraces the idea of advocacy on behalf of marginalized populations, as documented in the NASW Code of Ethics. NASW also takes political stands on a number of political issues and includes these in the 11th edition of its book, *Social Work Speaks* (2018) published by the NASW Press. *Social Work Speaks* describe the association's position on a wide range of public policy issues such as reproductive choice, health care, the death penalty, human trafficking, affirmative action, immigration, and LGBTQ rights issues, to name a few. However, as the above research shows, a significant minority of social workers identify as being politically conservative, including social work professor Bruce Thyer who argues that "conservative political ideology is both largely ignored and demonized by mainstream social work" and that "conservative principles are completely congruent with the value of social justice" (2010, p. 272). This creates some interesting tensions within the profession, but also creates opportunities for debate, reflection, tolerance, and critical thinking.

REFERENCES

Clark, E. J. (2007, October 20). What does unite social workers? *Washington Post*. Retrieved from http://www.washingtonpost.com/wp-dyn/content/article/2007/10/19/AR2007101902281.html

Duchovnay, M., Moore, C., & Masullo, G. M. (2020). How to talk to people who disagree with you politically. Center for Media Engagement. Retrieved from https://mediaengagement.org/research/divided-communities

Green Party of the United States. (n.d.). Ten key values. Retrieved from http://www.gp.org/ten_key_values_2016

Focus on the Family. (n.d.). Foundational values. Retrieved from https://www.focusonthefamily.com/about/foundational-values

Heritage Foundation (n.d.). About Heritage. Retrieved from https://www.heritage.org/about-heritage/mission

Klein, E. (2020). *Why we're polarized*. New York: Avid Reader Press.

Libertarian Party. (n.d). About the Libertarian Party. Retrieved from https://www.lp.org/about/

National Association of Social Workers. (2018). *Social work speaks: National Association of Social Workers Policy Statements 2018–2020* (11th ed.). Washington, D.C.: NASW Press.

National Election Studies. (2004). The ANES guide to public opinion and electoral behavior. http://www.electionstudies.org/nesguide/toptable/tab3_1.htm

Prigmore C., & Atherton, C. (1986). *Social welfare policy: Analysis and formulation*. Lexington, MA: D.C. Heath.

Ritter, J. A. (2007). Evaluating the political participation of licensed social workers in the new millennium. *Policy Practice Journal, 6*(4), 61–78.

Rosenwald, M. (2006). Exploring the political diversity of social workers. *Social Work Research, 30*(2), 121–126.

Thyer, B. (2010). Social justice: A conservative perspective. *Journal of Comparative Social Welfare, 26*(2–3), 261–274.

Will, G. (2007, October 14). Code of coercion. *Washington Post.* Retrieved from http://www.washingtonpost.com/wp-dyn/content/article/2007/10/12/AR2007101202151.html

Credits

CHAPTER 4   The Politics of Economics

"In this world nothing can be said to be certain, except death and taxes."

~Benjamin Franklin, 1789

"Like slavery and apartheid, poverty is not natural. It is man-made and it can be overcome and *eradicated by the actions of human beings.*"

~Nelson Mandela

"NASW supports a national economic policy that ... recognizes that a nation's well-being *derives not only from an economic balance sheet, but also from the well-being of its members.*"

~NASW, Social Work Speaks, 2009

Figure 4.1   Protester at the Occupy Wall Street demonstration in New York City

CHAPTER SUMMARY

Although many political debates are focused on social issues, some of the biggest political battles involve how the United States should spend its state and federal resources (i.e., taxpayer money). Indeed, a significant portion of political action by social workers involves trying to convince local, state, and federal governments to commit more public dollars to safety net programs, as well as programs that invest in human and social capital. By better understanding government budgets, social workers can learn what Americans prioritize as a society and where advocacy efforts are needed in order to ensure that vital social services are available to individuals and families in need. One of the primary tasks of advocacy groups is to be at the table explaining to lawmakers why more resources are needed to address a whole host of social problems—from child welfare, to poverty and homelessness, to mental health. Often there is stiff competition between various interest groups that are trying to get a bigger piece of the funding pie. However, getting increased funding has become increasingly challenging in recent years due to deficits at all levels of government. This requires great skill and creativity. Social work students are not always thrilled to have to learn about economics, but social work practitioners who have a basic working knowledge of economic issues and budgeting will be much more effective than those who do not.

Anyone who is heavily involved with politics and legislation understands the important connection between a country's political and economic systems. Political economy is the study of this interrelationship and seeks to understand (1) how government passes laws and policies that affect a society's allocation of resources and (2) how a society's economic system impacts the kinds of laws and policies that get passed by government. The strong connection between politics and economics cannot be overstated, and one of the major differences between liberals and conservatives concerns what the role of the government should be when it comes to taxation and wealth distribution.

Two sociologists used the term *welfare exceptionalism* to describe the reluctance of the United States to become a welfare state similar to other western industrialized countries. It is important for the social work profession to explore why the richest country in the world has such high rates of poverty and income inequality. One of the values of the social work profession is to promote social and economic justice, yet the profession has been accused of neglecting its commitment to the reduction of poverty on a macro level. This chapter will explore various policies that strive to promote poverty reduction in the United States.

STUDENT LEARNING OBJECTIVES

- Students will be able to explain the relationship between politics and the economy (political economy).
- Students will be able to summarize U.S. federal spending and explain the difference between discretionary and mandatory spending.

- ○ Students will be able to describe taxation in the United States and explain the relationship between taxation and economic inequality.

- ○ Students will be able to evaluate why the United States is in debt and to explain the difference between the deficit and the debt.

- ○ Students will be able to summarize both the strengths and shortcomings of poverty reduction strategies in the United States.

At first glance, this chapter might seem intimidating to some social work students because many of us have been give the message that economics is complicated and hard to understand. However, a significant portion of political action by social workers involves trying to convince local, state, and federal governments to commit more public dollars to social safety net programs that help keep people out of poverty, as well as programs that invest in human and social capital. Thus, social workers must learn the basic language and concepts of budgets and economics, which is completely doable. By better understanding government budgets, social workers can learn what we tend to prioritize as a society and where advocacy efforts are needed in order to ensure that vital health and social services are available to individuals and families in need. One of the primary tasks of advocacy groups is to be at the table explaining to lawmakers why more funding is needed to address a whole host of social problems—from child abuse and neglect, to poverty and homelessness, to mental illness. Often there is stiff competition between the various interest groups that are trying to get a bigger piece of the "funding pie." And arguing for increased funding for social programs requires skill and creativity in order to overcome those who argue for low taxes or small government. Although many political debates are focused on social issues, some of the biggest political battles involve how we should spend our state and federal resources (i.e., taxpayer money).

Policy Efforts That Promote Poverty Reduction

One of the core values of the social work profession is to promote social and economic justice, and there is perhaps no issue that is more deserving of social workers' attention than the reduction of poverty given that it has such negative impacts on people's lives and access to opportunity. Yet the social work profession has been accused of neglecting its commitment to the reduction of poverty on a macro level. Most would agree that poverty is not an easy social problem to solve. Social workers work with low-income individuals and families every day, and it can feel like a daunting endeavor to help people move out of poverty. To add to this complexity, how we define who is living in poverty in the United States is political and not without controversy. Some believe that the official poverty line underestimates the number of poor people in the United States, whereas others believe it is an overestimate.

Poverty is measured in the United States by comparing a person's or family's pretax cash income to a set poverty threshold or minimum amount of income needed to cover basic needs. People whose income falls under this threshold are considered poor. Shockingly, the **official poverty measure** was adopted in the 1960s and has not been revised since.

The formula was based on the idea that the average family spends about one-third of their income on food, so the cost of the least expensive food plan was calculated and that number was multiplied by three. The official poverty measure adjusts for various factors such as the number of children younger than 18 years, household size, and the age of householder. Additionally, it is adjusted for inflation based on the Consumer Price Index (CPI). According to the U.S. Census Bureau (2020), in 2019 the poverty line was as follows:

- Single person: $13,300
- Single parent with one child: $17,622
- Single parent with two children: $20,598
- Two adults with two children: $25,926

The poverty line is an **absolute measure** of poverty, which means that if you are below that line, you are in poverty, but if you are a few dollars above that line, you are not. Many government programs in the United States use the official poverty measure to determine whether people are eligible to receive benefits. Criticisms of the official poverty measure include the following: it does not take into account the fact that food is cheaper than it was in the 1960s, while costs for health care, housing, and child care have increased; when calculating household income, it does not include benefits such as SNAP and tax credits that people receive; and it does not adjust for geographic differences in housing costs (e.g., it is much more expensive to live in California than rural Alabama). As a result, the U.S. Census Bureau developed a new measure of poverty in 2011 called the Supplemental Poverty Measure (SPM) that includes a more expansive picture of a family's income and level of need. However, it is important to note that the SPM does not replace the official poverty measure, which remains the primary source for the government's official poverty statistics and for determining program eligibility.

According to the U.S. Census Bureau (2020), in 2019, 10.5% of people in the United States were living below the poverty line, which represents 34 million people. When describing people who are poor in the United States, generally two groups are identified: the working poor and those who are unemployed. Decades of research has consistently found that the following groups are disproportionately represented among the poor: women (referred to as the *feminization of poverty*), children, Blacks, and Latinos. The poverty rate in 2019 was 7.3% for Asian Americans, 9.1% for Whites, 15.7% for Latinos, and 18.8% for Blacks. The poverty rate for children under age 18 was 14.4%. The poverty rate was very high for those with disabilities (22.5%) and those without a high school degree (23.7%). It will be fascinating to see how these figures change for 2020 as a result of the pandemic and resulting economic recession.

In order to address poverty, it is important to understand why people are poor. Many researchers and poverty research centers are doing important work in this regard in order to gain more knowledge about this rather complex social problem (see Figure 4.2). The causes are often multifaceted. Social work professor Dr. Mark Rank explores the causes of poverty in his book *One Nation Underprivileged: Why American Poverty Affects Us All* (2004). The premise of his book is that the dominant perspective in the United States has viewed poverty as an individual failing, rather than the result of structural failings at the economic, political, and societal levels. He points to the impact of discrimination, the inability of the labor market to provide enough decent-paying jobs, and an American economy that has increasingly produced large numbers of low-paying jobs, part-time jobs, and jobs lacking in benefits.

Coalition on Human Needs
National Alliance to End Homelessness
National Coalition for the Homeless
The Alliance to End Hunger
National Low Income Housing Coalition
Half in Ten Campaign
The Urban League
National Center for Children in Poverty, Columbia University
National Poverty Center, University of Michigan
Center for Poverty Research, University of Kentucky
Institute for Research on Poverty, University of Wisconsin-Madison
West Coast Poverty Center, University of Washington

Figure 4.2 *Poverty advocacy organizations and research organizations*

According to Rank (2004), in the United States we have focused on *who* loses out at the economic game rather than *why* the game produces losers in the first place. The model that he puts forward is as follows:

- Opportunities and the acquisition of human capital (i.e., education, skill set, talents, abilities) are strongly influenced by your parents' social class.
- Lack of human capital places individuals in a vulnerable state when detrimental events and crises occur; life crises are experienced more often and with greater intensity.
- Structural forces ensure that there will be losers in the economic game.

Rank includes data in his book that show that a majority of Americans will experience poverty at some point during their adult years, as well as the societal costs to poverty (e.g., higher healthcare costs, less productive workers, and high rates of criminal activity).

There are three primary policy strategies that can be used to address poverty. The **alleviative approach** relies on programs that ease the suffering of the poor but do not ameliorate the causes of poverty (e.g., public assistance programs such as Food Stamps and welfare programs). The **preventive approach** attempts to prevent poverty from occurring in the first place and often employs social insurance strategies (e.g., Social Security, the unemployment insurance program). The **curative approach** targets the root causes of poverty and involves structural changes in society that would result in low levels of poverty (e.g., high taxes and redistribution of wealth similar to the social welfare systems used in many European countries). Even though the United States uses all three of these approaches in addressing poverty, we do not rely as much on the curative approach. The Scandinavian nations are known for relying heavily on this approach, and they have very low rates of poverty as a result. A number of policies have been recommended by experts as sound antipoverty strategies:

- **Make work pay.** This can be accomplished by raising the minimum wage and/or passing living wage ordinances (living wages are higher than minimum wages because they factor in how much money is needed to meet one's basic needs adequately). Below is a sample piece of testimony by a social worker in support of raising the minimum wage. Additionally, the federal Earned Income Tax Credit (EITC) and Child Tax Credit have been touted as the best antipoverty tools in existence today. They are targeted to low-income working families. The Child Tax Credit is worth up to $1,000 per each eligible child. The EITC decreases the tax burden on people making low and moderate incomes, and qualified workers receive a tax rebate from the federal government that exceeds the taxes they paid. In 2017, more than 25 million workers received this benefit, and the average EITC was about $2,470. For some families, the credit is enough to lift them over the poverty line. Finally, promoting unionization can be useful for ensuring that workers have fair wages and benefits.

- **Help people build wealth.** This can include asset-building strategies such as the use of individual development accounts (IDAs) where low-income people are encouraged to save, and whatever they put in is matched (by an outside funder), helping it to grow more quickly over time; funds can be used to buy a home, start a business, or to finance a college education. Another policy approach can include helping people become first-time home buyers, because this is a way to accumulate wealth and build equity. Finally, microfinance programs can be used to help people start a business.

Testimony in Support of Raising the Minimum Wage

February 15, 2016

Representative Paul Holvey, Chair
Members of the House Committee on Business and Labor
900 Court St. NE
Salem, Oregon 97301
Chair Holvey and Members of the Committee,

My name is Jessica Ritter, and I am a board member of Children First for Oregon. I am also an Associate Professor of Social Work at Pacific University Oregon. Children First wants Oregon to be **the best place to be a kid**. We strive to make change by advocating for policies that keep children healthy and safe while providing opportunities to allow them to succeed. Children First is the convener of the United for Kids 2016

Children's Agenda, which includes over 70 organizations and coalitions. Today, Children First is asking your support of SB 1532 A, a bill that would raise the minimum wage in Oregon.

As we all know, Oregon is a wonderful state, but unfortunately too many families are unable to provide their children with the basic necessities they need to thrive and succeed.

- More than 1 in 5 children in Oregon live in poverty, and the rate is much higher for children of color (38% of African American children; 33% of Pacific Islander children; 28% of Native American children; and 26% of Latino children).[1]
- Most families in poverty in Oregon are working families (71%), yet even working full-time, a minimum wage worker does not make enough to lift a family out of poverty.[2]
- Rents are 9% higher while family income is 7% lower than before the Great Recession.[3]
- So many Oregon workers are paid so little that the federal and state government spends $1.7 billion in taxpayer money each year on programs like food stamps and other income supports.[4]

When we think of a minimum wage hike we often think of adults, but **children are absolutely and deeply affected** by living in a home with inadequate financial resources. There has been extensive research documenting the negative effects of poverty on children and their ability to learn and develop. A 2015 study published in JAMA Pediatrics[5] found that children from families with incomes lower than the federal poverty level had regional gray matter volumes that were as much as eight to 10 percentage points less than those of children with normal development. There are serious human costs to children living in poverty, and this legislation has the power to break the often difficult-to-escape cycle of poverty.

The 2015 Kids Count Data Book from the Annie E. Casey Foundation **ranks Oregon as 35th in the nation with regard to economic well-being**. We can do better. When families earn enough money to support their families, everyone wins. Families that earn more, spend more, which helps to stimulate the state's economy. They also become taxpayers and are less reliant on social welfare programs. It's time for Oregon to help the hard-working parents of these children earn their way out of poverty and to make work pay. It's time to raise Oregon's minimum wage.

Please help us to make Oregon the best place to be a kid by voting yes on SB 1532 A. Thank you for your attention and your work on behalf of Oregon's children.

1   Oregon Center for Public Policy. October 2015. "Poverty in Oregon in Six Charts."
2   Oregon Center for Public Policy. December 2015. "Poverty Despite Work: A Growing Problem in Oregon."
3   Children First for Oregon. "2016 Children's Agenda: A Legislative Policy Agenda for Oregon's Kids."
4   Reddy, T., Morris, D., Scott, E. K., Bussel, B., & Dyer, S. (2015, January). The high cost of low wages in Oregon. *Oregon Workforce Report 2014.* University of Oregon Labor Education and Research Center.
5   Hair, N. L., Hanson, J. L., Wolfe, B. L., & Pollak, S. D. (2015). Association of child poverty, brain development, and academic achievement. *JAMA Pediatrics, 169*(9).

- **Provide opportunity for all.** Most people would agree that in a just and fair society, members of that society should have equal access to opportunity. It is a sign of a healthy society when members of one social class are able to advance to a higher social class, which has been termed **social mobility**. One way to help ensure that people have access to opportunity is to provide citizens with access to high-quality education, including higher education. Unfortunately, many Americans who live in high-poverty areas of the country are provided with substandard schools that puts them at a significant disadvantage. Additionally, the cost of housing and a college education has become unaffordable for many Americans. Advocates can push for policies that ask our legislators to make serious state and federal investments in public education, including higher education, and policies that make housing affordable for lower- and middle-class Americans.

• **Economic security and wealth redistribution.** The Scandinavian nations are perhaps the gold standard in their design of a social welfare system that includes high taxation to support a strong and generous "cradle to grave" social safety net that has resulted in the lowest levels of poverty and income inequality in the world (see Figure 4.3). Many Americans are quick to criticize this model because it includes high taxes, but Scandinavians are just as quick to point out all of the benefits that they receive from the taxes they pay and the security that comes from living a debt-free life, including no student loans to pay back. Scandinavia's system is an example of a Social Democracy, a system that blends capitalism with one of the most generous social welfare systems in the world.

"Cradle to grave" benefits that everyone pays for (via taxes) and everyone benefits from	Government subsidized child care so that it is very affordable for families
Free Universal Healthcare (including dental and mental health care)	Free college and/or vocational training (i.e., no student debt)
Monthly child allowance until child is 16 years old	Unemployment insurance and job training
Paid sick leave as a right of employees	Very generous benefits for senior citizens (e.g., social security; residential care)
Generous paid family leave after the birth/adoption of a child (480 days)	Housing subsidies to help make housing affordable
5 weeks paid vacation per year	Free school lunches for all children

Figure 4.3   Common model for social welfare benefits in Scandinavian nations

Two U.S. presidents, Franklin Delano Roosevelt and Lyndon B. Johnson, chose to prioritize poverty and to address it by passing far-reaching social welfare legislation. Johnson went as far as to declare a "War on Poverty." But since then, there has been no serious effort to address this social problem systematically as a nation, and this issue is often left off of the political agenda. It is up to social workers and other committed advocates to focus lawmakers and the greater public's attention onto this social problem that most people would rather ignore.

Political Economy

Social work students are not always thrilled to have to learn about economics, but social work practitioners who have a basic working knowledge of economic issues and budgeting will be much more effective than those who do not. Anyone who is heavily involved with politics and legislation understands the important connection between a country's political and economic systems. **Political economy** is the study of this interrelationship and seeks to understand (1) how government passes laws and policies that affect a society's allocation of resources and (2) how a society's economic system impacts the kinds of laws and policies that get passed by government. Some universities offer degree programs in political economy, and it is an important area of study and scholarship. The strong connection between politics and economics cannot be overstated, and one of the major differences between liberals and conservatives concerns what the role of the government should be when it comes to taxation and wealth distribution (see Table 4.1).

Current Events Spotlight: Stimulus Bills Passed During the Coronavirus Pandemic

One of the biggest economic debates that occurred between Democrats and Republicans during the coronavirus pandemic had to do with whether to offer **stimulus payments** (in the form of direct cash) and more generous unemployment benefits to Americans, many of whom were suffering economic hardship due to the economic downturn. Most Democrats were in favor of this type of immediate and direct aid, while many Republicans were not. Traditionally, Republicans do not support direct payments to citizens as they worry about fostering dependency in people. Democrats, on the other hand, believe that this kind of aid helps alleviate suffering and can boost the economy because most people end up spending these funds immediately on material goods such as food and other basic necessities.

The first stimulus bill, **the CARES Act**, was passed on March 27, 2020, and included a comprehensive array of benefits for individuals, small businesses, and other entities to help them weather the impending economic recession. The CARES Act, funded at $2 trillion dollars, was the largest economic stimulus package in modern U.S. history. It included:

- Direct payments of $1,200 to Americans making up to $75,000;
- An additional $500 for every eligible child under age 16;
- Expanded unemployment benefits, including an additional $600 a week in unemployment benefits (on top of the normal weekly benefit) until July 31, 2020;
- Deferment of federal student loan payments;
- Billions of dollars to support small businesses with federally guaranteed loans;
- Protections from being evicted (for eligible renters);
- Protections for homeowners who cannot pay their monthly mortgage payment (for those with federally backed mortgages);
- Funding to hospitals, medical providers, and state governments.

In December 2020, a second stimulus bill, funded at $900 billion was passed by the U.S. Congress. Democrats fought for more generous benefits, but had to compromise with Republicans in order to settle on a final bill, which included:

- Direct payments of $600 to those making up to $75,000;
- An additional $600 for every eligible child dependent;
- An additional $300 a week in unemployment benefits (on top of the normal weekly benefit) for 11 weeks;
- Additional loans for small businesses via the Paycheck Protection Program (with stricter terms to address the unfairness and fraud that occurred in the last round of benefits);
- Funding for vaccines and nursing homes;
- Funding for climate change;
- Ban on surprise medical bills;
- Extension of protections for eligible renters and homeowners who cannot pay their rent or mortgage;
- $25 billion in rental assistance;
- Billions of dollars for food security to support programs such as SNAP, food banks, food pantries, and Meals on Wheels;
- $7 billion for expanding access to high-speed Internet connections (assistance to low-income families to pay monthly Internet bills; funds to build out needed infrastructure in rural and tribal areas).

As soon as President-elect Joe Biden came into office, he introduced a $1.9 trillion coronavirus relief bill (dubbed the "American Rescue Plan") to help stimulate the economy and to aid the families and businesses who have been suffering terribly as a result of the economic recession caused by the coronavirus pandemic. The bill was one of largest stimulus plans in U.S. history and passed in the U.S. Congress along party lines. It did not receive a single Republican vote. Some of the features of this stimulus bill include the following:

- Extends a $300 per week unemployment aid supplement until Sept. 6, 2021 (on top of what individuals receive from their state).
- $1,400 direct payments to Americans making less than $75,000 a year and married couples making less than $150,000 a year.
- Expands the child tax credit for one year. Increases to $3,600 for children under six and $3,000 for kids between 6 and 17. Most American families will receive roughly $300 per child per month. Democrats hope to make this benefit permanent.
- $75 billion for Covid-19 vaccine distribution, testing, and contact tracing.
- $30 billion in rental and homeowner assistance.
- $350 billion in relief to state, local and tribal governments.
- $130 billion to help K–12 schools reopen safely.
- $40 billion to colleges and universities.
- Increases the Supplemental Nutrition Assistance Program benefit by 15% through September.
- $3 billion for states to help address mental health and substance use disorders, which have been exacerbated by the pandemic
- $7 billion of additional funding for the Paycheck Protection Program that provides relief to small businesses to help keep them afloat.
- $30 billion in aid to restaurants and bars.
- Subsidies to help Americans purchase health insurance through the Affordable Care Act exchanges.

Table 4.1. Conservatism Versus Liberalism

	Conservatism	Liberalism
View of the free market	A free market economy is the best mechanism for distributing a fair share of societal resources; competition is at the heart of free market economics.	The market is not equipped to meet basic needs; it produces an unequal distribution of income, resources, and life chances; and it fails to account for discriminatory barriers that stand in people's way.
Taxes	Lower taxes for corporations and the rich because this will allow businesses to expand and hire more workers. Conservatives embrace supply-side economics, which argues that the government should not meddle with the free market; oppose excessive government regulation.	Tax the wealthy and corporations to fund programs for the middle class and the poor. Liberals embrace Keynesian economics, which argues that the government must intervene into the affairs of the market in order to address its inadequacies and to ensure low unemployment; support policies that use taxation as a mechanism for redistributing wealth in society.

Taxation is one of the most contentious political issues in the United States, and there are distinct ideological differences between those on the left and those on the right, which often seem almost impossible to bridge. The Tea Party movement has made this one of their key issues, and their stance is that taxes take people's freedom away from them. Their position is that citizens should be allowed to keep the money that they earn and should not be heavily taxed. Those on the left maintain that taxes are necessary in order to ensure a level playing field and to fund education and important social programs that contribute to the greater public good.

Two dominant, and somewhat opposing, economic ideologies have had great influence in the United States: Keynesian economics (also called demand-side economics) and free market economics (also called supply-side economics). The father of **free market economics** is economist Milton Friedman, whose theories have been embraced by political conservatives and U.S. presidents such as Ronald Reagan. The basic idea behind this economic school of thought is that the government should not meddle in the affairs of the free market, and that the market works best when it is left to operate freely. Supporters advocate low taxes and minimal government regulation of corporations and argue that high taxes on corporations prevent businesses from being able to invest, expand their business, and hire more workers. "Supply-siders" also support the privatization of social services and other governmental functions, because, in their view, money spent on public welfare is money that could be spent in the private sector. They argue that economic growth is better than public welfare because it provides people with a job and a way to make a living (instead of people becoming dependent on government services). Opponents of supply-side economics have derisively labeled it "trickle-down economics" because it is predicated on the dubious belief that letting wealthy people keep more of their money (via low taxation) will trickle down to benefit the rest of society.

Critics of supply-side economics dispute the contention that the free market can be left to its own devices and have referred to ardent supporters of this economic philosophy as "free market fundamentalists." **Keynesian economics**, which is named after the economist John Maynard Keynes, is the economic philosophy embraced by those on the left. Supporters of this school of economic thought believe that there are times when the government must take an active role in addressing the inadequacies of the free market, particularly during economic recessions when people lose confidence in the system and save their cash instead of spending and/or investing. This model guided the economic policies of President Roosevelt in the aftermath of the Great Depression, and to some extent the policies of President Obama who came into office facing a serious economic recession. Keynesian economic philosophy posits that there are a range of options for spurring demand and ensuring that the economy can provide near-full employment: increasing or decreasing taxes; overseeing the transfer of public goods or services; printing more money; spending money to fund public works projects; and subsidizing demand via the provision of welfare entitlements. According to Keynes, social welfare spending boosts the economy because it increases people's spending capacity and increases productivity because social welfare programs are investments in human capital (i.e., provides people with education, training, and skills).

When we look around the world, we see various types of economic systems, the primary ones being **communism**, **capitalism**, and a **blend of capitalism and socialism**, what some have termed **social democracy** and "the Middle Way." Karl Marx is the brainchild of communism, but many of his ideas were not instituted in those nations that describe their economic system as communist. Marx was extremely critical of capitalism and believed it led to class warfare, where the working class end up being exploited and ruled by an elite, wealthy ruling class. Marx envisioned communism as a system where the working class controls the means of production, and a central tenet of this philosophy can be summarized with his famous phrase: "From each according to his ability, to each according to his needs." However, in many communist nations, such as Russia, North Korea, Cuba, and China, the state (not the workers) controls all aspects of the political and economic system, individual liberty is restricted, and they are sometimes led by malevolent leaders or dictators.

The United States is perhaps the best example of a nation that embraces capitalism and the free market. Some have referred to the United States as embracing "free market fundamentalism" because it has often been loath to institute rules and regulations to temper a system that can lead to greed, corruption, and vast economic inequality between the haves and the have-nots. The Scandinavian nations have embraced a system that blends a market economy with a strong and generous cradle-to-grave social welfare system. Their system is a modern form of **socialism** that has been called **social democracy**. Social democracy includes the redistribution of wealth via high taxation and a democratic government that coexists alongside a capitalist economy. Renowned scholar Jeffrey Sachs has studied the economic systems of nations around the world and has come to the conclusion that "the Middle Way" used in Scandinavia is the ideal economic model (see Figure 4.3 for more on their social welfare benefits). These nations are the happiest, healthiest, the most educated, and have the lowest poverty rates and level of economic inequality in the world. The word *socialism* is scary for many Americans, but the United States and many other nations around the world have parts of their system that can be described as socialism. In the United States, the best examples of this are Social Security, Medicare, the Veterans Administration, the U.S. Postal Service, and the public education system, because Americans pay for and receive benefits from these programs and social institutions.

Revenues ("Taxes 101")

To begin learning about the U.S. federal budget, first we will examine **revenues**, or how money comes into the government. Sometimes social workers are in the position of advocating for increased revenue (i.e., taxes) to pay for a variety of social welfare programs. This is often a hard sell to politicians who know this is not a popular stance with many constituents in their home districts who would prefer not to pay higher taxes. So, what is the purpose of taxation? Many discussions and debates surrounding taxation gloss over this question. Generally speaking, taxes provide the revenue needed to address the public good, and they are a major source of funding for many public programs. Taxes support the following (this list is not exhaustive):

- Public safety (police, child protection)
- Public education, including higher education (K–12 teachers, community colleges, state colleges, financial aid to college students)
- Infrastructure (roads, bridges, dams, airports, water systems, power plants/lines, schools, public transit)
- National defense and homeland security
- Research (science and technology)
- Health care (Medicare, Medicaid, public hospitals)
- Public housing
- Environmental protection (air, water, chemicals, and toxics)
- Consumer protection (food and drug safety)
- Social Security program
- Income support programs (TANF, WIC, SNAP)
- Public libraries
- Postal Service
- Public transportation

Progressive Versus Regressive Taxation

It is important for social workers to understand the difference between progressive and regressive taxes so they can weigh in appropriately when these issues are being considered by local or national lawmakers. **Progressive taxes** place a higher burden on wealthier citizens because the tax rate increases as income increases (e.g., income taxes). **Regressive taxes** are those taxes where the poor pay a higher percentage of their income than do wealthier individuals (e.g., sales taxes). Table 4.2 shows various types of taxes and whether they are considered regressive or progressive. At first glance, it may seem confusing that a sales tax is regressive because it is a set rate for everyone. For example, in a state with a 7% sales tax, all buyers would pay $70 in tax for a new laptop that costs $1,000. However, that $70 impacts a low-income person more than a higher-income individual because it represents a higher percentage of a lower-income person's overall budget. In other words, a person making $2,000 a month will feel that $70 much more than a person making $5,000 a month. The Social Security tax is also considered regressive because it has a tax ceiling, meaning that individuals are only taxed on the first $137,700 that they make (as of 2020). Thus, individuals making $1 million a year are only taxed on the first $137,700 of their earnings, while someone making $50,000 a year is taxed on their entire income. However, other economists argue that when you factor in the benefits that people receive over time, this tax is actually progressive, so this one is up for debate. The federal income tax is progressive because those who earn higher incomes pay more in taxes due to a graduated rate structure.

Table 4.2. Types of Taxes

Type of Tax	Progressive or Regressive?
Federal income tax	Progressive
State income tax (not all states have one)	Progressive
Sales tax	Regressive
Social Security withholding tax (i.e., payroll tax)	(Up for debate)
Real estate property tax (local tax)	(Up for debate)
Estate tax	Progressive
Luxury taxes (taxes on luxury goods)	Progressive
"Sin" taxes (e.g., tax on cigarettes/alcohol)	Regressive
Corporate income tax	Progressive (except when corporations pay less due to tax loopholes)

Taxes: Who Carries the Burden?

Many questions are debated with regard to taxation, such as: Who should bear the burden of taxation in our society? How much should they be asked to pay? To what extent should we use the tax system as a way to redistribute wealth and lessen economic inequality? And, finally, how should we spend our public resources? The National Association of Social Workers' (NASW) policy statement on poverty and economic justice indicates the profession's support for "federal tax, budget, and spending mechanisms that help to narrow gaps in the resources available to people" as well as "an adequate safety net for those unable to provide for themselves" (2009, p. 261).

According to the Center on Budget and Policy Priorities (CBPP, 2020a), total federal tax revenues for fiscal year 2019 were approximately $3.5 trillion. As Figure 4.4 shows,

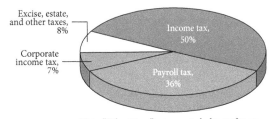

Note: "Other Taxes" category includes profits on assets held by the Federal Reserve. Figures may not add due to rounding.
Source: Office of Management and Budget.

Figure 4.4 Sources of federal tax revenue

Source: Center on Budget and Policy Priorities. (2020a). Policy basics: Where do federal tax revenues come from. Retrieved from https://www.cbpp.org/research/federal-tax/policy-basics-where-do-federal-tax-revenues-come-from

roughly 86% of these revenues were from individual income taxes and the payroll tax, which funds Social Security, Medicare, and unemployment insurance. Corporate income taxes represented about 7% of federal revenues, while the remaining 8% came from other taxes, such as excise taxes on goods such as alcohol and tobacco, and the estate tax, which is a tax on wealthy estates passed from deceased persons to their heirs.

The data show that since the 1940s the burden of taxation in the United States has increasingly been shifted from corporations to individuals. Between 1943 and 2015, corporate income taxes went from 40% of total federal revenues to 10.8% of total federal revenues (National Priorities Project, n.d.). Meanwhile, individual income taxes have remained relatively stable over the years. And according to a 2021 report by the Institute on Taxation and Economic Policy, 55 of the largest corporations in the United States, such as Nike, Fed Ex, and Excel Energy, paid $0 in federal taxes on billions of dollars in profit in 2020 (Gardner & Wamhoff, 2021). This is possible due to tax breaks by the government; strategies to avoid paying taxes, such as moving a business overseas; as well as corporations that hire tax attorneys who are very skilled at finding loopholes in the tax system. The practice of the government giving subsidies and tax breaks to corporations has been termed **corporate welfare**. Warren Buffett, one of the richest people in the world, famously remarked that his receptionist pays a higher share of her income in taxes than he does, which he believes is unfair. Other millionaires agree and have started a new website called Patriotic Millionaires for Fiscal Strength, where they are asking the president and government leaders to increase taxes for individuals and corporations making over $1 million a year.

Spending

Now that we understand how money comes into the government, it is time to focus on the spending side of the equation. Vigorous debate in the nation's capital has focused on government spending recently due to heightened concerns over the growing national debt. For fiscal year 2019, the federal government spent $4.4 trillion. Of this 4.4 trillion, 3.5 trillion was financed by tax revenues, and the remining amount was financed by borrowing. Many are not aware that there are three pieces of the pie when it comes to spending by the federal government (see Figure 4.5):

- Mandatory spending (61% of the budget)
- Discretionary spending (30% of the budget)
- Interest paid on the national debt (9% of the budget)

Mandatory spending in fiscal year 2019 was approximately $2.7 trillion (Congressional Budget Office, 2020). This is the part of the budget that funds the nation's **entitlement programs,** such as programs for older adults (Social Security), healthcare programs (Medicare and Medicaid), programs that provide income support (Veteran's Benefits; SNAP; unemployment compensation; Supplemental Security Income for the aged, blind, and disabled; federal student loans), as well as funds for transportation. This part of

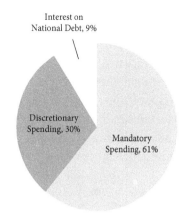

Figure 4.5   Federal spending, FY 2019

Source: Congressional Budget Office. (2020). The Federal Budget in 2019: An Infographic. Retrieved from https://www.cbo.gov/publication/56324

the budget does not go through the annual appropriation process because these expenditures are mandated by law. **Discretionary spending** in fiscal year 2019 was approximately $1.3 trillion (Congressional Budget Office, 2020). This is the part of the federal budget that is negotiated by the president and Congress, who may choose to increase or decrease funding on any of these programs in a given fiscal year. Roughly half of discretionary spending was devoted to military spending. The rest of the discretionary spending went to various government agencies that focus on education, housing, scientific research, veterans services, transportation, and more (National Priorities Project, 2020) (see Figure 4.6). Finally, paying **interest on the national debt** (which totaled roughly $22.8 trillion at the end

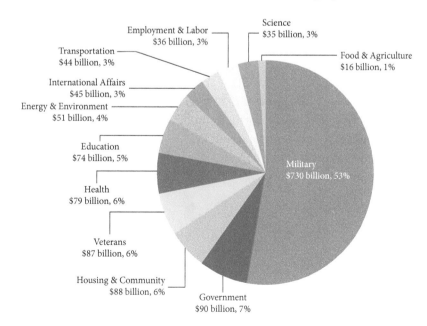

Figure 4.6   Federal discretionary spending, FY 2019

of 2019) cost the U.S. government roughly $400 billion in fiscal year 2019 (Congressional Budget Office, 2020).

However, when looking at the federal budget as a whole (mandatory and discretionary spending combined), 2019 data from the Center on Budget and Policy Priorities shows that the biggest budget items are healthcare programs (Medicare, Medicaid, CHIP, and marketplace subsidies; 25%), Social Security (23%), national defense (16%), safety net programs (8%), and interest on the national debt (8%) (see Figure 4.7). Federal spending on education (including higher education) is very low, at approximately 2% (not shown).

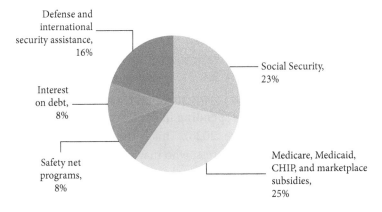

Note: Does not add to 100% due to rounding.
Source: 2019 figures from Office of Management and Budget, FY 2021 Historical Tables.

Figure 4.7   Overall federal government spending, FY 2019
Source: Center on Budget and Policy Priorities. (2020b). Policy basics: Where do our federal tax dollars go.
Retrieved from https://www.cbpp.org/research/federal-budget/policy-basics-where-do-our-federal-tax-dollars-go

An important theme of this chapter is that social workers need to be engaged with policymakers regarding spending priorities and how we spend our state and federal tax dollars. The box below shows a sample op-ed that could be submitted to a newspaper or online news website making the case of how we need to think differently when it comes to the nation's spending priorities.

Think seniors are the victims in the current federal budget debate? Think again.

One of the hottest political issues in the coming election year will no doubt be how to shore up the Social Security program when the baby boomers start to retire en masse. This is an important issue that must be addressed, but it greatly overshadows a little known fact—that it is children who get the short end of the stick when it comes to federal spending. The bulk of U.S. federal spending goes to defense, Social Security, and Medicare. Children are not a budget priority despite decades of solid research showing the importance of investing in children ages 0–5 since these are critical years for brain development.

According to a 2010 report from the Urban Institute and the Brookings Institution, in 2009 less than 10% of federal budget outlays were devoted to children. To put this another way, in 2007 total public spending (federal/state/local) on children was $10,642 per child while public spending on older adults was $24,300 per adult. More shockingly perhaps is their finding that children's share of domestic federal spending shrunk by 6 percentage points between 1960 and 2009 while spending on the *nonchild* portions of Social Security, Medicare, and Medicaid doubled during this time period. Is this the result of societal attitudes that devalue children or the fact that senior citizens are a strong and mobilized voting bloc?

According to Professor Lilian Katz, an expert in early childhood education, "Each of us must come to care about everyone else's children . . . The good life for our own children can be secured only if a good life is also secured for all other people's children." Indeed other western industrialized countries in Europe and Scandinavia have made this paradigm shift as demonstrated by public policies that invest in children such as family allowances (a monthly stipend given to families regardless of income that helps to cover the cost of raising children), universal health care, government-subsidized child care for working parents, and paid family leave, to name a few.

In comparison, U.S. rankings on international comparisons of child poverty, infant mortality, and student performance in math and science are embarrassingly poor. Federal and state governments have often failed the young by allowing millions to forgo healthcare coverage; ignoring countless children who attend highly segregated, substandard schools; and looking the other way when children are failed by the state child welfare agencies designed to protect them.

A recent story of a 4-year-old child who was killed by her mother, after being abused and severely malnourished, made front page news in the *New York Times*. The mother has been charged with murder, the grandmother with manslaughter. However, since this family was involved with child protection authorities, two city child welfare workers are being prosecuted for criminally negligent homicide.

For decades, child welfare advocates such as the Child Welfare League of America and the Children's Defense Fund have worked tirelessly to galvanize lawmakers to focus more on the welfare of children and the challenges facing child welfare systems that are severely under-resourced. However, there is one concrete step that could set us on the right path in seriously improving the lives of our nation's children.

President Obama should convene a White House Conference on Children (WHCC), which would bring together child welfare experts from across the country to review the current state of children in the United States and identify strategies for improvement. **Starting in 1909, this conference was held every 10 years. However, the last one was held in 1970.** Positive outcomes of previous conferences include the creation of the Child Welfare League of America; improvements in state regulation of child labor; the creation of the American Pediatric Society; and efforts to end the systematic institutionalization of children.

A White House Conference on Children would help to shine a spotlight on the needs of children. It could also help educate lawmakers on two important programs for children ages 0–5 that are supported by loads of research and offer a lot of bang for the buck: (1) early childhood education programs and (2) home visiting programs, which provide support and parenting education to new parents. Even a divided Oregon state legislature sees the light. This session, they passed a joint memorial (HJM 12) urging the U.S. Congress to convene a WHCC.

Our politicians often talk endlessly about "family values" echoing that "children are our future." In actuality, we are a nation that had a Society for the Prevention of Cruelty to Animals before a Society for the Prevention of Cruelty to Children. We are one of only two nations in the world that has failed to ratify the UN Convention on the Rights of the Child (the other is Somalia). And we are a nation that puts children at the bottom of the barrel when it comes to federal spending. A federal bill calling on the president to convene a WHCC failed in the 111th Congress.

Perhaps a new consciousness will emerge in the U.S., expressed eloquently by former author and activist Pearl S. Buck: "If our American way of life fails the child, it fails us all." Making sure that our parents and grandparents are taken care of in their golden years is priceless. Making sure that our children get a good start in life—equally priceless.

Source: Originally Published By Jessica Ritter, "Federal Spending: With Regard to Children's Welfare, Bucks Stop Here," *Oregonlive: The Oregonian.* Copyright © 2011 by Advance Local Media LLC.

How the Federal Government Creates the Budget Each Year

Each year, the president and the U.S. Congress must agree on what the budget will look like for the following fiscal year. According to the National Priorities Project (n.d.), the federal budget process has five key steps:

1. The president submits a budget request to Congress.
2. The House and Senate pass budget resolutions.
3. House and Senate Appropriations subcommittees "markup" appropriations bills.
4. The House and Senate vote on appropriations bills and reconcile differences.
5. The president signs each appropriations bill and the budget becomes law.

In some years, this process goes smoothly, and in other years it does not go smoothly at all. When Republicans and Democrats cannot agree on how funds are being appropriated in these spending bills, or when the president does not agree with what gets passed by the Congress, then the government will shut down until they can reach a compromise. When the government shuts down, some federal employees cannot get paid and some nonvital government functions come to a halt. Twenty-one government shutdowns occurred between 1974 and 2020, with some lasting only a day or two and others lasting 18 to 21 days. The longest shutdown in history was 35 days during the Trump administration, when the President demanded $5 billion in the federal budget to pay for his border wall with Mexico and the U.S. Congress would not agree to give him that much funding. It ended on January 25, 2019, when the President conceded.

Funding for Federal Programs

There are different types of federal funding. Most federal programs are either entitlement programs or block grant programs. An **entitlement program** is a program that eligible individuals or beneficiaries have a legal right to receive; in other words, they are "entitled" to receive these benefits if they meet eligibility requirements. However, do not let the terminology confuse you. Many entitlement programs such as Social Security, Medicare, and unemployment insurance are social insurance programs, which means that people have paid into these programs; in other words, people are not getting something for nothing. Social Security and Medicare are perhaps the most well-known entitlement programs because of their popularity and high costs, particularly now that the baby boomers are starting to retire en masse.

Because entitlement programs are under the realm of mandatory spending, they do not go through the annual appropriation process in Congress, thus the costs of these programs are more difficult for the government to control. This causes much consternation for political conservatives who complain about the inability of the government to continue to pay for these costly social programs. Some entitlement programs are administered through state governments in a cost-sharing or matching-funds framework, such as Medicaid (health care for low-income or disabled people) where the state may pay 30–40% of patient care costs while the federal government will pick up 60–70% of the costs. Generally, in entitlement programs there are some minimum standards imposed on states about services and populations that must be included, but states also have some flexibility to serve additional populations depending on their ability to generate the state financial resources to trigger the federal match.

Block grant programs have been increasingly popular in recent years due to efforts by federal lawmakers to rein in federal spending. Block grant funding is when the federal government gives states a specific lump sum to administer a particular program. Advocates of block grants like that states are given flexibility and decision-making power in designing the program and spending the funds to best suit local needs. Critics argue that block grants devolve responsibility for certain social problems from the federal government to the states, which in some cases are less sensitive to the needs of low-income individuals.

Also, block grants can be used to decrease funding for a specific program. Block grants are finite, so when the need exceeds the amount of the resources in the program either the services end or the implementing partners have to come up with additional resources to serve the clients from some other source, which could be state or local government funds, collecting client fees based on a sliding scale, or public-private partnerships. In fact, one strategy used by fiscal conservatives is to try to turn an entitlement program into a block grant program in order to shrink the size and funding of that program. Perhaps the best example of this occurred in 1996 when the nation's welfare program (Aid to Families with Dependent Children, or AFDC) was replaced with the Temporary Assistance for Needy Families (TANF) program. This ended the federal entitlement of public assistance to poor children and families, a practice that had been in place for 60 years in the United States.

Federal Entitlement Programs and Block Grants

Federal funds are distributed to states and communities through a variety of mechanisms. Each is designed to serve a particular purpose, and each comes with its own set of rules and requirements. Understanding the various types of funds is important because the funding mechanism of a particular funding source has an impact on the strategy employed to access funds. The following are the major types of federal funding:

- **Entitlement programs** guarantee that all individuals who meet the eligibility criteria are entitled to be served by that program. In other words, they have a legal right to these services. For many entitlement programs, the federal government and states combine funds to cover the costs. Examples of entitlement programs in the United States are social security, unemployment compensation, Veteran's Administration programs, and Medicare and Medicaid.
- **When a program is funded by block grant**, the federal government gives states or local governments a lump sum of money, and then states and local governments have a lot of discretion in how they manage that program. This is a way for the federal government to be able to control costs since they are able to cap funding for a block grant program. Unlike entitlements, block grants do not guarantee to cover everyone who is eligible. One famous example is the Temporary Assistance for Needy Families (TANF) program. The nation's "welfare" program used to be an entitlement program, but that changed when President Bill Clinton signed a law changing it to a block grant program.
- **Discretionary grants** fund a wide range of targeted federal efforts, for example, preventing juvenile delinquency or improving health outcomes, such as decreasing obesity. Depending on the program requirements, state and local governments, community-based organizations, or coalitions of community groups and agencies can apply directly to the sponsoring federal agency to gain access to these funds through a competitive bidding process. Many of these opportunities can be found on www.grants.gov.

Why Is the U.S. Government in Debt?

Many Americans grumble that the federal government is in debt, but when lawmakers begin talking about cutting specific popular social programs they are usually greeted with resistance from their constituents. Before exploring the rather complicated question of why the United States is in debt, it is important to understand the difference between the national debt and the deficit. The federal government has a balanced budget when revenues and government spending are equal in a given fiscal year. A **surplus** is a year when revenues exceed spending. The government runs a **deficit** when spending exceeds revenues in a given year. For example, in fiscal year 2019, the federal government ran a $984 billion deficit, because the tax revenues raised by individuals and corporations were not enough to cover the $4.4 trillion in federal spending (Center on Budget and Policy Priorities, 2020b). However, the **national debt** is the total money owed by the government over many years. When the United States has many years of running deficits, the accumulation of this is our national debt. The U.S. federal government is currently about $27 trillion in debt (as of January 10, 2020). To see the current status of the U.S. debt, visit www.usdebtclock.org.

When the U.S. government cannot pay for the programs and services that it needs to provide, it must borrow money. It does this by selling Treasury securities and savings bonds to other federal government agencies, individuals, corporations, state and local governments, associations, public and private organizations, as well as people, businesses, and governments from other countries. These various entities lend money to the U.S. government so that it can pay its bills, and over time the government must pay the money back with interest. Roughly three-quarters of the government's debt is public debt. Some Americans would be surprised to learn that foreign investors own a significant amount of U.S. debt. The countries that own the most U.S. debt are Japan, China, and the U.K.

One way that the U.S. Congress has tried to keep the federal government from amassing too much in debt is to pass a law enforcing a **debt ceiling**, a cap on the amount of debt the federal government can legally borrow. The debt ceiling has been raised many times over the years. Economists argue over whether running deficits is harmful to the U.S. economy, and deficit spending is often recommended during an economic recession to help spur economic activity. Fiscal conservatives argue that it is irresponsible for the government to be in debt in the same way that private individuals should not be in debt. However, running up high deficits has been used as a strategy by conservatives in order to cut government programs that we cannot afford (i.e., the "starve the beast" strategy) in their efforts to shrink the size of government.

So, the simple answer to the question of why the U.S. government is in debt is that it spends more money than it takes in. The president and the U.S. Congress continue to grapple over ways to bring the national debt down. Possibilities include raising revenues (taxes), cutting spending, or a combination of the two. Conservatives typically urge the president to cut spending, and are adamantly opposed to raising taxes on the wealthy. They argue that the rising costs of the Social Security and Medicare programs are unsustainable and that we have to get government spending under control. Progressives argue that it is unfair to balance the budget on the backs of the poor and the middle class, and advocate bringing down the deficit by raising taxes on the wealthy and corporations and cutting military spending. This is yet another example of how intertwined politics and economics are in the United States.

State Budgets

Though the focus of this chapter is on understanding the federal budget, there are a few important points to keep in mind when it comes to **state budgets**. In state budgets, there are generally three pots of money for state spending: social services, education, and public safety. And one major difference between the federal government and state governments is that states cannot run deficits or accumulate debt—when they are out of money, they must cut vital state services. When the country is in an economic recession, it is devastating for many states for several reasons. First, they rely on funding from the federal government, and when the federal government is struggling, this trickles down to state and local government. Additionally, many states rely on state income taxes, sales taxes, and property taxes, and when there are high rates of unemployment and home foreclosures, this results in less revenue for states. Like the federal government, states are also in the position of making tough decisions as to whether they need to raise revenues (taxes) or cut services and programs that serve vulnerable populations.

American Exceptionalism or *Welfare* Exceptionalism?

The term **American exceptionalism** has become part of the American lexicon in recent years as lawmakers and others have sought to make sense of the United States and its place in the world. It has an interesting history and means different things to different people, though it seems to attempt to define what makes America special or unique compared to other nations. Sociologist Seymour Martin Lipset (1996) wrote that "the nation's ideology can be described in five words: liberty, egalitarianism, individualism, populism, and laissez faire" (p. 19). It also has religious overtones, because many Americans believe that God has granted America a special role in human history (Tumulty, 2010). Some tend to embrace this terminology, whereas others are uncomfortable with the idea that the United States is superior to other nations around the world. The term has become very political and has been used to frame some lawmakers as anti-American when they criticize the United States or fail to embrace this idea.

However, two sociologists instead use the term **welfare exceptionalism** to describe the reluctance of the United States to become a welfare state similar to other western industrialized countries in Europe (Amenta & Skocpol, 1989). It is important for the social work profession to explore why the richest country in the world has such high rates of poverty and **income inequality**. When examining how the United States compares to other nations, we are often compared to other nations in the OECD (Organisation for Economic Co-operation and Development). Countries in the OECD are among the most wealthy and developed and are committed to democracy and a market economy. According to the latest report from the OECD (2019), out of the 36 OECD countries, the United States ranks:

- Fourth highest in highest household income (after taxes and benefits)
- Fourth highest on level of income inequality
- Number one on rate of poverty (18%, compared to an OECD average of 11.7%)
- Ninth lowest in life expectancy
- Twenty-first on percentage of GDP spent on social spending

- Eighteenth in life satisfaction
- Ninth lowest in electoral participation

So, the United States ranks extremely high in household income compared to other advanced nations, yet has high levels of poverty and income inequality. What explains this? One explanation is that there is a fairly consistent relationship between a nation's tax policy and its level of income inequality. As Table 4.3 shows, in most cases countries that have high taxes on individuals and corporations rank low in income inequality. For example, Denmark ranks highest in terms of tax revenues generated and also ranks very low on the Gini Index, a measure that is used to assess a nation's level of income inequality. It is fairly striking that four of the five countries with the lowest taxes (Mexico, Chile, Turkey, and the United States), are countries that rank very high on the Gini Index (meaning that these are the OECD countries with the highest levels of income inequality). The only outlier is Ireland, which has a low tax rate but also has a relatively low level of income inequality.

Another explanation for the high level of income inequality in the United States is that not all Americans enjoy the same level of prosperity when the economy as a whole grows. According to recent data from the Federal Reserve (2020), in the third quarter of 2020, the richest 10% of Americans owned 69% of the nation's wealth ($80 trillion). The bottom 50% of families owned just 2% of the wealth ($2 trillion). Feller and Stone (2009) point out that this is a trend that has been occurring in the United States since the late 1970s:

Table 4.3.   OECD Nations: Relationship Between Taxes and Income Inequality

OECD Nations with Highest Taxes as Percentage of GDP (2018)	Income Inequality (Gini Index)
Denmark	Low
France	Low
Belgium	Low
Finland	Low
Sweden	Low
OECD Nations with Lowest Taxes (2018)	
Mexico	High
Chile	High
Ireland	Low
Turkey	High
United States	High

Sources: Organisation for Economic Co-operation and Development (OECD). (2019). Society at a glance 2019—OECD social indicators. Retrieved from https://www.oecd.org/social/society-at-a-glance-19991290.htm; OECD. (2020). Revenue statistics 2020. OECD Publishing, Paris. Retrieved from https://www.oecd.org/tax/revenue-statistics-2522770x.htm

The uneven distribution of economic gains in recent years continues a longer-term trend that began in the late 1970s. In the three decades following World War II (1946–1976), robust economic gains were shared widely, with the incomes of the bottom 90 percent actually increasing more rapidly in percentage terms, on average, than the incomes of the top 1 percent. But in the three decades since 1976, the incomes of the bottom 90 percent of households have risen only slightly, on average, while the incomes of the top 1 percent have soared.

Data from the Economic Policy Institute show that, in 2019, CEOs of major U.S. corporations earned 320 times as much as a typical American worker; in 1965, the ratio was 21 to 1 (Mishel & Kandra, 2020).

When discussions of economic inequality arise, there is often someone who will state that it is impossible for societies to reach full economic equality. Although this is true, it is also true that many countries do have some control over the *degree* of inequality they are willing to accept. So a better question to ask would be: How much inequality are we prepared to accept as a society? And, why has the United States made different choices than many other industrialized nations when it comes to taxation and wealth distribution? Why is the United States "exceptional" in this regard? Possible explanations that have been posited by scholars include the following:

- The United States is less homogenous than other countries in Europe and Scandinavia (i.e., the United States has higher ethnic and religious diversity).
- The U.S. government is highly decentralized and values state's rights, making it difficult to have strong national strategies and policies.
- Powerful, well-financed corporate interest groups are able to bend economic policies in their favor.
- The worship of materialism and wealth in the United States prevents average Americans from challenging policies favoring the wealthy because they themselves aspire to be wealthy. The financial success of famous Americans like Bill Gates and Oprah Winfrey keep this mythology alive.
- The United States is rooted in the value of rugged individualism.
- Trade unions are weak in the United States.
- It has been observed that the United States is the only industrialized nation that does not have a Socialist Party or Labor Party.

Since the beginning of the social work profession, social workers have been concerned with issues of poverty and income inequality due to the deleterious effects they have on the lives of individuals and families and the health of communities. According to the NASW Code of Ethics, the profession has an ethical obligation to be focused on **economic justice**: "Social workers pursue social change, particularly with and on behalf of vulnerable and oppressed individuals and groups of people. Social workers' social change efforts are focused primarily on issues of poverty, unemployment, discrimination, and other forms of social injustice." The Code also states, "Social workers should engage in social and political action that seeks to ensure that all people have equal access to the resources, employment, services, and opportunities they require to meet their basic human needs and to develop fully" (NASW, 2017). Social workers can be important allies to other organizations that are focused on policy efforts to reduce poverty and income inequality in the United States.

REFERENCES

Amenta, E., & Skocpol, T. (1989). Taking exception: Explaining the distinctiveness of American public policies during the last century. In F. C. Castles (Ed.), *The comparative history of public policy*. New York: Oxford University Press.

Center on Budget and Policy Priorities. (2020a). *Policy basics: Where do federal tax revenues come from*. Retrieved from https://www.cbpp.org/research/federal-tax/policy-basics-where-do-federal-tax-revenues-come-from

Center on Budget and Policy Priorities. (2020b). *Policy basics: Where do our federal taxes go?* Retrieved from https://www.cbpp.org/research/federal-budget/policy-basics-where-do-our-federal-tax-dollars-go

Congressional Budget Office. (2020). *The federal budget in 2019: An infographic*. Retrieved from https://www.cbo.gov/publication/56324

Federal Reserve. (2020). *Distribution of household wealth in the U.S. since 1989*. Retrieved from https://www.federalreserve.gov/releases/z1/dataviz/dfa/distribute/chart/#quarter:0;series:Net%20worth;demographic:networth;population:1,3,5,7;units:levels;range:2005.2,2020.2

Feller, A., & Stone, C. (2009). *Top 1 percent of Americans reaped two-thirds of income gains in last economic expansion.* Center on Budget and Policy Priorities. Retrieved from http://www.cbpp.org/files/9–9-09pov.pdf

Gardner, M., & Wamhoff, S. (2021). *55 corporation paid $0 in federal taxes on 2020 profits* . Retrieved from https://itep.org/55-profitable-corporations-zero-corporate-tax/

Lipset, S. M. (1996). *American exceptionalism: A double-edged sword.* New York: W. W. Norton.

Mishel, L. & Kandra, J. (2020). *CEO compensation surged 14% in 2019 to $21.3 million: CEOs now earn 320 times as much as a typical worker.* Economic Policy Institute. Retrieved from https://www.epi.org/publication/ceo-compensation-surged-14-in-2019-to-21-3-million-ceos-now-earn-320-times-as-much-as-a-typical-worker/

National Association of Social Workers. (2009). *Social work speaks* (8th ed.). Washington, D.C.: NASW Press.

National Association of Social Workers. (2017). *Code of ethics. Approved by the 1996 NASW Delegate Assembly and revised by the 2017 NASW Delegate Assembly*. Retrieved from https://www.socialworkers.org/About/Ethics/Code-of-Ethics/Code-of-Ethics-English

National Priorities Project. (n.d.). *Budget process, federal budget 101*. Retrieved from https://www.nationalpriorities.org/budget-basics/federal-budget-101/federal-budget-process/

National Priorities Project. (2020). *The militarized budget 2020*. Retrieved from https://www.nationalpriorities.org/analysis/2020/militarized-budget-2020/

Organisation of Economic Co-operation and Development. (2019). *Society at a glance 2019: OECD social indicators.* Paris: OECD Publishing.

Organisation of Economic Co-operation and Development. (2020). *Revenue statistics 2020.* Paris: OECD Publishing. Retrieved from https://www.oecd.org/tax/revenue-statistics-2522770x.htm

Rank, M. (2004). *One nation underprivileged: Why American poverty affects us all.* New York: Oxford University Press.

Ritter, J. A. (2011, June 24). Federal spending: With regard to children's welfare, bucks stop here. *The Oregonian.* Retrieved from http://www.oregonlive.com/opinion/index.ssf/2011/06/with_regard_to_childrens_welfa.html

Tumulty, K. (2010, November 29). American exceptionalism: An old idea and a new political battle. *Washington Post.* Retrieved from http://www.washingtonpost.com/wp-dyn/content/article/2010/11/28/AR2010112804139.html?sid=ST2010112901818

U.S. Census Bureau. (2020). *Income and poverty in the United States: 2019.* Retrieved from https://www.census.gov/content/dam/Census/library/publications/2020/demo/p60-270.pdf

Credits

Part II

CHAPTER 5

Social Workers in Action
The Six Stages of the Policy Change Process

"About one-third of the American population can be characterized as politically apathetic or passive; in most cases they are unaware literally of the political part of the world around them. Another 60 percent play largely spectator roles in the political process; they watch, they cheer, they vote, but they do not battle. In the purest sense of the world, probably 1 or 2 percent of the American population could be called gladiators"

~ Lester Milbrath, political scientist, 1965

Figure 5.1   U.S. Capitol

CHAPTER SUMMARY

Social workers are in a unique position to play an important role in policy change efforts because they often work closely with populations who find it challenging to advocate for themselves before the U.S. Congress, state legislatures, or in other policy-making settings.

Social workers can either act as secondhand validators to a problem or concern or organize marginalized individuals or groups and assist them in speaking for themselves, or some combination of both. Many social workers initially find the legislative arena intimidating, but once they learn how the process works they realize it is not as daunting as originally perceived. Who makes policy in the United States? Unfortunately, most Americans picture political elites, and the average citizen does not easily come to mind when we think about who makes public policy in the United States. However, in order for a democracy to thrive, it is crucial to have high levels of civic and political participation among citizens from all walks of life, including social workers and the clients they serve. You may be surprised to learn that average citizens do affect the political process every day, though we often do not hear these stories. After her son Matthew Shepard was murdered in a hate crime incident where he was targeted for his sexual orientation, Judy Shepard worked tirelessly to get the Matthew Shepard and James Byrd, Jr. Hate Crimes Prevention Act passed into law. However, depending on whom you ask, you will get various perspectives regarding who actually makes policy in the United States.

In most social work courses, the planned change process is emphasized, and students learn that this process is used at the micro, mezzo, and macro levels. The six stages of the planned change process are engagement, assessment, planning, implementation, evaluation, and termination. The policy change process also has six stages and is similar in some ways to the planned change process used by social workers, though the terminology is somewhat different. When most people think about policy change, they usually focus primarily on stage 4, which is the "how a bill becomes a law" stage. However, it is important to know that there are five other important stages to facilitating change in the legislative arena.

Social workers engaged in policy practice must also be familiar with the judicial system, because sometimes legislation that is passed into law by policymakers is challenged in the courts when some individual or group tries to argue that it is unconstitutional. The makeup of the U.S. Supreme Court has gone through a significant shift since President Trump was able to appoint three justices to Court during his presidency (Neil Gorsuch, Brett Cavanaugh, and Amy Coney Barrett), making it the most conservative court since the 1930s, according to legal analysts. The court is now a 6–3 conservative–liberal majority, ending an era of 5–4 conservatism. Court cases have focused on a wide variety of hot-button social issues in recent years, including same-sex marriage, abortion rights, voting rights, and broader issues of racial justice, immigration, gun ownership, the constitutionality of the Affordable Care Act, and issues regarding religion.

STUDENT LEARNING OBJECTIVES

○ Students will be able to summarize who makes policy in the United States.

○ Students will be able to explain the six stages of the policy change process.

○ Students will be able to identify the branches of government at the federal, state, and local levels, as well as the major branches of the U.S. judiciary system.

Social workers are in a unique position to play an important role in policy change efforts because they work closely with populations who find it challenging to advocate for themselves before the U.S. Congress, state legislatures, or in other policy-making settings. Social workers can speak out on behalf of the client populations they work with, organize marginalized individuals or groups and assist them in speaking for themselves, or some combination of both. Many social workers initially find the legislative arena intimidating, but once they learn how the process works and gain some experience in policy making, they often find it is not as daunting as originally perceived.

Who Makes Policy in the United States?

Take a minute to think about the above question. What comes to mind for you? Unfortunately, most Americans picture political elites, and the average citizen does not quickly come to mind when we think about who makes public policy in this country. However, in order for a democracy to thrive, it is crucial to have high levels of **civic and political participation** among citizens from all walks of life, including social workers and the clients they serve. You may be surprised to learn that average citizens do affect the political process every day, though we often do not hear these stories. For example, in Chapter 9, Judy Shepard is profiled. After her son Matthew Shepard was murdered in a violent hate crime incident where he was targeted for his sexual orientation, she worked tirelessly to get the Matthew Shepard and James Byrd, Jr. Hate Crimes Prevention Act passed into law. Before this horrible incident happened to her son, Judy was an everyday American, but she was propelled into action to pass legislation that would help prevent similar incidents from occurring to other LGBTQ individuals like her son.

There are a number of political science theories to explain who makes public policy. According to **pluralism** theory, numerous groups and interests compete for influence in making policy, but all voices are heard equally and power is widely diffused. Other theories are more cynical. For example, according to **public choice** theory, all actors in the political arena are motivated to advance their own private self-interests (e.g., voters vote based on what is best for them personally; politicians make choices in order to get reelected and expand their base of power). Finally, according to **elitism** theory, policies are made primarily by political elites such as the wealthy, corporations, military institutions, and well-financed interest groups. Each of these theories probably has some truth and relevance. However, it is important to know that there are a number of key actors in the policy-making arena.

Legislators and their staff. It is imperative to build good relationships with elected officials and the staff who work in their offices. Although we often think of legislators in Washington, D.C., social workers most often work with legislators in their state capitol or in city government. Much of politics is done locally, and lawmakers at the local and state levels are much more accessible and open to working with members from the community. You might be shocked to learn how much easier policy change is at the local and state levels compared to the federal level, where gridlock is often the norm. Lawmakers who serve on the house side are referred to as Representative (insert last name here), and lawmakers who serve on the senate side are referred to as Senator (insert last name here). It is important to address lawmakers formally and with their correct title when you meet with them. Legislators are very busy, so much of the time you will be meeting with staff members who have public policy expertise in a variety of subject areas. These staffers (also called *legislative aides*) are very influential and can convince their "boss" to support you if you present a convincing policy proposal. Legislative staffers come from a variety of educational backgrounds, including social work.

Advocacy groups. There are thousands of advocacy groups across the country whose mission is to advocate for a specific cause or population (e.g., LGBTQ rights, those in poverty, women, immigrants, children, older adults, those with mental illness) in the legislative arena. Most are nonprofit organizations, and they are also sometimes referred to as *interest groups* or *special interests* (see list of U.S. advocacy organizations in Chapter 1). Advocacy organizations are a superb option for social workers who would like to do work in the policy arena at the local or federal level.

Political action committees (PACs). Political action committees are commonly referred to as *PACs*, and their sole purpose is to work to get people elected to public office who support their mission and goals. They do this by endorsing candidates, providing message or campaign training, engaging in grassroots activities (making calls or knocking on doors), and making financial contributions. However, PACs in and of themselves do not directly influence legislation. Structurally, a PAC is a controlled entity of an advocacy group, professional association, labor union, or industry. Many states have strict laws (or legislative rules) prohibiting or discouraging overt connections between policy making and PAC contributions—such as prohibiting campaign contributions while the legislature is in session. Generally what PACs "buy" is access, an open door, or clout that comes from the gratitude of an elected official for the efforts put forward during the election by an interest group. The National Association of Social Workers (NASW) has a federal PAC called PACE (Political Action for Candidate Election), and every election cycle the PAC makes endorsements and donates money to candidates running for political office at the federal level. State chapters of NASW have state PACs and are able to donate funds to political candidates running for office at the state level.

Lobbyists. Some people get confused about the difference between a PAC and a lobbyist, but they are trying to influence different parts of the political process. PACs try to influence *who* gets elected, while lobbyists try to influence actual legislation. Every day, lobbyists representing various special interests (from corporations to grassroots organizations) can be found in state capitals and the nation's capital trying to convince legislators to support their policy initiatives and legislative agenda. It is important to know that social workers can become registered lobbyists. The Lobbyist Spotlight highlights Maura Roche, a contract lobbyist in the state of Oregon.

Lobbyist Spotlight: Maura Roche, Contract Lobbyist

As a former lobbyist for a statewide group of social work professionals, I have experienced real challenges in getting social workers to narrow their policy focus enough to accomplish concrete changes at the state legislative level. Often when asked for policy priorities, what emerges are goals that are overly broad: improve the child welfare system or healthcare access for all. Of course, these are desirable to achieve, but not quite the right fit for a professional association of social workers to accomplish as the lead. Instead, it would be more productive to choose a smaller, more achievable goal such as increasing access to health care for low-income children with a concrete policy step of simplifying the state enrollment process for the State Children's Health Insurance Program or trying to secure a small amount of funding for better outreach so that more families who would qualify, actually know about the program. Who better than a social worker to identify that the eligibility determination process has some resolvable glitches or to recognize that far too many families don't know they are eligible for the service at all?

~Maura C. Roche, registered lobbyist, state of Oregon

Policy institutes or "think tanks." Think tanks have grown increasingly influential over the years in their efforts to shape public policy, both foreign and domestic. They are staffed by scholars and researchers who have developed an expertise on a range of important social or economic issues. Although some policy institutes are politically neutral and nonpartisan, many policy institutes lean left or right and operate from a distinct ideological framework—and are financially backed by individuals or organizations with a political agenda. Lawmakers, particularly at the federal level, have come to rely on the position papers and policy briefs produced by these policy institutes when deliberating on important public policy issues.

Six Stages of the Policy Change Process

In most social work courses the planned change process is emphasized, and students learn that this process is used at the micro, mezzo, and macro levels; thus, the planned change process is the same whether the target of intervention is an individual, family, group, organization, community, or society at large. The six stages of the planned change process include: engagement, assessment, planning, implementation, evaluation, and termination. The **policy change process** also has six stages and is similar in some ways to the planned change process used by social workers, though the terminology is somewhat different (see Figures 5.2 and 5.3).

1. **Problem Definition:** Identifying the problem and possible solutions
2. **Agenda Setting:** Getting your issue on the political agenda
3. **Policy Formulation:** Translating the solution into a proposed policy (e.g., a bill)
4. **Adoption/Passage of Proposed Policy:** Getting a bill passed into law
5. **Policy Implementation:** Implementing the new law so that it is carried out as intended
6. **Evaluating the Policy Change:** What was the impact or outcome of the new policy?

Figure 5.2   Six stages of the policy change process

When most people think about policy making in the United States, they usually focus primarily on stage 4, which is the "how a bill becomes a law" stage. However, there are five other important stages to facilitating change in the legislative arena. Similar to the planned change process used in social work, the policy change process outlined in this chapter is not always successfully achieved. This process involves a series of stages or steps, and it is possible to get derailed at each step along the way. It is not an easy, simple process and can only be achieved with concerted effort, persistence, and a little bit of luck. Like any job, doing policy practice requires gaining the requisite knowledge and skills, and you will need to receive training from someone with experience in this field (e.g., via volunteer experience, an internship, field practicum, on-the-job training). Finding a good mentor can be extremely valuable. Chapters 7 through 12 contain real-life stories that bring these policy stages to life.

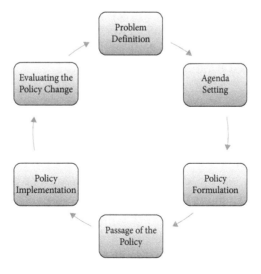

Figure 5.3   Visual Graphic of the six stages of the policy change process

I. Problem Definition

A proposed policy change always begins with the identification of a **problem** or **need.** Polices are proposed in order to address an **actual** or **perceived problem** that is affecting a significant number of people. This is a critically important stage of the process because before a policy can be formulated, the cause(s) of the problem must be very clearly understood. Oftentimes, people will agree that there is a problem, but disagree about the cause of the problem, and therefore have very different ideas regarding how that problem should be solved. This may be due to differences in political ideology. For example, progressives and conservatives may agree that the healthcare system needs to be reformed, that the immigration system is broken, or that poverty is a significant social problem in this country, but they would propose very different approaches to solving these problems based on their values, political ideology, and perception regarding the nature of these problems.

It is often easier to identify a problem than to come up with a solution. Because the causes of some problems are multifaceted and complex, it is harder than one would think to identify the best "fix" for the problem. One major decision that must be made during this stage is whether a large-scale, sweeping change will be sought or whether it makes more sense to use an incremental approach (e.g., identifying a series of small, meaningful steps that build to significant change over time). Even though social workers often prefer the idea of making significant changes, an incremental approach may be more politically feasible and lessen opposition from political opponents.

For example, in your state, social work leaders may identify the problem that social work salaries are too low and that social workers are burdened by high levels of student loan debt. At first glance, the state chapter of NASW may wish to pursue student loan forgiveness legislation. However, if the state is currently experiencing a budget crisis, it is very unlikely that this legislation will pass because it will require additional revenue from the state. Instead, as a first step, legislation could be proposed that would create a task force to examine workforce needs in the state as relates to the social work profession and come up with recommendations to improve the social work workforce in the coming years. One of these recommendations would likely include student loan forgiveness for social workers, and this could be proposed as future legislation.

How Do We Know That Something Is a Problem?

Experts and researchers often feel frustrated when policymakers fail to consult the latest research when designing a proposed policy change. As discussed earlier in the book, sometimes legislation gets proposed based on one's values or even one's "hunch" about what may solve a particular problem. Ideally, a policy would not be proposed until sufficient time has been devoted to studying the problem and the causes of the problem; however, the policy-making process is not a perfect process, and unfortunately it is often the case that this phase of the process is not given sufficient attention. However, because social workers are required to complete coursework on research, they understand how important it is that interventions are based on evidence and solid research whenever possible. Thus, proposed policy solutions that are backed up by a **policy analysis**, **needs assessment**, **program evaluation**, or **scientific research** study will have a better chance of successfully addressing the problem that has been identified. Social workers can help educate policymakers on this important point. These methods can be strengthened or enhanced with the addition of a social worker's **practice experience** and **anecdotal evidence.** Having clients and social workers tell compelling stories to legislators can also be very impactful.

Policy Analysis

For social workers, and others working in the policy arena, an important skill to have is the ability to conduct policy analysis. This work requires strong research, writing, and analytical skills. In its strictest definition, *policy analysis* means studying a proposed policy solution (or a set or policy solutions) to a social problem. For example, let's say that a legislator at the federal level wants to propose a piece of legislation that would help solve the growing opioid addiction problem in the United States. How would this legislator begin? Most policy experts would agree that this legislator cannot possibly introduce any sound or reasonable legislative concept until sufficient time has been devoted to fully understanding the causes of this social problem, which will then lead to possible alternatives for solution. Failure to do so will likely lead to bad policy with poor or unintended outcomes.

Policy analysis is an important service to provide because it helps legislators, stakeholders, and other interested individuals understand a problem that necessitates legislative action. Those who perform policy analysis often work for legislators, policy think tanks, or advocacy organizations. Legislative staff often conduct policy analysis to inform the policymakers whom they serve. It is also commonly performed by advocacy organizations and think tanks in order to inform those who have a strong interest in the issue at hand. It may also be performed by staff working in various federal, state, or local government agencies as they seek to better understand the complexities of a policy issue and to provide some input. The results of the policy analysis can be used as an advocacy tool by some organizations that wish to advocate for or against various strategies that are being proposed. Your arguments hold more sway when you can show that you did the research necessary to back up your claims.

There are numerous ways to organize your work when doing policy analysis, and many different frameworks exist, some that are more extensive than others. The culmination of this type of analysis is often the production of a **policy analysis brief** or **report**. The information in your brief can vary based on the audience. For example, if your readers are policy wonks, the policy analysis brief will be more sophisticated than if the audience consists of members of the general public. Understanding the problem would typically include the following pieces:

Case Example: Opioid Addiction in the United States

- **Description of the problem that necessitated the introduction of legislation**: How do experts define "opioids" and "opioid addiction"? Is this a new problem, or has this been a problem for some time (place the problem in historical context)? What attempts have been made to address this problem in the past? Describe the policies and programs that were previously developed to address this social problem and how effective or ineffective these initiatives were. Is this problem really an "epidemic" as it has been described in the media?

- **Who is affected by the problem and how are they affected?** Use data and statistics to document how widespread opioid addiction is and how many people in the United States are affected by it. What are the demographics of people affected by opioid addiction in the United States (e.g., gender, race/ethnicity, socioeconomic status, age, geography, etc.)? How does this problem impact vulnerable populations specifically?

- **What are the main causes of the problem?** What do researchers and experts conclude about the causes of opioid addiction in the United States? Make sure to include a range of diverse perspectives and cite credible experts and research studies. Do experts generally agree about the causes, or are there different opinions?

- **What are potential solutions to the problem, and what are the costs and benefits of each of these potential solutions?** This is where you would outline a few potential solutions to this problem based on the research you have conducted and the costs and benefits of each one. Potential solutions to the opioid epidemic might include: (1) increased federal funding for prevention and evidence-based treatment of opioid addiction, (2) new rules and safeguards in place for prescriptions of opioid painkillers to prevent overuse and overprescription, (3) implementation of harm-reduction interventions for those who cannot stop using these drugs, (4) increased civil and criminal penalties for opioid manufacturers if they fail to report suspicious orders, or (5) a combination of any of these solutions. Finally, make sure to address what the impact would be on vulnerable populations using a social justice perspective.

- **Recommendations:** Based on your analysis, what do you recommend as a proposed policy solution? How would this policy address the problem that has been identified, and why is it a better option than the alternatives that were explored? What are the costs and benefits of this policy approach? Can you identify any possible negative unintended consequences of this policy approach? Are the goals of this policy approach consistent with the values and ethics of the social work profession with regard to the promotion of human dignity and social justice? How can this policy approach later be evaluated to determine whether it improved the problem(s) that was identified?

Finally, at this stage, it is important to ask a very critical question: Is legislation the best way to solve this problem? In other words, can this problem be resolved best via the legislative process, or is there a better way to solve this problem? There is a saying that when you have a hammer every problem looks like a nail. However, not all problems can be solved via legislation. For example, based on research findings, a child advocacy organization might argue that it is harmful to spank children and may desire to follow the lead of other countries that have passed laws making it illegal for parents to hit or spank a child. However, a bill making spanking illegal is unlikely to pass in many states, and some would argue that it is bad public policy to penalize parents for this type of behavior. Perhaps a better approach might be to change people's attitudes on spanking by applying for grant funding to run creative antispanking public education campaigns.

The successful outcome of this stage depends on the ability of the participants to come to an adequate understanding of the problem, to consider various solutions to the problem, and to come up with a strong **legislative concept** or **legislative proposal** that has a reasonable success of passage. However, this is only the first step. The next step involves getting others, including at least one legislator, to care about and champion your issue.

II. Agenda Setting

This stage of the policy change process is often described as the "deciding what is to be decided" stage (DiNitto, 2011, p. 14). This is where you need to convince lawmakers that of all of the pressing issues facing our community or state or country, why they should care about this one. Those seeking policy change must think carefully about how to propel their issue onto the political agenda given that there is a finite number of bills that can be considered in any given legislative session. Agenda setting is a critical stage of the process because some issues get onto the "political agenda," and many issues do not make it there. Social workers often feel that many issues that affect poor and vulnerable people have a difficult time getting on the political agenda. There are numerous historical examples of issues that took a long time to get seriously considered by state and federal lawmakers, such as civil rights for women, people of color, LGBTQ individuals, and people with disabilities.

One strategy to getting your issue onto the political agenda is to get a strong, savvy advocacy organization with professional lobbyists support to adopt the issue you are trying to forward as one of its legislative priorities. This is the best and easiest way to get the technical support in the legislative process for your policy concept. However, do your homework, because if your concept gets picked up by a group that is not well regarded by lawmakers or the public, it can be very damaging. Another strategy is to **use the power of the mass media** to help propel your issue onto the agenda and to create the pressure needed to get state and/or federal lawmakers to pay attention. Sometimes an issue can suddenly be viewed as a "crisis" as a result of a sensational news story. For example, child welfare advocates may be able to get a piece of legislation to be taken more seriously after a serious case of child abuse is in the news. LGBTQ rights advocates may have an easier time introducing a piece of legislation focused on bullying after a series of news stories covering stories of adolescents who have committed suicide after being bullied by classmates. Unfortunately, it sometimes takes a tragic circumstance to create an opportunity to modify public policy, and occasionally circumstances align to help move an important social issue forward.

Finding a Legislative Champion

During the agenda setting stage, it is critical to find a legislator who will champion your policy proposal. In most states, hundreds or thousands of bills are introduced each session to be considered by lawmakers. Legislators are like the rest of us in that they gravitate toward working on things that they care about the most. When trying to secure a champion, a good starting place is to utilize legislative websites to scan legislators' educational background, occupation or work history, and personal biography. It would be important to know whether there are any legislators in your state with a degree in social work because they will be natural allies. Their biography may reveal important details such as experience being a foster parent, having a child with special needs, or a background as a mental health professional.

It is also important to get to know which legislators are assigned to committees or subcommittees with titles including "health care," "human services," "children," and "judiciary" because they are made up of people with an interest or expertise in those issues. Most state websites list the committees and which legislators serve on each committee. One advantage to working with professional lobbyists and advocacy organizations is that you can learn from those with more experience which legislators are known to be an advocate on a particular issue. Finally, once you gain more experience doing policy work in your community and/or state, you will slowly build relationships with legislators and the staff who work in their offices. When you are able to build a solid relationship based on mutual respect, a legislator will be more willing to spend her or his political capital on your issue.

Once you have a list of possibilities, start with the most obvious legislator (e.g., known to care about/work on the issue, sits on or chairs committee that deals with the issue), present your concept, and see if he or she would be willing to sponsor your bill. If they are unwilling, go to the next person on your list. It is ideal to have at least one champion in each chamber—House and Senate. Obviously it is easier to find legislative champions than to build them, but usually some combination is necessary in order to achieve the legislative support needed to pass a bill into law. Every now and then, an individual with an incredibly compelling personal story gets matched up with a legislator who is tenacious about resolving the issue. And sometimes we see the convergence of a high-profile media story, a compelling issue, and a persistent legislator—the perfect recipe for success.

Seeking Input from Political Allies and Opponents

During this stage, it is also wise to begin seeking input from allied individuals, groups, or organizations and to build support for your legislative proposal. This is also referred to as **coalition building**, a strategy that can be useful during this stage because it can indicate to legislators that there are a number of prominent or influential allied individuals, groups, and organizations that are supportive of your legislative proposal (see Chapter 6 for more on coalition building). Reaching out to allies is an important step and can help avoid problems later and hopefully identify unanticipated issues both with the politics of the issue and even with the technical aspects of what might be proposed. You may find a supportive legislator to forward your idea, but if the state's leading advocacy group shows up at the legislature to lobby or testify against your bill or point out a myriad of problems and unintended consequences, that is often the end of the road. Sometimes even if the differences are resolvable, it cannot be done within the timeline of that legislative session, and you will be delayed a year or more before you can come back with a modified proposal. During this stage, you will also begin to make decisions about **how to frame your policy**, and this can be done in collaboration with other members of your broad coalition. There are often many ways to frame an argument so that it is convincing and compelling to the lawmakers you are trying to convince, but much time needs to be devoted to finding the right angle (see Chapter 6 for more on framing).

Expect to begin identifying allies and meeting with them anywhere from six months to a year in advance of when the legislation would be introduced to start working to build support (or achieve neutrality, if that is the best that can be hoped for) and identify challenges with an eye toward resolving them in advance of getting into the more public arena of the legislative or rule-making process. In the process of identifying and reaching out to allies, it is also really important to anticipate which organizations or individuals (including policy makers) might lead the charge against what you are trying to accomplish. This is called doing **opposition research**. It is best to anticipate all the challenges and or objections to your proposal in advance so they might be resolved or, if irresolvable, so you can be better prepared to defend your proposal. Anytime you have a legislative proposal you will want to know what the arguments are against your proposal so you will be very prepared to answer those.

All of that being said, often when seeking change in the social services world, money is the enemy rather than any real opposition to the concept. Frequently, an issue you are working on is in need of greater financial resources to improve outcomes. When state budgets are tight, this can prove to be the greatest challenge of all, so anticipating this in advance is critical. Most legislative processes have a method for calculating and attaching a "fiscal" estimate to all bills, and sometimes you can obtain these estimates informally in advance of legislation being introduced. You will want to be able to answer the question, "How much is this bill going to cost exactly?"

III. Policy Formulation

In the previous two stages, the problem was studied, a solution to the problem was identified, allies and opponents were identified and consulted, and a legislative champion(s) was secured. The third stage of the process is not super exciting, but it involves getting the policy proposal drafted into an actual bill with the appropriate format and language. In some cases, the actual bill drafting is done by paid staff (legislative counsel) whose job it is to take a legislative concept and turn it into a bill or resolution. In other cases, the bill is drafted by the very advocates who are proposing the legislation. In either case, it is important to be involved in this part of the process to check the language for accuracy because sometimes mistakes are made or things get lost in translation when the legislative concept gets drafted into bill form. Despite everyone's best intentions, a bill can have grave, unintended consequences when it is not drafted accurately, as seen in Nebraska's safe haven law.

Nebraska's Safe Haven Law

In 2008, a safe haven law was passed in Nebraska. Safe haven laws have been passed in every state and provide a safe process for parents to surrender their newborn infants to the proper authorities without facing prosecution. These laws were developed to decrease the number of newborns who were abandoned in an unsafe way, which sometimes led to the baby's death. Most of the laws are written to apply to children younger than one year of age, but the Nebraska law failed to include an age limit. As a result, Nebraska saw a rash of cases where parents used the new law to abandon their children (ages 0 to 18) to the state. It was not long before the news media began reporting these stories, including the case of a father who dropped his nine children off (ranging in age from 20 months to 17 years) at the hospital after his wife died. The Nebraska state legislature later passed a fix to this law by stipulating that it only applies to children 30 days of age or younger.

Bills can be structured in a number of different ways, and different terms are used for those structures. These structures and terms also vary by level of government (federal, state, and local). However, at the federal level the four types of legislative measures are **bills, joint resolutions**, **concurrent resolutions**, and **simple resolutions**. The key distinction among them is that two make law (i.e., bills and joint resolutions) and two do not (i.e., concurrent and simple resolutions). There is little practical difference between a bill and a joint resolution, though bills are the most common. A bill originating in the U.S. House of Representatives is designated by the letters "H.R," followed by a bill number, whereas a bill originating in the U.S. Senate is designated by "S" followed by a bill number. Concurrent and simple resolutions normally are not legislative in character because they are not presented to the president for approval. They are often viewed as symbolic because they are used merely for expressing facts, principles, and opinions (e.g., proclaiming April as "National Child Abuse Prevention Month").

Another way to get a policy passed into law is through the use of **ballot measures**. However, only roughly half of states have this option. Ballot measures allow citizens or organizations in a state to place a measure onto the ballot for voters of that state to consider (after collecting the requisite number of signatures). They can either propose a new law or constitutional amendment (called an *initiative*), or they can propose that voters repeal a law that was passed by the state legislature (called a *referendum*). In the 2020 election, four states legalized marijuana using ballot measures (Arizona, Montana, New Jersey, and South Dakota), and Florida voters voted to raise the minimum wage to $15.00 an hour by 2026. Voters in states like Oregon and Washington State have used this process to legalize physician aid-in-dying for those who are terminally ill and wish to end their life (see Chapter 10 for how the Death with Dignity Act was passed into law). When advocates know that they cannot get a bill passed by the state legislature, they can consider getting it passed via a ballot measure.

IV. Passage of the Policy

This is the part of the policy change process that gets the most attention because this is when (potentially) a bill becomes a law. You may recall the song, "I'm Just a Bill," made famous on a Schoolhouse Rock video that shows the steps involved in this long, rather circuitous process at the federal level. During this stage, a proposed piece of legislation gets further refined and shaped through an ongoing process of compromise and negotiation. It is often said that politics is the art of compromise, so it is not unusual for a bill to change form as it makes its way through the process. It is remarkable that of the tens of thousands of bills that are presented in the U.S. Congress each session, only about 5–10% become law. Some find this statistic depressing because it is clear that it is not easy to successfully usher a piece of legislation through the legislative process; however, others point out that it should not be too easy to pass legislation because then we might see a lot of bad ideas passed into law (though this still happens sometimes, unfortunately).

An overview of the process at the federal level is as follows, and a visual diagram can be seen in Figure 5.4:

- The bill is introduced in at least one chamber of the legislature (House or Senate).
- It is then assigned to the committee that oversees the issue addressed by the bill.
- Sometimes a committee may refer a bill to a subcommittee for deeper consideration.
- Public hearings may be held where experts and members of the general public are allowed to voice their opinion on the bill to lawmakers.
- The committee decides whether to approve, amend, defeat, or table a bill (many bills "die" in committee and do not move forward).
- If the bill goes forward in either its original or amended form, the full chamber considers it, which means the entire body votes on the bill (additional amendments may be offered at that time).
- The bill is introduced in the other chamber and goes through this same process.
- If both chambers approve the bill, it goes to a conference committee to work out any differences between the two bills.
- If both chambers approve the final bill, it goes to the executive (president) for signature or veto.
- If the president signs it, it becomes law.
- If the president vetoes the bill, legislators must then attempt to override the veto; in the U.S. Congress, it must be passed by a two-thirds vote in both chambers.
- The third branch of government, the judiciary, can legally challenge existing legislation if it is deemed to violate the U.S. Constitution and is presented to them in the form of a lawsuit.

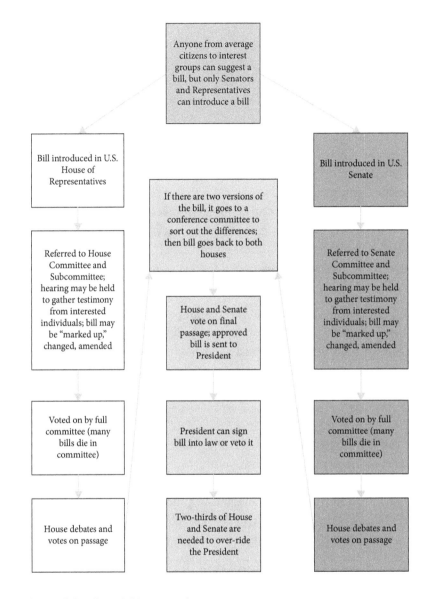

Figure 5.4   How a bill becomes a law

    Legislative bodies also have different rules about bill passage. Some, such as the U.S. Congress, typically have a bill introduced in both chambers, and then the bill goes through each chamber and may accumulate any number of amendments. Thus, two different versions of the bill may emerge. The two versions then must be reconciled via a conference committee. **Conference committees** are generally made up of members of the House and Senate committees who worked on the bill earlier in the process and are charged with ironing out the differences between the two bills. However, this may work differently in many state legislatures where bills start in one chamber, pass through the originating chamber, and then cross over to the other chamber where the bill may be amended further. Then there is usually a concurrence process (a simple vote by where the original chamber agrees to the changes made by the second chamber). Many, if not most, bills "die" in committee.

During this fourth stage, advocates of the policy are working diligently to shepherd their bill through the process. They are lobbying legislators, mobilizing others to contact legislators to urge passage of the bill, trying to get media coverage of their bill, and testifying in legislative committee hearings. It can be very helpful to work with a professional lobbyist because he or she will have the expertise needed to move the bill forward and to help it get unstuck at various points along the way. Social workers involved in policy change efforts become skilled in the art of persuasion and learn how to frame issues in a compelling way so that legislators are convinced to vote "yes." All these strategies and tactics are covered in Chapter 6.

V. Policy Implementation

This fifth stage is about what happens after a bill is passed into law. Once a bill is passed into law most assume that this is the end of the process, but this is a common misconception. Many complications may arise after a bill is passed into law, making implementation of the law problematic. In some cases, the language of the law was confusing or vague and those charged with implementing the law are not sure how to proceed, or they end up implementing the law incorrectly. For example, in the child welfare field policies are often written that instruct child welfare professionals to operate "in the best interest of the child." What does that mean exactly? Is it possible that people would have different interpretations about what is in the best interest of a child? Sometimes conflict continues when opponents decide to fight the new law by challenging it in court. A series of endless court battles may ensue, which delays the implementation of the new law (see end of chapter for more on the court system). Many times, the financial resources that are allocated to implement the law are inadequate. Finally, this is when the rulemaking process occurs.

The Rule-Making Process

Most social workers have never heard of **rule-making**, yet it is a part of the process where important decisions get made, and sometimes competing interests come to the table to try to influence the new "rules." Legislatures are charged with passing legislation, but then state and federal agencies have the power and the responsibility of creating more detailed **rules** or **regulations** in order to implement the new law. Often advocates or lawmakers do not want statutes to be highly specific in terms of implementation because it can mean having to amend the law repeatedly to keep it updated and current; laws should be crafted in a way to make them as timeless as possible. For example, many states have passed laws that require social workers to get licensed by the state, but the rule-making process is where many of the details get worked out (e.g., how much the fees will be, how often social workers have to renew their license, whether there will be an exam, how many CEUs will be required each year, etc.). State and federal agencies usually have fairly transparent and rigid rules of procedure for rule-making—though this process is more obscure and harder to know out about than the more public legislative process.

The rule-making process usually entails the writing of draft rules, the publication of the draft rules, a written comment period (typically 30, 60, or 90 days), and sometimes rule-making hearings. Some states have rule advisory groups made up of stakeholders convened by the agency charged with implementing the rule. Advocates can try to get a seat at that table or at least observe the meetings. In most cases, advocates will need to contact the state or federal agency charged with rule-making to find out what the process is and how they can be notified about participating. Rule-making is not always the "sexiest" part of the policy-making process, but it is an area where advocates can exert much influence in fleshing out critical details of a piece of legislation that has been passed into law.

Rule-Making Example at the State Level

In 2007, Oregon passed a bill prohibiting discrimination based on sexual orientation and gender identity and a bill establishing Oregon Registered Domestic Partnerships for same-sex couples. Afterwards, about a dozen state agencies had to promulgate rules in order to implement these new laws. For example, the Department of Human Services, Oregon Vital Records (the agency charged with recording births and deaths) had to change the form and procedure for collecting parents' names at the hospital after a birth for the purpose of birth certificates. The forms needed to say "birth parent" and "other parent" instead of "Mother's Name" and "Father's Name." This is a clear example of an implementation detail that would be inappropriate to write into law, but needed to be addressed in rule. This example may sound somewhat minor, but there were a number of glitches in the process that resulted in lesbian partners of birth mothers being told by hospital staff that they could not be listed as a parent on the paperwork for their child's birth certificate. Because these couples had anticipated being listed, they had not arranged for second-parent adoption in advance of the birth. Not being listed was painful and made partners feel legally vulnerable.

VI. Evaluating the Policy Change

The sixth and final phase of the policy change process is often overlooked, but it is crucial to conduct formal evaluations of social policies in order to determine the impact of new laws. In other words, did the new policy achieve what the sponsors hoped it would achieve, and was it ultimately successful in improving the situation? For example, in recent years, federal lawmakers passed legislation that limits the amount of time that parents can receive welfare benefits as well as legislation that shortens the time frame for the filing of termination of parental rights for those whose children have been removed from the home by child protection authorities. Afterwards, it would be important to find out how these new laws affected the parents and children served by these social service systems. For example, did a law that sought to get tough on people on welfare result in better or worse outcomes for children and families? Did a law that sought to free children in the custody of the state sooner result in better or worse outcomes for these youth?

In social work, we focus heavily on the need to evaluate our practice interventions, and it should be no different when it comes to evaluating the impact of social policies on the vulnerable individuals, families, and communities that we serve. This type of research is commonly conducted by researchers in universities, government agencies, and policy institutes or think tanks. Important questions for those who conduct this type of evaluation research from a social work perspective should include: "How did the new law impact vulnerable populations?" "Did the legislation result in any harmful, unintended consequences?" "Did the new law create positive change?" "Was the new law successful in achieving the specified goals?"

Policy-Making Settings in the United States

When working toward a particular change, it is critical to identify how the issue fits into the American system of government. If policy change is the right course to address the issue that has been identified, the branch of government where the change should occur must be determined. Are you seeking a change in federal law or regulation, state law or regulation, local law or regulation, or is there a way to change a policy or procedure without having to change the law directly? Could litigation cause the law or policy to be changed (i.e., using the judicial branch)? Is a state ballot measure the best avenue? Or, could the authority of an executive order issued by a governor or the president bring about the change you are seeking? And sometimes state or federal agencies have the authority by law to modify rules or regulations without requiring a change in the law at all.

Determining where the change should occur is one of the early pieces of research that will have to be done. Often, a policy change can be made at more than one level of government or by more than one route. Figuring this out is often part of the challenge. A couple of important factors to consider would be: (1) where you can garner the most support for the change and (2) where the desired change can be achieved most quickly. Or, in the case of litigation, how will it be paid for?

Policy Change Within Your Organization

The bulk of this book focuses on policy change within the political or legislative arena; however, it is important to keep in mind that policy practice also happens in the very organizations where social workers are employed. Almost every organization institutes its own policies that impact both employees (e.g., employee handbook; employee code of conduct) and the clients it serves (e.g., client rights and responsibilities). Some social workers are charged with implementing policies in their workplace as part of their job responsibilities, often as an administrator. It is not unusual for social workers to find themselves in a position to challenge a policy when they believe it is unethical or goes against social work values (e.g., dignity and worth of the individual, confidentiality, self-determination). It is right to question policies that are unethical, but it can be risky to challenge the status quo in one's own place of employment because it may be viewed as questioning the authority of those in charge. However, if done skillfully and professionally, this can be an important endeavor. Social workers employ some of the same skills and strategies when engaging in policy practice within their organization as they do when they are trying to get legislation passed (e.g., making a compelling argument, relationship building, coalition building; see Chapter 6).

Civics 101: Levels and Branches of Government

Despite the fact that we received this content in government or social studies class, it is always helpful to review, particularly in light of the fact that these days we receive little education on civics skills or what it means to be an active and engaged citizen. There are three branches of government at the federal, state, and local level: executive, legislative, and judicial. Having these separate branches ensures a "separation of powers" and provides for checks and balances in the system. As Figure 5.5 shows, the legislative branch makes laws, the executive branch carries out laws, and the judicial branch evaluates laws. The elected/appointed officials serve terms ranging from two years (U.S. Congress, state house, local elected officials), four years (presidents, mayors), six years (U.S. Senate, some state judges), to life (federal judges).

The Federal Government

The federal government can be the toughest to impact as an advocate, in part because of its size and distance from many local communities, the sheer volume of constituents the branches have to respond to, and because it has the most extensive and complex rules of engagement. Although change at this level can be slower than at other levels, on the upside, it tends to trump state and local laws or regulation, so changes in federal law can be the most profound and far reaching.

Executive Branch: The President of the United States, Cabinet, and Federal Agencies

The U.S. president is elected every four years through a nationwide election and is limited to two terms of service for a total of eight years. The election is conducted through the **Electoral College** instead of by national popular vote (simple majority of 50% plus one). The president chooses a running mate, who will be second in command as vice president. The United States is an outlier in how it selects its leader. Whereas most countries use the national popular vote, the United States uses the Electoral College, which some argue is not the most democratic way of electing a leader. On the first Tuesday in November, voters cast their ballots for a presidential candidate. However, these votes count toward a group of electors who pledge to vote for a specific candidate in the Electoral College. The Electoral College is the group of citizens selected by the people to cast votes for president and vice president. The president/vice president pair who wins the popular vote in any given state receives all of that state's Electoral College votes. Thus, the winner of the election is the candidate who receives a majority (270 or more) of the 538 Electoral College votes. A major criticism of the Electoral College is that it is possible for a presidential candidate to win the electoral college but lose the popular vote, and this has happened five times.

The president appoints the heads of each of the federal agencies and positions such as the U.S. Surgeon General. The president's cabinet typically includes the vice president and the heads of 15 executive departments—the secretaries of Agriculture, Commerce, Defense, Education, Energy, Health and Human Services, Homeland Security, Housing and Urban Development, Interior, Labor, State, Transportation, Treasury, and Veterans Affairs, as well as the Attorney General. The cabinet can also include the White House chief of staff and heads of the Environmental Protection Agency, Office of Management and Budget,

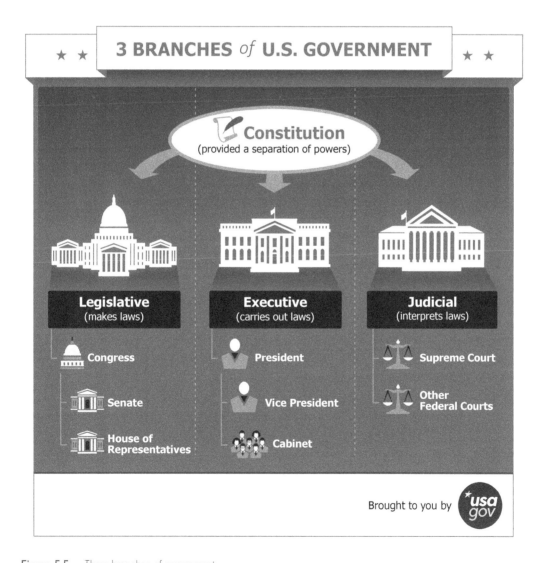

Figure 5.5   Three branches of government

United States Trade Representative, United States Mission to the United Nations, Council of Economic Advisors, Central Intelligence Agency, Office of the Director of National Intelligence, and Small Business Administration.

The president also has the power to reorganize federal agencies and their duties or create new ones. The most recent example of a newly created federal agency would be the Department of Homeland Security. The agency directors then have broad authority in hiring staff and setting policy within their agency's authority. This has a profound effect on how federal programs operate. Social workers should be familiar with the U.S. Department of Health and Human Services because this agency has a lot of impact on social service delivery in the United States.

Legislative Branch: The United States Congress

The United States House of Representatives and the United States Senate are the two legislative chambers at the federal level and are referred to as the United States Congress. There are no term limits for members of the U.S. Congress.

- **U.S. Senate**: Each state elects two members to the U.S. Senate (regardless of the state's population) every six years for a total of 100 members—aka "The Club of 100."
- **U.S. House of Representatives**: Each state elects members to the U.S. House of Representatives every two years, and the number of members representing a state is based on population and recalculated with the national census every decade. Each state gets one member per roughly 600,000 people in population, and each state is accorded at least one representative even if the state's population is less. There are 435 members of the U.S. House.

The structure and size of each chamber affects how they operate, and in a sense the chambers have different "personalities." The U.S. Senate is considered the "upper body." It is smaller than the U.S. House of Representatives, and therefore more power is concentrated in each member. It sits for reelection less often, and it is the body that is considered more deliberative and less reactive. The members tend to be more politically experienced because many of them have served in the U.S. House or other high office in their home state. The U.S. House can be much more raucous, and it can be difficult for a member (or their policy issues) to stand out or make their way into leadership due simply to the sheer number of members. The two bodies each have 20 committees with four joint committees, so obviously a higher percentage of Senate members are chairing committees than House members, and House committees have more members than Senate committees.

Partisanship and seniority matter in Congress and it shows, right down to the placement of the furniture. The party holding the most seats in each chamber occupies all of the presiding officer roles, such as Speaker of the House or President of the Senate. The presiding officers decide who will chair each committee, make all committee assignments for every member, and assign a majority of each committee's membership to the majority party. In fact, the desks on the "floor" of each chamber are arranged by party membership, with the center aisle moving left or right depending on the makeup of the chamber and perhaps the mood of the country.

Generally, to change or make policy via federal law a legislative concept must be introduced in both chambers and pass with a simple majority of 50% plus one. If the language that passes each chamber is not exactly the same, then the bills must go through a process to iron out the differences in language, and this is usually done through a conference committee.

Before each body can vote on a bill, the legislation will be assigned to a committee to be "worked." During this time, the committee will take testimony on the bill and entertain amendments. However, this is not the last opportunity for changes to the bill because amendments can be offered in either chamber at the time the bill is up for debate and final passage before the entire body. In fact, the rules pertaining to "germanity" are incredibly loose at the federal level, which can lead to attaching amendments to bills on topics that are seemingly unrelated.

Examples of committees that are most relevant to social workers are provided in Table 5.1. Some of these committees also have a number of smaller subcommittees attached to them. For example, the House Committee on Ways and Means has a subcommittee called the Subcommittee on Income Security and Family Support, while the Senate Committee on Finance has a subcommittee called the Subcommittee on Health Care.

Table 5.1.　U.S. House and Senate Committees

U.S. House Committees	U.S. Senate Committees
Appropriations	Appropriations
Budget	Budget
Education and Labor	Health, Education, Labor, and Pensions
Judiciary	Judiciary
Veterans' Affairs	Veterans' Affairs
Ways and Means	Agriculture, Nutrition and Forestry
Financial Services	Finance
	Banking, Housing, and Urban Affairs
	Indian Affairs
	Aging (Special)

State Government

State government is often much more accessible to citizen advocates as compared to the federal process, so this can be a good place to get experience. Advocates can have a great deal of influence at this level because policy changes at the state level impact the entire state. Similar to the federal government, state government has an executive branch overseen by the governor, a judicial branch with a state supreme court and state court of appeals, as well as state trial courts. Each state also has a state legislative body.

Executive Branch: Governors and State Agencies

Governors are the top elected official in a state's executive branch of government. In some states, the second-ranking state official (typically the lieutenant governor) runs on the same ticket as the governor, while in other states the lieutenant governor is elected separately so that the two top-ranking officials could be from different political parties. Six states do not have a lieutenant governor (Arizona, Maine, New Hampshire, Oregon, West Virginia, and Wyoming), thus the next person in line to succeed the governor is either the secretary of state, the president of the senate, or the speaker of the house. Governors appoint most state "agency heads" (though a few states have some positions that are elected) who oversee state programs, and the people appointed to run those programs have a profound effect on the philosophy and policies that are put in place in the state.

Legislative Branch: State Legislatures

State legislatures vary widely from state to state in size, structure, and rules of procedure. Some are structured similarly to the U.S. Congress, and some operate very differently. All but one state have bicameral institutions, meaning that they have a senate and a house of representatives or assembly. Nebraska is the only U.S. state with a unicameral system (only one legislative body).

How state legislatures structure representation of their populace can vary widely as well. It is fairly common to have representation based on population, which is reconfigured every decade with the U.S. Census. Most states have a roughly 2:1 or 3:1 house-to-senate ratio, with numbers such as 49 senate to 98 house as in Washington State, or 38 senate to 110 house as in Michigan. Some are structured very differently, such as Vermont, which has a house of representatives with 150 members (a representative for every 4,100 people) and a senate with only 30 members.

Many aspects with regard to partisan issues and majority rule are similar between the state- and federal-level processes. The majority party usually elects the presiding officers, such as the speaker of the house or assembly, the president of the senate, the whips and assistant leaders. Generally, the majority party gets to chair all of the committees and have numerical majorities on every committee. However, some states, such as Vermont, assign some committee chairmanships to minority party members (usually based on seniority) for a few committees as a way to create a more cohesive and less rancorous relationship between the majority and the minority parties.

The rules of procedure vary a great deal as well. Some common differences between state and federal rules of procedure have to do with the roles of committees, amendment procedures, and transparency of process. Many states do not allow amendments to be made on the floor while the entire body is deliberating on the bill. In those states, the committees are more powerful and there is a need to cultivate a champion for your issue on the "committee of jurisdiction." In states that allow amendments on the floor, committee structure is usually less powerful, and a legislator who is passionate about an issue but does not sit on the committee of those bills can still play a very powerful role on the issue.

Practice Exercise 5.1

Take a few minutes to find out who represents you in the U.S. Congress and who represents you in your state legislature. In most cases, this will be a total of five people. Two websites that may be helpful are Project Vote Smart (www.votesmart.org) and Congress.org (www. congress.org). Next, do some research on your city council. How many members are there, and who is the mayor?

Local Government: Councils, Commissions, Mayors, and Chairs

This is the level of government that is the closest and most personal to us. It tends to have a more limited scope of issues it addresses, with a fairly strong focus on law enforcement, transportation, land-use and development, public works, and infrastructure (sewer and water). However, some state programs are administered through local government. For example, advocates working on mental health issues often need to interact with local government because some of these programs may be administered at the local level. Local governments have policy-making functions similar to state or federal government, but most of these bodies are much smaller in size and do not share the bicameral structure. They often range from 3 to 15 elected officials in size and have both legislative and administrative functions (legislative and executive rolled into one); however, there are often county-level trial courts, creating some separation of powers.

The size and scope of local government varies widely from state to state. Louisiana has 302 municipal governments and Alaska has 145. Wyoming has 23 counties and 98 municipalities. Local governments have counties (in Louisiana they are called parishes and are headed by a parish president), which may be governed by boards of alderman or county commissions. Cities may have districts, wards, or boroughs. These may be governed by city councils and usually have a presiding officer, a mayor. School boards are also a local government function and are a good way for those interested in education policy to have some decision-making power regarding how local schools operate.

Overview of the U.S. Judicial System

Using the legislative process is a common and useful strategy for creating needed change on behalf of vulnerable and/or oppressed groups in this country. Indeed the bulk of this book is dedicated to exploring this aspect of macro-level change efforts. There are times when the court system can be used as a vehicle for social change when individuals or groups of individuals are not being treated equally under the law. Thus, it is important to understand when it makes sense to use the legislative system for change and when it makes sense to utilize the courts. Social workers engaged in policy practice must be familiar with the court system because sometimes legislation that is passed into law by policymakers is challenged in the courts when some individual or group tries to argue that it is unconstitutional. Court cases have focused on a wide variety of hot-button social issues over the years, including LGBTQ rights, abortion rights, gender discrimination, capital punishment, immigrant rights, and broader issues of racial justice. The Legal Advocacy Spotlight profiles a few legal organizations who advocate for those who have been wrongfully accused or who are treated unfairly in the criminal justice system.

Legal Advocacy Spotlight

Equal Justice Initiative (www.eji.org)

According to its website, the Equal Justice Initiative (EJI) "is committed to ending mass incarceration and excessive punishment in the United States, to challenging racial and economic injustice, and to protecting basic human rights for the most vulnerable people in American society. Founded in 1989 by Bryan Stevenson, a widely acclaimed public interest lawyer and bestselling author of Just Mercy, EJI is a private, 501(c)(3) nonprofit organization that provides legal representation to people who have been illegally convicted, unfairly sentenced, or abused in state jails and prisons. We challenge the death penalty and excessive punishment and we provide re-entry assistance to formerly incarcerated people."

Innocence Project (www.innocenceproject.org)

The Innocence Project (founded in 1992) is a nonprofit legal clinic affiliated with the Benjamin N. Cardozo School of Law at Yeshiva University. The project is a national litigation and public policy organization dedicated to exonerating wrongfully convicted people through DNA testing and reforming the criminal justice system to prevent future injustice. It operates as a clinic where law students handle case work while supervised by a team of attorneys and clinic staff.

The Sentencing Project (www.sentencingproject.org)

The Sentencing Project is a national organization that advocates for reforms of the criminal justice system so that it is fair and effective. It is concerned about inequities in the system given that "the U.S. is the world's leader in incarceration, that one in three young black men is under control of the criminal justice system, that five million Americans can't vote because of felony convictions, and that thousands of women and children have lost welfare, education and housing benefits as the result of convictions for minor drug offenses." It also promotes alternatives to incarceration.

The Federal Judiciary

The United States Supreme Court

The U.S. Supreme Court is the highest court in the land and therefore the court of last resort—there is no higher court to file appeal. It is made up of nine members (chief justice and eight associate justices) who have been appointed for life by a president and confirmed by the U.S. Senate. Their task is to ensure that state and federal laws, lower court decisions, and state constitutions are not in conflict with the U.S. Constitution. A limited number of cases come to them on appeal and from the federal court of appeals and state supreme courts, and the Court can decide to accept or reject a particular case.

The makeup of the Supreme Court has gone through a significant shift because President Trump was able to appoint three justices to the nation's highest court during his presidency (Neil Gorsuch, Brett Cavanaugh, and Amy Coney Barrett), making it the most conservative court since the 1930s, according to legal analysts. The court is now a 6–3 conservative–liberal majority, ending an era of 5–4 conservatism. Liberals across the country were dismayed when beloved feminist Supreme Court Justice Ruth Bader Ginsburg passed away on September 18, 2020. Justice Ginsberg was only the second woman to serve on the Supreme Court and was revered for her advocacy of women's rights over the course of her legal career. The country will now wait to see how this new court will rule on issues such as abortion rights, immigration, voting rights, gun rights, the constitutionality of the Affordable Care Act, and issues focused on faith and religion.

The Federal Circuit Court of Appeals

There are 12 regional circuits, each of which has a court of appeals that hears cases from the federal district courts below them. These courts are made up of judges from the region. Cases can be appealed from the circuit court of appeals to the U.S. Supreme Court.

The Federal District Courts

There are 94 district courts throughout the United States and territories. These are trial courts; both civil and criminal matters are tried in federal district court. Often these courts empanel juries who decide many of these cases.

State Supreme Courts, State Appeals Courts, and State Courts

The three levels of courts at the state level somewhat mirror the federal system with trial courts (district, county, or municipal), a court of appeals, and a supreme court.

State Supreme Courts

Every state has a court of last resort, and for most states it is a supreme court (except Maryland and New York, whose highest court is the court of appeals), and the justices are usually elected rather than appointed. Most states have a supreme court made up of five to nine justices and the chief justice may be elected by his or her peers or be based solely on seniority. Only the U.S. Supreme Court may overturn the decisions made by state supreme courts.

State Court of Appeals

Most, but not all, states have an appeals court, Nevada being an exception with no such court, which is an intermediary between the trial court and the supreme court. Utah's supreme court is the arbiter of cases going to the court of appeals. The structure and function of these courts varies somewhat from state to state. Most states have a website for their judiciary, and this can be a helpful tool in learning about the specifics where you live.

State Trial Courts and Specialty Courts

Again, although all states have trial-level courts, they vary widely. Some are district courts established by county, some are municipal. A few states have "chancery courts" and others have "courts of equity," which in modern times holds little distinction from "courts of law." In addition, there are specialty courts like drug courts, mental health courts, or juvenile courts that preside over a very narrow range of cases. Most states have a state government or state court website where you can find more information about your state.

Final Thoughts

It may seem overwhelming to read about the various levels of policy-making settings and the stages of the policy change process, but do not be daunted. Like anything else, it just takes some firsthand experience in these environments to learn how it works. Many advocates begin by working at the local or state level, because these levels of government tend to be more open and accessible. As a social worker seeking to engage in policy practice, it is important to have a working knowledge of the systems of government and the procedures for getting a policy passed into law. Since there is an ethical obligation for social workers to engage in political advocacy, every social worker should be familiar with the various levels of government where they can get engaged. Some will certainly choose to be more active than others, and some "political junkies" will make a career out of this field of social work practice. Being successful in this environment requires strong skills in written and oral communication, consensus building, and cultivating relationships—and these are certainly strengths for social workers.

REFERENCES

DiNitto, D. M. (2011). *Social welfare: Politics and public policy* (7th ed.). Boston, MA: Pearson.

Milbrath, L. W. (1965). *Political participation: How and why do people get involved in politics?* Chicago, IL: Rand McNally.

Credits

Fig 5.1: Source: https://commons.wikimedia.org/wiki/File:United_States_Capitol_-_west_front.jpg.

Fig. 5.5: USA.gov, https://www.usa.gov/branches-of-government.

CHAPTER 6

Tactics and Strategies for Creating Policy Change

"Never doubt that a small group of thoughtful people can change the world. Indeed it's the only thing that ever has."

~Margaret Mead

"Nice people made the best Nazis. My mom grew up next to them. They got along, refused to make waves, looked the other way when things got ugly and focused on happier things than 'politics.' They were lovely people who turned their heads as their neighbors were dragged away. You know who weren't nice people? Resisters."

~Naomi Shulman, writer

Figure 6.1 Two undergraduate social work students testifying before the Portland City Council

CHAPTER SUMMARY

It is understandable that many Americans feel frustrated and alienated from the political process and believe that the political system in the United States is broken and needs to be reformed. However, social workers cannot get off the hook that easily. Chapter 1 of this book details social work's special dedication to working for social and political change. Social work is the only profession in the United States that has a mission of social justice. The person-in-environment perspective embraced by social workers means that social workers assist individuals so that individuals can function better within their environment, but social workers also work on changing the environment so that it works better for many vulnerable populations—and changing the larger social environment often involves social and political action by committed social workers who are actively engaged in policy change efforts. Most policy junkies will advise you to find an issue that you are passionate about and then figure out how you can best contribute to that cause. This chapter will provide a range of ideas and suggestions regarding how social workers can get involved in policy change efforts on issues of interest, including the tactics that are used in the policy arena. The three broad categories include the following: (1) opportunities for social work students, (2) effecting policy change as a professional social worker, and (3) career options in the political arena.

Election Campaign Staff

Lobbyist (Contract versus On-Staff)

Legislative Staff

Consider Running for Office

STUDENT LEARNING OBJECTIVES

- ○ Students will demonstrate increased political efficacy with regard to various political skills (e.g., writing fact sheets, testimony, or op-eds; delivering oral testimony; conducting a successful lobby visit).

- ○ Students will be able to summarize how social workers can get involved politically as a student, volunteer, or employee, and identify the skills needed to carry out this work.

- ○ Students will be able to describe the barriers to social workers' political participation and how these barriers can be overcome.

Most Americans would agree that high levels of civic engagement (being an active participant in identifying and addressing issues of public concern) lead to stronger communities and societies. However, the news from researchers studying civic engagement in the United States has not been positive in recent years. Since the 1950s, voter turnout for presidential elections has ranged between 50% and 65%, which is much lower than in many other developed nations. Some blame individuals for this lack of participation, while others point to systemic barriers that create barriers for many Americans to become politically active (e.g., voter suppression; lack of civic education in K–12 schools). Harvard University professor Robert Putnam published the widely read book *Bowling Alone: The collapse and revival of American community* in 2000 that documented declining levels of civic engagement in the United States over the previous three decades. In the book, he cites data showing substantial decreases in voting and other forms of political participation, and declining membership in all kinds of clubs and organizations, such as the parent–teacher associations (PTAs), religions organizations, labor unions, civic organizations, and even recreational clubs such as bowling leagues. Putnam describes communities with decreasing levels of trust, cohesion, connectiveness, and reciprocity, which is often referred to as **social capital**. And the latest data from American National Election Studies (ANES) show that:

- In 2016, 82% of Americans felt the government is run by a few big interests looking out for themselves, whereas only 17% felt it is run for the benefit of all people.
- In 2016, 50% agreed with the statement: "People like me don't have any say about what the government does." In 1960, only 27% agreed with this statement.
- In 2016, 59% of Americans agreed with the statement: "I don't think public officials care much what people like me think." In 1960, only 25% agreed with this statement.
- In 2012, 64% of Americans felt that "quite a few government officials are crooked." In 1958, only 24% felt like this.
- In 2012, only 20% of Americans felt that they can trust the federal government to do what is right *most of the time*. In 1964, 62% of Americans felt this way.

It is understandable that many Americans feel frustrated and alienated from the political process and believe that the U.S. political system is broken and needs to be reformed. However, social workers cannot get off the hook that easily. Chapter 1 of this book details social work's special dedication to social and political change. Social work is the only profession in the United States that has a **mission of social justice**. The person-in-environment perspective embraced by social workers means that social workers assist individuals so that individuals can function better within their environment, but social workers also work on changing the environment so that it works better for many vulnerable populations—and changing the larger social environment often involves social and political action by committed social workers and others who are actively engaged in policy change efforts.

However, social workers may feel ambivalent about being involved with politics and legislation for a number of reasons. In the early 1990s, social work professor Mark Ezell (1993) observed that social workers avoid politics because (1) politics has to do with the pursuit and use of power, while social workers value equality; and (2) social workers believe politics is a dirty business, and they want nothing to do with the process, or the people involved in it. Social work education, which stresses a cooperative, strengths-based approach, may be viewed by some as incompatible with politics, an often adversarial process that involves skills in assertive communication and oral argumentation and persuasion. However, another valid perspective is that social workers are known for their exceptional communication and people skills such as listening, verbal communication, conflict mediation, problem-solving, and collaboration, all of which are excellent skills for the political arena. Figure 6.2

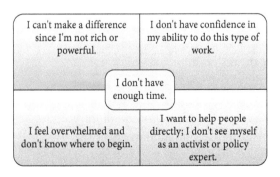

Figure 6.2   Obstacles to being involved politically

shows some common feelings that people have that prevent them from getting involved politically.

Social workers may also be reluctant due to fears of breaking legal codes that restrict the political activities of social workers in certain government and nonprofit settings and concerns that political activity will compromise their professional values, standing within the community, or one's place of employment. However, an article in *Social Work* by Rocha, Poe, and Thomas (2010) concluded that social workers employed in government and nonprofit organizations can be much more politically active than they realize. Their article explains in detail the lobbying activities permitted by the Internal Revenue Service (IRS) for those working in nonprofits as well as political activities permitted by the **Hatch Act** for those working for the government. According to the Rocha and colleagues (2010):

> Even after social workers feel competent to perform policy-related activities, it is important for them to know the laws regarding lobbying for nonprofit organizations, understand permitted and prohibited activities as state or federal employees, and not be afraid to participate in political advocacy. … Educating legislative bodies on issues important to clients and working with the executive branch agencies to implement regulations of laws are both important activities on which there are no restrictions whatsoever for either nonprofit organizations or public and private employees. Lobbying can be done legally by any employee and by nonprofits, as long as they watch how much they spend on these activities. The only real restriction that applies to public employees and some nonprofit employees is working in partisan political campaigns, and even these restrictions have been liberalized since 1993. The bottom line is that social workers, in organizations and individually, can advocate politically much more than they realize (p. 324).

Many social workers who lead busy lives find it challenging to find the time needed to devote to political activity. Others wonder whether their efforts can really make a difference. And then there are social workers who feel that political change takes too long and they are not patient enough to fight for an issue or a cause for years on end. They forget that helping individuals change can be equally daunting and time-consuming! Finally, some social workers find the political arena intimidating and do not have confidence in their skills and abilities when it comes to doing this kind of advocacy work, referred to as **political efficacy**. According to DiNitto (2011), "It is not enough for human service professionals to know the needs of people and to want to pass policies and provide services to help them. Policy advocates for the disenfranchised must both understand the political process and be adept at working within it if they are to have a voice in shaping social policy" (p. 32). Wolk, Pray, Weismiller, and Dempsey (1996) state that "Like any social work endeavor, political activity requires commitment, expertise, and training to be successful" (p. 91). Social work programs have an important role to play in order to ensure that students leave social work programs with the skills and knowledge needed to do work in the legislative arena (Ritter, 2007; 2008).

Most political junkies will advise you to find an issue that you are passionate about and then figure out how you can best contribute to that cause. This chapter provides a range of ideas and suggestions regarding how social workers can get involved in policy change efforts on issues of interest (see Top 10 Reasons for Social Workers to Be Engaged Politically). The three broad categories include the following: (1) how to gain knowledge and experience as a student, (2) effecting policy changes as a professional social worker, and (3) career options in the political arena.

Top 10 Reasons for Social Workers to Be Engaged Politically

1. Activism can be fun!
2. There is an issue that you are passionate about.
3. Someone you care about is affected by this issue.
4. You have the expertise to contribute to this cause.
5. It is an opportunity to gain new skills.
6. Policy change can result in change for a large number of vulnerable people.
7. Social workers have an ethical duty to do so.
8. It is a great way to develop relationships with others who are also passionate about your cause.
9. Policies can dramatically improve the lives of people we serve.
10. Some policies can be harmful to those we serve and should be changed or eliminated.

I. Opportunities for Social Work Students

The first step while a student is to choose a social issue that you are truly passionate about. There are a number of ways to get informed on a range of social problems and the politics surrounding these issues:

- Tune in to news/political programming on television (e.g., ABC's *This Week*; NBC's *Meet the Press*; Comedy Central's *The Daily Show*; HBO's *Real Time with Bill Maher* and *Last Week Tonight* with John Oliver; and TBS's *Full Frontal with* Samantha Bee).
- Read the political section of reputable newspapers (e.g., *New York Times*, *Washington Post*) and the local public affairs section of your local newspaper.
- Regularly read articles/blogs on reputable political websites (e.g., Politico, Slate, Daily Kos, Salon, RealClearPolitics, Huffington Post, local blogs in your state).
- Get a copy of *Social Work Speaks* published by the National Association of Social Workers to find out where the NASW stands on a number of political issues.
- Attend a social work "Lobby Day" at your state capitol if it is offered by your social work program or state NASW chapter.
- Become a member of NASW while a student when it is most affordable and then learn how to join your state chapter's legislative committee or political action committee.

- Listen to National Public Radio (NPR) and alternative media such as Democracy Now.
- Join, or start, a student group on campus that focuses on political advocacy (some social work programs have a student organization called the Social Welfare Action Alliance, or SWAA).
- Sign up for legislative alerts from local and national advocacy organizations that you care about; this is a great way to get informed about legislative issues.
- Visit the "Advocacy" section of NASW's website to learn more about legislative issues of interest to the social work profession.
- Attend community forums, town hall meetings, and other meetings in your community where important local issues are being discussed. (Tip: Go to your state legislature's website and use the "find your legislator" tabs to find out who your state representatives are. Then get on the e-list for your local representatives and they will send you invites for town hall meetings in your area.)

However, perhaps the most effective way to gain knowledge and skills in political advocacy is to choose a policy-focused practicum for the field education component of your social work education. Most social work programs have placement options for students interested in policy change efforts that may include legislator's offices and a range of diverse advocacy organizations at the local, state, national, and even international levels (see list of advocacy organizations in Chapter 1). Additionally, a number of master of social work (MSW) programs specialize in preparing students for social work in the political arena.

If you are interested in getting into the political arena as a career, completing a policy-focused internship or practicum will make you much more competitive on the job market because you will be able to demonstrate that you have acquired a beginning level of knowledge and skills in advocacy or legislative work. It is also a great opportunity to network and meet some of the key people who do this work in your city or state. Practicum experiences are invaluable because they give you the opportunity to discover whether you are well suited for this type of work. Additionally, you begin to learn the "lingo" and culture of this environment. Your practicum may provide you with the opportunity to learn how to lobby legislators, develop media and public education materials, recruit and organize volunteers, provide written and oral testimony, work on a campaign (issue or candidate), and bring groups of people together to work on an issue of concern.

II. Effecting Policy Change as a Professional Social Worker

Volunteer for an Organization

While you are a social work student, and once you become a practicing social worker, there are a number of ways to volunteer your time in order to meet the ethical duty of engaging in social and political action. The best piece of advice is to join an organization so that you are not doing this work alone. Although we often hear stories of remarkable individuals who made a huge impact when it comes to social and political change (e.g., Gandhi, Margaret

Sanger, Rosa Parks, Cesar Chavez, Dr. Martin Luther King, Jr., Dorothea Dix), the reality is that most people who engage in social change efforts do not work in isolation.

Many choose to volunteer their time and expertise for an advocacy organization in their field of interest. Social workers who work in mental health for example may want to donate some of their time to the National Alliance on Mental Illness (NAMI), whereas social workers who work with low-income children or children in foster care may want to join forces with an advocacy organization that is working on behalf of children (e.g., Our Children Oregon, Illuminate Colorado, Children's Defense Fund, Child Welfare League of America). Once you find an organization that you believe in and want to support with your time and energy, it is a good idea to sign up to receive legislative action alerts via email so that you stay up-to-date on the legislative "hot topics" in your chosen field.

Get Involved in Elections

Another important way to effect change is to volunteer to work on a political campaign. There are two types of **political campaigns**: "people" campaigns (aka "candidate" campaigns) and "issue" campaigns. An important component of political work is electing people who share your commitment to various issues and concerns in society. Social workers typically want to elect candidates who care about the needs of vulnerable people in society and are willing to dedicate financial resources to support social service programs that serve these populations. Social workers may also work on an issue campaign in their state when there is a ballot measure that is being considered by voters. Voters may be voting on rights for undocumented immigrants, whether to legalize marijuana, or whether to raise certain types of taxes in order to pay for vital state social services.

There are three main phases to election work: **voter identification** (learning where individual voters stand), **voter persuasion** (moving people from undecided to your side), and **getting out the vote**, or "GOTV" (turning out your base on Election Day). Social workers interested in this type of political work are typically engaged in the following activities: phone banking; creating and distributing campaign materials; canvassing neighborhoods and persuading voters to support an issue or candidate; organizing events that bring people together to educate them about an issue or candidate; using social media; and engaging in fundraising activities such as hosting a house party or "dialing for dollars." In recent years, voter suppression in the United States has become a serious issue of concern, as some in power believe it is in their interest to make it harder for some Americans to vote (e.g., typically for communities of color who tend to vote for the Democratic party). Instead of making it easy for all Americans to vote, many states have attempted to create barriers for some to vote by reducing the number of polling places, which creates long lines, passing strict voter ID laws, and opposing laws to make it easier to vote, such as mail-in voting.

Engage in Fundraising Efforts

Political candidates and organizations cannot survive or be effective without resources, thus grassroots fundraising can be incredibly effective. The cornerstone of **grassroots fundraising** is individual people asking people they know to make a contribution to a cause, political campaign, or organization. A lot of people find it uncomfortable to ask their friends and acquaintances to give money, and this is understandable. However, many organizations provide the training that is needed to give participants the confidence they need to be effective. There's a basic principle in grassroots fundraising, referred to as the ABCs:

- A: Asking people who have the "ability" to give.
- B: Asking people who have a "belief" in the issue or cause to give.
- C: Asking people who have a connection to the person asking or the organization itself to give.

Work to Influence Legislation at the Local, State, or Federal Level

Once candidates have been elected and government is in session, the focus becomes participating in various activities in order to influence legislation that is being considered. Sometimes social workers are in the position of working diligently to get legislation passed into law, and other times they are trying to defeat legislation that has been deemed harmful to a particular group or population. Social workers are often in the position of being the voice of those who are not able to advocate for themselves; however, it is very important to support clients in speaking for themselves whenever possible. When clients are able to speak directly to legislators about their struggles, it can be an empowering experience for them. It can also be very effective because legislators are often moved when they hear personal stories. One tool that can be very effective when trying to pass or defeat a piece of legislation is to develop a **one-to two-page fact sheet** about the bill and your organization's position on it. There is no one format for a fact sheet—some are very fancy and have impressive visuals (e.g., tables, graphs, photos, images) and others are more matter of fact. Because most people do not have the time to read an in-depth 10- to 20-page policy analysis paper, a fact sheet is a nice advocacy tool because it gives people a high-level overview of the policy and the arguments for or against. See the fact sheet example below ("Please Support Tuition Equity in Oregon, SB 742").

When social workers think about influencing legislation at the federal level, it seems very intimidating, not to mention that many of us live far away from Washington, D.C. However, social workers are often surprised to learn how easy it is to impact legislation locally (e.g., school board, city council, state legislature), because local and state lawmakers are often much more responsive and accessible to their constituents. There are a number of ways to influence legislation that is being considered, and some activities are more time consuming than others. Two very effective ways to impact legislation that is being considered is to make a lobby visit and to testify at a legislative committee hearing (see more below).

Lobby Your Local, State, or Federal Lawmakers (You Don't Have to Be a Professional Lobbyist!)

There are basically two types of lobbying—**direct lobbying** and **grassroots lobbying**. Direct lobbying occurs when a paid professional lobbies on behalf of a cause or issue or when individuals lobby decision-makers personally. Grassroots lobbying is when an organization

Please Support Tuition Equity in Oregon! (SB 742)

SB 742 is a bi-partisan piece of legislation that would make it possible for ALL Oregon Students, regardless of their documentation status, to be able to pay in-state tuition. Besides capitalizing on the investment in Oregon's K-12 students, SB 742 would boost the education level of Oregon's workforce and **bring in more tax dollars to the state's general fund**. These young adults want to live the American Dream which entails going to college, getting a job, and raising a family. **Please contact your state senator and representative and urge them to vote "yes" on SB 742!**

Fast Facts:

1. Roughly 65,000 undocumented students graduate from high school every year in the U.S.
2. Due to financial and other barriers, only 5 to 10 percent of undocumented graduates are able to attend college, according to a 2007 report from The Urban Institute.
3. Tuition and fees are nearly three times higher for undocumented students---$19,941 at the University of Oregon and $21,500 at PSU---a financial barrier that prevents most from attending college.
4. Undocumented students cannot legally receive any federally funded student financial aid, including loans, grants, scholarships, and work-study programs.
5. Ten other states have passed similar legislation to SB 742 including California, Illinois, New York, Texas, Utah and Washington.

What do supporters say?

"The bottom line is that this bill is about removing costly, unfair barriers that prevent hardworking Oregonians from continuing their education and giving back to our state. We'll all benefit from that."
~Portland State University President Wim Wiewel

"This young lady who worked hard, her desire to go to a university was foreclosed on. Why would we foreclose opportunity for life improvement for this young lady ... This is the right thing to raise the level of all society."
~Republican Senator Frank Morse

"We've already invested time and resources into these students in high school. Their dream of college has kept them going. They've taken the path we want all Oregonians to take but they've hit a roadblock that can be lifted with tuition equity."
~Democratic Representative Michael Dembrow

Overview of SB 742:

SB 742 would allow undocumented Oregon students who have grown up here and have attended Oregon schools to pay in-state tuition if they:

* Have attended an Oregon high school for at least three years;
* Have graduated from an Oregon high school;
* Are accepted at an Oregon University System institution; and
* Are actively working toward U.S. citizenship.

Chief sponsors of SB 742 include Senators Nelson (R-Pendleton) and Morse (R-Albany), and Representatives Dembrow (D-Portland) and Johnson (R-Hood River). This bill has bi-partisan support in the Oregon state legislature.

Who Supports SB 742?

- Oregon Students Association
- Oregon Dreamers
- National Association of Social Workers, Oregon Chapter
- SEIU
- Oregon Education Association
- Center for Intercultural Organizing
- CAUSA
- American Federation of Teachers
- Asian Pacific American Network of Oregon
- Presidents of PSU, Mount Hood Community College, OSU, and University of Oregon
- Oregonian Editorial Board

This fact sheet prepared by Dr. Jessica Ritter.

or campaign calls upon its members to lobby decision makers through email alerts, letter writing campaigns, and in-person lobby visits. Social workers can be involved in both direct and grassroots lobbying.

Generally, lobbying involves contacting or meeting with elected officials and asking them to support or oppose a piece of legislation. A personal visit to a legislator or elected official has the most influence. The degree of influence tends to correspond to the amount of effort a constituent puts into the lobbying effort. For example, a personal phone call into an office has more influence than a letter. A personal letter has more influence than a form letter or email.

Many citizens are intimidated by the idea of "lobbying" an elected official; however, the reality is that there is nothing to fear and it just takes some practice (see How to Make an Effective Lobby Visit). The staff members who work in legislative offices are paid to listen to their constituents and to be polite and considerate. The very essence of living in a democracy means that citizens have the right (some would say the obligation) to voice their concerns and opinions to those who were elected to represent them.

How to Make an Effective Lobby Visit

1. Be on time and organized. If you are going as a group, meet 15 minutes early near your appointment and get organized. Who is going to say what? Do a practice run-through.
2. Be informed. Go to the meeting having done preliminary research on where the decision-maker stands on your issue. If that is not possible to figure out, know what committees the member sits on.
3. Be prepared. Know what you are going to say in advance and stick to those points.
4. Be brief. Most office visits with a member are 15 to 20 minutes. If you meet with staff, you might get 30 minutes.
5. Start a visit with a round of introductions; clearly state the bill number and brief description and the position you hold. "Hi, my name is Sally Johnson, I am with Child Advocates Utah and we are here today to talk about SB 201, the Children's Health Bill and to ask for your support." Then share a compelling story about how this issue impacts the clients you serve.
6. Do not be afraid to say you do not know. If you don't know the answer to one of their questions, tell them you will get back to them. Then be sure you do it!
7. Leave them with a one-page fact sheet restating your main points that includes the bill number, your position on the legislation, and your contact information in case they want to follow up with you.
8. Never threaten a member with backing an opponent or launching a campaign against them if they say they are voting in opposition to your position.
9. Close your meeting by trying to get the member to actually say how he or she will vote. Elected officials are pretty good at not answering questions. You might say, "Rep So & So, can we count on you to vote in favor of SB 201?" Or if the member is noncommittal, ask what other information he or she might need to move to a yes/no position on the bill.
10. Thank them at the end of the meeting and then send a personal thank-you email or handwritten note afterward.

Get Your Message Out Through the Media

Advocates involved in policy change efforts understand the importance of getting media coverage. Many organizations and campaigns have professional or paid staff who are in charge of their messaging and media program. Maintaining "message discipline" can be critical to winning a victory. Political campaigns tend to be more effective when they are able to pay for television, radio, and newspaper ads (i.e., **paid media**), particularly when the opposition is using this as a strategy; however, paid media are very expensive. Grassroots organizations often do not have the resources necessary to buy ads and will often need to engage in various fundraising activities in order to finance this political strategy.

However, effective campaigns and organizations also understand and value the role that volunteers play in generating **earned media**, which is free. This includes writing and submitting letters to the editor and op-eds to newspapers for publication, using social media effectively (e.g., Facebook, Twitter, blogs), and participating in actions with the goal of getting free media attention such as rallies, marches, or civil disobedience. Publishing a letter to the editor or op-ed in a newspaper can be an extremely effective way to get attention focused on an issue because they are widely read by the public (see Tips for Writing an Effective Letter to the Editor or Op-ed). Letters to the editor are very brief (a couple of paragraphs) and are written in response to a previously published article. Op-eds are longer, comment on a current issue, and do not have to be in response to a previously published article in the newspaper. However, op-eds are more difficult to get published because you need to be viewed as someone with expertise on the topic.

Tips for Writing an Effective Letter to the Editor or Op-ed

1. Keep the focus on one single issue—why legislators in your state should vote "yes" on HB 201.
2. Think very carefully about the best arguments to make your case.
3. Write clearly and use language the general public will understand (avoid professional jargon).
4. Know the word limit and other submission rules (usually posted on the publication's website). You must be able to write succinctly.
5. Be timely if you are responding to a recent story in the paper because you will only get published if the editor views your piece as "newsworthy."
6. The most compelling letters and op-eds include compelling stories but also have pertinent facts and data.
7. Ask a trusted colleague to review your piece and give you feedback.
8. Edit your work several times before submitting to catch any writing errors and to improve your writing.
9. Include your contact information so the editor can contact you about publishing your piece.
10. Be very professional and measured in your tone. Extreme, outrageous views are not likely to be published.

Framing Your Argument

In order to engage in many advocacy-related activities, such as lobbying, testifying in a legislative hearing, or getting an op-ed published in a newspaper, advocates must become very skilled in how to **frame an argument** in a compelling way so that it resonates with and convinces those they are trying to influence (e.g., voters, legislators, funders). This can be harder and more time-consuming than it sounds, and advocates spend a lot of time figuring out the right "messaging" to use when they are working to get a policy passed. Sometimes focus groups are used to learn which messages people respond to the best. This may sound calculating, but when going up against a wealthier and more powerful opponent, this can be a smart strategy, because at the end of the day winning requires being able to make the most persuasive and compelling argument.

For example, in the chapter on mental health advocacy (Chapter 8), advocates who were trying to pass the Mental Health Parity Act argued that when health insurance companies provide less coverage for mental health care treatment than for physical health care treatment it is an act of discrimination. They could have framed the issue a number of ways but ultimately decided to frame the issue as one of fairness and discrimination. Once advocates have decided how to frame an issue, they must then maintain **"message discipline"** by sticking with their message and not straying to other arguments and messages unless there is a very good reason to.

Help to Build a Coalition

Bringing together groups of people, or **coalition building**, can be an effective tactic when trying to influence legislation. It is often said that there is power in numbers. When facing an opponent who is much better financed, often the only way to overcome this is through "power in numbers." For example, when an organization is lobbying on behalf of a particular piece of legislation it speaks loudly when it is able to say that 200 organizations in the state have signed on in support of the bill. Getting **endorsements from opinion leaders** can also be incredibly effective when trying to get a piece of legislation passed into law. Examples of opinion leaders can include scholars, experts, or researchers on the issue; local celebrities; editorial boards of newspapers; business leaders; prominent politicians, etc. The basic idea is that if you can get people who are widely respected to endorse your legislation you will be more likely to sway lawmakers to your position.

It is important to keep in mind that there are advantages and disadvantages when working as part of a coalition. The main advantages of coalitions is that they can increase the critical mass and visibility of an issue or campaign, help build relationships among member groups, save resources, and enable delegation of tasks across the participants. The potential downsides of coalitions is that they take time to form and maintain, groups differ in resources and may not be able to contribute equally, and compromises may have to be reached. Prior to joining a coalition, an organization may want to consider the following: Will it gain positive visibility from participating in the coalition? Will its membership increase because of the coalition? Will relationships be strengthened with other partners? Does it have the necessary resources to commit to the coalition? Will it have decision-making power as part of this coalition?

Provide Testimony at a Public Legislative Hearing

One of the most powerful ways that social workers can influence legislation is by sharing their experience and expertise with legislators on a particular issue. A very powerful action is to provide written and oral testimony on a bill when it has reached the stage of having a public hearing before a legislative committee (see Tips for Providing Effective Testimony in a Legislative Committee Hearing). Often, legislators do not have direct experience with the kinds of social problems that social workers are exposed to everyday, so it is extremely helpful to them to hear directly from social workers. When this does not happen, legislators are forced to make important decisions without the luxury of having all of the relevant facts and information. It is important to keep in mind that legislators vote on thousands of bills covering hundreds of issues; thus, they are "kindergarten experts" on a wide range of issues, but only true experts on a few. Therefore, *a social worker is likely to be more of an expert than a legislator* when it comes to the problems that many of our clients and communities face every day.

Tips for Providing Effective Testimony in a Legislative Committee Hearing

1. Prepare your written testimony in advance and bring the correct number of copies with you the day of the hearing.
2. Check your state's legislative website; it may provide tips for testifying or video examples of effective testimony. There may be audio/visual streaming of testimony in active committees or archived. Take a few moments to watch these so that you know the correct salutation/introduction to your testimony: "Chair Smith, members of the committee, my name is Jane Doe. I am here today on behalf of Child Advocates Montana to testify in favor of House Bill 2482."
3. It is best to prepare written testimony that is not too lengthy; in most cases, one to two pages should be sufficient.
4. It is okay to be nervous—most people are. But most people's butterflies will subside once they get going. Most of the time, this will be endearing to members of the committee and will show that you care.
5. You can use notes, but do not read your testimony word for word. If possible, paraphrase what you have written so that it sounds as conversational as possible.
6. Good eye contact is essential! You need to connect with the committee members.
7. Use the sandwich approach: clearly state your position right away, find creative ways to argue your position, then end by stating your position once again.
8. Do not be negative. Optimism always plays better. Do not talk down to the committee.

9. Back up your argument with empirical data whenever possible; however, do not overwhelm people with statistics. Using a few key pieces of data can be very powerful, but if you use too many people's eyes will start to glaze over.

10. Know the other side of the argument very well. One technique that can be effective is to preemptively respond to your opponent's argument: "The other side will tell you ... ; however, this flies in the face of all recent available research on this topic."

11. Whenever possible, create a compelling narrative. Stories resonate with people more than anything else.

12. Use creative language to frame the debate by using catchy phrases, colorful metaphors, and/or analogies.

13. Pull at people's heartstrings. A human interest angle can be effective, but choose carefully. Legislators respond better to an inspirational story rather than a "doom and gloom" story.

14. If a committee member asks you a question that you don't know the answer to, be honest, say you don't know, and that you will find out and get back to them. Then make sure you follow up.

15. Make sure to thank the members of the committee for the opportunity to testify.

Providing testimony is an important activity, yet very few social workers perform this critical role when their city council or state legislature is in session. The most likely reason is that it is perceived as an intimidating task to speak before a committee of legislators. For most people, this can be somewhat nerve-racking, but with experience, many social workers actually come to enjoy it. It can be incredibly gratifying to perform this kind of civic duty.

Social Worker Spotlight: Elaine Charpentier Philippi, BSW, MSW

On testifying before the Oregon State Legislature

As a BSW student, I believed that policy would be among my least favorite classes. I prematurely associated it with other required undergraduate credits like my early nemesis—algebra. Knowing this, you can imagine my surprise when I sat through my first policy lecture where my professor shared with us her goal—to turn us all into policy geeks by the end of the semester. What I came to rapidly understand in those early weeks of policy class was that my distaste for social policy could be more accurately translated as a misunderstanding of it.

Our class project was a great vehicle for converting me to a "policy geek." Our local NASW chapter was drafting a joint memorial bill that would be introduced in that year's legislative session asking our state lawmakers to urge the White House to convene a White House Conference on Children and Youth—something that had not been done in more than four decades.

Our assignment was to create a fact sheet for the joint memorial and then to meet with representatives in our districts to ask for their support of it. We ended the semester with a mock committee hearing in class where we were given the opportunity to sit before a "pretend" panel of legislators and offer testimony for the memorial. I was initially pretty intimidated by this assignment, but as I spent time researching child welfare issues for my testimony, I became deeply passionate about the need for the convening of a White House Conference on Children. I would soon discover that when you are passionate about an issue, and can translate that passion into an effective and eloquent piece of testimony, others will listen. An advocate was born.

Then a unique opportunity was presented to me at the end of the semester when I was asked by the NASW state chapter to read the testimony I had written for class before the House Committee on Human Services in my state. I was initially really excited about being part of a team of social workers who were petitioning our state legislators to give overdue attention to children affected by the child welfare system. Yet, at the same time, I was pretty sure that I would come off to the committee as nervous, stammering, and inexperienced. I decided to drag my family along—partially for moral support and also because it was a great opportunity to demonstrate to my children the power of being an active constituent and advocate. The experience was nothing short of fabulous! A committee co-chair spoke directly to my children after I finished testifying, thanking them for being there and telling them that they should be very proud of their mom. The experience eliminated my fear of the unknown and gave life to one of our profession's ethical standards—social and political action.

The more that I understand social policy and the diverse ways that social workers can engage in social and political action, the less afraid and more passionate I am about being a bridge between people and equal access to the resources, employment, services, and opportunities they require to be self-determining. I would encourage social work students to identify your distaste for policy and embrace it. At the very least you may be able to identify a social issue or marginalized population that you feel passionate about giving voice to. If a skeptical individual such as myself can be converted to a policy geek in just four short months, anything is possible!

Testimony from Elaine Charpentier Philippi

To: Senate Committee on Health Care, Human Services, and Rural Health Policy
From: Elaine Charpentier Philippi, Pacific University Social Work Undergraduate Student & Member of the National Association of Social Workers
Date: May 16, 2011
Re: Testimony in Favor of HJM 12

Chair Monnes Anderson and Members of the Committee:

My name is Elaine Charpentier Philippi, and I am an undergraduate student of Social Work and a member of the National Association of Social Workers. I am also a mom to three children. After receiving my bachelor's and master's degrees in social work, I plan on having a career focused on improving the lives of vulnerable children in Oregon. Today, I ask for your support of HJM 12, a bill that would urge our federal lawmakers to convene a White House Conference on Children.

The White House Conference on Children and Youth Act focuses on a myriad of child welfare issues. Included are actions for prevention and intervention in abuse and neglect, and increasing the number of foster children that are successfully and permanently placed through kinship care, adoptions, and reunification. It addresses issues like poverty and substance abuse, health and mental health care access, and the over-representation of minority populations served in child and youth systems.

Nationally, rates of child abuse and neglect, homelessness, and mental and physical health risks for children and youth are increasing exponentially. The current economic crisis is having a significant impact on the issues that impact our children and youth—it is also widening the margin of families that enter the system. Children and youth represent some of the largest populations of the homeless, the hungry, and the abused. Child abuse is costly on many levels—none of us are immune to this. In our global world we can no longer look at the issues plaguing our children and youth as someone else's problem.

In May of last year, msnbc.com ran an article reporting that the numbers of children hospitalized for shaken baby syndrome had risen since the onset of the recession. The article was based on research led by University of Pittsburgh's Medical Center/brain injury specialist, Dr. Rachel P. Berger.

Nineteen-month-old Leonard McIntire is named as one of the cases in the study. Leonard was reportedly bitten, beaten, and shaken by the mother's boyfriend. After he was taken into custody, the boyfriend admitted punching Leonard and shaking him violently. Leonard's injuries included a broken left arm and ligature marks on his neck. After five days on a ventilator, Leonard died.

Dr. Berger called our current fiscal and social climate the "perfect storm: increased stress, increased poverty and yet . . . social services [are] being cut." Understandably these cuts are largely the result of dramatic economic and budget reductions faced by many states. Obviously, there are no easy answers.

A quote from Lilian Katz says it best: "Each of us must come to care about everyone else's children. We must recognize that the welfare of our children is intimately linked to the welfare of all other people's children. After all, when one of our children needs life-saving surgery, someone else's child will perform it. If one of our children is harmed by violence, someone else's child will be responsible for the violent act. The good life for our own children can be secured only if a good life is also secured for all other people's children."

The White House Conference on Children would give child welfare advocates and professionals from all over the country the opportunity to review the best practices research pertaining to the prevention of child abuse and neglect and to make recommendations. This conference would help us to shine a spotlight on the needs of vulnerable children.

Thank you for hearing HJM 12 today. Today, I urge you to support HJM 12 and the White House Conference on Children and Youth Act.

Source: J. Aleccia. (2010, May 1). Shaken baby injuries rose in recession. MSN. Retrieved from http://www.msnbc.msn.com/id/36859272/ns/health-kids_and_parenting

Testimony in Support of HB 2787

To: Senate Committee on Education and Workforce Development
From: Jessica Ritter, PhD., MSSW, Associate Professor, Pacific University Oregon
Date: March 19, 2013
Re: Testimony in Support of HB 2787

Chair Hass and Members of the Committee:

My name is Jessica Ritter, and I am an Associate Professor of Social Work at Pacific University in Forest Grove, OR. I am here today to ask for your support of HB 2787, a bill that is crucial to the well-being of Oregon's youth. As a social work academic, I support policies that guarantee that the human services and education needs of all children and young adults are met, regardless of their, or their parent's, legal status.

Many of the undocumented youth in our state are remarkable young people. They are bright and motivated and have a strong desire to get their education, have a successful career, and make a meaningful contribution to their community. The young people that "tuition inequity" is preventing from contributing to our economy include those who wish to pursue careers in areas such as medicine, law, psychology, and social work. However, they cannot do so because they cannot afford the cost of higher education (Seibert and Ritter, 2011). **Tuition and fees are nearly three times higher for nonresident tuition, a financial barrier that prevents most from** attending college.

Unfortunately, the DREAM Act, which would have provided a path to citizenship for some undocumented youth, lost by a small margin in the last U.S. Congress. However, a federal solution to this issue is inevitable and Oregon has the opportunity to join at least 14 other states (including California, Illinois, New York, Texas, Utah, and Washington, and most recently Colorado) by passing this tuition equity bill. This is an important step in the right direction.

HB 2787 has the support of the Oregon Student Association, SEIU, Oregon Education Association, Center for Intercultural Organizing, CAUSA, American Federation of Teachers, Asian Pacific American Network of Oregon, the Presidents of all of the major public universities in Oregon, and the Oregonian Editorial Board. Portland State University President Wim Wiewel stated previously: "The bottom line is that this bill is about removing costly, unfair barriers that prevent hardworking Oregonians from continuing their education and giving back to our state. We'll all benefit from that."

Many of these youth were brought to the U.S. as young children and have lived in Oregon for most of their lives. We have invested our tax dollars in these students by supporting their education in Oregon public schools from Kindergarten through grade 12, and in turn, they've invested their time, energy and hard work. Why then would we effectively cripple them by preventing them from completing the two or four additional years of higher education needed to realize their dreams and to help them become contributing members of society? (Seibert and Ritter, 2011)

For many of these young people, not being able to attend college means the end of their American dream. **Helping more Oregon residents gain higher education degrees is good for all of us.** Those with college degrees earn higher wages and contribute to the economy as taxpayers and consumers. HB 2787 would benefit all Oregonians by promoting a more educated and thus more successful population (Seibert and Ritter, 2011).

It is important to understand that this bill is not a "handout." These youth grow up understanding all too well that they have to work 10 times harder than other young people due to the legal and psychological barriers they face. They will still have to work hard and earn good grades to graduate from high school. They will still have to compete with other students to gain acceptance to a public university. Then they will still have to pay in-state tuition without the benefit of receiving any state or federal financial aid.

Thank you very much for hearing HB 2787 today, and I respectfully ask the Committee to move this bill forward by voting "yes" on tuition equity.

Engage in Educational Outreach and Online Advocacy

One way to build support for a candidate, ballot measure, or piece of legislation is to plan and organize events in your community in order to educate people and to persuade them to support your position on the issue. Examples of this kind of outreach to the public have typically included town hall meetings, house parties, and community forums. However, society has changed a lot as a result of the technology age and the advent of the Internet. Today, people are less likely to attend community events like these in person and much more likely to receive information via the Internet and various forms of **social media.** These days, advocates use social media (e.g., Facebook, Twitter, email action alerts) as a communication tool in order to educate others and mobilize them to act. Before the Internet, Americans received their news by reading the major newspapers of the day and watching the evening news, but today they have endless options for how they choose to receive their news and other information. Hashtags are a new societal phenomenon, and we have seen new social movements use this successfully to gain momentum and support for their cause (#BlackLivesMatter, #MeToo, and #NeverAgain).

Paid Communication

Sometimes advocacy organizations are lucky to have resources to fund paid communication to get their message out to voters. This involves having staff members who are paid to (1) call voters on the telephone to urge them to vote a certain way (in a candidate campaign or issue campaign), (2) knock on doors and leave campaign materials with voters, and (3) educate and persuade voters out in the community at various community events. Paid communication also involves having resources to mail campaign literature out to voters via "snail mail." However, many groups are moving toward connecting with voters online and using social media, because this is where most people receive their information today.

Join a Social Movement

It is inspiring to think back to various social movements in the United States, such as the civil rights movement, the women's movement, and the environmental movement, and how much social and political change they were able to create in our society. Movements are powerful because they counter "money power" and "political power" with "people power" or "power in numbers." Change resulting from social movements does not usually happen overnight, so activists must stay focused on how to sustain their movement over time. There have recently been a host of new social movements in the United States, such as Black Lives Matter, the Me Too movement, and the youth movement for gun control. These movements have been very successful in galvanizing the nation's attention and changing the national discourse on police brutality against communities of color, sexual harassment/sexual violence against women, and the need for common sense gun control legislation. Movements use a range of tactics, and they often use various forms of political dissent, which is discussed next.

Engage in Political Dissent/Visibility

Some involved in advocacy work differentiate between "inside the system" tactics and "outside the system" tactics—sometimes referred to as **direct action** or **civil disobedience** or **political dissent** (e.g., rallies, protests, pickets, boycotts, marches, sit-ins/stand-ins, street theater, and demonstrations). Some social workers are more comfortable engaging as citizen lobbyists by understanding and using the system to forward an issue. However, when certain issues are being ignored by elected officials, sometimes advocates will plan a direct action (e.g., being forcibly removed or arrested; organizing a march) in order to attract media attention (i.e., visibility) and to pressure lawmakers to take action. When successful, direct action activities can demonstrate large-scale support for an issue and can be used to supplement other advocacy activities. In recent years, the United States has seen large marches and rallies in Washington, D.C., and across the country on a range of topics, including police brutality, immigration, gun control, and women's rights. Chapter 11 profiles some young immigration activists engaging in very interesting tactics involving political dissent that are similar to those used by previous social movements, such as the civil rights movement.

It is critical to understand the full ramifications of direct action when making strategic decisions about how extreme the action will be. Before this tactic is used, many considerations should be discussed: Is this the right tactic, or would the organization be better off using other methods of communication? Does it have the right people at the table to ensure that the action is well organized? Will the action bring more support from the public? Will it be well attended? Will it attract a good deal of media attention? How can the organization ensure that it will be a peaceful protest? What message is the action going to convey, and who are the best people to convey that message? And, most important, how can the organization make it safe and fun for the activists who attend?

Tactics Used by Advocates Engaging in Policy Practice

☒ Coalition building
☒ Direct lobbying (in-person lobby visits, sometimes by a professional lobbyist)
☒ Earned media (letters to the editor, actions that lead to media coverage)
☒ Grassroots lobbying (e.g., urging people to call, write, email legislators)
☒ Paid media (paying for TV/radio/newspaper ads)
☒ Educational outreach (town halls, house parties, community forums)
☒ Visibility (rallies, marches)
☒ Online advocacy (using social media)
☒ Political dissent (e.g., civil disobedience, protest)
☒ Paid communication (paid staff who call voters; materials mailed out)
☒ Providing testimony in a legislative committee hearing
☒ Fundraising activities

How Do I Find the Time to Get Involved Politically?

A common feeling among practicing social workers is that they want to be more active politically in order to meet the ethical obligation of advocating for the client populations they serve, but it is very challenging to find the time. This is understandable, and every social worker needs to find a method that works for them based on their homelife and work circumstances. There are times in people's lives when they have more time than others to devote to political advocacy. Sometimes people only have the time to contact a legislator by email or phone to convey a message about a particular bill that is under consideration, while other times they have the time to testify at a public hearing or attend a political rally or march.

III. Career Options in the Political Arena

Numerous jobs and career paths are available to social workers interested in policy practice. Today, those with MSWs are serving in the U.S. Congress, state legislatures, city councils, and school boards across the country. They are also are spearheading large-scale government programs, small nonprofits, and advocacy organizations. Senior positions may include executive director, development director, public affairs manager, and political director. Entry-level positions may include volunteer coordinator, grassroots organizer, government relations coordinator, event coordinator, or researcher.

Executive Director of an Advocacy Organization

As the chief executive, the executive director has a number of responsibilities, and the role will vary depending on the budget and overall staff size of an organization. Generally, the executive director will be responsible for strategic planning, fundraising and managing the budget, board development, program and policy development, communications, and staff hiring and management. Executive directors usually report to a board of directors.

Policy Staff (Related Titles: Director of Public Affairs, Policy Director, Policy Researcher/Analyst)

Many advocacy organizations, large and small, have full-time staff who are devoted to advancing the organization's policy agenda. They are usually headed by a director of public affairs or a policy director who is responsible for managing the following policy activities: developing and implementing a public affairs strategy to achieve the agency's advocacy goals; grant management; media and message development; electoral work and analysis; fundraising; policy analysis; advocacy and lobbying; public education; community organizing; and coalition building. Policy staff positions often focus on research, writing, analysis, and various aspects of policy development (see Social Worker Spotlight: Cathy Kaufmann, MSW). Policy analysis and research is used in advocating for policy, rule, or law changes. It may also be used in presenting testimony to a decision-making body or with the media to try to hold decision-makers accountable or raise the visibility of an issue. Staff in these kinds of positions will often write policy briefs and develop "report cards" that grade legislators or states on their level of support for various issues. It is not unusual for policy researchers to be found working in government agencies as well as advocacy nonprofits.

Social Worker Spotlight: Cathy Kaufmann, MSW

More Than 80,000 Oregon Children to Receive Health Insurance

Cathy Kaufmann was in sales briefly after graduating college, but quickly knew she wanted to do more with her life and career. She joined the staff of a nonprofit in Portland, Oregon, and went to work improving literacy for children. However, it wasn't long before Cathy realized she wanted to have a greater impact on social policies affecting children and their families. "We were conducting meaningful research showing that our literacy program was working, but it was just a band aid and not a long-term solution to the problem," says Kaufmann. So, while maintaining her position as a project coordinator, Kaufmann entered the MSW program at Portland State University: "I knew from the beginning of the program that I was interested in solving problems and advocacy was the solution. I wasn't personally interested in direct service."

In her first year of the program, Kaufmann's field placement was with the state's most populated county working on poverty issues. During her second year, she held a placement at the Juvenile Rights Project (JRP) (Note: this organization has been renamed Youth Rights Justice). The organization is dedicated to improving the lives of vulnerable children and families through legal representation and advocacy in the courts, legislature, schools, and community. At JRP, Kaufman worked for the School Works Program, advocating for educational access for formerly incarcerated youth and foster children. Upon completing her degree, Kaufmann worked for the university conducting research on child welfare. She again realized that while research is important the reports she worked on would quickly gather dust on a shelf. Kaufmann wanted more direct advocacy work and found it at Children First for Oregon (Note: this organization has been renamed Our Children Oregon), the state's most respected advocacy organization committed to improving the lives of Oregon's vulnerable children and families. Kaufmann found her calling at Children First starting as a policy associate; she was quickly elevated to the policy and communications director. It was at Children First that Kaufman saw all the pieces come together: "Issue expertise, strategic advocacy, targeted communications, direct lobbying and grassroots organizing combined to make a significant difference on policy issues."

For more than 10 years, the priority issue at Children First was the expansion of health insurance for children. They had built an extensive coalition and Kaufmann, among others, lobbied for the policy change in the state legislature. However, when the legislation failed to pass due to a lockdown by House Republicans, the Healthy Kids coalition worked to get the Oregon legislature to refer the issue directly to the ballot. Oregon voters would then have the opportunity to vote "yes" or "no" on Measure 50, a ballot measure that would expand health coverage for low-income children in Oregon by raising taxes on cigarettes and other tobacco products.

With the measure to appear on the ballot in less than five months, Kaufmann got "loaned" by Children First to serve as the campaign's communication director. Many aspects of Kaufmann's experience and skills were put to the test during the campaign. However, it proved impossible to overcome a four-to-one spending deferential. The Yes on Healthy Kids PAC spent $3.7 million; the tobacco industry answered by spending $12.1 million (this was the costliest measure in the state's history). Voters rejected the measure by 59% to 41%.

Despite the defeat at the ballot box, Kaufmann and the coalition went back to work and ultimately secured a legislative win when the governor prioritized spending for the Healthy Kids program during the 2009 legislature and came up with an alternative funding scheme.

Immediately following the passage of the legislation, Kaufmann was recruited by the director of the state's Department of Human Services to oversee the Office of Healthy Kids. As the program's administrator, Kaufmann had a staff of 17 and a budget of $13 million. In this position she was responsible for running the outreach, education and marketing programs associated with getting 80,000 Oregon children enrolled in health insurance and was able to see the impact of her work daily. Health and Human Services Secretary (HHS) Kathleen Sebelius said Cathy's program was a model for outreach and marketing.

"The work is certainly not always glamorous, but I know each and every day that I am making a difference. Whether your interest is macro or clinical, it is imperative to engage in political advocacy," Kaufmann says.

Election Campaign Staff

Most political campaigns require campaign staff, and the size of the staff will vary. A statewide campaign requires more staff than a legislative race. The following are some of the more common positions on a campaign:

- **Campaign director**. A campaign director is responsible for implementing all aspects of a campaign plan, such as crafting the campaign plan and ensuring that the resources are there to fully implement it.
- **Fundraising director**. A fundraising director is responsible for raising the funds. This may include major donor solicitation, direct mail, telemarketing, and online fundraising. In addition, a fundraising director will work with allied organizations to secure PAC donations.
- **Field director**. A field director is responsible for overseeing all aspects of the voter contact program. This includes voter identification, voter persuasion, and GOTV.

Lobbyist (Contract vs. On-Staff)

Lobbyists are responsible for developing legislation and getting it introduced and passed, as well as addressing legislation in opposition to the organization and planning and organizing for its defeat. Lobbyists are usually either "contract" or "in-house" depending on the size of the organization and its needs. A contract lobbyist usually works alone or as part of a firm and has contracts with a number of organizations. A staff lobbyist works "in-house" and may have other duties related to the overall public affairs program.

An experienced lobbyist with a lot of access to decision-makers can command a high salary, which might be challenging for an advocacy nonprofit to afford to have on staff. Hiring such a person on contract for a portion of their time gives a nonprofit a way to hire someone with experience and clout to work on its issues. Hiring a less experienced staff lobbyist ensures no conflicts of interest and the full focus of that staff person on the needs and concerns of the organization. There is no right or wrong answer regarding contract or in-house but rather meeting the needs of the organization.

Legislative Staff

Most elected public officials have staff who help them carry out many of the day-to-day tasks involved in legislative work. Positions may include chief of staff, legislative aide/assistant, policy liaison, and administrator. The chief of staff generally is responsible for the day-to-day management of an elected official's office and during campaign season may shift roles and become the candidate's campaign director. A chief of staff often represents the elected official at events or other functions. A legislative aide is often responsible for maintaining communication with an elected official's constituency, which includes in-person meetings as well as written communication. According to researchers, legislative casework is performed in many state and federal legislative offices, and social workers at the BSW and MSW levels are well suited for this type of work (Ortiz, Wirz, Semion, & Rodriguez, 2004). Nancy Walker is a MSW who worked as a legislative director for a Texas state representative (see Social Worker Spotlight: Nancy Walker, MSSW).

Social Worker Spotlight: Nancy Walker, MSSW

Legislative Director for former Texas State Representative Elliott Naishtat

Nancy Walker received her master's degree in social work from the University of Texas at Austin in 1999. Despite having little experience in the legislative arena, she completed her senior year MSW practicum with State Representative Elliott Naishtat, a state legislator with degrees in social work and law. Before receiving her bachelor's and master's degrees in social work, Nancy worked as a licensed chemical dependency counselor, and over time she began questioning who was making the decisions that were hampering the continuity of care of her patients (e.g., lack of community resources, funding cuts for programs serving her clients) and found out that many of these decisions were made at the State Capitol in Austin.

When she began her practicum in Representative Naishtat's office she was not sure she would be successful due to her lack of previous experience, but according to Ms. Walker, "I was hooked from day one!" She had a strong desire to learn everything about the legislative process and was able to focus on human services issues such as affordable housing for seniors and those with mental illness. Nancy learned that her social work skills were put to good use in this environment. Before long, she was learning how to assess a problem and gather information about the problem from a variety of perspectives, how to research and read laws/proposals, and how to write succinct bill analyses.

After graduating with her MSSW, Nancy was hired to work in Representative Naishtat's office. In her position as his legislative director, she helped him to develop his legislative package and was able to work on issues that she was passionate about that fall under the umbrella of health and human services (e.g., policies affecting children and families, mental health, disabilities, poverty, and housing). Ms. Walker worked with advocacy organizations and assisted them in developing policy proposals, responded to calls from constituents, did drop-in visits to government offices to ensure that the system is working properly, and lobbied other legislators in order to move Representative Naishtat's legislation forward. She received a lot of satisfaction from supervising social work students who completed their practicum in Naishtat's office to "watch the light bulbs go on."

Nancy loved every part of her job and states, "If a social worker is interested in the ultimate setting to have impact at the macro level, they should definitely consider a job with a legislator at the state or federal level!" The best part of her job was having the opportunity to have a positive impact on the lives of individuals and families who do not have much influence politically. One of Nancy's favorite wins was helping to pass a bill that created a "Texans conquer cancer" specialty license plate. Texas drivers pay a fee for this plate and the money funds a grant that nonprofit organizations can apply to in order to provide needed yet unfunded services to individuals and families affected by cancer. Every time she's driving down the road and sees a car with that license plate, it gives her a secret thrill.

Consider Running for Office

Too few people consider entering politics as a candidate. There are many good reasons for not running (e.g., pay often low, constantly campaigning, and opening self and family up to attacks). But what better way to effect change than to be in a position to legislate it? There are social workers all across the country who hold elected office at various levels of government, including Capitol Hill. In fact, six social workers served in the 116th U.S. Congress (see Table 6.1).

Table 6.1.   Social Workers in the 116th Congress

Representative Karen Bass (D-CA)	https://bass.house.gov
Representative Susan A. Davis (D-CA)	https://susandavis.house.gov
Representative Sylvia Garcia (D-TX)	http://sylviagarcia.house.gov
Representative Barbara Lee (D-CA)	http://lee.house.gov
Representative Kyrsten Sinema (D-AZ)	https://sinema.house.gov
Senator Debbie Stabenow (D-MI)	http://stabenow.senate.gov

Section 6 of the NASW Code of Ethics states:

> Social workers should engage in social and political action that seeks to ensure that all people have equal access to the resources, employment, services, and opportunities they require to meet their basic human needs and to develop fully. Social workers should be aware of the impact of the political arena on practice and should advocate for changes in policy and legislation to improve social conditions in order to meet basic human needs and promote social justice.

The Code says that social workers have an ethical duty to engage in political action, but it does not tell social workers what they need to do exactly in order to meet this ethical standard. Thus, individual social workers have the flexibility to decide how to best accomplish this. As this chapter demonstrates, there is a wide array of options available based on one's passions, skills, and abilities.

REFERENCES

American National Election Studies. (n.d.). *The ANES guide to public opinion and electoral behavior*. Retrieved from https://electionstudies.org/resources/anes-guide/

DiNitto, D. M. (2011*). Social welfare: Politics and public policy* (7th ed.). Boston, MA: Pearson.

Ezell, M. (1993). The political activities of social workers: A post-Reagan update. *Journal of Sociology and Social Welfare, 20*(4), 81–98.

National Association of Social Workers. (2017). Code of ethics. Approved by the 1996 NASW Delegate Assembly and revised by the 2017 NASW Delegate Assembly. Retrieved from https://www.socialworkers.org/About/Ethics/Code-of-Ethics/Code-of-Ethics-English

Ortiz, L. P., Wirz, C., Semion, K., & Rodriguez, C. (2004). Legislative casework: Where policy and practice intersect. *Journal of Sociology and Social Welfare, 31*(2), 49–68.

Putnam, R. D. (2000). *Bowling alone: The collapse and revival of American community*. New York: Simon & Schuster.

Ritter, J. A. (2007). Evaluating the political participation of licensed social workers in the new millennium. *Policy Practice Journal, 6*(4), 61–78.

Ritter, J. A. (2008). A national study predicting social workers' levels of political participation: The role of resources, psychological engagement, and recruitment networks. *Social Work, 53*(4), 347–357.

Rocha, C., Poe, B., & Thomas, V. (2010). Political activities of social workers: Addressing perceived barriers to political participation. *Social Work, 55*(4), 317–325.

Seibert, R. & Ritter, J. (April 8, 2011). Tuition equity is good for Oregon's youth—and our economy. *The Oregonian*. Retrieved from https://www.oregonlive.com/opinion/index.ssf/2011/04/tuition_equity_is_good_for_ore.html

Wolk, J. L., Pray, J. E., Weismiller, T., & Dempsey, D. (1996). Political practica: Educating social work students for policymaking. *Journal of Social Work Education, 32*(1), 91–100.

Part III

CHAPTER 7 Healthcare Policy and Advocacy

"The enjoyment of the highest attainable standard of health is one of the fundamental rights of every human being without the distinction of race, religion, political belief, economic or social condition."

~*World Health Organization Constitution (n.d.)*

Figure 7.1   Mad as Hell Doctors Winnebago

CHAPTER SUMMARY

The debate over universal health care in the United States is an interesting history lesson. A number of Democratic U.S. presidents were unsuccessful in their attempts to enact a national healthcare program, beginning with President Theodore Roosevelt. President Franklin Delano Roosevelt (FDR) was unable to include health care in the Social Security Act of 1935 due to heavy political opposition, particularly from the American Medical Association (AMA). President Truman, FDR's successor, proposed a single insurance system that would cover all Americans, but this also failed due to opposition from Republicans,

Southern Democrats who were leery of federal intervention into state matters (e.g., segregation), and a vigorous public campaign against "socialized medicine" by the AMA. In the 1960s, major progress was made when President Lyndon B. Johnson and a heavily Democratic Congress passed legislation to create the Medicaid and Medicare programs as part of Johnson's "Great Society" agenda, despite opposition from the AMA.

Since the beginning, the battle has raged on between conservatives who argue that the provision of medical services should be left in the marketplace (where doctors, drug companies, and other providers are free to establish the price of healthcare goods and services and to make a profit) and progressives who believe that health care is a basic human right and is too important to be left to the greed and uncertainties of the free market. The National Association of Social Workers (NASW) views health care as a right and supports a national healthcare system that provides individuals with universal access to a full range of health and mental health care throughout all stages of life. Chapter 7 tells two important stories: (1) how the Obama administration passed the Affordable Care Act into law and (2) the Mad As Hell Doctors who attempted to propel single-payer health care onto the political agenda.

STUDENT LEARNING OBJECTIVES

- Students will be able to define universal health care, single-payer health care, and socialized medicine, and provide examples of each.

- Students will be able to cite the major government-funded healthcare programs in the United States.

- Students will be able to analyze the political advocacy efforts of the Mad As Hell Doctors Tour.

- Students will be able to describe the Affordable Care Act that was passed into law and explain the strengths and weaknesses of the new law.

- Students will be able to cite healthcare advocacy organizations.

You would be hard-pressed to find a social worker in the United States who would disagree with the notion that health care should be a right, not a privilege, and that all Americans should have access to quality health care regardless of socioeconomic status. It is ironic that the richest nation in the world stands alone among the wealthy industrialized nations in not having some form of universal health care. The debate over **universal health care** in the United States is an interesting history lesson. A number of Democratic U.S. Presidents were unsuccessful in their attempts to enact a national healthcare program, beginning with President Franklin Delano Roosevelt (FDR). Roosevelt was unable to include health care in the Social Security Act of 1935 due to heavy political opposition, particularly from the American Medical Association (AMA). In the 1940s, encouraged by federal tax policies that allowed them to provide tax-exempt health insurance, businesses started offering healthcare benefits as a way to attract employees. Once the health insurance industry became established and financially lucrative, it was very difficult for anyone who argued for a different healthcare financing system.

President Truman, FDR's successor, proposed a single insurance system that would cover all Americans, but this also failed due to opposition from Republicans, Southern Democrats who were leery of federal intervention into state matters (e.g., racial segregation), the Chamber of Commerce, and a vigorous public campaign against "socialized medicine" by the AMA. In the 1960s, major progress was made when President Lyndon B. Johnson and a heavily Democratic Congress passed legislation to create the **Medicaid** and **Medicare** programs as part of Johnson's "Great Society" agenda, despite opposition from the AMA. These programs provide comprehensive medical coverage for people over 65, as well as those who are poor, blind, and disabled. President Truman was by Johnson's side when the legislation was signed into law. Yet, this still left millions of Americans without coverage.

In 1971, Senator Edward Kennedy from Massachusetts proposed single-payer healthcare legislation, and this marked the beginning of his career-long effort to reform the nation's healthcare system. However, it would take three decades until another U.S. president, Bill Clinton, would take up the cause of healthcare reform. President Clinton appointed the First Lady, Hillary Clinton, to head up this effort, and it was a spectacular failure. Some observers blame the administration for using a flawed closed-door process and emerging with a plan that was too complicated for many to understand. Others point to the successful efforts of powerful special interests, most notably the Health Insurance Association of America (HIAA) and the pharmaceutical industry, which worked with conservative lawmakers to preserve the status quo and defeat this effort. In Congress, the opposition was led by then Speaker of the House Newt Gingrich. The now infamous "Harry and Louise" television commercials were aired by the HIAA to scare the American public away from the Clinton health plan. After the Clinton health plan stalled in Congress, child welfare advocates were cheered when President Clinton signed legislation creating the State Children's Health Insurance Program (S-CHIP) in 1997 (with bipartisan support) so that more children would have access to health coverage.

President Clinton's healthcare failure was a stinging loss for the Democratic Party, and Democrats would not seriously revisit the issue until the election of President Obama, who had made healthcare reform one of his top campaign promises. In 2008, healthcare spending topped $2.3 trillion and an estimated 46 million Americans lacked healthcare coverage. Many believed that healthcare reform would be a relatively quick and painless process because the government was now controlled by a popular, new Democratic president and a heavily Democratic U.S. Congress. Also, Americans were increasingly disillusioned with their employer-based, HMO-style healthcare system. Obama promised that a bill would be signed by summer, but the road to healthcare reform under the new president was a rocky one. Defeat seemed imminent at several points along the way as Americans became increasingly confused and frustrated with the process.

Fifteen months later, in March 2010, after a long and arduous political battle, the **Patient Protection and Affordable Care Act** was signed into law by President Obama. The new law made some significant changes to the U.S. healthcare system but left many Americans disappointed. It was too radical for many conservative Tea Party activists who feared that this was the first step toward a "government takeover of health care," and not radical enough for progressive single-payer healthcare advocates who were stunned to find that the new law would not even include a public option, the compromise alternative to single-payer health care. The new law preserved the private insurance system and left many spectators around the world wondering why the United States remains the only western industrialized nation that does not ensure healthcare coverage for all of its citizens.

Since the beginning of this debate, the battle has raged on between conservatives who argue that the provision of medical services should be left in the marketplace (where doctors, drug companies, and other providers are free to establish the price of healthcare goods and services and make a profit) and progressives who believe that health care is a basic human right and is too important to be left to the uncertainties and greed of the marketplace. The National Association of Social Workers (2018) views health care as a right and supports a national healthcare policy that "ensures access to the full continuum of physical and mental health services for all people" (p. 149).

Timeline of Healthcare Advocacy and Achievements

- **1751,** first public hospital in the United States, Philadelphia Hospital, founded by Dr. Thomas Bond and Benjamin Franklin.
- **1812,** first national effort to provide medical care for disabled veterans, Naval Home, Philadelphia.
- **1872,** American Public Health Association is founded.
- **1901–1909,** President Theodore Roosevelt advocates for national health insurance.
- **1933–1945,** President Franklin D. Roosevelt advocates for national health insurance but is unable to include it in the Social Security Act due to political opposition.
- **1945–1953,** President Harry Truman proposes a single health insurance system but is not successful.
- **1965,** Medicaid and Medicare programs are created via legislation (supported by President Lyndon Johnson).
- **1971,** Senator Ted Kennedy of Massachusetts begins advocating for single-payer health care.
- **1987,** Physicians for a National Health Care Program (PNHP) is formed.
- **1997,** S-CHIP (State Children's Health Insurance Program) passed into law after President Clinton and First Lady's efforts to reform the nation's healthcare system fail.
- **2004,** Health Care Now! organization formed to advocate for a national single-payer healthcare system.
- **2009,** Mad As Hell Doctors is formed to advocate for passage of single-payer health care.

- **2010,** the Affordable Care Act is passed into law after heavy lobbying and support from President Obama.
- **2017,** Senator Bernie Sanders introduces Medicare for All legislation (single-payer legislation).

Current Events Spotlight: The Coronavirus Pandemic

In 2020, much of the globe was caught unprepared to deal with a virus that would turn into a worldwide pandemic. The last time the world had experienced a pandemic as severe was in 1918 with Spanish flu pandemic. According to the CDC (n.d.), the Spanish flu infected one-third of the world's population and killed 50 million people. The coronavirus pandemic is a fascinating lesson in how well local, state, and federal governments responded to a public health crisis and listened to the advice of public health experts; in other words, how well policymakers used research and science to inform public policy. Initially, President Trump downplayed the threat to the American people by comparing it to the seasonal flu and referring to it as an overblown hoax perpetuated by the Democratic Party, despite dire warnings he received from his own advisors. In an interview with journalist Bob Woodward, Trump shared that that he downplayed the dangers of the pandemic because he did not want to panic the general public (Gangel, Herb, & Stuart, 2020).

However, during the spring of 2020, it became clear that COVID-19 was a major public health threat that could lead to serious illness and even death for some people, particularly older adults and those with underlying health conditions. President Trump convened a coronavirus task force, and some members, such as Drs. Anthony Fauci and Deborah Birx, became household names. Because New York City was one of the early cities to suffer a large number of cases, New York governor Andrew Cuomo also became one of the famous public faces of the crisis and was on television daily to provide updates and relay public health recommendations.

The advice of leading public health officials was to wear masks when out in public, wash one's hands frequently, engage in social distancing of at least six feet, and avoid gathering in large groups, particularly indoors. In many major U.S. cities, state and local lawmakers enforced curfews and stay-at-home orders and forced certain businesses, such as restaurants, movie theaters, hair salons, and gyms, to temporarily close or change how they served their customers (e.g., permit restaurants to offer takeout service) in order to slow the spread of the virus.

President Trump voiced support for the recommendations of his task force, but most of his actions contradicted their advice. For example, he refused to wear a face mask in public, attended large rallies where the majority of his supporters did not wear masks, and he and many members of his administration ultimately contracted the virus. Trump blamed the crisis on China and often referred to it as the "Chinese virus." In May 2020, he announced that the United States would end its relationship with the World Health Organization (WHO) and accused the organization of mishandling the pandemic. The WHO designated the COVID-19 pandemic as a global health emergency on January 30; however, President Trump did not declare a national emergency until March 13.

To the surprise and dismay of many, public health recommendations related to the coronavirus—such as wearing a mask—became politicized in the United States. Many Trump supporters refused to wear masks, either claiming they were not effective or viewing mask mandates as an example of government coercion that infringed on their personal freedom. Unlike many other nations around the world that had a unified national strategy and were able to contain the number of cases by enforcing a lockdown when cases began to surge again, the United States largely left it to states and localities to decide how to address this crisis. As a result, the United States ended up leading the world with the highest number of coronavirus cases and deaths due to the virus, even when adjusting for population size. As of April 1, 2021, the United States had more than 30 million cases and 551,000 deaths due to COVID-19 (*New York Times*, 2021). In fact, Covid-19 was the third leading cause of death in the United States in 2020, behind heart disease and cancer. Worldwide, more than 129 million people have contracted the coronavirus as of April 1, 2021, and almost three million people have died. Due to socioeconomic factors, communities of color in the United States have been disproportionately affected by the pandemic as they become ill and die at higher rates than Whites.

The human costs of this pandemic to individuals and businesses cannot be overstated. When businesses were hit hard by the pandemic and had to lay off their employees or even close, the pain trickled down to American workers, many of whom lost their jobs and health insurance. Many also experienced food insecurity. It was distressing and shocking to see long lines of cars at drive-through food banks in many cities across the United States on the nightly news. People of color and low-income workers were disproportionately affected. Many working parents had to balance working from home while caring for their children who were learning virtually. In addition, the increased stress and isolation that many faced led to increased rates of people struggling with mental health issues such as anxiety, depression, substance abuse, and suicidal thoughts (Stephenson, 2020). The U.S. Congress passed two stimulus bills in 2020 and another one in 2021 to assist individuals, businesses, and other entities that were significantly impacted by the recession resulting from the coronavirus pandemic (see Chapter 4 for details on this legislation).

There was some good news at the end of 2020, when two vaccines, one by Pfizer and one by Moderna, showed that they were highly effective in preventing infections (over 90%). The speed at which these vaccines were developed is a truly remarkable scientific achievement. The vaccines were given emergency approval by the Food and Drug Administration (FDA), and Americans began receiving the vaccines in December 2020 via a priority system. Those with the highest priority included healthcare workers, workers and residents in residential care facilities, senior citizens, and people with underlying health conditions. President Trump promised to deliver 100 million vaccine doses by the end of 2020, but only about two million were administered by then. His administration faced immense criticism for not getting the vaccine out more quickly and efficiently.

President-elect Joe Biden vowed to make addressing the coronavirus one of his highest priorities. In his first 100 days in office, he focused on getting the vaccine out widely, enforcing a mask mandate, and getting children back into schools safely. He assembled a COVID-19 task force of 13 physicians and health experts and appointed two people to serve as high-level coordinators of the COVID-19 response. Biden asked Dr. Fauci to continue on in his current role and to serve as a chief medical advisor in his new administration. Biden also appointed new heads of Health and Human Services and the CDC, as well as a new U.S. Surgeon General. President Biden passed a $1.9 trillion coronavirus relief bill to support those most impacted by the pandemic and to get vaccines out to the public as quickly as possible. He reached his goal of delivering 100 million vaccine shots in his first 100 days in office early, and then increased the goal to 200 million. Americans are desperately hoping that the country will begin to turn the corner on this challenging episode and are anticipating when life will return to somewhat normal, pre-COVID times. One depressing statistic is that life expectancy in the United States fell by a full year in the first six months of 2020, the largest drop since World War II (Tavernise & Goodnough, 2021).

What Is the Problem With the U.S. Healthcare System?

Despite the fact that Americans have some of the best hospitals, doctors, medical treatment, and medical technology in the world, health experts and advocacy groups have identified a rather long list of problems with the current system. In 2000, the WHO ranked the United States 37th in the world on measures of medical outcomes (France and Italy were first and second). When compared to other developed countries, the United States does not fare well when it comes to life expectancy, rates of infant mortality, and other measures of health. A recent study (Schneider, Sarnak, Squires, Shah, & Doty, 2017) compared healthcare system performance in Australia, Canada, France, Germany, the Netherlands, New Zealand, Norway, Sweden, Switzerland, the United Kingdom, and the United States, and ranked the United States last in overall performance.

- **The United States has the most expensive healthcare system in the world**, yet millions of Americans do not have health coverage, and we do not have better health outcomes as a result. According to researchers from the Kaiser Family Foundation (Kurani & Cox, 2020), in 2018, the United States spent twice as much as comparable countries on health, driven mainly by higher payments to hospitals and physicians ($10,637 compared to $5,527 per person, on average).
- The United States has **a long history of employer-based health insurance**, and this creates problems for employees whose employers do not offer health insurance (e.g., part-time workers, those who work for small businesses, and those who work minimum wage jobs).
- The United States spends more than other advanced nations in large part because it **does not have a single-payer healthcare system** (this is defined later in the chapter). Single-payer healthcare systems are much less expensive because there is only one payer of health care (low administrative costs), and the government is able to negotiate the cost of healthcare services (i.e., regulating profits).
- Because the United States does not have a system of universal health care, **millions of Americans do not have healthcare coverage** (i.e., health insurance). According to researchers from the U.S. Census Bureau, in 2019, there were 26.1 million uninsured people in the United States (Keisler-Starkey & Bunch, 2020). However, this is roughly 20 million less than in 2010 due to the passage of the Affordable Care Act. Many Americans are not offered health insurance from their employer and cannot afford to purchase it on their own. Even with the new healthcare law, the cost of health insurance is simply unaffordable for many families. Additionally, some states have chosen not to expand their Medicaid system as allowed under the Affordable Care Act, leaving many people without access to the Medicaid program in their state. A 2009 Harvard study published in the *American Journal of Public Health* reported that 45,000 people die every year in the United States due to lack of health insurance (Wilper et al., 2009).

- **Roughly one-fifth of Americans with health insurance are underinsured.** According to the Commonwealth Fund, in the first half of 2020, 21% of U.S. adults who were insured all year were underinsured (Collins, Gunja, & Aboulafia, 2020). Being underinsured means that one's healthcare coverage does not adequately protect a person from high medical expenses due to high deductibles and out-of-pocket costs. Medical bills are a major cause of bankruptcy in the United States; this does not happen in nations with single-payer healthcare systems.
- The effects of poverty and lack of access to health care lead to **serious health disparities for many groups in the United States**. When researchers study the health of Americans, they find that certain groups, such as African Americans and Latinos, low-income people, and those with disabilities, have worse health outcomes than others.
- In the past, **health insurance companies were allowed to exclude people for various preexisting conditions.** This is now illegal thanks to the passage of the Affordable Care Act.
- **Very powerful special interests** have contributed vast amounts of money to our elected leaders in Washington, D.C., to prevent the United States from achieving meaningful healthcare reform.

Overview of the U.S. Healthcare System

The U.S. system of medical care is quite complicated and includes a number of pathways through which Americans can have health insurance, from both the private and public sectors. The various options include private insurance (employer based or self-contracted) or coverage provided through one of many government programs such as **Medicare**, **Medicaid**, the **Veterans Health Administration**, or the **Children's Health Insurance Program (CHIP)**. According to the U.S. Census Bureau, in 2016 the vast majority of Americans were covered by private health insurance (216 million), while 119 million were covered by government health insurance. The number of people without health insurance was 28 million (Barnett & Berchick, 2017).

- **Private:** Private health coverage includes health insurance that is provided by one's employer or union or coverage that is purchased directly by an individual from an insurance company or an exchange. The Affordable Care Act created healthcare exchanges to help people obtain health coverage if they could not previously afford to purchase it. Some people are eligible for federal subsidies to help cover the cost of coverage through a healthcare exchange. According to the U.S. Census Bureau, in 2016, 56% of Americans received health insurance from their employer (Barnett & Berchick, 2017).
- **Medicaid:** The Medicaid program was established in 1965 during the Johnson administration and was a major achievement in providing health insurance to America's

poorest individuals and families. It is also the largest single funding source for people with AIDS, for those living in nursing homes, and for those with developmental disabilities who live in a facility. Five groups are eligible for services: children, pregnant women, parents with dependent children, people with severe disabilities, and seniors. About half of Medicaid beneficiaries are children. The federal government and the states share the costs of Medicaid. According to the Census Bureau, in 2016, 19% of Americans were covered by the Medicaid program (Barnett & Berchick, 2017).

- **Medicare:** The Medicare program was also created in 1965 during the Johnson administration. Medicare is a health insurance program for people age 65 and older regardless of their income or medical history. In addition to serving seniors, the program also serves some people under age 65 with disabilities and those diagnosed with end-stage renal disease and amyotrophic lateral sclerosis (ALS). Medicare has a complicated structure and is organized into four parts: A, B, C, and D. According to the Census Bureau, in 2016, 17% of Americans were covered by the Medicare program (Barnett & Berchick, 2017). Medicare is financed by a combination of general revenues, payroll taxes, and beneficiary premiums. This is an example of a single-payer healthcare system because the government is the sole payer.

- **CHIP:** The Children's Health Insurance Program (CHIP) (originally called S-CHIP; the S was for "State") was created to cover uninsured children who are not eligible for Medicaid. In January 2018, Congress passed a six-year extension of the CHIP program, which means the federal government will fund this program through fiscal year 2023. The federal government and states share the costs of CHIP, but federal funds are capped.

- **VA system:** The Veterans Affairs (VA) healthcare system is set up to provide a full range of outpatient and inpatient services to living veterans of the U.S. military. The VA has almost 800 outpatient clinics and 152 hospitals. The VA is an example of socialized medicine because healthcare services are both (1) provided by the government and (2) paid for by the government.

What Is Single-Payer Health Care?

For those working in the area of healthcare policy and/or advocacy, a number of important questions need to be considered: How should healthcare resources be distributed? Should access to health care be based on one's income? Should it be linked to one's employment? Should quality and accessibility of health care vary from state to state? Is health care a right or a privilege? Do we want a healthcare *system* or a healthcare *industry*? The healthcare debate can get rather confusing at times because many terms get thrown around, such as *universal health care*, *single payer*, and *socialized medicine*.

When people talk about **universal health care,** they are referring to a system of care in which everyone is guaranteed to have healthcare coverage. The United States is virtually alone in the western industrialized world in not making this assurance to its citizens. In

single-payer healthcare systems, there is one payer, which is typically the government. The advantage to this is that administrative costs are very low because it is much more efficient to process claims when there is only one payer versus hundreds of payers (e.g., government programs, insurance companies, etc.). It would be incorrect to call this **socialized medicine**, however, if healthcare services are being provided in the private sector.

For example, Canada has a single-payer healthcare system because the government is the payer (though Canadians do pay for some costs out-of-pocket such as dental care, eye care, and prescription drugs); however, healthcare services are delivered by the private sector. For example, physicians in Canada do not work for the government. This is similar to the Medicare program in the United States. Canada's government is able to keep the costs of health care low because it is able to negotiate prices with hospitals, pharmaceutical companies, and other providers. It would be more accurate to call Britain's healthcare system socialized medicine because the government is not only the *payer of healthcare services*, but it is also the *provider of those services*. The British system is similar to the VA system in the United States. Hospitals are run by the government, and healthcare providers are government employees. The PNHP defines *single-payer health care* as, "A system in which a single public or quasi-public agency organizes health financing, but delivery of care remains largely private. Under a single-payer system, all Americans would be covered for all medically necessary services" (n.d.). Single-payer is sometimes called universal health insurance or improved Medicare for all.

Proponents of single-payer care believe that health insurance companies are a major source of the problem because they operate from a profit motive and are ultimately concerned about the bottom line. As evidence, critics point to the fact that they prefer to deny coverage to people with preexisting conditions, find creative ways to deny medical procedures that are recommended by a patient's physician (because anytime an insurance company has to pay for a medical procedure it is viewed as a financial "loss" for the company), and increase the costs of premiums making insurance unaffordable for many families. Doctors often feel frustrated that they cannot make medical decisions without the approval of an HMO (health maintenance organization) bureaucrat. A 2017 survey found that 56% of physicians support a single-payer healthcare system (Kaiser Health News, 2017), and Pew Research Center found that 33% of the public now favors a single-payer approach to health insurance (Kiley, 2017).

Debate continues over what kind of healthcare system is the best option. Ideally, healthcare systems would provide high-quality services to every citizen at a reasonable cost. Critics of the healthcare systems in Europe and Scandinavian countries argue that these countries have to ration (i.e., limit) services in order to cover everyone, and that, as a result, there are waiting lists for certain medical and surgical procedures. Others are quick to point out that the United States also rations healthcare services because healthcare services are provided for some citizens, while others go without.

Health Insurance Reform Under President Obama

When a group of people decide to embark on a policy change effort, they have to decide whether it is better to work for incremental change or whether it is feasible to achieve a more dramatic sweeping change. It cannot be overstated how incredibly contentious the political debate was surrounding President Obama's efforts to pass healthcare reform legislation after he became president. In February 2009, President Obama laid out eight principles of healthcare reform: protect families' financial health; make health coverage affordable; aim for universality; provide portability of coverage; guarantee choice; invest in prevention and wellness; improve patient safety and quality care; and maintain long-term fiscal sustainability (Politico staff, 2009). As Democratic lawmakers in Washington set out to draft legislation to reform the nation's healthcare system, there were a number of areas of consensus; for example, the practice of health insurance companies denying coverage to those with preexisting conditions had to end. Also, most agreed that the escalating costs of health care and health insurance had to be addressed and that health care reform had to be paid for so that it did not add to the federal deficit. There was also a consensus among Democrats on a number of areas, such as requiring Americans to have health insurance or pay a penalty, requiring businesses to offer health insurance to their employees or pay a penalty, and paying for health care, in part, by raising taxes on the wealthy.

However, large-scale social change is never easy, so there were a number of sticking points. The largest bone of contention among Democrats concerned whether reform should involve the creation of a new government insurance plan, or **public option**. Democrats were divided between conservative Democrats who opposed the public option and liberal lawmakers who embraced a government insurance plan that would be able to compete with private insurance. Health insurance companies and Republican lawmakers were unanimous in their opposition to the public option.

The first major task was to get lawmakers to reach consensus on a bill in each chamber. In the U.S. House of Representatives, bills from three committees had to be melded into a consensus bill that would win a House majority. The bill passed in the House on November 7, 2009, with a vote of 220 to 215. Only one Republican voted for it. It took a little longer to get a bill passed in the U.S. Senate due to disagreement over the public option from conservative Democrats. Despite Senator Harry Reid's advocacy for the public option, the Senate passed a compromise bill on December 24, 2009, without the public option; a compromise to allow people ages 55 to 64 to buy into Medicare was also unsuccessful. The bill passed with a vote of 60 to 39 after 25 straight days of debate.

However, while all of this activity was going on inside closed-door meetings and committee meetings on Capitol Hill, significant frustration was being expressed both inside and outside the Beltway. On the left, some liberals were revolting and advocating the defeat of the healthcare bill because it had become too compromised in their view. Single-payer activists were livid that the public option was off the table and that single-payer was not even allowed to be seriously considered and debated. Meanwhile crowds of Tea Party activists were disrupting town hall meetings by demonstrating; shouting down members of

Congress and hanging them, and Obama, in effigy based on their opposition to increased taxes and a larger government role in health care. Republican lawmakers were uniformly opposed to "Obamacare" and were doing everything they could to defeat the bill, including making claims that because end-of-life planning services were included in the legislation, the bill included "death panels" for older adults. After being criticized for not offering any of their own ideas, they offered their own plan in November 2009 (see "The Conservative Response to Healthcare Reform").

However, in February 2010, President Obama seemed to find new momentum as he seized his last opportunity to pass a historic healthcare bill. He planned a televised, bipartisan, half-day health summit where leaders on both sides of the aisle were encouraged to air their concerns and find areas of agreement. Obama vowed to listen to all ideas, from Republicans as well as Democrats. Then Anthem Blue Cross announced that premiums for its insurance policies would be raised anywhere between 25% and 39%. Obama took advantage of this opportunity and made an example out of Anthem in his talks and speeches. He then laid out a detailed White House plan for expanding health care to the uninsured that bridged elements of the House and Senate bills. In March he sold his plan to the public by giving speeches and attending political rallies. The White House worked diligently to line up the votes they needed and pressured Democrats to get on board.

On March 21, 2010, the House passed the Senate bill with not one single Republican vote. This was historic in modern history for a major piece of legislation to pass without a single vote from the opposite political party. Obama signed the Patient Protection and Affordable Care Act into law two days later surrounded by House and Senate lawmakers, the wife of deceased Senator Edward Kennedy (a longtime champion of U.S. healthcare reform), and individuals who had suffered greatly due to lack of health insurance. This was an incredible win based on the heavy opposition to the bill by the Republican Party and the many ups and downs that the bill experienced along the way. The Affordable Care Act was derisively called "Obamacare" by conservative critics, but Obama soon embraced the term and began referring to the legislation by this name since he was proud of this historic legislative achievement.

Overview of the Patient Protection and Affordable Care Act (aka "Obamacare")

Although the Affordable Care Act (ACA), or Obamacare, has its critics on both sides of the aisle, no one can dispute the fact this this was the most groundbreaking piece of healthcare legislation since the 1960s when the Medicaid and Medicare programs were created during the Johnson administration. The new Affordable Care Act is complicated, and we are still learning both the strengths and limitations of the new law as it is being fully implemented. The bill was over 2,000 pages long and was only supported by Democratic lawmakers, despite Obama's desire for bipartisan support. However, many liberals did not feel the bill went far enough and was too compromised; in their view, the new bill was *health insurance* reform, not *healthcare* reform. Conservatives, in contrast, saw this new effort as a slippery slope toward a government takeover of the healthcare system. However, one piece of data is very clear—the number of Americans without health insurance has declined significantly since the passage of the law. According to data from the National Center on Health Statistics (Cohen, Zammitti, & Martinez, 2017), in 2016, 28.6 million Americans were without health insurance, a decrease of 20 million since 2010. The following are some important features of the ACA (Kaiser Family Foundation, 2013):

- The health reform legislation required that all individuals have health insurance beginning in 2014, or else face paying a tax penalty.
- The poorest Americans would be covered under a Medicaid expansion.
- Those with low and middle incomes who do not have access to affordable coverage through their job will be able to purchase coverage with federal subsidies through new "American Health Benefit Exchanges."
- Imposes a tax penalty on employers with 50 or more full-time employees that do not offer health coverage. Small businesses will be able to access more plans through a separate exchange.
- Tax credits will be provided to small employers, with no more than 25 employees and average annual wages of less than $50,000, that purchase health insurance for employees.
- Health plans will not be allowed to deny coverage to people for any reason, including a preexisting condition (this took effect in 2010 for children and 2014 for adults).
- Assistance for Medicare beneficiaries with high drug costs will be provided (helps to close the "doughnut hole").
- The legislation includes a focus on prevention by covering proven preventive services, providing grants for up to five years to small employers that establish wellness programs (starting in 2011), and requiring chain restaurants and food sold from vending machines to disclose the nutritional content of each item (starting in 2011).
- Investments in community health centers, school-based health centers, and various strategies to improve the healthcare workforce, including social workers, are included.
- Young adults now have the option of being covered under their parents' plan up to age 26 (starting in 2010).
- The final bill did not include a public option, but some Democrats vowed to get this passed in a separate bill in the future (did not happen).
- The Congressional Budget Office estimated that the bill would provide coverage to 32 million uninsured people, but still leave 23 million uninsured, thus falling short of the goal of ensuring that all Americans have health insurance coverage.

The Conservative Response to Healthcare Reform

President Obama's hope that healthcare reform could be a bipartisan effort was dashed when it became clear that the Republicans and Democrats had completely different ideas about how the nation's healthcare system should be reformed. Once again, it became clear how polarized and politicized the environment is in the nation's capital. Republicans complained that they were being shut out of the process and that the Democratic plan was a "government takeover of health care." Democrats portrayed Republicans as the "party of no" and countered that many Republican ideas were included in the health reform legislation.

In November 2009, Republicans offered their own healthcare plan, which involved limiting damages in medical malpractice lawsuits, allowing small businesses to join together to buy insurance exempt from most state regulation, and rewarding states for reducing the number of uninsured. It was similar to the Democratic legislation in that it would allow young adults to stay on their parents' health plans at least through age 24 (compared with 26 under the Democrats' bill) and would prohibit insurers from imposing annual or lifetime limits on spending for covered benefits (Pear & Herszenhorn, 2009).

However, there were also some key differences between the Democratic and Republican plans. The Republican plan would not require citizens to have health insurance nor employers to offer it, nor would it expand government programs such as Medicaid (Pear & Herszenhorn, 2009). The Republican plan would not provide subsidies to individuals to help them purchase insurance, nor would it impose any new taxes. Finally, the Republican bill would not prohibit health insurance companies from denying coverage to people due to a preexisting condition. When the new bill was signed into law by President Obama, Democrats lauded it as major historic reform, while House Republican leader John Boehner stated, "This is a somber day for the American people. By signing this bill, President Obama is abandoning our founding principle that government governs best when it governs closest to the people" (Stolberg & Pear, 2010).

The ACA has been challenged in the U.S. Congress and the courts; however, thus far, none of these efforts have been successful in dismantling the legislation. According to Abbe Gluck writing for the *New York Times* (2020):

> It is the most challenged statute in modern American history. In addition to the Supreme Court cases, there have been more than 1,700 cases in the lower courts; Republicans in Congress have tried more than 70 times to repeal it; the Trump administration has engaged in an unprecedented array of executive actions to undermine the insurance markets and financially starve the law; red states rebelled against it from the day it was passed; and state initiatives have been enacted by supporters to force states to effectuate it.

In 2012, the U.S. Supreme Court ruled that the ACA is constitutional and that Congress has the right to enforce the individual mandate because the penalty that individuals must pay if they refuse to buy insurance is a kind of tax that is within the power of Congress to impose. There have been more than 70 attempts by Republican lawmakers in the U.S. Congress to undo or seriously undermine the ACA (often referred to as "repeal and replace") since it became law, and President Trump vowed to dismantle it when he campaigned for president, though he was ultimately unsuccessful. However, Republicans and President

Trump were successful in repealing the financial penalty for not having health insurance. In March 2020, the U.S. Supreme Court agreed to hear another legal challenge to the ACA (*California v. Texas*) that was brought by 18 Republican state attorneys general and two Republican governors who argue that the ACA is unconstitutional now that there is no tax penalty for the individual mandate. The Court is expected to issue their ruling by June 2021.

Did the Affordable Care Act Address the Root Problems of the Healthcare System?

Going back in time, we now know that there were a number of options that could have been pursued as the best way to solve the nation's healthcare problems. One option would have been to eliminate health insurance companies and move to a single-payer healthcare system, like those used in other advanced nations. There are three primary models that are used by other nations with universal healthcare systems:

- **Beveridge model**: Paid for by taxation; government is both the provider and payer of health care; the government negotiates prices and costs (United Kingdom, Spain, Italy, Scandinavia, Hong Kong, and our VA system are all examples).
- **National health insurance model**: Providers of health care are private but the payer is a government-run insurance program that citizens pay into via monthly premiums; includes some rationing of services; government is able to negotiate for lower prices (Canada; Medicare program in United States; Taiwan and South Korea have variations of this model).
- **Bismarck model**: Uses private health insurance plans that are financed jointly by employers and employees via a payroll deduction; however, the insurance companies are basically nonprofit organizations that do not generate profit; tight regulation leads to cost control (Germany, Japan, Belgium, Switzerland, and parts of Latin America use this model).

A compromise alternative could have included a **public option** where Americans would be able to choose a government program for their health insurance (similar to Medicare) that would compete with the private health insurance companies. However, the option that was finally chosen and pursued by Democratic lawmakers was not to radically change the U.S. healthcare system but rather to reform the way that health insurance companies operate by placing new rules and regulations on them (e.g., not allowing them to deny people coverage for preexisting conditions; requiring them to include certain preventative services for no cost). The law also aimed to get more people covered thorough a large expansion of the Medicaid program and by allowing young people to stay on their parent's health insurance until age 26.

Has the ACA been successful? The answer is both yes and no. The good news is that since the passage of the law, 20 million more people have health insurance coverage than before the law went into effect. This includes many people who were previously unable to get insurance due to a preexisting health condition. However, the goal of universality has not been achieved, because there are roughly 28 million Americans without health insurance. Due to the political divide between Republican and Democratic lawmakers, as of November 2020, 12 states have refused to expand their Medicaid program to allow more low-income people to have access to that program.

However, the biggest problem with the ACA has to do with affordability and access. In some parts of the country, some insurers are not willing to sell plans through the ACA marketplaces, which leaves many without coverage. Additionally, many who have plans through the ACA marketplaces face high premiums and deductibles leading them to be underinsured. The ACA includes federal subsidies to help offset costs, but not everyone qualifies. Finally, the high cost of prescription drugs continues to be a serious problem for many Americans. Thus, healthcare advocates must choose to either continue making incremental improvements to the ACA, or scrap the ACA altogether and embrace single-payer health care. The Mad As Hell Doctors, most of whom belong to the advocacy group PNHP mentioned earlier, prefer the latter.

The Mad As Hell Doctors Tour

Many Americans were hopeful that with the election of Barack Obama the United States would finally be able to make universal health care a reality. However, when the debate over healthcare reform in Congress heated up, single-payer proponents were extremely disappointed when they learned that a single-payer system would not be one of the options under consideration. In fact, Democratic U.S. Senator Max Baucus, chairman of the Senate Finance Committee, did not invite any representatives from groups advocating for single-payer health care to the series of meetings held before his committee where healthcare reform was discussed. He had 13 protesters (doctors, nurses, and activists) removed by Capitol police for demanding that single-payer advocates be given a seat at the table. They were arrested and soon became known as *The Baucus 13*.

After much pressure, Senator Baucus later agreed to have a meeting with five prominent single-payer advocates. At the meeting were Dr. David Himmelstein, associate professor of medicine at Harvard Medical School and cofounder of the PNHP; Dr. Marcia Angell, senior lecturer, Harvard Medical School, and former editor-in-chief of the *New England Journal of Medicine*; Dr. Oliver Fein, associate dean, Cornell Weill Medical School and president of the PNHP; Rose Ann DeMoro, executive director of the California Nurses Association; and Geri Jenkins, president of California Nurses Association, each of whom pleaded their case for allowing single payer to be considered and debated (see Advocacy Spotlight for a description of healthcare advocacy organizations). Baucus later admitted that he made a mistake by not leaving single payer on the table, despite the fact that he did not believe that it was politically feasible. He agreed to use the power of his office to have the charges dropped against the Baucus 13.

Advocacy Spotlight

California Nurses Association (www.calnurses.org)

Founded in 1903, the California Nurses Association/National Nurses Organizing Committee/AFL-CIO is an organization of registered nurses with more than 86,000 members in hospitals, clinics, and home health agencies in all 50 states. CNA/NNOC is also a founding member of the 150,000-member National Nurses United, which in 2009 united CNA/NNOC, the United American Nurses, and the Massachusetts Nurses Association to create the largest union and professional association of nurses in U.S. history.

CNA/NNOC activities have included advocating for guaranteed health care by expanding and updating Medicare to cover all Americans, negotiating collective bargaining contracts for RNs in the nation, and fighting for regulatory protections for patients and nurses.

Healthcare-NOW! (www.healthcare-now.org)

Healthcare-NOW is fighting to win a national single-payer healthcare system because access to health care is basic to human dignity. To win, we must build a powerful social movement through education and action, so our work focuses on raising up the voices of patients who feel isolated in their struggles with the healthcare system, educating activists to gain the knowledge and skills they need to become leaders, and mobilizing our movement through collective action.

Physicians for a National Health Program (www.pnhp.org)

PNHP is the only physician organization in the country dedicated to a single issue—the implementation of a universal, comprehensive single-payer national health program. They began advocating for reform of the U.S. healthcare system in 1987 and today they have more than 17,000 members. They do this by educating physicians and other health professionals about the benefits of a single-payer system, publishing scholarly research articles, and educating the public by speaking at community forums, town hall meetings, and through interviews with the media.

Mad As Hell Doctors (www.madashelldoctors.com)

In 2009, they drove a Winnebago across the country organizing town hall meetings and rallies in 30 towns and cities in 15 states to educate the public and stakeholders about the benefits of a single-payer healthcare system. Read more about their story later in this chapter.

In August 2009, Mad As Hell Doctors was formed by media expert Adam Klugman, campaign organizer Gary Jelenik, and a group of five Oregon physicians who are members of **Physicians for a National Health Program (PNHP).** Of all of the stories in this book, the Mad As Hell Doctors is a good example of a grassroots policy change effort. They decided that something drastic was needed to bring attention to single-payer health care, which was being excluded by lawmakers in Washington, D.C. Their strategy was to embark on three-week road trip through the American heartland in fall of 2009, and they would call it the *Mad as Hell Doctors Tour*. They would get their message out to the public through education, advocacy, and entertainment. Their Winnebago (see photo at beginning of chapter), which was decorated with the name of their cause, was used to carry them across the country so they could speak at single-payer rallies and town hall meetings in churches, union halls, universities, public parks, and arts centers.

The Goal and the Strategy

The Mad As Hell Doctors Tour was run by a few paid people with expertise in political campaigns, along with many people who volunteered their time to this cause. Adam Klugman was hired to do the media work, which involved designing the logo, initial concept, and messaging of the campaign and putting together the website. Gary Jelenik was hired as the campaign organizer and was responsible for planning the nuts and bolts of the road tour, which involved contacting people in the various cities they would visit, putting together a "ground crew" in those cities, and planning the events. A third person was paid to staff the phones and help with set-up. The goal of the campaign would be to (1) educate the public about single-payer healthcare systems (via the political rallies and media coverage), (2) strengthen linkages between organizations interested in advocating for single payer, and (3) to try to propel single payer onto the national policy agenda (e.g., agenda setting). There was a six- to eight-week planning period before kicking off the road tour.

Advocacy Tip

When embarking on a policy change effort, having paid staff with expertise in working with the media and designing a website can be instrumental to winning.

Rallies. The heart of this campaign were the organized rallies and town hall meetings. All in all, the doctors made stops in 30 towns and cities in 15 states. The kick-off event was held in Portland, Oregon, on September 8, 2009, and the final stop was in Washington, D.C., where they hoped to have a meeting with President Obama. The tour started with five physicians who made the entire trip, and they were joined by four other physicians who were able to travel on various segments of the trip. There were also a few critical people who volunteered their time to work as support crew, such as social work professor Bill Whitaker (see photo below and Dr. Whitaker's personal account of his experience on the Mad As Hell Doctors Tour at the end of this chapter).

Advocacy Tip

Deciding whether (and when) to organize a rally is a strategic decision that must be carefully considered. If carefully planned and organized, it can be an effective way to get media attention and mobilize supporters **but** you have to be able to turn people out.

The Winnebago, affectionately nicknamed "Winnie," was useful in generating interest and enthusiasm as they traveled across the country. Over time, they refined the format of the rallies, which typically went as follows:

- People attending the rally were filmed talking about why they are upset about the current healthcare system, and this was projected on a screen for all to see.
- The physicians were introduced at the beginning of the rally, and each one spoke from their experience for a couple of minutes about why they were "Mad As Hell."

Figure 7.2 Social work professor William Whitaker, PhD, traveled with the Mad As Hell Doctors on the tour and provided logistics support. See his first-person account of his experience at end of chapter.

- An excerpt of a video was shown to educate the audience about single payer (produced by Dr. Paul Hochfeld).
- Mad As Hell Minutes: Anyone at the rally could talk for one minute to tell their story and explain why they were "Mad as Hell." These were all filmed and posted on the Mad As Hell Doctors website.
- Sometimes there was musical entertainment, such as singing by the "Mad As Hell Nurses" at the rally in Portland, Oregon.
- At the end of the rally, attendees were asked to engage in some sort of action. They were asked to contact the White House asking the White House to meet with the Mad As Hell Doctors. The White House later blocked any emails sent from the Mad As Hell Doctors website, so people had to send emails from other email accounts. Attendees were asked to sign a petition at the rally. Finally, they were asked to contribute money to the Mad As Hell Doctors Tour to support their road tour.
- There was a table at the rallies that had literature, campaign materials for sale (buttons, T-shirts, etc.), and white ribbons that could be tied near government buildings to represent people who die every year due to having no health insurance.

Framing the issue. Because healthcare reform is a rather complicated topic, it is important to be able to break the issue down into key messages that will resonate with the people you are trying to influence. On the tour, the doctors developed a working definition of *single payer*, which was, "A system of payment that redirects all current health care monies, both public and private, into a single public fund that covers everyone." Other key messages were:

- "Single payer is the fiscally conservative approach to universal coverage, the only affordable approach for the long haul."
- "We need a single risk pool—everyone in, nobody out."
- "Stop insurance company 'cherry picking'—limiting insurance to the most healthy and denying coverage to those most likely to need medical care."
- "The current health care funding system is broken and cannot be repaired incrementally."
- "Under single payer, health care delivery (physicians, hospitals, etc.) remains as is. Only health care funding is carried out by the government."
- "Single-payer is essentially an improved Medicare for All system."
- "Thirty percent of all health care dollars go to insurance company overhead and profits."
- "Under a single-payer system, current levels of health care expenditures would be enough to provide universal coverage at no additional cost."
- "The U.S. is the only industrialized country lacking universal, publicly funded health care."
- "The U.S. spends nearly twice as much per capita on health care, leaves many millions uncovered, and has poorer health outcomes than any other industrialized country."

Advocacy Tip

A significant amount of time in issue campaigns is spent on messaging or "framing" the issue. Your message must be persuasive and resonate with those you are trying to influence. This is much easier said than done!

Funding. As you can imagine, this tour required funds in order to be successful. The physicians funded much of this effort, and this was supplemented by generous donations from people passionate about this cause. The funding was used to pay for work performed by the three paid staff members, the Winnebago, as well as gas, meals, and motel stays along the way. People who donated $500 or more were made an honorary "Mad As Hell Doctor."

Media coverage. The Mad As Hell doctors were disappointed that they did not get as much national media coverage as the "anti-groups" such as the Tea Party protesters. However, they were successful in getting coverage in local media (radio, television, and newspaper), and they did get some coverage on national news programs such as MSNBC's *Countdown with Keith Olbermann*. On the tour, each physician averaged three to four media interviews per day. Finally, the Mad As Hell Doctors made a documentary film showcasing their travel experience across the country, which could be viewed on their website.

Social media. The Mad As Hell Doctors had a professional website developed, and followers were able to visit the website to learn about their progress as they made their way across the country. They also communicated with their "fans" on Facebook.

Tactics Used by Mad As Hell Doctors

- ☒ Coalition building
- ☐ Direct lobbying (in-person lobby visits, sometimes by a professional lobbyist)
- ☒ Earned media (letters to the editor, actions that lead to media coverage)
- ☒ Grassroots lobbying (e.g., urging people to call, write, email legislators)
- ☐ Paid media (paying for TV/radio ads)
- ☒ Educational outreach (town halls, house parties, community forums)
- ☒ Visibility (rallies, marches)
- ☒ Online advocacy (using social media)
- ☐ Political dissent (e.g., civil disobedience, protest)
- ☐ Paid communication (paid staff who call voters, materials mailed out)
- ☐ Providing testimony in a legislative committee hearing
- ☒ Fundraising activities

Was the Mad As Hell Doctors Tour a Success?

In the end, the Mad As Hell Doctors did not win this battle. Single payer never made it on the political agenda and was not taken seriously as an option by lawmakers in Washington, D.C. However, advocates cannot get discouraged and have to come to terms with the fact that significant progress can take a long time when working on causes that represent a significant change to the status quo. Even though they did not ultimately win this round, progress was made, and there are many lessons that can be learned from this story. The White House would not agree to meet with the doctors; however, their final rally in D.C. included a rousing speech by Congressman Dennis Kucinich, a single-payer supporter. A single-payer bill (H.R. 676) introduced in the 111th Congress sponsored by Representative John Conyers (D-MI) had 87 cosponsors. Members of the Mad As Hell Doctors Tour were able to educate thousands of Americans who turned out to attend their rallies or heard their message in various media outlets.

This was also the beginning of a new organization, Mad As Hell Doctors, which has a website full of helpful information on single-payer health care. They did a tour in California in 2010 to advocate for passage of a single-payer healthcare bill at the state level, and another tour in Oregon in 2011 in efforts to continue to press for a single-payer healthcare system in the United States. They also work in collaboration with other coalition partners, such as the California Nurses Association, the PNHP, Health Care for all Oregon, and HealthCare-Now! These organizations are currently working to support passage of the Medicare for All Act of 2017 (H.R. 676) that was introduced by Senator Bernie Sanders.

Practice Exercise 7.1

There were a lot of Mad As Hell Doctors and Mad As Hell Nurses involved in this effort, along with a very dedicated social work professor. If more social workers were involved, what could they add to this effort? Visit their website to learn about their current activities: http://madashelldoctors.com/

In Closing

Social workers who work in health care, or are passionate about issues related to health care, should advocate for policies at all levels of government that align with the mission and values of the social work profession, such as health care access for all, working to eliminate health disparities, and policies that support the self-determination, dignity, and worth of the individual within the healthcare system. In some cases, social workers may be advocating for major healthcare system reform policies, while other times they may be working for incremental changes. Examples include, but are not limited to, end-of-life care policies, enhanced funding for research focused on various diseases, policies that promote health and disease prevention, policies that promote the healthcare workforce, cultural competency training for healthcare workers, sick leave policies, and policies that impact substance abuse and prescription drugs.

On the Road with the Mad As Hell Doctors' Health Care-a-Van

By Bill Whitaker, PhD, ACSW

On September 8, 2009, as the healthcare debate raged in Congress, a group of five doctors from Oregon embarked on an historic road trip through the heartland of America, arriving on September 30th at the doors of Congress and the White House. Other doctors, nurses, social workers, and concerned citizens joined our caravan for varying lengths of time.

Our mission was to promote single-payer health insurance as a fiscally conservative, affordable way to provide universal health care to the 47 million Americans who are currently uninsured; to improve coverage for the many millions more of us who currently have catastrophic insurance at best; and to help every insured American cope with declining benefits accompanied by increasingly high premiums, deductibles and copays.

Through our Health Care-A-Van we educated Americans about the advantages of single risk pool, single-payer health care and recorded the stories of countless individuals and families whose lives have been shattered by lack of access to affordable health care.

Our proposal is simple. The United States needs single-payer health care, a system of payment that redirects all current health care monies, both public and private, into a single public fund that covers everyone.

A single-payer system is built on a single risk pool with "everybody in and nobody out." We believe a single-payer health care system is the only means to lasting, substantive healthcare reform for the United States.

"I'm mad as hell and I'm not going to take it anymore!" This refrain was heard over and over again as the Mad As Hell Doctors' Health Care-A-Van traveled through state capitals, major cities and rural communities in 15 states. Enthusiastic crowds greeted us at rallies and town halls in 30 cities large and small. More than 6,000 persons attended the 46 rallies and town halls we held in churches and union halls, in universities, public parks, and arts centers.

Our journey took us from Sequim, Washington, to Portland to Seattle and on to Spokane, Bozeman, Idaho Falls, Pocatello, Salt Lake City, Fort Collins, Denver, Des Moines, Mankato, Minneapolis/St. Paul, Madison, Gary, Bloomington, Nashville, Louisville, Xenia, Yellow Springs, Detroit, Chicago, Toledo, Pt. Clinton, Cleveland, and Pittsburgh before arriving at a rally at Lafayette Park across from the White House on September 30.

We began our rallies and town meetings by distinguishing between anger and rage. Anger is a normal human feeling, a healthy feeling which can be channeled productively to generate change and work for social justice. Anger is what the Mad As Hell Doctors expressed and attempted to harness with the tour. Rage is the type of feeling fostered by those funding Tea Party attempts to disrupt public discourse and to prevent others from exercising their freedom of speech.

We explained that we support the full expression of all points of view whether or not they agree with us. Each of our events included a series of "mad as hell minutes" in which any person could say anything uninterrupted for 60 seconds. Perhaps as a consequence we encountered no organized disruption. There was only one organized opposing demonstration.

In the mad as hell minutes we heard heartbreaking story after story of the crushing impacts of the lack of health insurance on human lives. In one case a man was fired from his job in a small firm when his wife was diagnosed with MS—if he had been permitted to continue employment, health insurance would have been too costly for anyone who worked there. We heard repeatedly about bankruptcies resulting from medical expenses. We heard about couples being advised to divorce so one member could be insured or to avoid total loss of family assets through medical bills.

A woman, a doctor from Spokane, spoke for many: "I'm mad because medicine should be a human enterprise, not a commercial enterprise, because we don't have access to health care for all, because there are unneeded disparities in health outcomes between poor and rich, between blacks and whites." A veteran put it this way: "I'm mad as hell because I have excellent socialized medicine from the Veteran's Administration but not everyone has access like I do."

Some of the most moving stories will be included in a full-length documentary of our campaign.

We asked President Obama to do two things: (1) meet with us so we could share with him what we have learned in our travels, and (2) appoint a White Ribbon Commission consisting of public health experts and healthcare professionals—but no health insurance or pharmaceutical corporation representatives—to compare healthcare systems throughout the world and to develop a uniquely American system that will provide access to health care for every American. We posted our requests on our website and asked supporters to contact President Obama in support of our requests.

Several days into the trip we received a phone call from a White House staffer. "When," he asked, "are you going to take that request off your website? We are receiving so many emails that our mailbox is being flooded." Our reply was straight forward. "We'll remove the request when President Obama agrees to meet with us." The White House responded by blocking emails from our site. We asked our supporters to cut and paste the request into their own email addresses. Emails continued to flood the White House.

President Obama has not yet met with the Mad As Hell Doctors. From our perspective he has missed the opportunity to make history by bringing us healthcare reform we can believe in.

This is disappointing but not surprising. The systematic exclusion of full and fair consideration of single risk pool, single-payer options in congressional deliberations on health insurance reform demonstrates the near stranglehold of corporate interests on Congress. Billions of dollars in profits are at stake. It is no surprise that health insurance and pharmaceutical special interests are employing six full-time health insurance lobbyists for every member of Congress and are spending more than $1.4 million daily to prevent even the most modest reform of the system. If we follow the money trail, it is increasingly clear that we do have the best Congress that money can buy.

As organizers we know that breaking the hold of corporate greed on Congress is a daunting task. But it is essential for progressive change. It will require mobilization of the growing outrage we encountered throughout the nation.

Might a "White Ribbon Campaign" help spark the continuation of the civil rights movement? Dr. Martin Luther King, Jr. put it this way some 40 years ago: "Of all the forms of inequality, injustice in health care is the most shocking and inhumane." His words continue to resound today.

In communities throughout the nation, concerned and angry citizens are placing flowers and lighting candles at city halls and in front of health insurance company offices—mourning the 45,000 persons who die needlessly in the United States each year from lack of health insurance. They are tying white ribbons to symbolize the hope for enactment of single-payer health-care legislation that will prevent these unnecessary deaths. And increasingly, protestors are putting their bodies on the line, being arrested for civil disobedience. Perhaps an aroused citizenry can even reclaim the democratic structure of the United States.

Bill Whitaker is Professor Emeritus of social welfare at the Boise State University School of Social Work. He lives in La Grande, Oregon, where he is active in local and state issues and politics, single-payer advocacy, and work to mitigate the effects of global warming on climate change. He may be contacted at wwhitak@boisestate.edu.

More information about Mad As Hell Doctors can be found at www.madashelldoctors.com. For comprehensive information about single-payer health programs, see Physicians for a National Health Program (PNHP), at www.phhp.org.

REFERENCES

Barnett, J. C., & Berchick, E. R. (2017). *Health insurance coverage in the United States: 2016. Current Population Reports, P60–260.* Washington, D.C.: Government Printing Office. Retrieved from https://www.census.gov/content/dam/Census/library/publications/2017/demo/p60–260.pdf

Bluth, R. (2017). Doctors warm to single-payer health care. Kaiser Health News. Retrieved from https://khn.org/news/doctors-warm-to-single-payer-health-care/

Centers for Disease Control and Prevention. (n.d.). History of 1918 flu pandemic. Retrieved from https://www.cdc.gov/flu/pandemic-resources/1918-commemoration/1918-pandemic-history.htm#:~:text=It%20is%20estimated%20that%20about,occurring%20in%20the%20United%20States.

Cohen, R. A., Zammitti, E. P., & Martinez, M. E. (2017). Health insurance coverage: Early release of estimates from the National Health Interview Survey, 2016. National Center for Health Statistics. Retrieved from https://www.cdc.gov/nchs/data/nhis/earlyrelease/insur201705.pdf

Collins, S. R., Gunja, M. Z., & Aboulafia, G. N. (2020, August 19). U.S. health insurance coverage in 2020: A looming crisis in affordability. Findings from the Commonwealth Fund Biennial Health Insurance Survey, 2020. Retrieved from https://www.commonwealthfund.org/publications/issue-briefs/2020/aug/looming-crisis-health-coverage-2020-biennial

Gangel, J., Herb, J., & Stuart, E. (2020, September 9). Play it down: Trump admits to concealing the true threat of coronavirus in new Woodward book. *CNN*. Retrieved from https://www.cnn.com/2020/09/09/politics/bob-woodward-rage-book-trump-coronavirus/index.html

Gluck, A. R. (2020, November 10). The Court is taking on the most challenged statute in our history. Again. *New York Times*. Retrieved from https://www.nytimes.com/2020/11/10/opinion/obamacare-supreme-court.html

Kaiser Family Foundation. (2013). Summary of the Affordable Care Act. Retrieved from https://www.kff.org/health-reform/fact-sheet/summary-of-the-affordable-care-act/

Keisler-Starkey, K., & Bunch, L. N. (2020, September 15). Health insurance coverage in the United States: 2019. Retrieved from https://www.census.gov/library/publications/2020/demo/p60-271.html

Kiley, J. (2017). Public support for 'single payer' health coverage grows, driven by Democrats. Pew Research Center. Retrieved from http://www.pewresearch.org/fact-tank/2017/06/23/public-support-for-single-payer-health-coverage-grows-driven-by-democrats/

Kurani, N., & Cox, C. (2020, September 25). What drives health spending in U.S. compared to other countries. Retrieved from https://www.healthsystemtracker.org/brief/what-drives-health-spending-in-the-u-s-compared-to-other-countries/

National Association of Social Workers. (2018). *Social work speaks* (11th ed.). Washington, D.C.: NASW Press.

New York Times. (2021, April 1). Coronavirus in the U.S.: Latest map and case count. Retrieved from https://www.nytimes.com/interactive/2020/us/coronavirus-us-cases.html

Pear, R., & Herszenhorn, D. M. (2009, November 3). GOP counters with a health plan of its own. *New York Times*. Retrieved from https://www.nytimes.com/2009/11/04/health/policy/04health.html

Physicians for a National Health Program. (n.d.). What is single payer? Retrieved from http://www.pnhp.org/facts/what-is-single-payer

Politico staff. (2009, February 26). Obama-care 101: The president's 8 principles. *Politico*. Retrieved from https://www.politico.com/story/2009/02/obama-care-101-the-presidents-8-principles-019362

Schneider, E. C., Sarnak, D. O., Squires, D., Shah, A., & Doty, M. M. (2017). Mirror, mirror 2017: International comparison reflects flaws and opportunities for better U.S. health care. The Commonwealth Fund. Retrieved from http://www.commonwealthfund.org/Publications/Fund-Reports/2017/Jul/Mirror-Mirror-International-Comparisons-2017

Stephenson, J. (2020). CDC report reveals "considerably elevated" mental health toll from COVID-19 stresses. *JAMA Health Forum*. Retrieved from https://jamanetwork.com/channels/health-forum/fullarticle/2770050

Stolberg, S. G., & Pear R. (2010, March 23). Obama signs health care overhaul bill, with a flourish. *New York Times*. Retrieved from http://www.nytimes.com/2010/03/24/health/policy/24health.html

Tavernise, S., & Goodnough, A. (2021, February 18). A grim measure of Covid's toll: Life expectancy drops sharply in U.S. *New York Times*. Retrieved from https://www.nytimes.com/2021/02/18/us/covid-life-expectancy.html?campaign_id=60&emc=edit_na_20210218&instance_id=0&nl=breaking-news&ref=cta&regi_id=16076514&segment_id=51867&user_id=73336ca6dc759a-620714ce751393911c

Wilper, A. P., Woolhandler, S., Lasser, K. E., McCormick, D., Bor, D.H., & Himmelstein, D. U. (2009, December). Health insurance and mortality in U.S. adults. *American Journal of Public Health*, *99*(12).

World Health Organization (WHO). (n.d.). Constitution of WHO: Principles. Retrieved from http://www.who.int/about/mission/en/

Credit

CHAPTER 8

Mental Health Policy and Advocacy

"Everyday language tends to encourage a misperception that mental health or mental illness is unrelated to physical health or physical illness. In fact, the two are inseparable."

~*The Surgeon General's Report on Mental Health, 1999*

CHAPTER SUMMARY

For decades, mental health advocates have fought against mental health stigma and for a system of care where those affected by a mental health disorder have access to quality care. Unfortunately, the United States has a long history of stigmatizing mental disorders and providing dehumanizing and degrading care to those with mental illness. It is somewhat surprising that there is so much stigma surrounding mental illness, because according to the National Institute of Mental Health (NIMH) 20.6% of U.S. adults suffered from a diagnosable mental disorder in 2019 (this represented 51.5 million people). One of the biggest legislative battles in the field of mental health has been the fight to get leaders in Washington, D.C. to pass a strong federal bill to address discrimination against those with mental health problems who require treatment. Simply put, mental health parity is the principle that health insurance plans should include equal coverage for medical care and mental health care, when policies cover both. For social workers, this is not a radical idea, because there is an overwhelming body of research that shows that mental illnesses have biological causes and are diseases of the brain. The National Association of Social Workers (NASW) has been an ardent supporter of mental health parity legislation, and its position has been formalized in its book of policy statements, *Social Work Speaks*. Efforts to pass mental health parity legislation at the state and federal level began in the early 1990s, and a strong federal bill was not passed until 2008. Legislation seeking social change often involves taking on powerful special interests with significant financial resources. The story has a long and winding path, but this legislation would not have been successfully passed into law without the ongoing efforts of committed mental health advocacy organizations.

STUDENT LEARNING OBJECTIVES

- Students will be able to define mental illness, serious mental illness, and mental health parity.

- Students will be able to describe the major sectors of the mental health system.

- Students will be able to analyze the political advocacy efforts of mental health advocates who worked for passage of the Mental Health Parity Act.

- Students will be able to describe the Paul Wellstone and Pete Domenici Mental Health Parity and Addiction Equality Act that was passed into law.

- Students will be able to cite mental health advocacy organizations in the United States.

Leading mental health experts have voiced concern about the impact of the coronavirus pandemic on people's mental health, and some early data suggests that Americans are suffering more with anxiety, depression, substance abuse, and suicidal thoughts. However, it will likely take researchers a few years to gather good data about the impact of this health crisis on Americans' mental health functioning. For decades, committed mental health advocates have fought tirelessly for a system of care that is less fragmented and provides access to quality care for those in need of treatment. Unfortunately, the United States has a long history of stigmatizing mental health disorders and providing inadequate care to those with mental illness, especially as compared to medical care. In many ways, the mental health sector has been treated as the stepchild of the U.S. healthcare system. This issue is of primary concern to social workers because they perform the majority of mental health treatment in the United States; they outnumber other mental health professionals such as licensed professional counselors and psychologists. It is somewhat surprising that there is so much stigma surrounding mental illness, because mental health disorders are so prevalent (see statistics below under *Mental Illness*).

In order for mental health advocates to make progress politically, it has been necessary to address the stigma surrounding mental disorders by spending significant time and resources focused on public education. Another strategy has been to join forces with legislators who have firsthand experience with mental illness in their family. Thanks to government-funded research on mental health disorders, and increased knowledge about the causes and treatment of these disorders, there is a new understanding that mental illness is a disease of the brain and body and should not be viewed separately from physical illness.

Lawmakers, and the American public, are sometimes forced to focus on the failings of the U.S. mental health system when examples of untreated mental health disorders result in unspeakable tragedy. Recent high-profile examples include the many school shootings across the country, such as the one in February 2018 at Marjory Stoneman Douglas High School in Parkland, Florida, that resulted in 17 casualties. When a person with a mental illness commits a violent act, it is normal and right to ask what could have been done to prevent this and to search for policy solutions. In the aftermath of these school shootings, some lawmakers have advocated preventing those with mental illness from purchasing and owning a gun. On its face, this may sound like a reasonable policy response; however, upon deeper critical reflection, gun control policies focused on those with mental illness may not be the best answer to this problem.

This policy approach raises number of questions: What percentage of people with a mental health disorder commit violent crimes? Which types of disorders are more likely to result in violence against others? Would the law apply to everyone with a mental health disorder (e.g., depression, substance abuse, posttraumatic stress disorder [PTSD], etc.; there are over 200 mental health disorders listed in the *Diagnostic and Statistical Manual of Mental Disorders* [DSM])? Are those with mental illness more likely to be self-harming and to commit suicide or to engage in violent acts against others? If someone has never come to the attention of a mental health professional, how would that person be prevented from purchasing a gun? Do discussions of mental illness and guns lead to false notions of persons with mental illness when a small percentage are actually violent toward others? Would it be better to restrict gun ownership more generally, as many other advanced nations have done? Finally, instead of focusing solely on guns, should we work to fix our broken mental health system so that people in need have access to care and treatment?

Mental Illness

Mental illness generally refers collectively to all mental disorders that can be diagnosed in the *Diagnostic and Statistical Manual of Mental Disorders* published by the American Psychiatric Association (APA). Mental disorders are health conditions that are characterized by alterations in thinking, mood, or behavior (or some combination of these three) associated with impaired functioning and/or distress. Examples of mental disorders include mood disorders (e.g., depression, bipolar disorder), anxiety disorders (e.g., PTSD, social phobia, obsessive compulsive disorder [OCD]), autism, attention deficit hyperactivity disorder (ADHD), schizophrenia, and eating disorders. Collectively, anxiety disorders are the most common type of disorder experienced by Americans.

Mental disorders are often viewed on a continuum from mild to severe. According to data reported by the NIMH (n.d.), 20.6% of U.S. adults suffered from a diagnosable mental disorder in 2019 (this represented 51.5 million people). Young adults aged 18 to 25 years had the highest prevalence of mental illness (29.4%) compared to adults aged 26 to 49 years (25%) and those aged 50 and older (14.1%). Suicide is the 10th leading cause of death in the

United States. Serious **mental illness** is defined as a serious functional impairment that substantially interferes with or limits one or more major life activities (NIMH, n.d.). About 5% of U.S. adults suffer from serious mental illness. Because treating those with mental illness sometimes involves involuntary hospitalization and treatment, this requires social workers and other treatment providers to carefully balance a client's right to self-determination with the safety of family members and the community. Due to the tireless efforts of advocates in the United States, such as Clifford Beers and Dorothea Dix, it is now considered unacceptable to warehouse the mentally ill in prisons or to allow inhumane treatment in overcrowded state mental hospitals.

Timeline of Mental Health Advocacy in the United States

- **1840s**, Dorothea Dix advocates on behalf of mentally ill people who are incarcerated, many of whom are beaten and chained. Her 40 years of dedicated advocacy work leads to the establishment of 32 state hospitals for the mentally ill (see the Activist Spotlight).
- **1909**, Clifford Beers founds the National Mental Health Association after publishing an autobiography titled, *A Mind That Found Itself*, which detailed his negative experience in a Connecticut mental institution.
- **1946**, President Truman signs the National Mental Health Act calling for a National Institute of Mental Health (NIMH) to conduct research on mental illness.
- **1949**, NIMH is formally established.
- **1962**, author Ken Kesey publishes *One Flew Over the Cuckoo's Nest*, which becomes a national bestseller and later is made into a Hollywood film starring Jack Nicholson.
- **1963**, the Mental Retardation Facilities and Community Mental Health Centers Construction Act is signed into law by President Kennedy. This marked the beginning of the deinstitutionalization movement, and this new law aimed to shift resources away from large state mental institutions towards community-based mental health centers; however, the funding provided was not adequate to realize these aims, so many people let out of state hospitals had nowhere to go for treatment.
- **Mid-1960s**, the deinstitutionalization movement begins in the United States, which results in the removal of hundreds of thousands of patients from mental institutions. The goal was to serve these newly released patients in community-based facilities and mental health centers; however, many become homeless due to inadequate funding and infrastructure.
- **1979**, the National Alliance for the Mentally Ill (NAMI) is founded.
- **1986**, the National Alliance for Research on Schizophrenia and Depression is formed.
- **1992**, Congress establishes the Substance Abuse and Mental Health Services Administration (SAMHSA), whose mission is to reduce the impact of substance abuse and mental illness on America's communities.

- **1996**, the first federal Mental Health Parity act is passed and signed into law by President Clinton (however, this law is very compromised and does not solve the parity problem).
- **2008**, federal Mental Health Parity legislation is passed, championed by Senators Paul Wellstone and Pete Domenici, which significantly improves the 1996 law.
- **2010**, under the Affordable Care Act, beginning in 2014 all new small group and individual market plans are required to include mental health and substance use disorder services in the 10 Essential Health Benefit categories and are required to cover them at parity with medical and surgical benefits.

Activist Spotlight: Dorothea Dix

In the 1840s, Dorothea Dix began her life's work, advocating on behalf of the mentally ill in the Unites States. She traveled all across the United States (more than 60,000 miles) documenting the deplorable condition of the mentally ill who were housed in prisons, poorhouses, and other types of institutions. In her appeal to the U.S. Congress where she suggested federal aid to the states so that they could provide humane treatment to the mentally ill, she stated,

I myself have seen more than nine thousand idiots, epileptics, and insane, in the United States, destitute of appropriate care and protection; and of this vast and most miserable company, sought out in jails, in poorhouses, and in private dwellings, there have been hundreds, nay, rather thousands, bound with galling chains, bowed beneath fetters and heavy iron balls, attached to drag-chains, lacerated with ropes, scourged with rods, and terrified beneath storms of profane execrations and cruel blows; now subject to jibes and scorn, and torturing kicks—now abandoned to the most loathsome necessities, or subject to the vilest and most outrageous violations. These are strong terms, but language fails to convey the astounding truths.

("Dorothea L. Dix and Federal Aid," 1927, p. 120)

Her measure passed both houses of Congress but was vetoed by President Franklin Pierce. Her first success came in 1843 when she presented the state of Massachusetts with her findings and the state legislature agreed to fund a state hospital in Worchester. Other states were soon to follow.

Overview of the U.S. Mental Health System

The U.S. mental health system is often described as a fragmented, loosely coordinated system of care. There are four major sectors of this system where clients may be served:

- **The specialty mental health sector**, which consists of mental health professionals such as psychiatrists, psychologists, and psychiatric nurses and social workers who are trained to treat those with mental disorders.

- **The general medical care sector**, which consists of healthcare professionals such as physicians, nurse practitioners, and social workers in medical settings.
- **Human service organizations,** such as nonprofit organizations, school-based counseling services, residential programs, criminal justice settings, and faith-based organizations.
- **The voluntary support sector**, which consists of self-help groups such as 12-step programs and peer counselors. This is often where people with mental illness and their family members assist others dealing with the same problem.

The mental health service system can also be categorized by whether services are provided by the public sector or the private sector. Services provided by the public sector include services directly operated by government agencies (e.g., state and county mental hospitals) and services financed with government resources (e.g., Medicaid and Medicare). It is important to note that publicly financed services may be provided by private organizations. In contrast, services provided by the private sector include those directly operated by nongovernmental agencies and services that are financed with private resources (e.g., employer-provided insurance).

People pay for their care in a variety of ways. Some access treatment through private health insurance provided by their employer. Others access care through funding provided by the government. State and local government is the major payer of public mental health services. But since the mid-1960s, states have largely divested and the role of the federal government has increased through the Medicare and Medicaid programs, as well as special programs for adults with serious mental illness and children with serious emotional disability. Historically, mental health services have not been prioritized within the healthcare industry, and as a result, treatment has been inaccessible to many patients. According to data reported by the NIMH (n.d.), in 2019, only 44.8% of those diagnosed with a mental disorder received treatment in the past year.

What Are the Biggest Issues Addressed by Mental Health Advocates?

- Decreasing mental health stigma within U.S. society.
- Working to ensure that mental health treatment is available to those who need it, particularly in rural communities where mental health services often are not available.
- Ensuring that culturally responsive mental health services are available due to the ethnic diversity of the U.S. population.
- Concerns over the criminalization of mental illness. Due to the current shortage of community mental health centers and state hospitals, and other barriers to treatment, many experts have noted that "prisons are the new asylums" as correctional facilities have become the nation's de facto mental health providers.
- Working to increase early mental health screening of youth in schools and by doctors.
- Ensuring that veterans with mental health struggles have access to treatment and are adequately served.

- Increased funding for mental health research.
- Funding programs that provide assistance with employment, housing, and independent living skills for those with mental illness.
- Public policies to address the growing opioid crisis in the United States.
- And mental health parity, the major focus of this chapter.

Current Events Spotlight: Mental Health Days for Students in Oregon

In 2019, Oregon Governor Kate Brown signed a new bill into law that allows students in Oregon to have excused absences for mental health reasons, broadening the definition of "taking a sick day." But the best part of this story is that it was pushed by youth activists from around the state who argued that it was time for schools to treat mental health and physical health equally and to decrease the stigma surrounding mental health struggles in schools. Some of these activists reported being inspired to get involved politically after witnessing high school students from Parkland High School who were using their voices to change gun control laws in Florida. These Oregon activists used data showing alarming rates of suicide and suicidal ideation among youth in their state to argue in support of the legislation. With this new law, youth will no longer need to lie and pretend that they are physically ill when they need to take a day off from school. According to Debbie Plotnick of Mental Health America, this will be a model for other states to follow. According to Plotnick, "As a matter of public policy, for decades we have waited until stage four, until crisis, and then treating it only through incarceration or having kids thrown out of school. We think that this kind of legislation will help people reach out when they need to, not be afraid to do so and not be ashamed" (Bryson Taylor, 2019). The law allows students to take five mental health days in a three-month period. Similar legislation has been passed in Utah and Colorado.

What Is Mental Health Parity?

One of the biggest legislative battles in the field of mental health has been the fight to get leaders in Washington, D.C. to pass a strong federal bill to address discrimination against those with mental health problems who require treatment. Simply put, **mental health parity** is the principle that health insurance plans should include equal coverage for medical care and mental health care, when policies cover both. For social workers, this is not a radical idea because there is an overwhelming body of research that shows that mental illnesses have biological causes and are diseases of the brain. The National Association of Social Workers (NASW) has been an ardent supporter of mental health parity legislation, and its position has been formalized in its book of policy statements, *Social Work Speaks*. In a 1999 report on mental health, U.S. Surgeon General David Satcher stated that one of the most important contributions of mental health research in recent years is the extent to which it has debunked the misconception that there is a division between "mental" health and "physical" health.

However, for decades, it has been legal for insurers to provide less coverage for mental health care than for the treatment of conditions such as heart disease, diabetes, or cancer.

Before strong mental health parity legislation was passed into law, many were not aware of this inequity until a family member required treatment for severe depression, schizophrenia, or substance abuse, and were shocked to discover that their insurance plan provided limited mental health coverage, which was quickly exhausted. Most plans limited the number of outpatient visits and hospital days covered for those with a mental disorder. Mental health benefits were also typically more costly and involved higher copays.

How the Paul Wellstone and Pete Domenici Mental Health Parity and Addiction Equality Act of 2008 Was Passed into Law

Efforts to pass legislation at the state and federal levels began in the early 1990s, and a strong federal bill was not passed until 2008. Legislation seeking social change often involves taking on powerful special interests with significant financial resources. This story has a long and winding path. But as you will see, this legislation would not have been successfully passed into law without the ongoing efforts of committed mental health advocacy organizations. These kinds of work settings are ideal for social workers who have a desire to effect change in the legislative arena at the local and/or national levels.

Phase I: First Parity Bill Is Passed (Small Step Forward)

Policy change efforts are much more likely to achieve success when they are spearheaded by organizations with sufficient funding and resources to devote to the issue. It is also crucial to have lobbyists and professional staff with knowledge and expertise in how to work with lawmakers and key stakeholders to get legislation passed. Two nonprofit organizations worked tirelessly to get a strong mental health parity bill passed: the National Alliance on Mental Illness (NAMI) and Mental Health America (formerly the National Mental Health Association). Andrew Sperling, lobbyist for NAMI, was a key player in this effort.

Advocacy Spotlight

National Alliance on Mental Illness (www.nami.org)

Started in 1979, NAMI is one of the most prominent mental health advocacy organizations in the United States. NAMI describes itself as a grassroots organization made up of families, friends, and other individuals who seek to improve the lives of those affected by mental illness through awareness, education, and advocacy. NAMI has hundreds of local affiliates spanning all 50 states.

Mental Health America (www.mentalhealthamerica.net)

Mental Health America is another leading national organization that advocates on behalf of those with mental and substance use conditions. It has more than 200 affiliates in 41 states and the District of Columbia. Visit the organization's website to learn more about the important work it carries out on an annual basis.

As described in Chapter 6, when working on a policy change effort it is important to find legislators who will passionately take up and champion your cause. Two legislators were key in this effort: **Republican Senator Pete Domenici**, who had a daughter with schizophrenia, and **Democratic Senator Paul Wellstone**, who had a brother with severe mental illness. Senator Wellstone also worked with a female constituent who had a 22-year-old daughter with anorexia who later committed suicide. The family's insurance company, Blue Cross and Blue Shield of Minnesota, denied some coverage for her daughter's condition and later settled with the family. In a separate settlement with the state of Minnesota, Blue Cross and Blue Shield agreed to cover more mental health claims. The first serious effort to get a federal bill passed occurred in 1996 under President Bill Clinton when Wellstone and Domenici introduced legislation requiring parity for mental health and substance abuse. The primary opponents were insurance companies and businesses that argued that expanding coverage for mental health conditions would be too costly.

Advocacy Tip: Agenda Setting

Find legislators who have a personal connection to the issue to help champion your bill. It will take time to do the background research needed on various legislators, but this is definitely time well spent.

The first blow came when the bill (which was offered as an amendment to another piece of legislation) was dropped during final negotiations due to heavy opposition and lobbying from health insurers. As a result, 150 NAMI members protested across the street from the White House, which was not good for President Clinton as it was a reelection year. Less than two months later, Congress passed an extremely compromised mental health parity bill, and President Clinton signed it into law on September 22, 1996. Advocates were less than enthusiastic because the new law was such a small step in the right direction and did not result in true parity. The new law prevented employers with more than 50 employees from imposing more restrictive annual or lifetime dollar limits on these services than they do on medical or surgical care. However, the legislation:

- Allowed insurers to limit the number of outpatient visits and hospital days covered for mental health services;
- Did not include substance abuse;
- Did not address parity regarding copays, deductibles, and out-of-pocket maximums; and
- Allowed employers and health plans to waive the parity requirement if the cost of compliance exceeded 1%.

Advocacy Tip

Deciding whether (and when) to organize a protest is a strategic decision that must be carefully considered. If carefully planned and organized, this can be a good way to get media attention, mobilize supporters, and apply political pressure.

By the end of 1996, eight states had passed some form of mental health parity legislation. But it would take another 12 years before a strong mental health parity bill was passed by the U.S. Congress. On June 7, 1999, President Clinton signed an executive order directing the Office of Personnel Management (OPM) to require all health plans in the Federal Employee Health Benefits Program (FEHBP) to meet a standard of equitable coverage for mental health and substance abuse benefits. On May 18, 2000, a public hearing was held before the Health, Education, Labor, and Pensions Committee in the U.S. Senate. See testimony provided by Jacqueline Shannon, a mother of a child with schizophrenia and then-executive director of the NAMI, at the end of this chapter.

Advocacy Tip

Providing written and/or in-person oral testimony at a committee hearing is a fantastic way for social workers to influence legislation in a very direct way. Helping our clients do this can be even more powerful. Get to know the protocol in your state or locality and get coached by an experienced person the first time around.

Phase II: Stagnation Due to Political Opposition from the Republican Party

On March 15, 2001, Senators Domenici and Wellstone introduced parity legislation requiring parity for all *DSM-IV* diagnoses. However, according to another champion of the federal mental health parity bill, Republican Representative Jim Ramstad, little progress was made during the next 10 years of a Republican-controlled Congress. Ramstad, a recovered alcoholic, sponsored the bill in the House of Representatives for years despite opposition from his own party. According to Ramstad, "I couldn't get a hearing, let alone a vote" (Frommer, 2008).

However, things started looking up when the Democrats took over the Senate in 2001 and when President George W. Bush voiced his support for it during a speech at the University of New Mexico in 2002 (Bush had signed a state mental health parity bill when he was governor of Texas). Bush stated, "Senator Domenici and I share this commitment. Health plans should not be allowed to apply unfair treatment limitations or financial requirements on mental health benefits" (National Public Radio, 2007). On June 6, 2002, a political rally was held in support of mental health parity in Washington, D.C. Senators Paul Wellstone (D-MN) and Pete Domenici (R-NM) and Representatives Marge Roukema (R-NJ) and Patrick Kennedy (D-RI) spoke at the rally as well as former NAMI president, Jim McNulty who detailed his history with mental illness and barriers to getting treatment (see his remarks below).

Pass Parity Now: Statement of Jim McNulty, President, National Alliance for the Mentally Ill at U.S. Capitol Rally

My name is Jim McNulty. I am president of the National Board of Directors of the National Alliance for the Mentally Ill (NAMI). I also suffer from bipolar disorder (manic depression). I am on the podium today because I am living proof of the profound, positive effects that parity has for people with mental illnesses.

In 1987, when I was first diagnosed, my health insurance plan provided virtually no coverage for treatment of mental illness. I desperately needed psychiatric medications and therapy, but my insurance wouldn't pay for them. I was forced to seek treatment from my primary care physician, who knew nothing about treating manic depression. The negative consequences on my life were traumatic and extreme. I lost my job, my home, and my family. Were it not for the kindness of friends, I would have become homeless.

I can't even begin to explain how devastating the consequences were. And if it happened to me, it can happen to anyone. I had been a successful businessperson. I was an elected Alderman. A family man. All of these roles and identities were lost, because I could not get the treatment I needed for what was a medical illness—as much as diabetes, heart disease, or cancer. Had it affected any other part of my body, my insurance would have covered the treatment I needed. But because my illness affected my brain, I was discriminated against. I was denied. I could not get my treatment covered.

Then, in 1994, Rhode Island enacted one of the first parity laws in the nation. Finally, I was able to see a psychiatrist for medication prescription and regular monitoring. I also was able to see a therapist for help in coping with the profound losses I had suffered and the changes that were needed because of my illness. The results of good treatment were rapid. I recovered from the depths of despair. I started a business as a computer consultant. Most importantly, I started to get involved in helping others with similar problems.

I initiated local self-help groups for people with bipolar disorder. I became active in NAMI Rhode Island and the Manic-Depressive and Depressive Association of Rhode Island. In 1999, the governor of Rhode Island appointed me to the Governor's Council on Mental Health, a statutory body that advises the executive branch of Rhode Island on mental health issues. This past year, as a consumer, a person with a mental illness, I was proud to be elected national board president of NAMI—the nation's voice on mental illness.

I am telling you this not because I want to try to impress anyone with lofty titles. Instead it is to make a point. I could be anyone. There are literally tens of thousands of people with mental illnesses in this country who lead highly productive lives and many more who could if they had access to treatment through adequate insurance coverage.

This year, Congress has the opportunity to follow the recommendations of the Office of the U.S. Surgeon General to end discrimination against mental illnesses in insurance coverage. The cost is modest and outweighed by the benefits. They include decreased hospitalizations or emergency costs and increased productivity. As a society, we already know this. Thirty-four states have passed parity laws and the experiences in those states have demonstrated that parity is cost-effective. Now it's time to cover those Americans who aren't already covered by these laws.

In the last 20 years, scientific progress in understanding and treating mental illness has been phenomenal. Today, we have the ability to diagnose and treat people with schizophrenia, bipolar disorder, major depression, and severe anxiety disorders as accurately and effectively as other illnesses. People with mental illnesses, their families, and advocates know that **treatment works, but only if we can** get it.

I am humbled and moved as I look out today and see so many people like me rallying for parity. After this rally, we will visit our representatives to remind them how important parity is and that **it is a priority that must be enacted into law this year**. President Bush has recognized this fact and pledged his support. Now, it's time for Congress to recognize it too by passing the Domenici-Wellstone mental health parity bill.

No more excuses. No more games. No more backroom deals. Insurance discrimination kills. Parity saves lives. Give Americans the coverage that members of Congress and other federal workers already have. Invest in recoveries like my own. Invest in our return to productivity. Invest in America's future.

Source: Jim McNulty, "Pass Parity Now: Statement of Jim McNulty, President, National Alliance for the Mentally Ill at U.S. Capitol Rally."

However, soon there were a couple of serious setbacks. The legislation moved to the backburner after the September 11th attacks and then Senator Paul Wellstone, one of the bill's champions, was killed in a plane crash just before Election Day in 2002. Senator Wellstone's son, David Wellstone, continued to lobby Congress for mental health parity in the years following his father's death. A very interesting development occurred in 2004 when Senators Pete Domenici and Edward Kennedy invited insurers and business leaders to work with mental health advocates on drafting the legislation. Since they could see growing, bipartisan support for the legislation, the insurance and business lobbies realized it was in their interest to come to the table. "It was an incredible process," said E. Neil Trautwein, a vice president of the National Retail Federation. "We built the bill piece by piece from the ground up" (Pear, 2008).

Phase III: True Parity Is Finally Achieved!

When the Democrats took control of Congress in 2007, they were able to put mental health parity on the fast track. When it was introduced in the 110th Congress, it had 57 cosponsors in the Senate (S.558), and 274 cosponsors in the House (H.R.1424). On March 24, 2007, the *New York Times* published an editorial calling on the House and Senate to pass the legislation, stating that it "would be a boon to the millions of Americans who suffer from mental illness or addiction and find it hard to afford treatment. It should also reduce the high productivity losses from depressed or stressed workers."

A number of legislators were key in getting the bill through Congress, including both senators from the state of Minnesota (Republican Senator Norm Coleman and Democratic

Senator Amy Klobuchar), as well as Senator Edward Kennedy (D-MA), his son Representative Patrick Kennedy, who has suffered from addiction and mental health problems, (D-RI), Republican Senator Mike Enzi, and Democratic Senator Chris Dodd. Other prominent individuals who promoted passage of the legislation included Tipper Gore and former first ladies Betty Ford and Roslyn Carter.

In early 2007, Representatives Patrick Kennedy and Jim Ramstad participated in a series of forums that were held in major cities across the country in order to gather testimony from citizens affected by mental illness and addiction as well as business leaders and mental health experts. The "Equity Campaign Tour" was sponsored by NAMI and Mental Health America (see press statement below).

Congressmen Kennedy and Ramstad Embark on Nationwide Tour to Promote Mental Health Parity Bill

The Campaign to Insure Mental Health and Addiction Equity
FOR IMMEDIATE RELEASE January 12, 2007
WASHINGTON Congressmen Patrick J. Kennedy (D-RI) and Jim Ramstad (R-MN) are embarking on a nationwide tour, traveling to forums taking place in major cities all across the country. The national tour entitled, "*The Campaign to Insure Mental Health and Addiction Equity*," will hear testimony from ordinary American citizens whose lives have been touched by mental illness and addiction.

The first forum in the series is scheduled for Tuesday, January 16, 2006, at the Rhode Island State House. Members of the public, employers, mental health advocates, and health care professionals will share personal stories pertaining to their experience negotiating the health care system as it relates to mental health. The sessions will also include the leadership of all three commercial insurers in Rhode Island. The testimony will be used to help facilitate a comprehensive debate over equal access to health care for mental health and addiction treatment.

"Our goal is to compile testimony from Americans across the country in an effort to pass the most responsible and comprehensive federal equity bill possible," said Congressman Kennedy. "Americans with these physiological diseases of the brain pay their premiums like everyone else and their insurance should be there when they need it, like it is for everyone else. Every family in America has, in some way, come face to face with the burden of these diseases and the difficulty in getting care. We pay enormously, as individuals and as a society, the costs of leaving these diseases untreated. It's time for action."

The Congressmen are preparing to reintroduce federal legislation aimed at ensuring that health plans offer fair coverage for mental health and addiction care. The bill, called the Paul Wellstone Mental Health and Addiction Equity Act, after the late Senator who championed the cause, had majority support in past Congresses but was blocked from consideration by House leadership. The new House Leaders have promised Congressmen Kennedy and Ramstad that they will bring the bill up for a vote.

"The American people should not be forced to wait any longer for Congress to knock down the barriers to treatment for mental illness and chemical addiction," said Congressman Ramstad. "Congress must hear their call and pass the Paul Wellstone Mental Health and Addiction Equity Act."

Additional forums are being organized across the country by Mental Health America (formerly the National Mental Health Association) and the National Alliance for the Mentally Ill (NAMI). Congressmen Kennedy and Ramstad will join other Members of Congress at scheduled forums in Minnesota, Maryland, Los Angeles, and Washington State leading up to Congressional hearings in Washington, D.C.

The Paul Wellstone Mental Health and Addiction Equity Act expands the Mental Health Parity Act of 1996 by requiring group health plans to offer benefits for mental health and addiction on the same terms as care for other diseases. The legislation closes the loopholes that allow plans to charge higher copayments, coinsurance, deductibles, and maximum out-of-pocket limits and impose lower day and visit limits on mental health addiction care.

"Every day that we allow insurance discrimination against mental illnesses is another day 82 Americans will die of suicide," said Kennedy. "It's another day that American business will lose $85 million in lost productivity to depression alone. It's another day that thousands of children will be in state custody instead of home with their parents. It's another night on the streets for 200,000 homeless Americans living with mental illness and addictions. We cannot afford the status quo."

According to the Government Accountability Office, nearly 90 percent of plans impose such financial limitations and treatment restrictions on mental health and addiction care despite voluminous scientific research documenting the biological, genetic, and chemical nature of these diseases, and the effectiveness of treatment. The bill applies to group health plans of 50 or more people.

The legislation is modeled after the Federal Employees Health Benefit Program, which covers Members of Congress and other federal workers and dependents and which implemented parity in 2001. According to an exhaustive study published earlier this year by the Department of Health and Human Services, the federal employees' parity policy was implemented with "little or no increase in total MH/SA [mental health/substance abuse] spending."

A majority of respondents to a Mental Health America survey indicated that they would support equity legislation even if it meant a $1 per month increase to their premiums. The Congressional Budget Office has estimated that such legislation will increase health care costs by far less than that amount.

Forum Schedule:
- Jan. 16 Providence, RI District of Rep. Patrick Kennedy
- Jan. 22 Minneapolis, MN District of Rep. Jim Ramstad
- Jan 29 Rockville, MD District of Rep. Chris Van Hollen
- Feb. 10 Los Angeles, CA District of Rep. Grace Napolitano
- Feb. 17 Vancouver, WA District of Rep. Brian Baird

*dates pending in many other locations
Source: http://www.dbsalliance.org/site/PageServer?pagename=advocacy_01292007&printer_friendly=1.

The Senate passed a mental health parity bill in September 2007, and the House passed a different version in March 2008. Some interesting tensions emerged, because many advocates, including Representative Patrick Kennedy, felt that the House bill was a stronger piece of legislation. His father, Senator Edward Kennedy, however, felt that the Senate bill would have more success passing because it included a number of compromises that had the support of insurance and business lobbies who helped write the legislation, along with mental health advocates. The standoff ended when sponsors of the House bill agreed to drop a provision that required insurers to cover treatment for *any* condition listed in the *Diagnostic and Statistical Manual of Mental Disorders*.

Advocacy Tip

Legislators work with advocates behind the scenes and consult with them when making difficult decisions regarding when (and if) to make political compromises in order to get legislation passed. Deciding whether to compromise can be a tough decision.

The Paul Wellstone and Pete Domenici Mental Health Parity and Addiction Equality Act of 2008 was attached to the $700 billion Wall Street bailout bill and was signed into law by President Bush on October 3, 2008. After passage, Senator Edward Kennedy stated, "Congress has finally agreed to end the senseless discrimination in health insurance coverage that plagues persons living with mental illness for so long" (Frommer, 2008). Mental Health America's president and CEO hailed the new law as a civil rights victory for the millions of Americans with mental disorders who have been unable to gain access to treatment.

Figure 8.1   President Bush signing the Mental Health Parity Act

The new mental health parity legislation outlaws health insurance discrimination by requiring insurance companies to treat mental health on an equal basis with physical illnesses, when policies cover both. It is important to understand that the act does not mandate that group insurance health plans include mental health and addiction, but when mental health is included on a plan it must be on par with medical treatment with regard to the following categories of coverage:

- Copays
- Deductibles

- Inpatient hospital days
- Number of outpatient visits

A managed care company can refuse to pay for care on the grounds that it is not medically necessary, but the new law will require them to disclose their reason for denying any particular claim for mental health treatment. When the bill was passed, federal officials stated that the new law would improve coverage for 113 million people and only increase premiums by an average of about two-tenths of 1%. Businesses with fewer than 50 employees are exempt. A separate bill passed three months earlier eliminated discriminatory copayments in the Medicare program.

The Strategy

Many lessons can be learned from the successful effort to get mental health parity legislation passed by federal lawmakers in Washington, D.C. The first lesson is that some policy change efforts turn into rather lengthy battles. Major changes to a large system of care often require many years of hard work on behalf of dedicated individuals and organizations. In this case, various strategies were used in order to raise awareness of this issue and to create the political pressure needed for passage:

- **Lobbying**. Individuals and organizations lobbied federal lawmakers for years, including paid lobbyists with expertise in mental health, as well as friends and relatives of people with mental illness and addiction, including those directly affected.
- **Securing legislative champions.** The impassioned and aggressive support of a number of key legislators, most of whom were personally affected by the issue, was key [Sen. Pete Domenici (R-NM); Sen. Edward M. Kennedy (D-MA); Sen. Paul Wellstone (D-MN); Rep. Patrick Kennedy (D-RI); and Rep. Jim Ramstad (R-MN)].
- **Coalition building and grassroots lobbying.** Prominent advocacy organizations such as NAMI and the National Mental Health Association (now named Mental Health America) worked together and urged their own members and members of the public to contact their legislators. These organizations did a lot of work in the area of public education and awareness (dispelling the myths) by posting information on their websites and getting information out through various media outlets.
- **Visibility**. Well-attended political rallies held in Washington, D.C., with people who were able to speak eloquently raised visibility on the issue.
- **Framing the issue as discrimination**. "Health insurance plans should include equal coverage for medical care and mental health care, when policies cover both."
- **Compromise.** Sitting at the table with the opposition in order to find common ground and areas of compromise was key. Negotiating with business leaders and demonstrating to employers that state parity laws, as well as the health insurance program for federal employees, have not broken the bank.

- **Testimony.** The Equity Campaign Tour, a series of community forums that were held in major cities across the country, allowed the gathering of testimony from citizens affected by mental illness and addiction as well as business leaders and mental health experts.
- **Providing testimony to Congress**. To see an appropriate format for written testimony, see the statement from former NAMI president, Jackie Shannon.

Tactics Used by Mental Health Advocates to Pass This Act into Law

- ☒ Coalition building
- ☒ Direct lobbying (in-person lobby visits, sometimes by a professional lobbyist)
- ☒ Earned media (letters to the editor, actions that lead to media coverage)
- ☒ Grassroots lobbying (e.g., urging people to call, write, email legislators)
- ☐ Paid media (paying for TV/radio ads)
- ☒ Educational outreach (town halls, house parties, community forums)
- ☒ Visibility (rallies, marches)
- ☒ Online advocacy (using social media)
- ☒ Political dissent (e.g., civil disobedience, protest)
- ☐ Paid communication (paid staff who call voters, materials mailed out)
- ☒ Providing testimony in a legislative committee hearing
- ☐ Fundraising activities

Did the Mental Health Parity Act Lead to Meaningful Change?

In Chapter 5, the six stages of the policy change process were outlined, and the final stage discussed was evaluation. Once a policy is passed into law, most would like to believe that this is the end of the story—that the law was implemented as intended and the problem was improved as a result of the new law. Unfortunately, this is not always the case, and this is why it is so important that policies are evaluated to ascertain whether the new law is being followed and whether it has had an impact. There are three possibilities when a new law is passed: it improved the situation; it had no impact; or it made the situation worse. The Mental Health Parity Act is a great example of why evaluation of social policies is so crucial.

In 2016, a presidential task force organized by President Obama made some findings and recommendations with regard to how well the Mental Health Parity Act was faring, and whether it was being appropriately enforced. The good news was that insurers were following the cost provisions of the law and were not charging more for mental health treatment than they were for medical treatment in the areas of copays, deductibles, and annual limits. Thus, there has been progress in more people having coverage for mental health and substance abuse treatment. The bad news was that some insurers were limiting treatment by holding patients with mental illness to a stricter "medical necessity" standard than those with other medical conditions. The other problem was that patients and their families did not know how to file a complaint if they believe their insurance company was not following the law. As a result of the findings, $9.3 million was awarded to states to help enforce parity protections, a government website was launched to help consumers file complaints, a consumer guide was created to help explain patient rights under the parity law, and the Department of Labor was tasked with reporting each year on its investigations into parity violations. However, Benjamin Miller, director of the health policy center at the University of Colorado School of Medicine, says that true parity will only come from erasing the lines between mental and physical health care. "Separate is not equal—mental health is core to health," said Miller (Gold, 2016).

NAMI President Jackie Shannon Gives Testimony on Mental Health Parity

NAMI Members Encouraged to Make Strong Advocacy Push
For Immediate Release, June 2, 2000

On May 18, the Senate Health, Education, Labor, and Pensions Committee held a hearing on mental illness parity focusing on implementation of the Mental Health Parity Act of 1996 as well as legislative proposals at the federal level that would expand previous efforts to full parity.

STATEMENT OF JACQUELINE SHANNON, PRESIDENT NATIONAL ALLIANCE FOR THE MENTALLY ILL (NAMI), REGARDING MENTAL HEALTH PARITY FOR THE COMMITTEE ON HEALTH, EDUCATION, LABOR AND PENSIONS UNITED STATES SENATE

MAY 18, 2000
Chairman Jeffords, Senator Kennedy and members of the Committee, I am Jacqueline Shannon of San Angelo, Texas, President of the National Alliance for the Mentally Ill (NAMI). In addition to serving as NAMI's president, I am also the mother of Greg Shannon. Greg was diagnosed with schizophrenia in 1985, during his senior year in college. For the past 15 years, Greg and our entire family have struggled with his illness. We have experienced discrimination in health insurance firsthand. Our health insurance had a lifetime maximum benefit for mental illness of six thousand dollars. Greg exhausted this benefit during his first hospitalization.

For the past decade, insurance parity has remained NAMI's top legislative priority. As the nation's largest organization representing individuals with serious brain disorders and their families, 210,000 members and 1,200 affiliates, we know why a minimum standard for parity in insurance coverage is desperately needed. Our members—individuals with mental illnesses and their families—know firsthand what it means to face discrimination in health insurance.

NAMI members understand what it is like to exhaust their coverage with a single hospital stay, to be forced to pay higher deductibles and copayments, to run through unfair limits on inpatient days and outpatient visits.

What makes these discriminatory limits so unjust is that they apply only to illnesses of the brain and not to any other organ or system of the body. As I will discuss in greater detail in my testimony, NAMI believes strongly that insurance parity for the treatment of severe mental illness is at its core an issue of discrimination. We believe that mental illnesses are brain disorders, and that treatment for these illnesses are just as (if not more) effective than for other diseases. We therefore believe that health plans should not be allowed to impose limits and conditions in insurance plans that do not apply to all other diseases. In short, we are not asking for special treatment, merely the coverage that any of us expect when we need treatment.

1. **Mental Illnesses Are Brain Disorders**

   A mental illness is, more accurately, a brain disorder; and brain disorders—like epilepsy—are biologically based medical problems. The newest medical technology can take "pictures" that show differences between brains with disorders and normal brains. In any given year, about five million American adults suffer from an acute episode of one of five serious brain disorders: schizophrenia, bipolar disorder (manic depression), severe depression, obsessive-compulsive disorder, and severe anxiety disorders. Even many of America's children—more than three million—suffer from these disorders.

   Untreated, disorders of the brain profoundly disrupt a person's ability to think, feel, and relate to others and to his or her environment. Despite age-old myths and misinformation, "mental illnesses" are not caused by bad character, poor child rearing, or an individual's behavior.

   Brain disorders are shrouded in stigma and discrimination. For centuries they have been misunderstood, feared, hidden, and often ignored by science. Only in the last few decades has the first real hope for people with mental illnesses surfaced, and that hope has grown from pioneering research that found both a biological basis for brain disorders and treatments that work. NAMI's efforts to combat discrimination and stigma received a major boost in December 1999 with the release of the U.S. Surgeon General's Report on Mental Health. This historic report documents the scientific evidence that treatment is effective and concludes that there is no justification for health plans to cover treatment for serious brain disorders such as schizophrenia and bipolar disorder differently from any other disease.

2. **Treatment Works**

   As the Surgeon General documented, science has proven that severe mental illnesses are treatable. The current success rate for treating schizophrenia is 60 percent. The success rate for treating manic depression is 65 percent, and for major depression it is 80 percent. By contrast, treatment efficacy rates for interventions such as angioplasty (41 percent) and atherectomy (52 percent) are lower. Mental illnesses can now be diagnosed and treated as precisely and effectively as other medical disorders. Tragically, the stigma associated with these illnesses too often prevents people from seeking the treatment that science has proven is effective. More importantly, the fact that health insurance plans have historically imposed limitations and conditions on coverage for treatment for severe mental illness compounds this stigma.

3. **Discrimination Is Wrong**

   Discrimination in health insurance takes many forms. The most common techniques to avoid fair coverage of mental illness treatment are: higher cost-sharing requirements for outpatient visits and prescriptions, fewer allowed inpatient days and outpatient visits, and greater annual and lifetime dollar limits. The use of these discriminatory limits and conditions has been well documented.

   Numerous studies compiled prior to the enactment of parity laws (including surveys of plans by the U.S. Bureau of Labor Statistics) found that 85 percent of all plans limit inpatient care and more than 98 percent limit outpatient care. In 1991–92, the BLS Employee Benefit Survey also found that one-half of plans were restricting hospitalization to 30 to 60 days. More than 70 percent of plans were found to have limited either the dollar value of outpatient benefits or the actual number of visits. These surveys also found that arbitrary limits were often unrelated to actual treatment needs. While the federal Mental Health Parity Act (MHPA) and the 31 state parity laws are changing this discrimination, clearly a legacy of discrimination still exists in the private health insurance market.

Mr. Chairman, while these studies are persuasive, the experience of Bonnie Putnam of Florence, South Carolina, more clearly articulates what NAMI members go through every day to get coverage for the treatment they need. Every year, we at NAMI receive hundreds of these personal stories that demonstrate how health insurance plans discriminate against individuals with severe mental illness and their families.

Bonnie is from Florence, South Carolina, and has been diagnosed with major depression since 1979. Even though she has worked for the same company for more than 25 years, she is on the verge of having to leave her job because she cannot afford to pay for the treatment she needs on her own, the very treatment that keeps her well enough to work. Her employer qualifies for the small-business exemption under the MHPA. South Carolina's parity law is of little benefit to Bonnie because it still allows her health plan to strictly limit coverage for outpatient medication and therapy—limits she long ago exceeded. Passage of South Carolina's law actually made things worse for Bonnie since her health plan responded by further limiting outpatient coverage. Bonnie Putnam needs true parity.

4. **The 1996 Mental Health Parity Act Was an Important Step Forward**

The first major step toward ending discrimination in health insurance came in 1996 when President Clinton signed the federal Mental Health Parity Act (P.L. 104–204) into law. With the leadership of Senators Pete Domenici (R-NM) and Paul Wellstone (D-MN), this landmark law establishes a standard of parity for annual and lifetime dollar limits only. The law applies only to employers that offer mental health benefits; i.e., it does not mandate such coverage. More important, the MHPA allows many cost-shifting mechanisms, such as adjusting limits on mental illness inpatient days, prescription drugs, outpatient visits, raising co-insurance and deductibles, and modifying the definition of medical necessity.

As the General Accounting Office (GAO) noted in their testimony before this Committee, lower limits for inpatient and outpatient mental illness treatments have continued and, in some cases actually expanded to help keep costs down. However, it is important to note that the MHPA does apply to both fully insured state-regulated health plans and self-insured plans that are exempt from state laws under the Employee Retirement Income Security Act (ERISA), which are regulated by the Department of Labor. Existing state parity laws are not preempted by the MHPA (i.e., a state law requiring more comprehensive coverage is not weakened by the federal law, nor does it preclude a state from enacting stronger parity legislation, which many have). Other critical limitations in the MHPA include a small-business exemption (for firms with 50 or fewer employees) and an increased cost exemption for employers that can demonstrate a one percent or more rise in costs due to parity implementation will be allowed to exempt themselves from the law.

NAMI is encouraged by the GAO findings presented at this hearing that 86 percent of surveyed health plans are complying with the MHPA. While it is alarming that 14 percent of the surveyed plans are not in compliance, we view this as a lack of effort on the part of state insurance commissioners, the Health Care Financing Administration (HCFA), and the Pension and Welfare Benefits Administration (PWBA) to educate employers about the new law. Likewise, as the GAO noted, compliance is based largely on a complaint-driven process, that places responsibility on aggrieved plan participants to come forward—which often fails because of the stigma associated with mental illness. To ensure greater compliance with the MHPA and all future federal parity efforts, NAMI urges Congress to push HCFA and PWBA to do more to educate employers and health plans about their responsibilities under the law and to randomly audit representative samples of large, medium, and small employers for compliance.

Mr. Chairman, it is interesting to note that while the opponents of the MHPA attempted to vastly expand the scope of this increased cost exemption during regulatory implementation of the MHPA, relatively few employers have used it. NAMI believes that this is due in part to accountability measures included in the regulations (by retrospective examination of claims data, disclosure to employees when a firm seeks an exemption, etc.). However, the fact that fewer than ten employers have sought the one-percent cost exemption is more than likely due to the fact that parity is affordable and costs simply have not gone up because of it.

5. **31 States and FEHBP Have Adopted Parity**

As is often the case, states have taken the lead ahead of Congress in ending insurance discrimination. The original idea behind parity was modeled on legislation in the 1960s that prohibited cancer exclusions in insurance coverage. Mental health parity was first successful with state employees in Texas, then in Maine, New Hampshire, Rhode Island, and Maryland. By the early 1990s, parity laws had been passed in six states. Although these laws do not apply to ERISA self-insured companies, they give employees some protection and they serve to statistically validate the fact that parity is affordable. After enactment of the federal MHPA in 1996, we saw the passage of nine more state parity laws in 1997 and seven (unfortunately three were vetoed) in 1998. In 1999, 11 more states enacted parity laws, bringing the total number of states with such laws to 28. With the addition of California, now more than half the population lives in States that require non-discriminatory coverage.

Already in 2000, Kentucky, Massachusetts, and New Mexico have passed parity laws, which brings the total to 31 states. Clearly, the trend to pass state parity legislation is picking up momentum. Even today, NAMI affiliates are continuing to seek out legislative leaders to sponsor State parity bills of all types with the ultimate goal of ending all insurance discrimination against those who suffer from mental illnesses. NAMI will continue to provide documentation of the experiences of the states that passed parity laws in the early 1990s and other evidence of the affordability of parity and the effectiveness of treatment. NAMI will seek coverage equal to that of other medical conditions covered in each policy written, and we will not turn away from this effort until the discrimination has ceased.

Even though Congress has not acted to expand the modest protections in the Mental Health Parity Act since its passage nearly four years ago, the Clinton Administration has moved to expand the scope of parity. In June of 1999, as part of the historic White House Conference on Mental Health, the President announced that the Federal Employees Health Benefits Program (FEHBP) would require parity beginning in January 2001. FEHBP is the largest health insurance program in the nation, covering 9.5 million federal employees, retirees, and their families.

6. **Parity Is Affordable**

One of the principal lessons learned from the experience in the states that have enacted parity laws—as well as from preliminary estimates by the Office of Personnel Management (OPM) for FEHBP—is that parity is unquestionably affordable. This affordability is especially evident under the laws that focus the parity requirement on a categorical list of severe diagnoses.

As has been made clear at this hearing, the cost of paying for health insurance parity for mental illness unfortunately remains a hotly debated issue. This is disturbing to us at NAMI since overwhelming evidence from multiple studies controversy demonstrates the minimal cost impact resulting from parity. As the GAO found in its report on MHPA implementation, only 3 percent of surveyed plan administrators found that their insurance costs went up as a result of compliance. For the record, I would like to briefly summarize just a few of these studies—most of them from independent sources with no stake in the policy debate over parity—that have provided data in recent years:

- Background Report: Effects of the Mental Health Parity Act of 1996 (March 30, 1999)—Issued by the Substance Abuse and Mental Health Services Administration (SAMHSA), results of this national survey showed that 86 percent of employers who made changes in health plans to comply with the 1996 federal law did not make any compensatory reductions in other benefits because the cost of compliance was minimal or nonexistent.

- Parity in Financing Mental Health Services: Managed Care Effects on Cost, Access & Quality (July 15, 1998)—The second in a series of reports to Congress issued by the National Advisory Mental Health Council found that full parity costs less than one percent of annual healthcare costs. When implemented in conjunction with managed care, parity can reduce costs by 30 to 50 percent.

- Rand Corporation Study (November 12, 1997)—This study found that equalizing annual limits (typically $25,000)—a key provision of the Mental Health Parity Act of 1996—will increase costs by only about $1 per employee per year under managed care. An even more comprehensive change required by some state laws (i.e., removing limits on inpatient days and outpatient visits) will increase costs by less than $7 per enrollee per year. The main beneficiaries of parity were found to be families with children who, under current conditions, are more likely than adult users to quickly exceed their annual benefit limits and go uninsured for the remainder of the year.

- Mercer Study (October 23, 1997)—The findings of this study indicated that 85 percent of American companies are either in compliance with the federal law or plan to comply with the Mental Health Parity Act of 1996 by January 1, 1998. Seven out of ten of those same employers agree that mental health parity is a reasonable national policy goal and that parity is important to their employees.

- National Advisory Mental Health Council's Interim Report on Parity Costs (April 29, 1997)—This report found that the introduction of parity in combination with managed care results in, at worst, very modest cost increases. In fact, lowered costs and lower premiums were reported within the first year of parity. Maryland reported a 0.2 percent decrease after the implementation of full parity at the state level. Rhode Island reported a less than 1 percent (0.33 percent) increase of total plan costs under state parity. Texas experienced a 47.9 percent decrease in costs for state employees enrolled in its managed care plan under parity.

- Lewin Study (April 8, 1997)—In this survey of New Hampshire insurance providers, no-cost increases were reported as a result of a state law requiring health insurance parity for severe mental illnesses.

7. **Let's Finish the Job—S. 796**

As I noted above, the combined effect of the MHPA, the 31 state laws, and parity for FEHBP participants, while substantial and historic, still leave too many individuals with mental illness behind. Parity has become a reality in our country, but discrimination persists—particularly for individuals in ERISA self-insured plans and in cost-sharing requirements that apply only to mental illness treatment.

NAMI believes strongly that S. 796, the Mental Health Equitable Treatment Act, is needed to address these gaps in parity and finish the job of ending discrimination for persons living with the most severe and disabling forms of mental illness. NAMI's consumer and family membership is extremely grateful for the leadership of Senators Domenici and Wellstone in seeking to once and for all end discrimination.

The Mental Health Equitable Treatment Act requires that limitations on the coverage of benefits for "severe biologically based mental illnesses" may not be imposed unless comparable limitations are imposed on medical and surgical benefits. This provision provides full insurance parity for treatment for people with severe mental illnesses and effectively removes all inequitable limits on co-pays, deductibles, inpatient days, and outpatient visits.

S. 796 targets specific adult and childhood mental illnesses and defines the term "severe biologically based mental illnesses" as illnesses determined by medical science in conjunction with the *Diagnostic and Statistical Manual of Mental Disorders* (DSM-IV) to be severe and biologically-based. These illnesses are listed in the bill as: schizophrenia, bipolar disorder (manic depression), major depression, obsessive compulsive disorder, panic disorder, post-traumatic stress disorder, autism and other severe and disabling mental disorders such as anorexia nervosa and attention deficit/hyperactivity disorder.

S. 796 also prohibits unequal limits on the number of covered inpatient days and outpatient visits for people seeking treatment for all mental illnesses. Under this provision, the number of covered impatient days and outpatient visits for mental illnesses must be equal with covered medical/surgical inpatient days and outpatient visits.

Other key features of S. 796 include a small-business exemption for firms with 25 or fewer employees. This change from the 1996 MHPA (its small-employer exemption is 50 or fewer workers) will result in an additional 15 million workers and their families being covered by parity. S. 796 also eliminates the existing expiration provision in the MHPA that sunsets its requirements on October 1, 2001. In addition, S. 796 eliminates the "one percent" cost exemption in the MHPA mentioned above.

S. 796 is core to NAMI's vision of ensuring that the next generation of individuals with mental illness and their families will not have to live out their lives on disability or in public institutions, unable to get the very care that would give them back productive lives. Insurance discrimination enforces the invalid message that mental illnesses are "untreatable" and "hopeless." As I have noted above, parity is both affordable and cost-effective. With parity as envisioned in S. 796, businesses in fact stand to gain: from reduced absenteeism, reduced healthcare costs for physical ailments related to mental illnesses, increased employee morale, and increased productivity overall.

Conclusion

Chairman Jeffords and Senator Kennedy, thank you for the opportunity to share NAMI's views on this important issue. We look forward to working with you and all members of this Committee to ensure that the Senate acts on S. 796 this year.

Source: Jackie Shannon, "Nami President Jackie Shannon Gives Testimony On Mental Health Parity."

REFERENCES

Advocates renew push for mental health 'parity' bill. (2007, January 8). National Public Radio. Retrieved from https://www.npr.org/templates/story/story.php?storyId=6740128

Bryson Taylor, D. (July 24, 2019). Need a mental health day? Some states give students the option. *New York Times*. Retrieved from https://www.nytimes.com/2019/07/24/health/oregon-mental-health-days.html

Dorothea L. Dix and Federal Aid (1927). *Social Service Review*, The University of Chicago Press, *1*(1), 117–137.

Fairness for mental health. (2007, March 24). *New York Times*. Retrieved from https://www.nytimes.com/2007/03/24/opinion/24sat1.html

Frommer, F. (2008, October 3). After 12 years, Wellstone mental health parity act is law. Minnesota Public Radio. Retrieved from http://minnesota.publicradio.org/display/web/2008/10/03/parity_finalpassage/?refid=0

Gold, J. (2016). Federal panel calls for stricter enforcement of mental health care parity law. National Public Radio. Retrieved from https://www.npr.org/sections/health-shots/2016/10/31/500056803/federal-panel-calls-for-stricter-enforcement-of-mental-health-care-parity-law

National Institute of Mental Health (NIMH). (n.d.). Mental illness. Retrieved from https://www.nimh.nih.gov/health/statistics/mental-illness.shtml

Pear, R. (2008, October 5). Bailout provides more mental health coverage. *New York Times*. Retrieved from https://www.nytimes.com/2008/10/06/washington/06mental.html

U.S. Department of Health and Human Services. (1999). *Mental health: A report of the Surgeon General—executive summary*. Rockville, MD: U.S. Department of Health and Human Services, Substance Abuse and Mental Health Services Administration, Center for Mental Health Services, National Institutes of Health, National Institute of Mental Health.

Credits

Child Welfare Policy and Children's Rights

"If our American way of life fails the child, it fails us all."

~Pearl S. Buck

Figure 9.1

CHAPTER SUMMARY

The idea that children should have certain rights and need special protection based on their vulnerable status is not a controversial idea to most social workers. Even though the United States has experienced thriving social movements on behalf of ethnic minorities, the poor, women, older adults, and people with disabilities, a social movement for children has not occurred, perhaps because children cannot vote, are dependent upon adults for their care and protection, and cannot mobilize on their own behalf in the same way that adults can. Thus, children, more than many other vulnerable groups, depend on committed adults who will advocate for them in the public sphere. Child maltreatment is not a new social problem. Historically, children have been viewed as the property of their parents, and too many have been victims of abuse, neglect, and exploitation at the hands of adults, both inside and outside of the family. The government has also failed children at times by allowing millions of them to be without healthcare coverage, not outlawing child labor until the 1920s, and looking the other way when they are abused by powerful people (e.g., priests) and institutions designed to protect them. To child welfare advocates, it is shocking that there was a Society for the Prevention of Cruelty to Animals (SPCA) in the United States before there was a Society for the Prevention of Cruelty to Children (SPCC).

Child welfare policies govern how the United States responds to children who are maltreated by their parents and caregivers in an effort to keep children safe and free from abuse and neglect. These policies are often fraught with controversy because they involve the government's intrusion into the family home, a place most Americans view as sacred. State child protection systems find themselves in a no-win situation because many Americans believe they do not go far enough in protecting the nation's children from abuse and neglect, whereas others believe they are overly intrusive into the private lives of families. Throughout most of American history, children were considered the property of their parents, and it was not the role of the government to intervene. Societal attitudes slowly began changing after the "discovery" of parental child abuse by pediatric radiologists in the 1940s and when Dr. Henry Kempe and colleagues coined the term *battered child syndrome* in 1962 to describe children who had suffered from serious physical abuse. Since then, child welfare advocates have grappled over whether child welfare policies should focus primarily on preserving the family or protecting the child, and whether it is possible to do both.

Social workers are committed to improving the welfare of children in the United States and around the world; however, most have never heard of the United Nations Convention on the Rights of the Child (CRC) despite the fact that the National Association of Social Workers (NASW) supports its passage. The CRC is a human rights treaty that outlines the rights that every child should be entitled to regardless of national boundaries. The CRC is widely recognized as the first legally binding international instrument that incorporates the full range of human rights (civil, cultural, economic, political, and social) into a single text. The convention includes basic standards that individual nations agree to pursue on behalf of children. This chapter explores why the United States is the only nation in the world (that is a party to the UN) that has not ratified the CRC.

STUDENT LEARNING OBJECTIVES

- ○ Students will be able to summarize the major problems experienced by children in the United States.

- ○ Students will be able to cite examples of child advocacy efforts at the local, state, national, and international levels.

- ○ Students will be able to describe the UN Convention on the Rights of the Child.

- ○ Students will be able to evaluate the political advocacy efforts of the Campaign for U.S. Ratification of the CRC.

- ○ Students will be able to analyze the arguments in favor of and against the CRC.

- ○ Students will be able to explain the purpose of international human rights treaties overseen by the United Nations.

The idea that children should have certain rights and need special protections based on their vulnerable status is not a controversial idea to most social workers. Even though the United States has experienced thriving social movements on behalf of ethnic minorities, the poor, women, older adults, and people with disabilities, a social movement for children has not occurred most likely because they cannot vote, are dependent upon adults for their care and protection, and cannot mobilize on their own behalf in the same way that adults can. Thus, children, more than many other vulnerable groups, depend on committed adults who will advocate for them in the political realm. Even though most Americans and lawmakers will say that they value children and that they should be a top public policy priority, the reality is that children are not prioritized in public policy. Unfortunately, many Americans have been unwilling to pay higher taxes to fund programs that serve children and youth (e.g., K–12 education, child protection, health care, etc.). There are a number of broad categories of child welfare policy (see Figure 9.2), but this chapter will focus primarily on child maltreatment (i.e., child abuse and neglect).

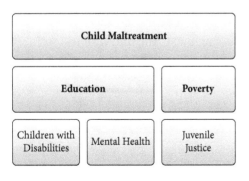

Figure 9.2   Types of child welfare policy

Child welfare policies at the state and federal level govern how the United States responds to children who are maltreated by their parents and caregivers in an effort to keep them safe from abuse and neglect. However, these policies are often fraught with controversy because they involve the government's intrusion into the family home, a place most Americans view as sacred. State child protection systems find themselves in a no-win situation because many Americans believe they do not go far enough in protecting the nation's children from abuse and neglect, whereas others believe they are overly intrusive into the private lives of families. Historically, children have been considered the property of their parents, and many believed it was not the role of the government to intervene when a child was being mistreated. Societal attitudes slowly began changing after the "discovery" of parental child abuse by pediatric radiologists in the 1940s and when Dr. Henry Kempe and colleagues coined the term *battered child syndrome* in 1962 to describe children who had suffered from serious physical abuse. Since then, child welfare advocates have grappled over whether child welfare policies should focus primarily on preserving the family or protecting the child, and whether it is possible to do both.

Child Maltreatment in the United States

Child maltreatment is not a new social problem, and too many children have been victims of abuse, neglect, and exploitation at the hands of adults, both inside and outside of the family. The government has also failed children at times by allowing millions of them to be without healthcare coverage, not outlawing child labor until the 1920s, and looking the other way when they are abused by powerful people (e.g., priests) and institutions designed to protect them. To child welfare advocates, it is shocking that there was a Society for the Prevention of Cruelty to Animals (SPCA; founded in 1824) in the United States before there was a **Society for the Prevention of Cruelty to Children** (SPCC; founded in 1875).

Each state operates a child welfare system that is responsible for investigating reports of child maltreatment, which consists of both abuse and neglect. **Abuse** includes physical abuse, sexual abuse, and emotional or psychological abuse. **Neglect** involves failing to provide a child with needed food, clothing, shelter, medical care, or supervision to the extent that there is a serious risk to the child's health and safety. Many states also include abandonment and parental substance abuse in their definition of child maltreatment. The Child Abuse Prevention and Treatment Act defines child abuse and neglect as, "Any recent act or failure to act on the part of a parent or caretaker which results in death, serious physical or emotional harm, sexual abuse or exploitation; or an act or failure to act, which presents an imminent risk of serious harm." In fiscal year 2018, child protective services (CPS) agencies across the country received an estimated 4.3 million reports of suspected child abuse and neglect, representing approximately 7.8 million children. (U.S. Department of Health and Human Services, Children's Bureau, 2020). Sometimes reports are not investigated at all because the situation does not fall under the state's rules for investigation or the case is not given a high priority and the state lacks the resources to follow up on every report.

After screening, approximately 3.5 million children received an investigation in 2018, and of those, approximately 17% were **substantiated** (i.e., evidence of maltreatment was found) or indicated (i.e., there was reason to suspect maltreatment). This means that in 2018 there were approximately 678,000 victims of child abuse or neglect. The other 83% of reports were not substantiated because CPS investigations found either no evidence or insufficient evidence to indicate that the children in these cases were maltreated. Children younger than three years old had the highest rate of victimization (29%). About 61% of substantiated child victims suffered neglect only; 11% suffered physical abuse only; and 7% suffered sexual abuse only. Roughly 15% of victims suffered two or more maltreatment types. A nationally estimated 1,770 children died from abuse and neglect in 2018 (U.S. Department of Health and Human Services, Children's Bureau, 2020).

Child Welfare Policies and Programs

The history of the development of child welfare policies and programs is fascinating. In 1853, Minister Charles Loring Brace founded the **Children's Aid Society** to assist the thousands of orphaned, abandoned, and unwanted children living on the streets of New York City. Horrified by the living conditions of these children, Brace believed that they needed to get out of their harmful environment and could have better lives with kind, Christian families in the country who were in need of farm labor. Between 1854 and 1929, an estimated 200,000 children were put on a train (later termed the **Orphan Trains**) and sent to various U.S. states to be placed with rural families, many of them farming families. Some children were lucky to be placed with loving families, whereas others were mistreated and wanted only for their labor. The Orphan Trains were a precursor to the U.S. foster care system. This is one example of a child welfare practice or policy that emerged in response to the social problem of orphaned, abandoned, or abused children. To learn more about this fascinating period of child welfare history, watch *American Experience: The Orphan Trains* on DVD (PBS Home Video).

The **first juvenile court** was founded in 1899 due to the tireless work of social reformers who had persuaded lawmakers that juvenile offenders should be separated from adult offenders and that the focus should be on rehabilitation. The federal government's initial involvement in the welfare of children began with the first **White House Conference on Children** in 1909 and the establishment of the **Children's Bureau** in 1912. The first **compulsory education laws** were passed in the 1920s, and in 1938, the Fair Standards Labor Act placed serious limits on child labor.

The Social Security Act of 1935 authorized the first federal funding for child welfare services and allowed states to develop local agencies and programs, and in the 1960s, **mandatory child abuse reporting laws** started being passed in the United States. However, a fully funded, formalized child welfare system was not in place in the United States until the 1970s when the **Child Abuse Prevention and Treatment Act (CAPTA)** was passed (sponsored by Senator Walter Mondale) and significant levels of federal dollars were dedicated to aiding states in the investigation and treatment of child abuse. This was a huge step forward, and since CAPTA was passed many important pieces of legislation have been passed over the years in an attempt to better address the needs of vulnerable children, particularly those in state foster care (see the Timeline). Child welfare policies have focused on many aspects of child welfare practice, including the prevention of child abuse and neglect, foster care, adoption, kinship care, and foster youth emancipating from the foster care system when they reach adulthood. The most recent significant piece of legislation to impact children and families at risk of child maltreatment served by the child welfare system is the Family First Prevention Services Act of 2018. This act came out of an effort to enable federal dollars to be used to help prevent children from entering foster care by providing preventive services to families such as mental health services, substance use treatment, and in-home parenting skill training. Child welfare advocates are hoping that this legislation will be a game changer in child welfare.

Timeline of Child Welfare Advocacy in the United States

- **1854–1929**, Orphan Trains via Children's Aid Society.
- **1875**, Society for the Prevention of Cruelty to Children founded (51 years after the SPCA!).
- **1899**, first juvenile court in the United States, Cook County, Illinois.
- **1909**, first White House Conference on Children.
- **1912**, U.S. Children's Bureau established; first government agency in the world dedicated solely to improving the lives of children and their families.
- **1921**, Child Welfare League of America founded.
- **1920s**, first compulsory education laws in United States.
- **1935**, Social Security Act of 1935 (first federal funding for child welfare; Aid to Dependent Children program created).
- **1938**, Fair Standards Labor Act passed into law (placed limits on child labor in the United States).
- **1962**, Dr. Henry Kempe discovers "battered child syndrome."
- **1965**, Head Start Program established by LBJ administration.
- **1960s**, mandatory child abuse reporting laws in the United States.
- **1973**, Children's Defense Fund founded by Marian Wright Edelman.
- **1974**, Child Abuse Prevention and Treatment Act (landmark legislation).
- **1974**, Juvenile Justice and Delinquency Prevention Act.
- **1975**, Education for all Handicapped Children Act.
- **1978**, Indian Child Welfare Act.
- **1980**, Adoption Assistance and Child Welfare Act of 1980.
- **1994**, Multi-Ethnic Placement Act.
- **1996**, Inter-Ethnic Placement Provisions Act.
- **1997**, Adoption and Safe Families Act (termination of parental rights petition must be filed by 15 months).
- **1997,** S-CHIP (State Children's Health Insurance) program created.
- **1999**, Foster Care Independence Act (focused on youth who leave the foster care system when they reach adulthood).
- **1999**, Texas is first state to pass Safe Haven or "Baby Moses" law.
- **2008**, Fostering Connections to Success and Increasing Adoptions Act.
- **2018**, Family First Prevention Services Act of 2018

The United States has also witnessed the development of a number of prominent child welfare advocacy organizations, such as the **Child Welfare League of America** and the **Children's Defense Fund**, whose mission is to advocate on behalf of vulnerable children and the organizations that serve them (see Advocacy Spotlight: Child Advocacy Organizations). However, despite this progress, state child protection systems continue to be underfunded and understaffed, creating a revolving door for caseworkers who burn out too soon. The qualifications of child protection caseworkers are also cause for concern because many states do not require a social work or related degree.

Advocacy Spotlight: Child Advocacy Organizations

Two of the country's leading child welfare advocacy organizations are the **Child Welfare League of America (www.cwla.org)** (founded in 1921) and the **Children's Defense Fund** (www.childrens-defense.org) (founded in 1973).

Court Appointed Special Advocates for Children (CASA) (www.casaforchildren.org) is a national organization that advocates for youth served in the child welfare system. The focus of their work is to provide CASA or guardian ad litem volunteers: "CASA/GAL volunteers are appointed by judges to watch over and advocate for abused and neglected children, to make sure they don't get lost in the overburdened legal and social service system or languish in inappropriate group or foster homes. Volunteers stay with each case until it is closed and the child is placed in a safe, permanent home. For many abused children, their CASA/GAL volunteer will be the one constant adult presence in their lives."

Child Rights International Network (www.crin.org): According to CRIN's website,

"Our foundation is the United Nations Convention on the Rights of the Child (CRC), which we use to bring children's rights to the top of the international agenda and to put pressure on national governments to promote and protect children's rights. We also do our best to empower local people to campaign for children's rights in their country and promote the use of the law as a powerful advocacy tool. We are proactive and campaign on specific issues that need urgent attention, and also advocate for long term change and legal reform. We want children's rights to be taken seriously, and do not avoid tackling controversial issues" (CRIN, What we do, n.d.).

Every Child Matters (www.everychildmatters.org) and **Children's Rights (www.childrensrights.org)** are newer organizations that are also at the forefront in fighting to make children one of the nation's priorities. For social workers interested in the macro side of child welfare, organizations like this at the state or national level will be of interest. A great organization at the state level to check out is Children First for Oregon.

Visit the websites of each of these organizations in order to learn more about their missions, their public policy issues of interest, and their current legislative agenda. What was most surprising to you about the work of these organizations? Next, do some research online to find out about child welfare advocacy organizations in your city or state. How many exist?

In 2018, a new law, the Family First Prevention Services Act of 2018, was passed by the U.S. Congress. It has been lauded as the most important piece of child welfare legislation in more than a decade by experts such as the Child Welfare League of America since it was intended to make important improvements to the child welfare system. Do some research on this act. What are the major components of this legislation?

The timeline lists a number of important pieces of legislation that have been passed into law to address the needs of children and families served by state child welfare systems in the United States. Sometimes legislation is introduced to try to remedy harmful and/or discriminatory practices against racial and ethnic minorities. The **Indian Child Welfare Act** (ICWA) was passed into law in 1978 to address the problem of Native children being separated from their extended families, tribes, and communities. The new law demanded that any child welfare case involving a Native child must follow certain rules and procedures, such as making special efforts to place the child with a relative and actively involving the tribe in child welfare proceedings. This law later led to a best practice in child welfare, the notion that a child should be placed with relatives over foster care when there are relatives who are safe and appropriate for the child.

In the 1990s, many states were being criticized for delaying the placement of African American and Latino children because they were attempting to place them with families that matched their ethnicity. In response to the concern over the disproportionate number of children in the child welfare system who are ethnic minorities, Congress passed the **Multi-Ethnic Placement Act** (MEPA) in 1994. MEPA prohibited states from delaying or denying adoption and foster placements on the basis of race or ethnicity, but allowed states to consider race *as one of many factors* in making placement decisions. Then in 1996, the **Inter-Ethnic Placement Provisions Ac**t made it illegal for states to include race as a factor at all. Some social workers agree with these federal policies and believe that adoption should be a color-blind process where race is not a major factor when making placement decisions. In other words, they are not concerned over the practice of placing Latino or African American children into the homes of White families. However, other social workers (many social workers of color) disagree and believe that children of color are better off when they are placed with families, and live in communities, that match and can thus preserve their cultural background. This is an example of how social policies are sometimes controversial.

Social workers in child welfare were similarly divided over one provision of the **Adoptions and Safe Families Act** (1997) that significantly shortened the timeline when child welfare officials are required to file a petition to terminate parental rights. Supporters of this provision felt this was important so that children do not languish in the foster care system waiting for their parents to get rehabilitated. Others disagreed and argued that parents with serious substance abuse problems, for example, cannot possibly recover successfully within this more stringent 15-month time frame. In child welfare policies, there are often competing values at play, such as the rights and well-being of children versus the rights and well-being of parents. This values debate can be clearly seen when examining the United Nations (UN) Convention on the Rights of the Child, which is the focus of the rest of this chapter.

Current Events Spotlight: Child Allowances

Most Americans have never heard of **child allowances**, despite the fact that the vast majority of industrialized nations around the world, such as Canada, and many nations in Europe, have them as part of their social welfare system. The basic idea behind a child allowance is that the government should provide some support to families, regardless of income, with the financial costs of raising a child by sending families a monthly check (typically in the range of $200-300 per child per month until the child reaches adulthood). Historically this kind of universal welfare benefit would have a tough time gaining support in the U.S. since it goes against the strong American social value of rugged individualism. However, the times might be changing. The 2021 $1.9 trillion coronavirus relief bill that was passed into law by Democrats and the Biden administration included a provision that will operate like a child allowance by expanding the child tax credit temporarily for one year. As a result, most American families, (except the very wealthy) will receive roughly $250-300 per month per child, amounting to roughly $3600.00 a year per child. Poverty researchers estimate that this policy will decrease the child poverty rate significantly and will help prevent the harmful effects of living in poverty on a child's development. Democrats plan to work to make this benefit permanent, but they will face a tough fight from Republican lawmakers in the U.S. Congress who argue that this kind of a benefit discourages work. According to DeParle (2021), "The child benefit has the makings of a policy revolution. Though framed in technocratic terms as an expansion of an existing tax credit, it is essentially a guaranteed income for families with children, akin to children's allowances that are common in other rich countries."

What Is the UN Convention on the Rights of the Child?

Social workers are committed to improving the welfare of children in the United States and around the world; however, most have never heard of the UN Convention on the Rights of the Child despite the fact that the National Association of Social Workers (NASW) supports its passage. The UN Convention on the Rights of the Child (CRC) is a human rights treaty that outlines the rights that every child should be entitled to regardless of national boundaries (see Summary of the UN Convention on the Rights of the Child). According to the childrightscampaign.org, "The CRC recognizes all children's rights to develop physically, mentally, and socially to their fullest potential, to express their opinions freely, and to participate in decisions affecting their future" (Child Rights Campaign, n.d.c). The CRC, which was adopted by the United Nations in 1989, has a preamble and 54 articles that spell out the rights that all children should have including civil rights, political rights, economic rights, social rights, and cultural rights. These rights can be organized under the following four themes:

- The right to Survival;
- The right to **Develop** to the fullest potential;
- The right to **Protection** from abuse, neglect, and exploitation; and
- The right to **Participate** in family, cultural, and social life and in decisions that affect them (Child Rights Campaign, n.d.b).

Nations that ratify the CRC are asked to implement policies and programs that promote and protect children's best interests.

Summary of the UN Convention on the Rights of the Child

(The United States is the only UN member state that has not ratified it.)

Children have the right to:

- Nondiscrimination
- Survive and develop healthily
- A legally registered name
- A nationality
- Know and be cared for by their parents
- An identity
- Live with their parents unless it is bad for them
- Move between different countries to visit their parents
- Say what they think should happen and have their opinions taken into account
- Freedom of expression
- Freedom of thought, conscience, and religion
- Freedom of association
- Right to privacy
- Have access to information that is important to their health and well-being (mass media)
- Protection from all forms of violence
- Special protection if they are a refugee
- Be cared for by people who respect their ethnic group, religion, culture, & language
- Special care and support if they have disabilities
- Good quality health care
- Help from the government if they are poor or in need
- Adequate standard of living
- An education (special focus on girls)
- Relax and play
- Be protected from child labor that is harmful and exploitative
- Be protected from drugs
- Be protected from sexual exploitation and abuse

- Not be abducted, sold, or trafficked
- Not be punished in a cruel or harmful way
- Protected from war; not be forced to take part in a war or join the armed forces
- Receive special help to recover from abuse and neglect
- Fair treatment in a justice system that respects their rights; minimum age set below which children cannot be held criminally responsible.

Full text of the CRC can be found at http://www.ohchr.org/EN/ProfessionalInterest/Pages/CRC.aspx.

International Human Rights Treaties

The CRC is just one example of a body of international law that is designed to protect human rights for individuals and groups of people around the world. Early examples that mark the beginning of human rights include the American Bill of Rights adopted in 1791 and the **Universal Declaration of Human Rights of 1948**. Other examples include the Convention on the Elimination of all Forms of Racial Discrimination, the Convention Against Torture, and the Convention on the Elimination of all Forms of Discrimination Against Women. For a complete list of international human rights instruments, please visit http://www.ohchr.org/EN/ProfessionalInterest/Pages/CoreInstruments.aspx housed at the United Nations website.

The purpose of **international human rights treaties** is to persuade nations around the world to commit to protect the rights of various vulnerable and oppressed populations. Nations that ratify these treaties are asked to make a commitment to abide by the treaty, to set goals and benchmarks, and to measure progress over time. Some critics argue that international treaties are not very effective since enforcement is weak and there are often no real consequences for violating them. Supporters disagree and believe that it can be an effective mechanism to require nations to focus on the needs of oppressed populations, which are often ignored. They point to a number of examples where nations have made concerted efforts to improve their domestic laws as a result of ratifying an international treaty.

Nations that are a party to the UN must decide whether they will ratify these international human rights treaties, which commits them to ensuring that their own domestic laws are compatible with the treaty. The United States has ratified a number of these treaties (e.g., the Convention on the Prevention and Punishment of the Crime of Genocide; the Convention on the Elimination of all Forms of Racial Discrimination; the Convention Against Torture) but has not yet ratified others (e.g., the Convention on the Elimination of all Forms of Discrimination Against Women; the Convention on the Rights of the Child). It is noteworthy that the United States is the only UN member state that has not ratified the CRC, making it the most widely ratified UN treaty. The box below describes the steps involved with ratifying an international treaty in the United States.

Steps Involved in Ratifying an International Treaty

1. Signing by the president.
2. Transmittal to the U.S. Senate by the president.
3. Referral to the Senate Committee on Foreign Relations.
4. Senate committee recommends approval to ratify (may include reservations, which modify U.S. obligations without changing the treaty language).
5. Two-thirds of Senate approves ratification of treaty.
6. Ratification by the president.

What Is the Problem That the CRC Is Addressing?

It is not a surprise to most social workers that there is much room for improvement when it comes to measures of child well-being in the United States and around the world. Because children are not a strong voting bloc and rely on adults for their care and protection, their needs are often neglected, and problems facing children are often not prioritized by policymakers. Living conditions of children in developing countries are cause for serious concern; however, many Americans would be surprised to learn about the numerous challenges facing children in the United States, the richest country in the world.

Child Poverty and Homelessness

According to a report by the Children's Defense Fund (2020), children are overrepresented among the nation's poor. For example, children are more than twice as likely as adults 65 years and older to be poor. Among all children under age 18 in the United States, about one in six were poor in 2018, which represented 11.9 million children. In 2018, African American, American Indian/Alaska Native, and Latinx children were disproportionately poor compared to White children:

- 8.9%% of White children were poor (1 in 11);
- 23.7% of Latinx children (1 in 4);
- 29.1% of American Indian/Alaska Native children (1 in 3);
- 30.1% of African American children (1 in 3).

The United States ranks high in levels of child poverty compared to other wealthy industrialized countries, and has been criticized for not doing more to decrease child poverty through government spending on family and social benefits. The United States is in the company of nations such as Chile, Israel, Spain, and Turkey, which have child poverty rates of over 20%. The Nordic nations have the lowest child poverty rates in the world. For example, in Denmark and Finland the child poverty rate is 3% to 4% (OECD Family Database, n.d.). Almost 1.4 million children enrolled in U.S. public schools experienced homelessness during the 2016–2017 school year—double the number at the start of the Great Recession between 2007 and 2009 (Children's Defense Fund, 2020).

Child Abuse and Neglect

A primary measure of child well-being is the prevalence of child abuse and neglect in a society. A previous section "Child Maltreatment in the United States" provides an overview of this social problem in the United States, including the latest child abuse statistics.

Infant Mortality

In January 2018, the *LA Times* ran an article titled, "Why the United States is 'the most dangerous of wealthy nations for a child to be born into'" (Kaplan, 2018). The article reports the findings of a study that compared the United States to 19 other advanced wealthy nations and found that the United States ranks last in child mortality (deaths of children ages 0 to 19 years) due to in large part to its high rates of child poverty, fragmented healthcare system, and weak social safety net. The researchers found that from 2001 to 2010 the risk of death in the United States was 76% greater for infants and 57% greater for children ages 1 to 19. During this decade, children ages 15 to 19 were 82 times more likely to die from gun homicide in the United States. The study authors concluded that more than 600,000 childhood deaths could have been avoided if the United States had performed as well as its peer countries between 1961 and 2010 (Thakrar, Forrest, Maltenfort, & Forrest, 2018). Many are surprised to learn that the richest country in the world ranks so poorly on measures of child mortality compared to other western industrialized nations.

Health Care

The number of uninsured children in the United States has dropped significantly since the passage of the Affordable Care Act, but there are still children who go without health insurance. According to the National Center for Health Statistics, 5% of children in the United States were uninsured in 2018 (Cohen, Terlizzi, & Martinez, 2019). Again, the United States is an outlier on this measure of child well-being because virtually every other western industrialized nation guarantees health insurance for children.

The Controversy Over the CRC in the United States

In 1979, over a 10-year period, child welfare experts from around the world (government and nongovernmental organizations, or NGOs) worked on drafting the language of the CRC. They wanted to set forth basic standards that nations agree to pursue on behalf of children in their country and to create a human rights treaty that outlines the basic rights and protections of children, no matter which country they live in. The CRC was adopted by the UN General Assembly in 1989 and instituted in international law in 1990. In the early 1990s, several attempts were made in the U.S. Congress to ratify the CRC; however, these attempts were ultimately unsuccessful. In 1990, resolutions were adopted in the U.S. House and Senate; however, President H. W. Bush failed to sign or pursue ratification of the CRC due to concerns about the CRC's impact on state and federal laws, U.S. sovereignty, and parental rights.

In 1994, another CRC resolution was introduced in the Senate by Senator Bill Bradley (D-NJ), along with 54 cosponsors. The following year, the White House issued a press release stating that President Clinton would sign the CRC and send it to the Senate for advice and consent to ratification. On February 16, 1995, Secretary of State Madeleine Albright signed the CRC on behalf of the United States. However, it soon faced political opposition from the right. Senator Jesse Helms, a staunch conservative, exclaimed that as long as he was chairman of the Senate Committee on Foreign Relations, he would do everything he could to prevent the CRC from being given a hearing. He went as far as introducing a separate resolution (S. RES. 133), in the 104th Congress, along with 26 cosponsors, urging the president not to support the CRC because it is "incompatible with the God given right and responsibility of parents to raise their children" and because "the United States Constitution is the ultimate guarantor or rights and privileges to every American, including children" (S. RES 133). The strong opposition from several members of Congress prevented the Clinton administration from moving forward. The George W. Bush administration opposed the CRC and argued that it conflicted with U.S. laws regarding family rights and privacy.

Even though the CRC has widespread support from child welfare experts and advocates, there are some who view it as extremely controversial. It has been described by the Home School Legal Defense Association (HSLDA) as "the most dangerous attack on parental rights ever." According to the HSLDA, the CRC would "undermine families by granting to children a list of radical rights . . . these new radical rights would include the right to privacy, the right to freedom of thought and association, and the right to freedom of expression." Groups such as Focus on the Family and the Christian Coalition have joined the HSLDA in working to defeat passage of the CRC.

In 2002, the United States decided to ratify the two optional protocols in lieu of ratifying the entire CRC. These two protocols are the Optional Protocol on the Sale of Children, Child Prostitution, and Child Pornography, which protects the rights and interests of children affected by these issues, and the Optional Protocol on the Involvement of Children in Armed Conflict, which states that children under 18 should not be recruited or required to enter the armed forces. As of 2018, the CRC has been ratified by all nations who are a party to the UN; only the United States has not.

Why Has the United States Failed to Ratify the CRC?

Many who first learn about the CRC immediately want to understand why the United States has failed to ratify this human rights treaty for children when 193 nations around the world have done so. The first answer is that there is a rather lengthy review process in the United States, and the U.S. government typically considers one international treaty at a time. For example, the **Convention on the Prevention and Punishment of the Crime of Genocide** took more than 30 years to be ratified in the United States, and the **Convention on the Elimination of All Forms of Racial Discrimination (CERD)** was ratified 28 years after being signed by President Johnson. If the treaty is controversial (or depicted as such), it can become politicized, which often lengthens the process even more.

Widespread misconceptions about the CRC's intent and potential impact have created obstacles to moving the CRC ahead expeditiously. For example, opponents of the CRC have pitted children's rights against parent's rights and have argued that if the United States ratifies the CRC, children will be able to get an abortion without their parent's consent, the government will tell parents how they should raise their children, schools would be required to distribute contraceptives, and children will be allowed to choose their own religion and sue their parents. Supporters of the CRC have tried to correct these misconceptions and explain that the CRC includes language that speaks to the pivotal role that parents play in their children's lives. For example, in emphasizing the **primacy and importance of the role and authority of parents**, the treaty calls for governments to respect the responsibilities, rights, and duties of parents to provide direction and guidance to their children. However, these misconceptions have resulted in opposition to the treaty within the U.S. Senate and in some sectors of the general public.

Finally, some policymakers do not like the idea of ratifying international treaties and believe that doing so threatens U.S. national and state sovereignty. In other words, they do not like the idea that an international treaty could supersede national, state, and local U.S. laws. The CRC may conflict with current U.S. law in a number of areas, particularly in the areas of ensuring that all children have access to health care and laws that govern criminal justice.

The Emergence of the Campaign for the Ratification of the CRC

As a result of this stalemate, child welfare advocates in the United States had to figure out a plan to get lawmakers to ratify the CRC. Through the leadership of the Child Welfare League of America (CWLA), a core group of advocates convened the first meeting of the Campaign for U.S. Ratification of the Convention on the Rights of the Child in August 2002. Participants focused on efforts needed to build a national coalition. Then in 2003, representatives from more than 50 U.S. nongovernmental organizations met in Washington, D.C., for a two-day strategy session titled, "Moving the CRC Forward in the United States." Out of this effort, the Campaign for U.S. Ratification of the CRC was born (see Campaign for U.S. Ratification of the UN Convention on the Rights of the Child). One of the cochairs of the campaign was social worker Martin Scherr.

Coalition building. According to childrightscampaign.org, the Campaign "is a volunteer-driven network of academics, attorneys, child and human rights advocates, educators, members of religious and faith-based communities, physicians, representatives from non-governmental organizations (NGOs), students, and other concerned citizens" (Child Rights Campaign, n.d.a).

Advocacy Tip

Coalition building is an advocacy strategy that can be very useful because it demonstrates "power in numbers" and allows groups to share their resources and expertise.

Campaign for U.S. Ratification of the UN Convention on the Rights of the Child

According to the Child Rights Campaign:

> The Campaign is a volunteer-driven network of academics, attorneys, child and human rights advocates, educators, members of religious and faith-based communities, physicians, representatives from non-governmental organizations, students, and other concerned citizens, dedicated to the ratification and implementation of this extraordinary human rights treaty that our country helped to create.
>
> Our mission is to bring about ratification and implementation of the CRC in the United States. We will achieve this through mobilizing our diverse network to educate communities on the Convention, thereby creating a groundswell of national support for the treaty, and by advocating directly with our government on behalf of ratification.

Visit their website at: www.childrightscampaign.org.

Educational outreach. Early on, the focus of the Campaign was to educate the public and raise awareness of the CRC, because most Americans are unaware of this human rights treaty for children. A series of events were planned for this purpose, as described on the website of the Campaign for U.S. Ratification of the CRC.

In the Spring of 2006, the CRC Campaign convened its first National Summit, "Convention on the Rights of the Child: Mobilizing Communities for Ratification," on the campus of American University in Washington, D.C. This event was attended by over 300 individuals, including 100 youth, from 29 states, Puerto Rico, and 11 countries. Professionals working in the civil and human rights, educational, legal, medical, religious, and social services fields were present at the Summit, alongside youth from Covenant House, Homeschoolers UN Club, High School for Human Rights (Brooklyn, New York), and the Children's Theater Company. Participants took part in and attended various workshops, panels, plenary sessions, and artistic presentations designed to educate individuals on the CRC, implications of U.S. ratification, best practice models for advancing children's rights, and how to organize efforts at the local, state, and national levels (Summit for the Convention on the Rights of the Child (n.d.).

Next, the Campaign cohosted a Senate Briefing on Juvenile Justice in April 2007 along with the following sponsors: Georgetown University's Center for Juvenile Justice Reform and Systems Integration, the Children and Family Justice Center at Northwestern University School of Law, the Juvenile Justice Initiative of Illinois, and the National Juvenile Justice Network. Speakers included individuals from the UN Committee on the Rights of the Child, the Center for Children's Law and Policy, the University of Chicago Law School, and Georgetown University (Senate Briefing on Juvenile Justice, n.d.).

Advocacy Tip

Sometimes organizations will organize a **congressional briefing** to educate lawmakers and/or members of their staff about a particular issue. Some briefings have even involved showing a compelling documentary film.

In celebration of Universal Children's Day and the CRC's 18th Anniversary, local and state CRC Briefing Days were convened at universities across the country in November 2007. More than 800 individuals attended these events, which were held in the following cities: Atlanta; Boston; Denver; Hartford; Honolulu; Los Angeles; New Orleans; New York City; Suffern, New York (suburban New York City); and Washington, D.C. Participants included academics, legal and healthcare professionals, social workers, representatives from child advocacy and humanitarian organizations, students, elected officials, and members of the media. Topics discussed ranged from education, health, juvenile justice, poverty, and welfare to the historical importance of the treaty and the need for U.S. ratification.

In commemoration of the 19th Anniversary of the adoption of the Convention on the Rights of the Child by the UN General Assembly, the Campaign convened its second Senate Briefing, "Children's Health Issues and the Convention on the Rights of the Child." This initiative was cohosted by the American Academy of Pediatrics (AAP), the American Psychological Association (APA), and Child Welfare League of America (CWLA). The briefing was moderated by an attorney with the American Bar Association Center on Children and the Law.

The next major event for the Campaign included organizing a National Symposium June 1–2, 2009, in Washington, D.C., at the Georgetown University Law Center. This event was cosponsored by the Georgetown University Law Center's Juvenile Justice Clinic. The focus of the Symposium, "The Convention on the Rights of the Child: Why It is Time to Ratify," was to look at the Convention through the lens of its impact on U.S. children. The Symposium brought together a multidisciplinary group of experts representing the fields of child and human development, education, health/medicine, law, psychology, public policy, and social work.

The development of a professional website. The Campaign has spent much of their time developing and hosting a professional website full of information about the CRC (http://childrightscampaign.org) and why it should be ratified, including campaign materials that are used to educate people about the CRC, such as fact sheets, campaign brochures, and flyers. The website provides an incredible array of advocacy materials and toolkits on the website that people can download (includes templates so that advocates do not have to reinvent the wheel). A social media toolkit was added in 2016.

Encouraging advocates to get op-eds published in area newspapers. One way for advocates to educate the public about an issue is to get an op-ed published in a local newspaper. Most newspapers are online now and many op-eds get reposted on other websites or shared via social media such as Facebook and Twitter. Because an op-ed needs to be viewed as current and newsworthy, advocates need to be strategic about finding a good hook (e.g., submit it during Child Abuse Prevention Month, or when a research study is published documenting outcomes related to child well-being in the United States, or when a high-profile child abuse case is in the news, etc.). A sample op-ed follows.

Example of Newspaper Op-Ed

U.S. may soon become the only nation to shun the UN Convention on the Rights of the Child

The U.S. ranks 28 out of 29 advanced nations in child poverty. Yet the issue of children's well-being receives little attention in the United States. And perhaps not accidentally, the U.S. could soon become the only country to not ratify the United Nations Convention on the Rights of the Child (CRC), underscoring how child welfare is not one of our public policy priorities.

Adopted by the U.N. General Assembly in 1989, the CRC outlines the rights and protections that every child should be entitled to regardless of national boundaries, including the right to survival, to develop to one's fullest potential, to protection from abuse, neglect and exploitation and to participate in family, cultural and social life. It calls on states to develop and implement policies and programs that ensure that all children will grow up in supportive family and community environments.

At the beginning of 2015 there were only three countries that did not ratify the CRC—Somalia, South Sudan and the United States. South Sudan ratified the treaty in May. Somalia started the ratification process in January and is expected to formalize it once the paperwork is deposited with the U.N.

Partisan fear mongering and widespread misconceptions about the CRC's intent and potential effect continue to create obstacles to expeditiously moving the treaty forward in the United States. Opponents of the CRC, which includes a coalition of religious conservative groups, have pitted children's rights against parents' rights suggesting that the treaty would allow the government to tell parents how they should raise their children and grant children autonomous rights such as accessing birth control and abortion without parental consent. Supporters of the CRC insist that it includes language that emphasizes the primacy and importance of the role and authority of parents.

The U.S. does not have a good record on the rights of children. Child labor was abolished only in 1938 following decades of lobbying efforts. The American Society for the Prevention of Cruelty to Animals was established in 1866, nearly a decade before the formation of the American Society for the Prevention of Cruelty to Children. And it took another 100 years before a fully funded, formalized child welfare system was in place when Congress passed the Child Abuse Prevention and Treatment Act of 1974 and federal dollars were allocated to assisting states in the investigation and prosecution of child abuse. It's only in 2005 that the U.S. Supreme Court ruled the sentencing of juveniles to death was a cruel and unusual punishment. Poor and minority children in the U.S. still attend substandard schools that are as racially segregated as they were in the 1950s.

Ratifying the CRC would signal to the rest of the world that the United States is interested in joining the community of nations that are working for the betterment of their children and youth.

A powerful minority of social and religious conservatives have repeatedly obstructed any progress on the CRC, citing unfounded fears that ensuring *children's* rights leads to the infringement of *parental* rights, forcing the U.S. to stand alone on the issue within the global human rights community. In the early 1990s, Congress made several attempts to ratify the CRC amid opposition from President George H. W. Bush. His successor, President Bill Clinton, was widely expected to sign the CRC and send it to the Senate for advice and consent to ratification. However, the administration faced stiff resistance from the right.

Former Sen. Jesse Helms, R-N.C., then the chairman of the Senate Committee on Foreign Relations, vowed to prevent a hearing on the CRC. He then introduced a separate resolution, backed by 26 cosponsors, opposing the treaty, arguing that it is "incompatible with the God given right and responsibility of parents to raise their children" and that "the United States Constitution is the ultimate guarantor or rights and privileges to every American, including children." The George W. Bush administration also opposed the CRC, arguing that it conflicted with U.S. laws on privacy and family rights.

Despite lobbying by child welfare advocates and organizations, President Barack Obama has made no serious efforts to push for the CRC's ratification. It is a shame because the U.S. does not fare well on a number of social and health indicators that measure child welfare when compared to other industrialized countries. In fact, a 2013 UNICEF report (Adamson, 2013) ranks the U.S. in the bottom on five important indicators of child well-being compared to other 29 economically advanced nations:

- **Overall ranking: 24.8.** The bottom four places in the ranking are occupied by three of the poorest countries in the survey, Latvia, Lithuania and Romania, and by one of the richest, the United States.
- **Material well-being ranking: 26.**
- **Health & Safety ranking: 25.** The only countries with infant mortality rates higher than 6 per 1,000 births are Latvia, Romania, Slovakia and the U.S.
- **Education ranking: 27.** The U.S. also ranks near the bottom on provision of early childhood education and in rates of young adults participating in higher education.
- **Behaviors & risk ranking: 23.** The U.S. ranks last in childhood obesity and teenage births.
- **Housing & environment ranking: 23.** The U.S. ranks 27th in children's exposure to violence as measured by the nation's homicide rate.

It is perplexing that the richest nation in the world has such appalling rates of child poverty and educational attainment. The U.S. also stands out for not guaranteeing healthcare coverage for children and for prosecuting children as adults and sending them to adult prisons. Ratifying the CRC would signal to the rest of the world that we are indeed interested in joining the community of nations that are working for the betterment of their children and youth.

Source: J. A. Ritter. (2015, June 20). America's shameful child rights record. Al Jazeera. Retrieved from http://america.aljazeera.com/opinions/2015/6/americas-shameful-child-rights-record.html

Encouraging advocates to enact state and local resolutions in support of ratification. There is an interesting tactic that can be used by advocates when legislation needs to get passed at the federal level, but federal lawmakers are not taking action. Sometimes advocates in various states and cities will get resolutions passed in support of the federal legislation and, when enough of these have been passed into law, it can be used to pressure federal lawmakers. In the case of the CRC, resolutions have been passed in a number of states and cities urging the U.S. Senate and the President of the United States to ratify the UN Convention on the Rights of the Child. An example of a resolution passed by the Portland City Council follows.

Case Example: Social Work Students at Pacific University Oregon, *Think Globally, Act Locally*
During the Spring of 2008, social work undergraduate students in a course titled Macro Social Work, embarked on a class project with the goal of increasing awareness of the CRC in the greater Portland, Oregon area. Students broke out into three groups. One group focused on community education and did this by creating a Myspace page, canvassing in the community and handing out literature, and getting an op-ed published in a community newspaper. Another group organized a forum at Portland State University and invited community members and child welfare professionals who were likely to be interested in this topic. The third group set out to get a resolution passed by the Portland City Council.

Advocacy Tip

One strategy that can be used to pressure federal lawmakers to pass a piece of legislation is to **pass a resolution** at the state or local level urging the U.S. Congress to pass said legislation.

The first step in getting a resolution passed was finding a Portland City Council member who would be interested in sponsoring the resolution. Students did some research on the city council members and discovered that there was a connection between the university and one of the council members because there were two Pacific University alumni who work in this council member's office. Students then contacted the office of council member Randy Leonard and arranged a meeting with one of his staff members to discuss the resolution.

At this meeting, students brought materials on the CRC to share with the staff member and gave a brief overview of the issue. Students explained how similar resolutions have been passed in other cities and states. Students then requested that Commissioner Leonard sponsor this resolution. The students later heard from Commissioner Leonard's office that he had agreed to sponsor the resolution.

The next step was writing the resolution and crafting language that would be most appropriate for this local city resolution. Luckily, the Campaign for the Ratification of the CRC had a sample resolution that cities and states could use as a template and then tailor to their own needs. Students used this template but included some facts and figures related to the welfare of children in Portland, Oregon. Students stayed in good communication with Commissioner Leonard's office throughout the process and sent them the resolution after the students agreed on a final version. Students were then told when they were scheduled to speak to the Portland City Council.

Figure 9.3 Social Work Students from Pacific University, Oregon, Jean Laschever and Celeste Goulding, Testifying before the Portland City Council, May 2008

It was agreed that two students would address the Portland City Council since they felt most comfortable doing public speaking. However, ahead of time, these students prepared their remarks and practiced. Luckily, everything went very smoothly on the day the students addressed the City Council. They read their prepared remarks, answered a couple of questions from the city council members, and then the council voted unanimously to pass the resolution. A photo of two students testifying before the Portland City Council and a copy of the resolution that passed are provided here (Figure 9.3 and Resolution from Portland City Council).

Resolution from Portland City Council

RESOLUTION No. 36604
Urge the United States Congress to pass binding legislation that ratifies the United Nations Convention on the Rights of the Child. (Resolution)

WHEREAS, In Oregon children are still 5% more likely to live below the poverty line that the general population, trend that has existed for over eight years; and

WHEREAS, In a recent United Nations study of the 21 wealthiest nations, the United States ranged 20th in child welfare; and

WHEREAS, Globally, an average of 26,000 children under the age of five die every day mostly due to preventable causes; and

WHEREAS, After almost twenty years the United States remains one of the two countries still needed to ratify the United Nations Convention of the Rights of the Child; and

WHEREAS, Portland has already adopted a Bill of Rights for Children and this resolution would be the first step in expanding these rights to all children; and

WHEREAS, Oregon's Congressional delegation should unite in support of the binding legislation proposed by the United Nations Convention on the Rights of the Child to help ensure the mental, physical, and emotional prosperity of all children everywhere.

NOW, THEREFORE BE IT RESOLVED, that the Council of the City Portland, on behalf of the people of Portland, urges the United States Congress to ratify the United Nations Convention on the Rights of the Child; and

BE IT FURTHER RESOLVED, that a suitable copy of this resolution shall be sent to George W. Bush, President of the United States, and the members of the Oregon Congressional delegation.

Adopted by the Council: **MAY 14, 2008**

Gary Blackmer
Auditor of the City of Portland

By:

Susan Parson

Commissioner Randy Leonard
Mayor Tom Potter, Commissioner Sam
Adams, Commissioner Dan Saltzman
Sara Petrocine :sp

Deputy

May 6, 2008

Source: Portland City Council, "Resolution from Portland City Council," Resolution No. 36604.

Practice Exercise 9.2

Visit the website of the Campaign (www.childrightscampaign.org) and review their campaign materials and other information on their website. Having a good website is crucial for most advocacy organizations and campaigns in order to get their message out and educate the public. What do you like about their website? What would make this website more effective, in your opinion?

What Is the Current Status of the UN Convention on the Rights of the Child in the United States?

In order for the United States to ratify an international treaty, the president must send it to the U.S. Senate, and two-thirds of the Senate must consent—that is, 67 "yes" votes. Thus, it needs to have the support of the president and two-thirds of the Senate. The Campaign for the CRC was hopeful that this would be possible with the election of President Obama in 2009 and a heavily Democratic Congress. President Obama indicated his overall support for the objectives of the CRC and stated that his administration would conduct a legal review of the treaty. At her confirmation hearing, Susan Rice, the U.S. Permanent Representative to the United Nations, reiterated this commitment to reviewing the CRC. Unfortunately, this did not end up being a top priority of the Obama administration due to other pressing issues. CRC advocates will have to wait to see whether this ends up being a priority for the Biden administration. The Campaign is currently using the following strategies to try to get the United States to ratify the CRC:

- Actively lobbying members of the U.S. Senate;
- Using the campaign website to inform the general public about the CRC and providing campaign materials to those who want to advocate on behalf of the CRC (www.childrightscampaign.org);
- Getting people and organizations to become members of the Campaign and join their email listserv in efforts to broaden their coalition;
- Encouraging supporters to engage in educational outreach in their local communities;
- Asking advocates and supporters to submit Letters to the Editor and Op-eds in local newspapers; and
- Asking people to contact their U.S. Senators and the president (e.g., writing; calling; lobbying in person) to urge ratification of the CRC.

Tactics Used to Get the CRC Ratified

- ☒ Coalition building
- ☒ Direct lobbying (in-person lobby visits, sometimes by a professional lobbyist)
- ☒ Earned media (letters to the editor, actions that lead to media coverage)
- ☒ Grassroots lobbying (e.g., urging people to call, write, email legislators)
- ☐ Paid media (paying for TV/radio ads)
- ☒ Educational outreach (town halls, house parties, community forums)
- ☐ Visibility (rallies, marches)
- ☒ Online advocacy (using social media)
- ☐ Political dissent (e.g., civil disobedience, protest)
- ☐ Paid communication (paid staff who call voters, materials mailed out)
- ☐ Providing testimony in a legislative committee hearing
- ☐ Fundraising activities

State-Level Child Welfare Advocacy Efforts: Our Children Oregon

The UN Convention on the Rights of the Child is a great example of a policy at the international level that can effect positive change for children. But there are a number of child advocacy organizations across the country that advocate for children at the state level. Children First for Oregon (CFFO) was founded in 1991 to inform state lawmakers about the challenges faced by vulnerable children in the state of Oregon, primarily those in foster care and those living in poverty. In January 2020, Children First for Oregon (CFFO) and the Children's Trust Fund of Oregon (CTFO) merged to form Our Children Oregon (see www.ourchildrenoregon.org). Our Children Oregon hires professional lobbyists to pass legislation that would help children in Oregon succeed and thrive. They do incredible work, but two aspects of the organization will be highlighted as innovative best practices in child advocacy.

Building a Statewide Coalition for Children: "The Children's Agenda"

In 2015, CFFO identified an obstacle that was preventing child advocates from achieving more for children in the state in Oregon. In most states, a number of organizations provide advocacy for children, but they often work in silos. For example, individual organizations provide advocacy around issues such as education, child care, mental health, health care, foster youth, disabilities, poverty, homelessness, and children in communities of color. Thus, CFFO set out to build a statewide coalition of child advocacy organizations that would work together to pass legislation each legislative session in order to benefit youth in their state. Each legislative session, the coalition comes to a consensus on their legislative priorities and publishes it in a "Children's Agenda" that is posted on the organization's website and shared with state lawmakers and the general public. The state coalition has more than 120 partner organizations. Their legislative successes in 2018 and 2019 included legislation that expanded health coverage to children in Oregon who were previously denied coverage due to their immigration status, a new law that raised the age of tobacco sales to age 21, a new law that requires children younger than two years of age to be secured in rear-facing car seats, legislation that raises the minimum wage in the state of Oregon, universally offered home visiting for families with newborns, and paid family and medical leave.

Foster Youth Advocacy

Our Children Oregon has a program called the Oregon Foster Youth Connection that aims to bring foster youth across the state together to provide them with a sense of community and also to promote leadership development. From a social work perspective, Our Children Oregon does something very impressive and exciting on behalf of foster youth—instead of relying on professionals to be the voice of foster in their advocacy work, they train foster youth to advocate for themselves in the Oregon state legislature each session. Each summer, foster youth are brought together in a working retreat to decide which issue they would like to address in the upcoming legislative session in Oregon. This is based on identifying a pressing challenge that foster youth face across the state that could be improved with a piece of legislation. Trained lobbyists teach the youth how to lobby legislators and testify in legislative hearings, and then these brave youth tell their stories, which are often heartbreaking and compelling. The following are the pieces of state legislation they have successfully passed into law in the state of Oregon:

- **2009**, a bill that requires the Department of Human Services (DHS) to provide assistance to foster youth in obtaining a driver's license.
- **2010**, a bill that extends healthcare coverage for all youth in Oregon's foster care system when they turn 18.
- **2011**, a bill that waives tuition and fees at state universities and community colleges for youth who have spent time in Oregon's foster care system.
- **2013**, Foster Youth Bill of Rights bill passed, which established clear requirements for informing foster youth about their legal rights and established a hotline answered by the Foster Care Ombudsman, an independent resource to investigate complaints, concerns, or violation of rights for children in the custody of Oregon DHS Foster Care.
- **2015**, a bill that ensures that foster youth 12 years or older receive direct assistance from DHS in establishing their own savings accounts.
- **2015**, a bill that ensures that the Oregon DHS and foster parents work together to support youth in joining at least one ongoing extracurricular activity.
- **2017**, Sibling Bill of Rights legislation, which ensures that youth in care are supported in preserving and strengthening relationships with their siblings.

Final Thoughts

In summary, this chapter demonstrates that in every social work field of practice, there are opportunities to impact the legislative process at multiple levels from the local level to the international level. Some social workers prefer to work locally, while others enjoy working on the national or international stage. This is good news for social workers because it provides an array of opportunities to choose from in their ongoing work to effect positive change of behalf of the individuals and families they serve.

REFERENCES

Adamson, P. (2013). Child well-being in rich countries: A comparative overview. Innocenti Report Card no. 11. Unicef. Retrieved from https://www.unicef-irc.org/publications/683-child-well-being-in-rich-countries-a-comparative-overview.html

Child Rights Campaign. (n.d.a). About the campaign. Retrieved from http://www.childrightscampaign.org/about

Child Rights Campaign. (n.d.b). Themes of the child rights convention (n.d.). Retrieved from http://www.childrightscampaign.org/what-is-the-crc/the-themes-of-the-crc

Child Rights Campaign. (n.d.c). What is the CRC? Retrieved from http://www.childrightscampaign.org/what-is-the-crc

Child Rights International Network. (n.d.). *What we do.* Retrieved from https://www.crin.org/en/home/what-we-do

Children's Defense Fund. (2020). The state of America's children 2020. Retrieved from https://www.childrensdefense.org/the-state-of-americas-children-2020/

Cohen, R. A., Terlizzi, E. P., & Martinez, E. P. (2019). *Health insurance coverage: Early release of estimates from the National Health Interview Survey, 2018*. U.S. Department of Health and Human Services. Centers for Disease Control and Prevention. National Center for Health Statistics. Retrieved from https://www.cdc.gov/nchs/data/nhis/earlyrelease/insur201905.pdf

DeParle, J. (2021, March 7). In the stimulus bill, a policy revolution in aid for children. *New York Times*. Retrieved from https://www.nytimes.com/2021/03/07/us/politics/child-tax-credit-stimulus.html

Kaplan, K. (2018, January 8). Why the United States is 'the most dangerous of wealthy nations for a child to be born into.' *LA Times*. Retrieved from http://www.latimes.com/science/sciencenow/la-sci-sn-childhood-mortality-usa-20180108-story.html

Kempe, C. H., Silverman, F. N., Steele, B. F., Droegemueller, W., & Silver, H. K. (1962). The battered child syndrome. *Journal of American Medical Association*, *181*, 105–112.

Home School Legal Defense Association. (2002, May 3). United Nations special session on children set to meet. Retrieved from http://www.hslda.org/docs/nche/000010/200205060.asp

Organisation for Economic Co-operation and Development (OECD). Family database. Child poverty. Retrieved from http://www.oecd.org/els/soc/CO_2_2_Child_Poverty.pdf

Senate Briefing on Juvenile Justice (n.d.). Retrieved from https://web.archive.org/web/20101212165642/http://childrightscampaign.org/crcindex.php?sNav=events_snav.php&sDat=briefing07_dat.php

Senate Resolution 133. Library of Congress (THOMAS). Retrieved from http://thomas.loc.gov/cgi-bin/query/z?c104:S.RES.133

Summit for the Convention on the Rights of the Child. (n.d.). Retrieved from https://web.archive.org/web/20101212165438/http:/childrightscampaign.org/crcindex.php?sNav=events_snav.php&sDat=summit_dat.php

Thakrar, A. P., Forrest, A. D., Maltenfort, M. G., & Forrest, C. B. (2018). Child mortality in the US and 19 OECD comparator nations: A 50-year time-trend analysis. *Health Affairs*, *37*(1). Retrieved from https://www.healthaffairs.org/doi/abs/10.1377/hlthaff.2017.0767

U.S. Department of Health & Human Services, Administration for Children and Families, Administration on Children, Youth and Families, Children's Bureau. (2020). Child maltreatment 2018. Retrieved from https://www.acf.hhs.gov/cb/resource/child-maltreatment-2018

CHAPTER 10　Aging Policy and Advocacy

"Death is not the greatest of evils; it is worse to want to die, and not be able to."

         ~Sophocles, Greek playwright

Figure 10.1　Maggie Kuhn, founder of the Gray Panthers

CHAPTER SUMMARY

Social workers who work in the field of aging know firsthand the many challenges faced by individuals as they grow older and leave the work-force. The coronavirus pandemic put a spotlight on adults 65 years and older, because they were one of the populations most at risk of illness and death and many live in congregate, residential settings. As a result, they were prioritized when the vaccines came out. However, in contrast to children, seniors are a strong and organized voting bloc with the ability to mobilize and advocate for themselves in the social and political spheres. According to the Administration on Aging (2020), in 2018 the number of adults age 65 and older was 52.4 million, or approximately one in seven Americans. This was an increase of 35% over the previous decade. The proportion of older adults in the United States will continue to grow in the coming years as the baby boomers continue to retire en masse. Current estimates indicate that in 2040 there will be about 80.8 million older persons, more than twice as many as in 2000, with the number of older adults reaching 94.7 million by 2060. This is one of the nation's most pressing social issues; the "graying of America" will soon begin to stress federal programs such as Social Security and Medicare that are set up to meet the needs of older Americans. Social Security is the most expensive social program in the United States and has been successful in keeping millions of older Americans out of poverty in their old age. This chapter will explore whether the Social Security program is in crisis and possible policy solutions.

Policymakers need to carefully consider whether current programs will be able to meet the needs of these new retirees, and social workers certainly have an important role to play in these policy discussions. Potential problems facing older adults include lack of income security and poverty; deteriorating health, including mental health; the need for affordable housing and caregiver support; elder abuse; discrimination in the workplace; and issues of death and dying, which is the focus of this chapter. Each of these is an opportunity for advocates to help address the needs of older adults in the legislative arena.

This chapter will profile a successful policy change effort by a professional campaign. It will also provide an opportunity for readers to examine their own values and beliefs in relation to an issue that is controversial and complex. The Death with Dignity Act is a good example of an issue that divides Americans who have different views about whether people should have the right to end their life with a physician's assistance when they have a terminal or debilitating illness. Oregon was the first U.S. state to have a physician-assisted death law, and since then seven other states (Washington, Maine, Vermont, California, Colorado, Hawaii, and New Jersey) and Washington, D.C., have legalized it. These state laws are part of a larger right-to-die movement that advocates on behalf of individuals' right to die with dignity and to make their own end-of-life decisions.

STUDENT LEARNING OBJECTIVES

- Students will be able to summarize challenges experienced by older adults in the United States that require a policy solution.

- Students will be able to describe advocacy efforts in the United States that led to the development of social programs that are designed to support people 65 years and older.

○ Students will be able to describe the major features of the Death with Dignity Act (DWDA).

○ Students will be able to evaluate the political advocacy efforts of the advocates who fought to pass the DWDA in Washington State.

○ Students will be able to analyze the arguments in favor of, and opposed to, the DWDA.

S ocial workers who work in the field of aging know firsthand the many challenges faced by individuals as they grow older and leave the workforce. The coronavirus pandemic put a spotlight on adults 65 years and older because they are one of the populations most at risk of illness and death due to the virus and many live in congregate, supportive residential settings. Social workers work with older adults (defined as people older than 65 years) in a variety of settings, such as health care, hospice and palliative care, and residential care. Healthcare problems such as heart disease, obesity, cancer, and dementia grow more common as people age. Some older adults experience economic insecurity after they stop working. Seniors are vulnerable to elder abuse and exploitation. The need for caregiving increases with age, and older adults must face important decisions regarding end-of-life care. As a society, we continue to grapple with how to best respond to the needs of older adults via social welfare legislation that promotes their **dignity**, **independence,** and **self-determination** as much as possible. However, in contrast to children, senior citizens are a strong and organized voting bloc with the ability to mobilize and advocate for themselves in the social and political spheres. This chapter will highlight advocacy efforts that have led to an incredible array of legislation and programs designed to protect the rights and well-being of older adults in the United States, including the rights of terminally ill patients to end their life.

There has been a lot of media coverage about the "graying of America," which refers to the demographic shift where a higher proportion of the U.S. population consists of older adults, in part due to longer **life expectancy** and decreasing fertility rates. According to the Administration on Aging (2020), in 2018 the number of adults age 65 and older was 52.4 million, or approximately one in seven Americans. This was an increase of 35% over the previous decade. The proportion of older adults in the United States will continue to grow in the coming years as the baby boomers continue to retire en masse. Current estimates indicate that in 2040 there will be about 80.8 million older persons, more than twice as many as in 2000, and that the number of older adults will reach 94.7 million by 2060. Additionally, those who are 85 and older are projected to more than double from 6.5 million in 2018 to 14.4 million in 2040, a 123% increase. Older women outnumbered older men in 2018 (29.1 million to 23.3 million) (Administration on Aging, 2020).

This is one of the country's most pressing social issues, because the "graying of America" will soon begin to stress federal programs such as Social Security and Medicare that are set up to meet the needs of older Americans. Social Security is the most expensive social program in the United States and has been successful in keeping millions of older

Americans out of poverty in their old age. Policymakers will need to carefully consider whether current social programs are able to meet the needs of these new retirees, and social workers certainly have an important role to play in these policy discussions.

Problems Faced by Older Adults

Potential problems facing older adults include lack of income security; deteriorating health, including mental health; the need for affordable housing and caregiver support; elder abuse; discrimination in the workplace; and issues surrounding death and dying, a major focus of this chapter. Each of these is an opportunity for advocates to help address the needs of older adults in the legislative arena. Even though the Social Security program lifts millions of older Americans above the poverty line, approximately 9% of older adults were below the poverty line in 2018, nearly 1 in 10. The median income for older adults was $34,267 for males and $20,431 for females, a significant gender disparity (Administration on Aging, 2020). Social Security is a major source of income for the majority of seniors.

Most people older than 65 years have at least one chronic health condition, and many have multiple conditions. The top five chronic conditions for older Americans in recent years were arthritis (54%), heart disease (28%), diabetes (28%), cancer (19%), and stroke (9%). Some type of disability was reported by 34% of adults older than 65 years (e.g., hearing, vision, cognition, ambulation). Obesity is also a major concern for older adults; from 2013 to 2016, more than 60% of adults age 55 and older were overweight or obese. Older adults face challenges with regard to the need for **caregiving**. Data show that 33% of people older than 65 years needed help with personal care in 2018. In addition, some older adults must be the caregiver to a spouse or other family member, such as a grandchild, which can take an emotional toll (Administration on Aging, 2020).

In most states, **elder abuse** must be reported to the authorities by law, and elder abuse allegations are investigated similar to child abuse allegations. The primary difference is that older adults have more autonomy and decision-making power in adult protective services cases, whereas in child protection cases the "best interests of the child" are decided by the caseworkers and other legal officials. Elder abuse includes physical abuse, sexual abuse, psychological abuse, neglect, abandonment, and financial exploitation. It is difficult to know the true prevalence of elder abuse because it is greatly underreported and no national data are collected. However, one study found the prevalence to be 10% and that the perpetrators are most likely to be spouses and adult children (Lachs & Pillemer, 2015). Older adults can also be abused and/or neglected in nursing homes and long-term care facilities.

Timeline of Older Adult Advocacy in the United States

- **1935**, Social Security Act of 1935 passed.
- **1954**, American Society on Aging founded.

- **1958**, American Association of Retired Persons founded.
- **1961**, first White House Conference on Aging.
- **1965**, Medicare and Medicaid established as part of the Social Security Act.
- **1965**, Older Americans Act passed by Congress to help each state develop a comprehensive and coordinated network that would provide services, opportunities, and protections for older Americans to help them maintain health and independence in their homes and to be able to continue to function as a part of their community.
- **1965**, Administration on Aging established by the Older Americans Act
- **1967**, Age Discrimination in Employment Act.
- **1970**, Gray Panthers founded by Maggie Kuhn.
- **1972**, National Senior Citizens Law Center (fights senior poverty) (renamed Justice in Aging).
- **1974**, broad language in Title XX of the Social Security Act in 1974 gave permission for states to use Social Services Block Grant (SSBG) funds for the protection of adults as well as children (Adult Protective Services).
- **1978**, SAGE founded (advocacy for LGBT older adults).
- **1980**, Alzheimer's Association formed,
- **1988**, National Center on Elder Abuse established by the Administration on Aging.
- **1994**, Oregon's Death with Dignity Act.
- **2008**, Washington State's Death with Dignity Act.
- **2010**, Elder Justice Act.
- **2015**, White House Conference on Aging.

Policies and Programs Impacting Older Adults

The Social Security Program

Perhaps the most significant piece of legislation impacting the lives of older adults is the **Social Security Act of 1935**, which created the Social Security program. Social Security is a federal entitlement program and is the most expensive social program in the United States, requiring roughly one-quarter of the total federal budget. According to the Social Security Administration (2019), at the end of 2018, 62.9 million people received Social Security benefits, totaling $988 billion. The Social Security system is actually called the **OASDI program**, which stands for Old Age, Survivors and Disability. At the end of 2018, this program served 46 million retired workers and dependents of retired workers, almost six million survivors of deceased workers, and 10 million disabled workers and dependents of disabled workers.

The philosophy of the program centers on the idea of an **intergenerational compact** whereby current workers in the workforce contribute to a program that funds the retirement of former workers who are now retired. It is an insurance program that insures people against their own poverty after they leave the workforce. Tax revenues for the Social

Security program come from the FICA payroll tax that is split evenly between employers and employees, and the money goes into the Social Security trust fund, where it earns interest. When you retire, your benefits are in proportion to your contribution. Retirement benefit calculations are based on one's average earnings during a lifetime of work under the Social Security system. Social Security was meant to be part of a three-legged stool (personal savings, pension, and Social Security) that Americans relied on after their retirement, but for many reasons, most people rely on Social Security as a major source of income after leaving the workforce. For most current and future retirees, one's 35 highest years of earnings are averaged. According to the Social Security Administration (2019), the average monthly payment for retired workers at the end of 2018 was $1,461 a month, whereas the maximum payment for a worker retiring at age 66 in 2018 was about $2,788 a month. According to the Organisation for Economic Co-operation and Development (OECD), the United States ranks in the bottom third of developed nations with regard to social security payments. The top five countries are Italy, Luxembourg, Austria, Portugal, and Denmark (Van de Water & Romig, 2020).

The Social Security system has been touted as one of the country's most effective social welfare programs for many reasons. Because Social Security is the major source of income for a majority of retirees, it successfully keeps millions of older adults above the poverty line. The program has significantly reduced poverty rates among older adults (lowered from about 40% to 10% over the past 50 years). It is a very efficient program because it costs less than one cent per dollar to administer the program. It helps the unemployment rate because when older adults leave the workforce there are more jobs for younger workers, and it helps the economy because senior citizens remain viable consumers. It takes the financial burden away from the children and grandchildren who otherwise would be responsible for the financial support of their aging parents and/or grandparents. There is no stigma due to collecting Social Security because all Americans participate and benefit from this social program. Finally, the program adjusts for inflation, and the benefits are portable from job to job.

Americans are living much longer than they did when the program was first devised during the 1930s. Increasingly, Americans have been hearing about the "crisis" of the Social Security system due to the current and impending retirement of millions of baby boomers, which will cause financial stress to the Social Security system. For many years, the Social Security system collected more tax revenues than needed to pay benefits and was able to put the additional funds into an interest-bearing trust fund for reserve spending. Social Security is "healthy" when there is enough funding at the beginning of the year to pay out all of the benefits owed for that year. Since the beginning of the program, this has not been a problem; in fact, in most years until recently, collected taxes have been sufficient to pay for the program and there have been significant surpluses in the trust fund. In 2019, for example, OASDI had a balance of $2.9 trillion and owed $1,048 billion in benefits (Social Security Administration, 2020). For this reason, the U.S. government sometimes borrows money from the Social Security trust fund when it is running a deficit.

However, current projections estimate that the trust fund will begin to have a budget shortfall in the coming years due to demographic factors such as declines in fertility rates among current workers and increases in life expectancy. As a result, there will be too few workers in the workforce compared to those who are retired, which is referred to as the dependency ratio. The **dependency ratio** is the ratio of current workers in the workforce to beneficiaries. For example, in 1950, there were 16 workers for every 1 person on Social Security. The ratio is projected to drop to 2.3 to 1 by 2035 (Congressional Research Service, 2020). Unless something is done, in the not too distant future the Social Security trust fund will not have enough funding to pay out to its beneficiaries, and the trust fund will be depleted by 2035. Beginning in 2010, Social Security began dipping into the trust fund in order to pay scheduled benefits. According to a recent congressional report, "In 2021, Social Security's cost is projected to exceed total income (i.e., tax revenues plus interest income). Trust fund reserves are projected to decline steadily from their peak of $2.9 trillion to zero in 2035. Following the depletion of trust fund reserves, scheduled tax revenues are projected to be sufficient to pay 79% of scheduled benefits initially, declining to 73% by 2094" (Congressional Research Service, 2020).

Thus, policymakers will need to make some tough choices in order to keep the Social Security program solvent, some of which will be more popular than others with Americans. Potential options include: decreasing benefits for retirees, raising the retirement age, raising the payroll tax, eliminating the earning ceiling, which taxes only the first $137,700 that individuals make (this means that for someone earning $10 million a year, only his or her first $137,700 is taxed), and cutting wealthier Americans off from collecting at all (i.e., creating a means test). Some conservatives have advocated privatizing the Social Security system, but this has not been popular with a majority of Americans who are fearful about a program that relies on investments in the stock market. Thus, the good news is that there are a number of ways to save the Social Security program, but strong leadership will be needed to find the right solution.

Medicare Program

In some ways, the Medicare program goes hand in hand with the Social Security program because both programs are designed to support people over the age of 65. The Medicare program was started in 1965 and signed into law by President Lyndon B. Johnson. Most people ages 65 and over are entitled to Medicare Part A if they or their spouse are eligible for Social Security payments and have paid payroll taxes for 10 or more years. Most Americans have paid into Medicare via the FICA payroll tax; thus, like Social Security, it is a social insurance program. In 1972, the program was expanded to cover people under 65 who have permanent disabilities.

According to Kaiser Family Foundation (KFF), while there is a two-year waiting period for those under 65 with permanent disabilities, those diagnosed with end-stage renal disease (ESRD) and amyotrophic lateral sclerosis (ALS) become eligible for Medicare with no waiting period. The program helps seniors to pay for "many medical care services, including hospitalizations, physician visits, and prescription drugs, along with post-acute care, skilled nursing facility care, home health care, hospice care, and preventive services" (Kasier Family Foundation, 2017). However, due to gaps in coverage, deductibles, and out-of-pocket expenses, many older Americans must purchase supplemental health insurance to help cover these costs and fill in the gaps. Some older Americans are also covered by the Medicaid program that is designed to provide health coverage for low-income Americans. After Social Security, Medicare is the next most expensive federal program, representing approximately 15% of the total federal budget.

Older Americans Act of 1965

The Older Americans Act (OAA), signed into law by President Lyndon B. Johnson, was a groundbreaking piece of legislation for older adults. The spirit of the law was to provide a range of home-based and community-based supportive services to older adults to promote independence, "aging in place," and remaining engaged citizens of their community. It also established the Administration on Aging. The original **10 objectives** identified in Title I of the Older Americans Act recognized the rights of older persons to:

- An adequate income
- The best possible physical and mental health
- Suitable housing
- Full restorative services
- Employment without age discrimination
- Retirement in health, honor, and dignity
- Participation in civic, cultural and recreational activities
- Opportunities for community service
- Immediate benefit from research
- Freedom and independence

Programs offered to seniors (many of whom are homebound) include meals-on-wheels and other nutrition programs, in-home services, transportation, legal services, elder abuse prevention, and caregiver support. It is also based on the idea that if you can provide supportive services to older adults in their home, it will be much cheaper than nursing home care and hospitalization. According to the Administration for Community Living (n.d.):

> The OAA is considered to be a major vehicle for the organization and delivery of social and nutrition services to this group and their caregivers. It authorizes a wide array of service programs through a national network of 56 state agencies on aging, 629 area agencies on aging, nearly 20,000 service providers, 244 Tribal organizations, and 2 Native Hawaiian organizations representing 400 Tribes.

The OAA has been reauthorized through fiscal year 2019. Each state receives OAA funds according to a formula based on the state's share of the U.S. population age 60 and older; however, many experts assert that the funding has not kept pace with the growth of the older adult population. See the Activist Spotlight for a profile of activist Maggie Kuhn, who founded the Gray Panthers.

Activist Spotlight: Maggie Kuhn, Gray Panthers

It is a shame that more Americans are not familiar with Maggie Kuhn, a pioneer and founder of the Gray Panthers. Kuhn founded the Gray Panthers (inspired by the Black Panthers) after she was let go from her job at the age of 65, the mandatory retirement age at the time. She had been a champion of social causes long before her work with the Gray Panthers, but this work made her famous. Her work with the Gray Panthers focused on the issue of age discrimination, and this group successfully lobbied against the mandatory retirement age, which the U.S. Congress eliminated in 1986. Since 1977, the Gray Panthers have lobbied on behalf of a healthcare system paid by the government. According to Kuhn (1974),

> The Gray Panthers can best be described simply as a rapidly growing network of people old and young drawn together by deeply felt concerns for human liberation and social change. The old and young live outside the mainstream of society. Agism—discrimination against persons on the basis of chronological age—deprives both groups of power and influence. The Gray Panthers believe that the old and the young have much to contribute to make our society more just and humane, and that each needs to reinforce the other in goals, strategy, and action.

Maggie Kuhn died at the age of 89.
Source: Gray Panthers New York City. (1974). The Gray Panthers movement. Retrieved from http://www.graypanthersnyc.org/gray-panthers-movement--.pdf

Elder Justice Act (2010)

The Elder Justice Act is regarded as the most comprehensive federal legislation ever passed to combat elder abuse, neglect, and exploitation via Adult Protective Services (APS). It was signed into law by President Obama as part of the Affordable Care Act after advocates, such as the Elder Justice Coalition, fought for more than a decade for its passage. The act authorizes millions of dollars in federal funding to local and state APS programs and to implement other aspects of the bill. Historically, federal funding for APS agencies has lagged behind Child Protective Services (CPS) programs due to child abuse being more visible than elder abuse. The primary goal of the law is to better coordinate responses to elder abuse across federal and state agencies and to ramp up efforts to better detect and prevent elder abuse in the United States. The act also provides grant funding to support the development of elder abuse forensic centers and clarifies reporting requirements as well as penalties for failing to report elder abuse. Advocates must now monitor the legislation to ensure that funds are being appropriated as hoped.

End-of-Life Policies

When many people think about working for social change, they often visualize grassroots movements that are low in financial resources but high in passion and "people" resources. Many social workers have been a part of one of these efforts at the local or national level. However, some policy change efforts are well financed, and social workers may be hired to work on a professional campaign that is charged with getting a policy passed into law. This requires a skillset that involves the ability to (1) frame an issue in a way that resonates with lawmakers and the public and (2) communicate that message effectively and persuasively. This chapter will profile a successful policy change effort by a professional campaign. It will also provide an opportunity for readers to examine their own values and beliefs in relation to an issue that is quite controversial and complex.

Some political issues are much more controversial than others. In recent years, conversations about **end-of-life care** have entered the national discourse, and this topic is being discussed more frequently than ever before, perhaps due to the impending retirement of millions of baby boomers. End-of-life care is a broad term that encompasses a range of issues such as living wills, advance directives, pain management (also referred to as palliative care), hospice care, do not resuscitate orders, who can make decisions for those who lack decision-making capacity (i.e., durable power of attorney), and how to help people live out their final years with dignity. It is important to understand the difference between palliative care and hospice care. **Hospice care** is provided to patients who have six months or less to live. They are provided a range of services such as pain relief, nursing care, and emotional and spiritual support. **Palliative care** is not subject to any time restrictions and is focused on pain management to ensure that the patient suffers as little as possible.

Americans saw firsthand how heated this issue can be when it emerged as a hot topic during the debate over healthcare reform under President Obama. A provision of the massive healthcare bill would have required the Medicare program to reimburse healthcare practitioners when consulting with patients on end-of-life care. Former vice presidential candidate Sarah Palin took to Facebook and referred to this provision as "death panels" made up of government bureaucrats who would have the power to decide who should live and who should die. Although the myth that the provision would encourage euthanasia was debunked by a number of reputable fact check sites and news organizations, it caught on like wildfire and was soon used by some Republicans to scare older adults in their efforts to denounce the new healthcare reform legislation. Due to the controversy, Democrats were forced to drop the provision from the healthcare bill, but the Obama administration later achieved the same goal through a new Medicare regulation that went into effect on January 1, 2011.

The Death with Dignity Act

The **Death with Dignity Act** is a good example of an issue that divides Americans who have different views about whether someone should have the right to end their life with a physician's assistance when they have a terminal or debilitating illness. Oregon was the first U.S. state to have a physician-assisted death law, and since then seven other states (Washington, Maine, Vermont, California, Colorado, Hawaii, and New Jersey) and Washington, D.C., have legalized it. These laws are part of a larger **right-to-die movement** that advocates on behalf of an individual's right to die with dignity and to make his or her own end-of-life decisions. The debate not only concerns what the laws should be, but also what terminology should be used. Many right-to-die activists prefer the terms *physician-assisted death*, *physician aid-in-dying* (**PAD**), or *hastened death* over *physician-assisted suicide*, which they see as a politically loaded term used by the opposition. (Note: For the rest of this chapter, PAD will be used.) Opponents of these laws include the American Medical Association, the Catholic Church, pro-life Christian organizations, and disability advocacy groups. PAD is legal in a few other countries, such as Belgium, Luxembourg, the Netherlands, and Switzerland, but this debate is far from over in the United States.

What Is the Difference Between Euthanasia and Physician Aid-in-Dying?

It depends on *who* performs the last act.
- **Euthanasia:** A third party performs the act that hastens the patient's death (e.g., patient given a lethal injection).
- **Physician aid-in-dying:** The person who dies hastens his or her own death (e.g., swallows an overdose of drugs) with the assistance of a physician.

What Was the Impetus Behind the Death with Dignity Act?

The aid-in-dying movement is a fascinating story of a diverse range of committed individuals determined to change U.S. laws that govern whether, and under what circumstances, individuals have the right to end their life with the assistance of a medical professional. A number of organizations were formed to further their cause, such as the Hemlock Society, Compassion in Dying, Compassion & Choices, and the Death with Dignity National Center (see Advocacy Spotlight: End of Life). Members of these organizations typically include citizens who are directly affected by this issue, scholars, and medical and legal experts. Right-to-die activist Dr. Jack Kevorkian, and former Washington Governor Booth Gardner are examples of prominent citizens who have become the public face of this issue. A right-to-die bill was first introduced in the Florida legislature in 1967, and the Hemlock Society was formed in 1980. Oregon passed the Death with Dignity Act in 1994, and it took until 2008 for another state (Washington) to join Oregon. This is yet another example of how some policy change efforts take a long time until a legislative victory is achieved. Thus, advocates often have to be patient and work year after year to raise awareness until attitudes change and a tipping point is reached.

Advocacy Spotlight: End of Life

The following two organizations work to enable people to make their own decisions regarding their end-of-life care, including policies that allow individuals under certain circumstances to hasten their own death. Please visit their websites to learn more.

Death with Dignity National Center (www.deathwithdignity.org)
Compassion & Choices (www.compassionandchoices.org)

What Is the Death with Dignity Act?

Seven U.S. states and Washington, D.C., have a Death with Dignity Act. Oregon was the first state to pass such a law, and other states have based their law on Oregon's statute because it is considered model legislation. The law allows terminally ill patients to obtain a prescription from their physician for a lethal dose of medication. The medication must be self-administered. People unable to use the law include those with debilitating illnesses that are not terminal, such as Parkinson's disease, anyone deemed not mentally competent to make this decision, and those who are unable to self-administer the medication (e.g., those with paralysis).

According to the Oregon Health Authority (n.d.), to use the Oregon law, a patient must be 18 years of age or older, an Oregon resident, able to make and communicate their own healthcare decisions, and diagnosed with a terminal illness with six months or less to live. A patient must provide the attending physician proof of Oregon residency. There is no minimum residency requirement. The attending physician must decide whether these criteria have been met.

The Oregon law requires that the patient:

- Make two verbal requests—separated by 15 days—to the physician,
- Make a written request to the attending physician, and the request is witnessed by two individuals who are not primary caregivers or family members,
- Is able to rescind the verbal and written requests at any time, and
- Is able to self-administer the prescription (lethal dose of medication is ingested).

The law further requires that:

- The attending physician must be Oregon-licensed.
- The physician's diagnosis must include terminal illness, with 6 months or less to live.
- The diagnosis must be certified by a consulting physician, who must also certify that the patient is mentally competent to make and communicate healthcare decisions.
- If either physician determines that the patient's judgment is impaired, the patient must be referred for a psychological examination.

- The attending physician must inform the patient of alternatives, including palliative care, hospice, and pain management options.
- The attending physician must request that the patient notify his or her next-of-kin of the prescription request.

The Oregon Department of Human Services (DHS) enforces compliance with the law. Physicians are required by law to report all lethal prescriptions to DHS. Physicians and patients who comply with the law are protected from criminal prosecution. The use of the Death with Dignity Act cannot affect the status of a patient's health or life insurance policies. Physicians and healthcare systems are not obligated to participate in Oregon's Death with Dignity Act (DWDA).

One of the criticisms of the act was that people from other states would move to Oregon to use the law to hasten their death. This same accusation gets leveled at countries like Switzerland where the term **suicide tourism** has been coined to describe the phenomenon of people who visit another country in order to take advantage of a PAD law. However, this does not seem to be the case in Oregon. According to the Oregon Health Authority, Public Health Division (2019), 2,518 terminally-ill patients have used the Oregon law to hasten their own deaths since the law was passed in 1997. In 2019, 188 people died from ingesting medication prescribed by the DWDA. Approximately 75% were aged 65 years or older and 96% were White. Most patients had cancer (68%), neurological disease (14%) and respiratory disease (7%). The majority of patients (94%) died at home, and most (90%) were enrolled in hospice care. The three most frequently reported end-of-life concerns were decreasing ability to participate in activities that made life enjoyable (90%), loss of autonomy (87%), and loss of dignity (82%). The time from ingestion to death ranged from 1 minute to 47 hours, and the median was 51 minutes.

The Controversy over the Death with Dignity Act

Earlier in this book, the role of values in the political process was discussed, and the fact that many of the positions that people take on various political issues stem from their personal values or belief system. This is particularly true when it comes to the debate over PAD. This debate has religious overtones, and much of the opposition comes from the Catholic Church and various prolife organizations that oppose the Death with Dignity Act on moral grounds. The opposition of the Catholic Church is clearly explained in the *Catechism of the Catholic Church* (#2277), which condemns "an act or omission which, of itself or by intention, causes death in order to eliminate suffering." Many Catholic Church leaders remind their flock that human life is sacred and of the commandment "Thou shall not kill." The Catholic Church poured large sums of money into the 2008 Death with Dignity campaign in Washington State in its efforts to defeat the measure.

Despite the fact that many physicians support this act, the medical establishment does not. Some physicians believe that PAD violates the Hippocratic Oath. The state medical associations in most states oppose PAD, as does the AMA. During the debate over the Death with Dignity Act in Washington State in 2008, the president of the Washington State

Medical Association stated that PAD is dangerous and "fundamentally incompatible with the role of physicians as healers" (Washington State Medical Association, 2008).

Another argument that is used to oppose the Death with Dignity Act is that the law will be abused by doctors and healthcare workers, and that individuals from certain vulnerable or oppressed groups will be disproportionately targeted. In particular, concerns have been raised about patients with mental health conditions such as clinical depression, and groups who may be more prone to ending their life in order to avoid being a burden to their families, such as women and those with serious disabilities. The overriding fear is that certain lives are deemed as less valuable or worthy than others. Many **disability rights groups** have entered the fray in opposing Death with Dignity state laws. One such group is a national organization named Not Dead Yet.

About Not Dead Yet

The organization Not Dead Yet strongly opposes legalized physician aid-in-dying and the euthanasia movement. The organization was founded in 1996, shortly after physician Jack Kevorkian was acquitted in the physician assisted deaths of two women. They take credit for helping to put Kevorkian behind bars in 1999. In 2003–2005, alongside other national disability rights groups, they fought to save Terri Schiavo and opposed her guardian's "right to starve and dehydrate her to death."

Proponents of the Death with Dignity Act are just as passionate as the opposition. Most advocates believe it is cruel and inhumane to let people suffer a slow, painful death. They frame the issue as "death with dignity" because many have the experience of witnessing the passing of a loved one who was not allowed to die in a dignified manner. After the passage of the Death with Dignity Act in Washington, the president of Compassion & Choices, Barbara Coombs Lee, exclaimed that the new law was "a turning point on the path to human liberty." She went on to say, "No terminal Washingtonian will ever have to shoot themselves or use other violent means again. We hope someday to be able to say the same for patients in the other 48 states" (Compassion & Choices, 2008).

Advocates also believe that it should be an individual's right or choice to determine when life has become too unbearable and to end his or her suffering. They cite freedom of religion and decry the fact that certain religious institutions would force their beliefs onto others who do not share those same beliefs. However, like any social movement, not every member has the same opinions and perspective, and a small number of members have views that would be considered more radical. The right to die movement is a broad movement, and the Death with Dignity movement is a subset of this movement. For instance, some advocates do not believe that the current Death with Dignity state laws go far enough and believe that people who are depressed should be able to end their life with assistance. Others, such as the **Final Exit Network**, support the idea that it is a basic human right to end one's life when that individual's quality of life has been seriously threatened (e.g., individual does not have to be diagnosed with a terminal illness). They believe this is an individual choice that should not be restricted by "the law, clergy, medical profession, even friends and relatives no matter how well intentioned" (visit www.finalexitnetwork.org).

When visiting the websites of the various right-to-die organizations, you will find personal testimonies of those with a terminal illness who are desperate for the right to hasten their death, as well as family members who have had to witness the prolonged suffering of a loved one. Compassion & Choices (2009) issued a press release about the first patient in Washington State, Linda Fleming, to use the Death with Dignity Act:

> Linda Fleming of Sequim, Washington was stunned last month to receive a terminal diagnosis of advanced pancreatic cancer. "I had only recently learned how to live in the world as I had always wanted to, and now I will no longer be here." With deep regret and firm conviction, Linda's life ended May 21st on the terms she chose. She was the first Washington resident to die using the choices offered under Washington's recently passed Death with Dignity law. Linda worked with her physician and with Compassion & Choices Client Support volunteers to carefully consider her choices and make her end-of-life decisions. "I am a very spiritual person," Linda explained, "and it was very important to me to be conscious, clear-minded and alert at the time of my death. The powerful pain medications were making it difficult to maintain the state of mind I wanted to have at my death. And I knew I would have to increase them." On a spring evening, in her home, Linda took her prescribed medication with her family, her physician and her dog at her bedside.

The right to-die-movement is also full of physicians, scholars, and church leaders who believe strongly in a patient's right to die with the aid of a physician. Perhaps the most famous and controversial right-to-die activist was **Dr. Jack Kevorkian** who served eight years in prison for euthanizing a patient (read Dr. Kevorkian's story below). He died in 2011. His detractors called him "Doctor Death." He believed that the U.S. government's opposition to PAD is tyrannical. Dr. Kevorkian was critical of the Death with Dignity Act, a law in his view that does not go far enough because it excludes people who cannot administer the legal drugs themselves. Many right-to-die activists view Dr. Kevorkian as a controversial renegade and are quick to point out that he would be prosecuted under the Death with Dignity Act since he violated many of the safeguards and protocols of this law.

Dr. Jack Kevorkian

Most Americans know the name Dr. Kevorkian. He is either famous or infamous, depending on your viewpoint. Dr. Kevorkian was the first doctor in the United States to become known for his advocacy of a patient's right to die. He steadfastly believed that it is a physician's role to help people live, but also to help them die when it is their wish or desire. In his heyday, he was on the cover of major magazines like *Time Magazine*, interviewed by journalists such as Barbara Walters, and featured on news programs like *60 Minutes*. Over the course of his career, he helped 130 patients hasten their death and was tried in court several times for these actions. His medical license was revoked as well. He was always acquitted of the charges in court until he helped Thomas Youk, a patient who was suffering from Lou Gehrig's disease. In each of Kevorkian's cases, the patients administered the medication themselves, but with Youk, Kevorkian administered the lethal injection himself (with the consent of the patient and the patient's family). He then went on *60 Minutes* where the footage of Mr. Youk's hastened death was shown on national television. He was quickly charged with first-degree murder, yet the jury found him guilty of second-degree homicide. The judge sentenced Kevorkian to serve 10 to 25 years in prison, but he was released after eight years for good behavior. Upon his release, he vowed to stop his practice of physician aid-in-dying and to instead work toward the decriminalization of this practice in the United States. In 2008, Kevorkian ran for the U.S. Congress in Michigan as an Independent but did not win the election. An HBO movie about his life called *You Don't Know Jack* aired in 2010, with Oscar-winning actor Al Pacino playing the title role.

Former Washington Governor Booth Gardner initially made statements that he views the Death with Dignity Act as a first step because he would be unable to take advantage of the law but cannot because he has Parkinson's disease, a debilitating disease that is not terminal. Some in this movement, such as Derek Humphry, look forward to the day when the Death with Dignity laws include more people who in his view are deserving of assisted dying, such as the law in the Netherlands that permits lethal prescriptions for those whose suffering is unbearable. Humphry is an important and influential person in the right-to-die movement because he was the founder of the Hemlock Society in 1980 and has published many books on the topic, including the controversial and bestselling book *Final Exit*, published in 1991.

Practice Exercise 10.1

In your opinion, how should a social worker handle the following situation: Martha is a social worker in a medical clinic in Washington State where the Death with Dignity Act is law. She has a terminally ill male client who wants her help to begin the process of learning about this law and making a decision on whether or not he would like to use it to hasten his own death. The patient would like Martha's support throughout this process because he does not have many friends and his relationships with his grown children are strained. However, due to her religious beliefs, Martha does not agree with PAD, and she feels very strongly about this. As a professional social worker, what are Martha's ethical obligations to her patient in this scenario? Given that her personal and professional values are in conflict, how can she best sort this out?

How the Death with Dignity Act Became Law

Some policies consist of minor tweaks or changes to existing laws. The Death with Dignity Act, however, is an example of what we might refer to as landmark legislation or a groundbreaking policy change effort. This act has the power to radically change the way society thinks about and responds to terminally ill people who wish to hasten their death with the aid of a medical professional. These kinds of change efforts can take many decades before progress is made in order to change public opinion and build a movement that is able to take on more powerful interests. When the time is right, a number of possible strategies must be considered. Should advocates try to get a bill passed at the federal level? Should they try to get a bill passed at the state level? Would it make sense to use the judicial system by filing a lawsuit? How about a ballot measure and letting the voters decide? Which approach is most feasible?

Oregon's Death with Dignity Act (ODWDA)

The story begins in Oregon, in the early 1990s, when the first Death with Dignity Act was developed by a group of Oregonians with a strong interest in changing the law. These advocates were able to learn from the experiences of two other states that lost their battles, Washington State in 1991 and California in 1992. In these two states, voters were voting on whether to allow euthanasia by lethal injection. In Washington, the initiative failed by a margin of 46% to 54%, and in California it failed by the same exact margin. Oregon did two things differently, which seemed to make the difference. First, the Death with Dignity Act that was crafted prohibited lethal injection and active euthanasia and only allowed the patient to self-administer the lethal medication with many safeguards in place. This had the advantage of silencing many of the critics' arguments. Second, advocates learned that in order to defeat the well-financed opposition, it would be necessary to run a professional campaign. A grassroots effort would not cut it.

Advocacy Tip

A **ballot measure** is a good strategy to use when the policy is not likely to pass by the state legislature but when the public is behind it.

The campaign was able to gather the signatures needed to get the issue on the ballot so that the voters in Oregon could decide the outcome. A **ballot initiative** is a process that allows citizens to draft legislation, place it on a ballot, and submit it to the voters to decide instead of being adopted by a state legislature. A predetermined number of signatures are needed to qualify a measure for the ballot, and the number needed varies by state. Measure 16 established the Death with Dignity Act in Oregon in November 1994 when it was approved by a narrow margin of 51% to 49%. However, that was just the beginning of the story as opponents tried to repeal the ODWDA using a number of strategies over the next several years (Death with Dignity National Center, n.d.):

- November 1994, Oregon voters approve Measure 16 by a slim margin (51% to 49%) establishing the Death with Dignity Act.
- In December 1994, *Lee v. State of Oregon* becomes the ODWDA's first legal challenge. The plaintiffs in the case were doctors and patients who contended that the Oregon law violated the Constitution's First and Fourteenth Amendments. (*Lee v. State of Oregon* eventually made its way to the U.S. Supreme Court, which refused to hear the case.)
- In 1995, District Judge Hogan rules that ODWDA violates the U.S. Constitution's Equal Protection clause. The ruling was immediately appealed to the U.S. Circuit Court of Appeals.
- In 1997, a three-judge panel of the Ninth Circuit Appeals Court dismisses the District Court's challenge to Oregon's Death with Dignity Act.
- In 1997, in two related rulings, *Vacco v. Quill* and *Washington v. Glucksberg*, the U.S. Supreme Court rules that physician aid-in-dying is not a Constitutional right. However, according to the Court, the issue would be best addressed in the "laboratory of the states," which are free to prohibit or legalize physician-assisted dying.
- In 1997, the Oregon state legislature sends Measure 51 to voters in an attempt to repeal the Death with Dignity Act, but it is defeated by voters (60% voted against it).
- In 1997, Drug Enforcement Administration (DEA) chief Thomas Constantine states that Oregon physicians participating under the law's guidelines would be in violation of the Controlled Substances Act.
- In 1998, Attorney General Reno issues a reversal of the DEA's position, saying that the Department of Justice would not prosecute physicians who had assisted their patient's deaths in compliance with the Oregon law.
- In 1998, the Death with Dignity Act is implemented. During the first year of implementation, 15 patients died after taking lethal medication.
- In 1998, congressional opponents to physician-assisted dying introduce the Lethal Drug Abuse Prevention Act (HR 4006/S 2151), designed to overturn the Oregon law. However, it did not pass due to opposition from President Clinton, healthcare organizations, and congressional legislators.
- In 1999, the U.S. House of Representatives passes the Pain Relief Promotion Act to bar physicians from prescribing medications as allowed by the ODWDA. However, it does not pass because it never makes it to the floor of the U.S. Senate for a full vote.
- In 2001, U.S. Attorney General John Ashcroft attempts to block the ODWDA by authorizing DEA agents to investigate and prosecute doctors who prescribe federally controlled drugs to help terminally ill patients die.
- Over the next several years, Ashcroft's case is heard in various court cases and was eventually appealed all the way to the U.S. Supreme Court.
- On January 17, 2006, the Supreme Court votes 6–3 to uphold an Oregon physician aid-in-dying law in the case *Gonzales v. Oregon* (formerly *Oregon v. Ashcroft*), ruling

that former Attorney General John Ashcroft overstepped his authority in seeking to punish doctors who prescribed drugs to help terminally ill patients end their lives. In the decision, the Supreme Court rules that the Oregon law supersedes federal authority to regulate physicians and that the Bush administration improperly attempted to use the Controlled Substances Act to prosecute Oregon physicians who assist in patient aid-in-dying.

- In 2006, U.S. Senator Sam Brownback introduced the Assisted Suicide Prevention Act, which would prohibit doctors from prescribing federally controlled substances for the purpose of physician aid-in-dying. Oregon Senator Ron Wyden announced that he will block the bill indefinitely through a legislative hold. The bill was eventually withdrawn.
- Since its passage in 1997, 1,275 terminally ill patients have used the Oregon law to hasten their own deaths.
- In 2011, HBO aired a documentary film titled *How to Die in Oregon*, winner of the 2011 Sundance Film Festival U.S. Documentary Grand Jury Award.

Washington State's Death with Dignity Act

In November 2008, Washington became the second U.S. state to pass a Death with Dignity Act. However, it was a long road to get there. The Washington law was modeled on the Oregon law because it was deemed to be model aid-in-dying legislation. The ballot measure in 2008 won by a sizeable margin, with 58% voting to approve and 42% opposed. An important lesson to be learned is that most successful policy change efforts are not achieved by individuals, but rather by an organized effort or coalition of individuals and groups working together.

Social Worker Spotlight: Peg Sandeen, PhD, MSW

Social worker Dr. Peg Sandeen is the executive director of the **Death with Dignity National Center** in Portland, Oregon, a policy organization that advocates for expanded end-of-life options in the form of Death with Dignity legislation.

Sandeen has been a policy-level social worker her entire career, starting out as an intern in the Iowa House of Representatives during the final year of her master's degree. She was a multiclient lobbyist in the Iowa Statehouse for two years, working to strengthen domestic violence and sexual assault laws, as well as to promote civil rights protections for individuals from the lesbian, gay, bisexual, and transgender (LGBT) community.

In her professional capacities, as well as through personal loss, Sandeen has felt firsthand how legal and medical interaction affects people's lives in both positive and negative ways. As a result, her scholarly and professional efforts have increasingly focused on health-related ethical concerns, particularly end-of-life decisions, privacy issues, and mental health.

At the AIDS Project of Center Iowa, she was a public policy specialist (and later executive director) advocating at both the state and federal levels to achieve funding for HIV prevention and care services. As a result of her exploration of ethical, legal and medical issues related to HIV care in social work, Sandeen was named 2002 Price Fellow in HIV Prevention Leadership by the Centers for Disease Control and Prevention.

As a volunteer, she helped to found two LGBT-oriented groups, the Iowa Coalition for Human Rights and the Queer Youth Alliance, and she worked for the Bridges Project of the American Friends Service Committee as a research volunteer.

In her position at the Death with Dignity National Center, she led the organization through the complexities of a public opinion campaign during the U.S. Supreme Court case *Gonzales v. Oregon*. She was a member of the political strategy team that successfully worked to pass a Death with Dignity ballot initiative in the state of Washington.

Sandeen earned her PhD in Social Work and Social Research at Portland State University.

How the Washington State Death with Dignity Act Was Passed

In April 2005, the Death with Dignity National Center decided to pursue a ballot initiative in Washington State for the 2008 election. According to Eli Stutsman, one of the chief architects of the Oregon and Washington laws, "Political success demands a well framed message delivered by well-chosen messengers against a well-defined opponent" (Quill & Batton, 2004, p. 259). He believes that initiatives failed in other states (despite popular support) because they failed to run an effective, professional political campaign. The moral of the story is that if you want to win, you must organize and raise money even if public opinion is on your side. Paid media are necessary to beat a wealthy opponent. Some policy change campaigns are grassroots, "outside the system" efforts; however, the Death with Dignity movement is an example of a professional campaign that was operating within the system in order to achieve a win. Various phases of the successful effort are described here.

I. A Coalition Was Formed

In February 2006, a coalition was formed, and it had its first official meeting. The coalition included the Death with Dignity National Center, Compassion & Choices, Compassion & Choices of Washington, and former Washington Governor Booth Gardner who formed his own group called Dignity 2000. Each of these four groups had three representatives for a total of 12 coalition members. Putting a coalition together takes a lot of time and energy and is not an easy feat. Governor Gardner was a key person in this effort since he had name recognition and was able to put a public face on the issue due to his Parkinson's disease diagnosis. He helped the coalition early on by conducting focus groups to ensure that Oregon's law is the best policy for Washington.

Advocacy Tip

Coalition building is an advocacy strategy that can be very useful because it allows groups to share their resources and expertise. Having famous and/or influential people in your coalition can also be useful.

II. Official Campaign Was Launched

At the end of 2007, the campaign became official. The campaign was named, It's My Decision Committee, and a campaign office was opened in Seattle. The Oregon Death with Dignity Political Action Fund donated $200,000 in seed money to jump-start the campaign. All of the money was raised by donors. One of the tricky parts to raising money in the early phase of a campaign is doing this under the radar without alerting the opposition. In February 2008, the campaign was renamed Yes on I-1000 (I-1000 was the name of the ballot measure that Washington voters would vote on). In May 2008, a campaign manager was hired.

III. The Death with Dignity Act Was Certified for the Ballot

The lead author of ODWDA drafted the Washington Death with Dignity Act. More than 3,600 volunteers assisted in the gathering of signatures. However, in order to gather the number of signatures needed, it was necessary for the campaign to hire paid signature gatherers, which cost the campaign roughly a quarter of a million dollars. In July 2008, Governor Booth Gardner turned in 320,000 signatures to the Secretary of State's Office (100,000 more than was needed), and the proposed act was officially certified for the November 2008 ballot. The Coalition Against Assisted Suicide challenged the language of the ballot title and wanted it to include the phrase "physician assisted suicide." Judge Wickham ruled against this challenge and explained that, according to the statute, the language used should be as neutral as possible. In the ruling, the judge stated that the term is too broad and politically loaded. The language that was on the actual ballot can be seen in Figure 10.2.

BALLOT TITLE

Statement of Subject: Initiative Measure No. 1000 concerns allowing certain terminally ill competent adults to obtain lethal prescriptions.

Concise Description: This measure would permit terminally ill, competent, adult Washington residents, who are medically predicted to have six months or less to live, to request and self-administer lethal medication prescribed by a physician.

Should this measure be enacted into law? Yes[ ] No[ ]

BALLOT MEASURE SUMMARY

This measure would permit terminally ill, competent, adult Washington residents medically predicted to die within six months, to request and self-administer lethal medication prescribed by a physician. The measure requires two oral and one written request, two physicians to diagnose the patient and determine the patient is competent, a waiting period, and physician verification of an informed patient decision. Physicians, patients and others acting in good faith compliance would have criminal and civil immunity.

Figure 10.2   Death with Dignity ballot measure, Washington State

IV. Money Was Raised

In September 2008, former Governor Booth Gardner donated $300,000 to the campaign, making him the campaign's single largest donor. The Oregon Death with Dignity Fund donated $615,000 to the campaign, which was the largest check from a single organization. By the end of October 2008, the campaign had raised a total of $4.8 million, far outspending the opposition.

V. Allies Lent Their Support and Endorsed the Campaign

Organizations that publicly supported Yes on I-1000 included the American Medical Student Association, the American Medical Women's Association, the Lifelong AIDS Association, the ACLU, the National Women's Law Center, the Washington Chapter of the National Association of Social Workers, and the Washington State Public Health Association. The position paper of the Washington Chapter of NASW is provided below.

NASW/WASHINGTON CHAPTER, 2008 Legislative Session Position Paper[1,2]

Support the Death With Dignity Initiative to legalize the option of assisted death for terminally ill, mentally competent adults.

ISSUE

End of life care has improved with the expansion of hospice programs which are justifiably recognized as expert in the provision of palliative care to terminally ill people. However there are those who reach a point where they want an additional service not offered by hospice, they want assisted death. They want to control the manner and timing of their deaths and they want the option whether or not they use it. Most of Dr. Kevorkian's patients were in hospice programs and 86% of those who have used the Oregonian Death With Dignity Act were hospice patients. LAC priorities for the 2008 legislative agenda include "legislative issues related to civil rights." The option of hastened death may be regarded as the ultimate civil right.

BACKGROUND

The Hemlock Society of Washington State was founded in 1988 to promote end of life options for terminally ill, qualified adults. In 1990 they co-sponsored a Death With Dignity initiative campaign to legalize physician assisted death. NASW/WA State was one of the first organizations to endorse this Initiative, followed by several special interest social work groups. In 1991 it was on the ballot and narrowly failed, 46%–54%. However the extensive support for this issue led to practice changes by oncologists and other physicians caring for the dying.

---

1   Disclaimer: All views expressed in this document represent opinions of the National Association of Social Workers/Washington Chapter and do not necessarily reflect views of the organization as a whole.

2   This document was originally published in 2008, and is reflective of the National Association of Social Workers' Washington state Chapter during this time. The nomenclature, as well as other things, have since been updated.

Following this effort Oregon passed a similar law in 1994 with some modifications. It was subjected to a series of attacks by then Attorney General John Ashcroft but has been operating in exemplary fashion since 1997. Over nine years of implementation only 292 people have used prescriptions to hasten death, although 455 requested prescriptions. Their primary concern was loss of autonomy (96%) decreasing ability to participate in meaningful activities (96%) and loss of dignity (76%). Less than 50% were concerned about pain control.

The WA Hemlock Society changed its name and subsequently merged with a sister right-to-die organization to become Compassion & Choices of WA. Their mission includes advocating for "excellent end-of-life care, . . . and, for terminally ill, competent adults, aid in dying to avoid intolerable suffering."

This issue has always involved social workers and attracted their support. Social workers were members and officers of the National Hemlock Board since its formation in the 80s and continue to take leadership positions in WA. Many if not most WA NASW members work in medical settings and many are involved in end of life care. Oregonian social workers play a key role in the practice of their law, promoting client self -determination and working with patients and their families to ensure that all other options have been explored.

Opposition to hastened death comes primarily from the religious right and anti-pro-choice groups. Opposition from the hospice administration does not seem to represent their staff, the social workers and nurses providing direct care are generally supportive.

ACTION

Support for the Death With Dignity Initiative which is modeled on the Oregon law and will be launched in Jan 2008. Endorsement by the Board of WA/NASW following the recommendation of LAC, with publicity through Currents. Education about this issue through classroom teaching, conferences, mailings, with specific reference to the role of the social worker following the successful passage of the law.

Source: NASW/Washington Chapter. (2008). 2008 legislative session position paper. Retrieved from http://nasw-wa.org/wp-content/uploads/2013/06/DeathwithDignityPaper08.pdf

---

VI. Media Campaign and the Importance of Framing the Issue

In June 2008, the Yes on I-1000 Campaign hired a political consulting firm based out of Tennessee to coordinate and produce all of its media efforts. It is often said that an issue is lost or won in the last 6 weeks of the campaign. During this phase, the campaign manager, pollster, and media firm work very closely in order to run an effective media campaign. Many activities are performed in order to get the campaign's message out to voters including door knocking, radio spots, making presentations to various audiences across the state, and meeting with opinion leaders such as mayors and newspaper editorial boards in order to win endorsements. However, nothing is more effective in getting your message out than running television commercials in major metropolitan markets. The campaign ran a number of television spots in the last weeks of the campaign, which cost around $650,000. Links to these commercials can be found at: https://www.youtube.com/watch?v=O2JSBgRkyws (features a doctor whose mother used the Oregon law to hasten her death); https://www.youtube.com/watch?v=yribAiWGBEs&feature=relmfu (responds to the No on 1000 commercial featuring actor Martin Sheen); and https://www.youtube.com/watch?v=Tx5K4rjsZtM&feature=relmfu (features former Oregon governor Barbara Roberts).

Framing is critical in terms of communicating with the target audience and persuading others to your side of the issue. This has to be very carefully considered, and often focus groups and polling are used to find out the best way to frame an issue so that the message resonates with the public. The individuals delivering the message are also key. It would not have been effective if only right-to-die advocates delivered the message. In the commercials, doctors, nurses, and surviving family members were featured. In Washington the issue was framed in the following ways:

- It is compassionate to allow terminally ill patients to end their suffering.
- It is based on the Oregon law, which has been proven safe and effective.
- There are many safeguards in place, and public oversight, to ensure a high standard of care (e.g., competency and age requirements, written request by patient, two physicians approve, waiting period, informed decision, witnesses, residency requirement).
- The law is *not* euthanasia or mercy killing; it is self-administered by the patient.
- It is for people with a terminal illness only—not for those with chronic illness.
- The opposition is lying and making distortions.

Tactics Used to Get the Death with Dignity Ballot Measure Passed into Law

- ☒ Coalition building
- ☐ Direct lobbying (in-person lobby visits, sometimes by a professional lobbyist)
- ☒ Earned media (letters to the editor, actions that lead to media coverage)
- ☐ Grassroots lobbying (e.g., urging people to call, write, email legislators)
- ☒ Paid media (paying for TV/radio ads)
- ☐ Educational outreach (town halls, house parties, community forums)
- ☐ Visibility (rallies, marches)
- ☐ Online advocacy (using social media)
- ☐ Political dissent (e.g., civil disobedience, protest)
- ☒ Paid communication (paid staff who call voters, materials mailed out)
- ☐ Providing testimony in a legislative committee hearing
- ☒ Fundraising activities

The Opposition

Major opposition to Yes on I-1000 came from the Coalition Against Assisted Suicide. This coalition consisted of a range of individuals who are opposed to PAD, including doctors, nurses, hospice workers, disability rights advocates, pro-life Christian organizations, and politicians from both major parties, and then governor of Washington, Christine Gregoire. However, the largest block of opposition came from the Catholic Church, which was also the largest financial contributor. Money was raised from Catholic parishes, dioceses, and organizations from all over the country. Initiative opponents raised and spent $1.6 million in their efforts to defeat the ballot measure. The biggest donors included Catholic groups such as the Knights of Columbus, the Washington State Catholic Conference, the Seattle Archdiocese, and the Catholic Health Association. The Washington Medical Association was also strongly opposed to I-1000. Its president, Brian P. Wicks, MD stated:

> We believe physician-assisted suicide is fundamentally incompatible with the role of physicians as healers. Patients put their trust in physicians and that bond of trust would be irrevocably harmed by the provisions of this dangerous initiative … . The initiative is a dangerous distraction from symptom-directed end-of-life care that provides comfort for dying patients and their families. Our focus should remain on caring for terminally ill patients and should never shift toward helping them kill themselves.

> *(Frankham, 2008)*

The No on I-1000 campaign also had a famous face in actor Martin Sheen, known for his role as the U.S. President in the television drama *The West Wing* and films such as *Apocalypse Now*. Sheen, whose politics usually lean left, is a staunch Catholic. He was featured in television ads opposing I-1000 (see http://www.youtube.com/watch?v=zGLaZmOZFxo). In the ad, Sheen states that the law would endanger the poor, the disabled, and those suffering from depression. He goes on to say that "people who are ill need real medical care and compassion, not lethal drugs."

Next Steps for the Death with Dignity Movement

The Death with Dignity National Center will continue to make efforts to get the Death with Dignity Act passed in other U.S. states. According to its website, 17 states are currently considering DWDA laws (as of December 2020). Because the national center has limited resources for these campaigns, it does careful research to select states where it is sure to win. Part of this research includes public opinion polling and assessing factors such as cost, demographic profile, geography, and leadership in said state.

REFERENCES

Administration on Aging, Administration for Community Living, U.S. Department of Health and Human Services. (2020). 2019 profile of older Americans. Retrieved from https://acl.gov/sites/default/files/Aging%20and%20Disability%20in%20America/2019ProfileOlderAmericans508.pdf

Administration for Community Living. (n.d.). Older Americans Act. Retrieved from https://www.acl.gov/about-acl/authorizing-statutes/older-americans-act

Compassion & Choices. (2008, November 4). Washington becomes second state to legalize aid in dying: Campaign has moved patients' rights forward. Retrieved from https://www.compassionandchoices.org/washington-voters-approve-death-with-dignity-act-59–41-initiative-i-1000/

Compassion & Choices. (2009, May 22). First terminally ill Washingtonian uses Death with Dignity Act. Retrieved from https://www.compassionandchoices.org/terminally-ill-woman-becomes-first-to-use-washingtons-death-with-dignity-act/

Congressional Research Service. (2020). Social Security's funding shortfall. Retrieved from https://fas.org/sgp/crs/misc/IF10522.pdf

Death with Dignity National Center (n.d.). Oregon death with dignity act: A History. Retrieved from https://www.deathwithdignity.org/oregon-death-with-dignity-act-history/

Frankham, J. (2008, November 7). Health care providers in Washington State refuse to perform assisted suicide. Retrieved from https://www.lifesitenews.com/news/health-care-providers-in-washington-state-refuse-to-perform-assisted-suicid

Gray Panthers New York City. (n.d.). The Gray Panthers movement. Retrieved from http://www.graypanthersnyc.org/gray-panthers-movement--.pdf

Kaiser Family Foundation (2017). Overview of Medicare. Retrieved from https://www.kff.org/medicare/issue-brief/an-overview-of-medicare/

Lachs, M., & Pillemer, K. (2015). Elder abuse. *New England Journal of Medicine, 373*, 1947–1956.

Oregon Health Authority (n.d.). About the death with dignity act. Retrieved from https://www.oregon.gov/oha/PH/PROVIDERPARTNERRESOURCES/EVALUATIONRESEARCH/DEATHWITHDIGNITYACT/Pages/faqs.aspx#whocan

Oregon Health Authority, Public Health Division. (2019). Oregon Death with Dignity Act, 2019 data summary. Retrieved from https://www.oregon.gov/oha/PH/PROVIDERPARTNERRES-OURCES/EVALUATIONRESEARCH/DEATHWITHDIGNITYACT/Documents/year22.pdf

Quill, T. E., & Battin, M. P. (Eds.). (2004). *Physician assisted dying: The case for palliative care and patient choice*. Baltimore, MD: Johns Hopkins University Press.

Social Security Administration. (2019). Annual statistical supplement to the Social Security bulletin, 2019. Retrieved from https://www.ssa.gov/policy/docs/statcomps/supplement/2019/supplement19.pdf

Social Security Administration. (2020). Summary: Actuarial status of the Social Security trust funds. Retrieved from https://www.ssa.gov/policy/trust-funds-summary.html#:~:text=A%202019%20annual%20surplus%20of,estimated%20annual%20expenditures%20for%202020

Van de Water, P. N., & Romig, K. (2020). Social security benefits are modest. Center on Budget and Policy Priorities. Retrieved from https://www.cbpp.org/research/social-security/social-security-benefits-are-modest

CHAPTER 11

Advocacy for Racial Justice and Immigrant Rights

"We shall overcome. We shall overcome. Deep in my heart I do believe we shall overcome. And I believe it because somehow the arc of the moral universe is long, but it bends towards justice."

~Dr. Martin Luther King, Jr.

"No human being is illegal."

~Elie Wiesel, Nobel Laureate, author, and Holocaust survivor

Figure 11.1   Jim Crow laws

CHAPTER SUMMARY

Despite the fact of its cherished ideals of freedom, the right of citizens to pursue happiness, and belief that all men are created equal, the United States has often faced great difficulty living up to the principles of tolerance, equality, and inclusion. Historically, women, racial and ethnic minorities, those who are gay or lesbian, immigrants, and people with disabilities have been systematically shut out of participating in the public sphere. Although each of these social movements has its own unique story, disenfranchised groups share many common experiences. The subjugation of these groups was achieved at least in part by policies that were passed and codified into law by local, state, and federal lawmakers, including the executive branch, as well as Supreme Court decisions. It is often assumed that legislation is passed in order to solve a pressing social problem in a constructive way. However, it is important to keep in mind that legislation can be harmful to vulnerable groups in society. Significant progress has been made by each of these groups who over time rose up, banded together in social movements, and demanded social justice by challenging the larger power structure and status quo. A powerful recent example of this is the Black Lives Matter movement. This chapter will profile advocacy groups and examples of policies that have been used to outlaw discrimination and advance opportunity for marginalized groups.

From the beginning, the United States has had an uneasy and somewhat contradictory relationship with immigrants. On the one hand, this country often touts itself as "a nation of immigrants." In 1964, John F. Kennedy published a book by this very name. Indeed, every citizen of the United States is a descendent of immigrants except those who are descended from Native Americans. Many people around the world long to come to the United States for a better life, job opportunities, and to pursue the American dream. And large business sectors have taken advantage of the benefit immigrants provide in the form of cheap labor. On the other hand, some Americans fear and resent newly arriving immigrants. From the beginning of America's founding, each new generation of immigrants has had to face racism and discrimination and hear complaints that the newly arrived immigrants are taking jobs away from other low-wage earners and keeping wages low, do not share American values, and are a drain on public resources. As soon as immigrants arrive, they are expected to quickly assimilate and to learn to speak English.

President Trump faced immense criticism for his tough immigration policies while he was in office, which were viewed as inhumane and draconian by his critics. The task now falls to President Biden to find a federal solution to fix a broken immigration system, which he has vowed to do. The goal of immigration advocates is to get a comprehensive immigration bill passed into law that would provide a path to citizenship for the roughly 10–11 million individuals residing in the United States with no legal status. However, because this has proven very difficult politically, advocates also support the Development, Relief, and Education of Alien Minors (DREAM) Act, which would provide a path to citizenship for undocumented youth who were brought to the United States as minors by their parents, have grown up here, and consider the United States their home. Because they do not have "papers," these young people cannot obtain a driver's license, get a job, or qualify for federal student loans in order to attend college. This chapter tells the story of the young immigration activists and their efforts to get the U.S. Congress to pass the DREAM Act.

STUDENT LEARNING OBJECTIVES

- Students will be able to cite policies that have caused harm to marginalized groups, as well as policies that have advanced social justice.

- Students will be able to define concepts such as amnesty, migrants, asylum seekers, refugees, and comprehensive immigration reform.

- Students will be able to describe the goal and main features of the DREAM Act.

- Students will be able to evaluate the political advocacy efforts of DREAM Act activists who have worked for passage of the act.

- Students will be able to analyze the arguments in favor of, and opposed to, comprehensive immigration reform and the DREAM Act.

- Students will become familiar with advocacy groups in the United States that advocate for communities of color and immigrants.

Despite the fact of its cherished ideals of freedom, the right of citizens to pursue happiness, and belief that all men are created equal, the United States has often faced great difficulty living up to the principles of **equal opportunity** and inclusion. Historically, women; racial and ethnic minorities; individuals who are gay, lesbian, or transgender; immigrants; and people with disabilities have been viewed as lesser than and systematically shut out of participating in many important aspects of social and political life in the public sphere. These groups have endured discriminatory attitudes and behaviors and even violence at the hands of those in power who have sought to keep them marginalized by denying them access to the vote, education, equality in the workplace, and other basic **human rights**. Public policy can be used to counteract privilege and institutional discrimination in society.

Privilege refers to the unearned advantages that certain groups in society are afforded simply by being part of that group. Examples of privilege are white privilege, male privilege, heterosexual privilege, and wealth privilege. **Institutional discrimination** is when discrimination is built into the norms, systems, and institutions in society and is enforced by those in power through force, violence, or restriction of resources. Large institutions such as education systems and criminal justice systems can include policies and practices that are evidence of institutional discrimination. Significant progress has been made by each of these groups who over time rose up, banded together in **social movements**, and demanded social justice by challenging the power structure and status quo. A powerful recent example of this is the Black Lives Matter movement. Though each of these social movements has its own unique story, disenfranchised groups share many common experiences, as can be seen in the Table 11.1.

This chapter will outline the following ways that public policy has been used to advance **civil rights** in our society: (1) policies that outlaw discrimination; (2) policies that provide protection to groups vulnerable to violence and exploitation; and (3) policies that promote equal opportunity for low-income and oppressed groups by providing funding for programs that invest in human capital and address structural barriers to equality (e.g., Head Start, job training programs, affordable housing, financial support to attend higher education, etc.).

Table 11.1. Discrimination

	Women	Black/Indigenous/People of Color (BIPOC)	Gay/Lesbian/Transgender Individuals
Legal discrimination	Once barred from voting; Civil Rights Act of 1964 outlawed discrimination based on sex	Once barred from voting; Jim Crow laws; no federal protection against racial discrimination until the Civil Rights Act of 1964	No federal law prohibiting employment discrimination due to sexual orientation or gender identity
Violence	Domestic violence and sexual assault	Violence and hate crimes (lynchings, bombings, mob violence, police brutality)	Hate crimes; sexual orientation and gender identity was not included in federal hate crimes legislation until 2009
Segregation	Historically, women were not allowed in certain settings (universities, politics, men's clubs, military schools, etc.)	Segregation in schools and many other settings: buses, restaurants, separate restrooms and drinking fountains	"Don't ask don't tell" policy in the military; Gay people must often segregate themselves since it is not socially acceptable for them to show physical affection in public (e.g., gay bars & clubs); transgender bathroom laws
Hurtful and degrading stereotypes	Viewed as "less than" and not as intelligent as men	Viewed as "less than" and not as intelligent as white people	Viewed as "abnormal" or deviant
Family	Women could not divorce or own property; birth control was illegal; abortion continues to be debated	During slavery, denied the opportunity to marry and have families; many states had laws forbidding Blacks and Whites to marry	Denied the opportunity to marry; a number of states do not allow gay people to adopt; sodomy laws that made sex acts between men illegal (outlawed in 2003 by Supreme Court)
Religion	Bible is/was used to argue the traditional role of women in society and that women are subservient to men	Bible was used to justify slavery and to argue that Whites and Blacks should not be allowed to marry	Bible is used to argue that gay people should not marry and that sexual acts between same-sex couples are immoral and forbidden by God
Representation	Underrepresented in U.S. Congress; no female president	Underrepresented in U.S. Congress	Underrepresented in U.S. Congress

continued

Table 11.1.   Continued

	Women	Black/Indigenous/People of Color (BIPOC)	Gay/Lesbian/Transgender Individuals
Income	Feminization of poverty, wage gap, glass ceiling	Disproportionate number of Black, Indigenous, People of Color living in poverty; serious wealth disparities	No federal protection from discrimination in the workplace
Role of social movements	Women's movement	Civil rights movement	Gay rights movement and transgender rights movement

Policies and Social Movements to Advance Racial Justice in the United States

Slavery has been referred to as the United States' mortal sin, and Americans continue to grapple with the legacy of it. The United States has never engaged in any sort of truth and reconciliation process similar to that which was used in South Africa after apartheid was ended. As a result, Americans have a very difficult time talking about issues of race and racial inequality. After slavery was abolished in the United States after the end of the Civil War, **Jim Crow laws** were instituted across the South in attempts to keep White people segregated from Black people in almost all aspects of social life. The most famous example is the signs that were commonly posted to indicate "Whites Only" and "Colored" (see Figure 11.1) with regard to everything from drinking fountains to movie theaters and public transportation. This was a horrific system of racial apartheid that was codified by state laws across the South. See Examples of Jim Crow Laws in Selected States.

Examples of Jim Crow Laws in Selected States

Alabama

Health Care
No person or corporation shall require any white female nurse to nurse in wards or rooms in hospitals, either public or private, in which negro men are placed.

Public Facilities
It shall be unlawful for a negro and white person to play together or in company with each other at any game of pool or billiards.

It shall be unlawful to conduct a restaurant or other place for the serving of food in the city, at which white and colored people are served in the same room, unless such white and colored persons are effectually separated by a solid partition extending from the floor upward to a distance of seven feet or higher, and unless a separate entrance from the street is provided for each compartment.

Florida

Marriage/Cohabitation

All marriages between a white person and a negro, or between a white person and a person of negro descent to the fourth generation inclusive, are hereby forever prohibited.

Any negro man and white woman, or any white man and negro woman, who are not married to each other, who shall habitually live in and occupy in the nighttime the same room shall each be punished by imprisonment not exceeding 12 months, or by fine not exceeding five hundred dollars.

Education

The schools for white children and the schools for negro children shall be conducted separately.

Georgia

Public Facilities

No colored barber shall serve as a barber [to] white women or girls.

The officer in charge shall not bury, or allow to be buried, any colored persons upon ground set apart or used for the burial of white persons.

All persons licensed to conduct a restaurant, shall serve either white people exclusively or colored people exclusively and shall not sell to the two races within the same room or serve the two races anywhere under the same license.

It shall be unlawful for colored people to frequent any park owned or maintained by the city for the benefit, use and enjoyment of white persons . . . and unlawful for any white person to frequent any park owned or maintained by the city for the use and benefit of colored persons.

Mississippi

Free Speech

Any person . . . who shall be guilty of printing, publishing or circulating printed, typewritten or written matter urging or presenting for public acceptance or general information, arguments or suggestions in favor of social equality or of intermarriage between whites and negroes, shall be guilty of a misdemeanor and subject to fine or not exceeding five hundred dollars or imprisonment not exceeding six months or both.

Hospital Entrances

There shall be maintained by the governing authorities of every hospital maintained by the state for treatment of white and colored patients separate entrances for white and colored patients and visitors, and such entrances shall be used by the race only for which they are prepared.

Texas

Education

The County Board of Education shall provide schools of two kinds; those for white children and those for colored children.

North Carolina

Textbooks

Books shall not be interchangeable between the white and colored schools, but shall continue to be used by the race first using them.

Source: National Park Service, U.S. Department of the Interior. (n.d.). Jim Crow laws. Retrieved from www. nps.gov/malu/forteachers/jim_crow_laws.htm

Perhaps the most famous and groundbreaking piece of civil rights legislation in the United States is the **Civil Rights Act of 1964**, signed into law by President Lyndon B. Johnson. President Johnson famously stated,

> You do not take a person who, for years, has been hobbled by chains and liberate him, bring him up to the starting line of a race and then say, "You are free to compete with all the others," and still justly believe that you have been completely fair. Thus it is not enough just to open the gates of opportunity. All our citizens must have the ability to walk through those gates.

The Civil Rights Act passed after a long-fought battle by the **civil rights movement** and civil rights leaders, such as **Dr. Martin Luther King, Jr.** Dr. King is perhaps the most famous civil rights activist in U.S. history, and many other social movements have replicated his peaceful civil disobedience tactics (e.g., marches; demonstrations; boycotts, etc.) (see Figure 11.2). The Civil Rights Act is historic because it ended racial segregation in public places and banned employment discrimination on the basis of sex, race, color, religion, or national origin. One year later, President Johnson singed the **Voting Rights Act of 1965** into law, which addressed the barriers that many African Americans were facing when they tried to exercise their right to vote (e.g., poll taxes, literacy tests, harassment, intimidation, and violence). And in 1968, in the days after the assassination of Dr. Martin Luther King, Jr., President Johnson signed the **Fair Housing Act of 1968** into law because many African Americans were unable to rent or purchase a home in certain residential areas due to the color of their skin. This new law prohibited discrimination with regard to the sale, rental, and financing of housing based on race, religion, national origin, or sex.

After President Obama was elected, some argued that the United States had entered a **post-racial era** where racism was no longer a problem because the nation had elected its first African American president. One research study found that White respondents believe that bias against Black people has *decreased* while bias against White people has *increased* (Norton & Summer, 2011). Others disagree

Figure 11.2   Dr. Martin Luther King, Jr.

and cite social science data that shows that African Americans and Latinos continue to lag behind Whites on indicators such as wealth and median household income, poverty rate, high school and college graduation rate, health and life expectancy, and incarceration rate. Social science data also shows that public schools are as racially segregated today as they were in the 1960s.

Current Events Spotlight: Police Brutality and #BlackLivesMatter

A new social movement, #**BlackLivesMatter,** emerged on the national scene in 2013 after a number of shootings of unarmed Black women and men by police were profiled in the media, many as a result of these shootings being captured on video by police or bystanders. #BlackLivesMatter was started by three Black activists, Alicia Garza, Patrisse Cullors, and Opal Tometi, after George Zimmerman was acquitted of murdering 17-year-old Trayvon Martin in Florida. Other high-profile cases followed, such as Mike Brown, Sandra Bland, Breonna Taylor, Eric Garner, Philando Castille, Tamir Rice, Elijah McClain, and too many other names to include here. Initially, #Black Lives Matter led to a contentious debate in the United States as famous athletes, such as football player Colin Kaepernick, kneeled during the National Anthem in protest, and detractors chanted, "All Lives Matter" and "Blue Lives Matter." President Trump appeared to side with the critics and failed to criticize the actions of law enforcement or White supremacists while he was in office. Some have observed that overtly racist speech and behaviors became more commonplace in the United States after Donald Trump became president. The Southern Poverty Law Center reports that the number of hate groups increased during Trump's presidency:

If 2016 was the year of white supremacists being electrified by the rise of Donald Trump, his inauguration in January sent them into a frenzy. They believed they finally had a sympathizer in the White House and an administration that would enact policies to match their anti-immigrant, anti-Muslim and racist ideas. Throughout the year, Trump thrilled and comforted them with his apparent kinship and pugilistic style, his refusal to condemn hate crimes committed in his name and his outrageous statements equating neo-Nazis and anti-racist activists after the deadly violence in Charlottesville.

(Beirich & Buchanan, 2018)

But the Black Lives Matter movement was raised to a whole new level and became a mainstream social movement after the horrific murder of George Floyd in Minneapolis by a police officer on May 25, 2020. Police arrested Mr. Floyd after he attempted to purchase cigarettes with a counterfeit $20 bill. During the arrest, police officer Derek Chauvin pinned Mr. Garner on the ground by keeping his knee on Mr. Garner's neck for approximately eight minutes as Mr. Garner pleaded for help, repeatedly stating that he could not breathe. Three other police officers watched and did not intervene. Even though there were many other senseless deaths at the hands of law enforcement before George Floyd, this incident shook the nation in a way that the others had not. The four police officers face various charges in the death of Mr. Floyd. Derek Chauvin was charged with second-degree murder, third-degree murder, and second-degree manslaughter. On April 20, 2021, a jury found him guilty on all three counts.

Soon after Americans watched a video of Mr. Floyd's murder, protests broke out in across major cities across the United States and around the globe, and "I Can't Breathe" became a rallying call for the need to address systemic racism in the criminal justice system and other sectors of society. The protests were made up of people of all ages, races, and socioeconomic statuses, though young Americans were particularly motivated. Some of the protests erupted into looting and violence, and it is often unclear which groups were responsible, though the vast majority of antiracism protesters were peaceful. President Trump acknowledged that the murder of George Floyd was tragic but did not support the Black Lives Matter movement. He instead inflamed racial tensions by failing to condemn White supremacy, supporting the Confederate flag, criticizing the violent activity at the protests, and denying that a disproportionate number of Black men and women are victims of police brutality.

Meanwhile #BlackLivesMatter became an organized global social movement with chapters around the world and a website (see www.blacklivesmatter.com). According to the website, "Black Lives Matter is an ideological and political intervention in a world where Black lives are systematically and intentionally targeted for demise. It is an affirmation of Black folks' humanity, our contributions to this society, and our resilience in the face of deadly oppression" (n.d.).

Like all social movements, Black Lives Matter does have its critics. Those who oppose the ideas of the Black Lives Matter movement counter with the slogans "All Lives Matter" and "Blue Lives Matter" and argue that the movement unfairly portrays all law enforcement as bad and racially insensitive. One of these critics is the **alt-right,** a movement that is not new in the United States but that became more vocal and empowered when Donald Trump became president. The alt-right lacks a formal structure and much of its activity occurs on social media; however, they are united as White nationalists who seek to preserve White identity and Western civilization. White nationalists, led by Richard Spencer and David Duke, organize political rallies in support of their cause, such as the one in Charlottesville, Virginia, in February 2017, which was a protest of the city's removal of a Confederate statue. The rally turned deadly when a car plowed through the crowd of antiracist counter-protesters, injuring 35 people and killing a 32-year-old woman. President Trump was criticized by Democratic and Republican lawmakers alike when he failed to condemn the White supremacists explicitly and said there were "very fine people on both sides."

The impact of this social movement and its power in focusing the nation's attention on systemic racism in U.S. society cannot be underestimated. Police departments around the country are being asked to change harmful practices (e.g., banning chokeholds; removing criminal immunity from prosecution) and get better training, and some states and localities are considering reallocating funds for criminal justice to education and social services. This movement has had a ripple effect on corporations (e.g., changing the name and image of the Aunt Jemima brand; Band-Aid making brown and black bandages), Hollywood (with calls to be more inclusive of actors of color), state symbols (e.g., Mississippi changing its state flag), historical monuments (e.g., removal of Confederate statues), and the sports world (e.g., Nascar banning Confederate flags). It is unclear how much real legislative change will come as a result of this movement, but President Biden has promised to make this a focus when he is president.

However, this is only one piece of the larger story that is mass incarceration and the disproportionate treatment of Blacks and Hispanics in the criminal justice system. In the book *The New Jim Crow* (2010), author Michelle Alexander argues that the new way that Black and Brown people are systematically subjugated in U.S. society is through the criminal justice system. She cites mounds of social science data that shows that African Americans and Latinos are incarcerated at higher rates than Whites and are given harsher sentences than Whites for the same crimes. She argues that this relegates Blacks and Latinos to a permanent second-class status because many felons find it impossible to secure employment and have basic rights taken away from them, such as voting and receiving certain social welfare benefits after they have served their time. The Advocacy Spotlight provides a list of prominent advocacy groups that advocate on behalf of various communities of color.

Advocacy Spotlight: Organizations for Communities of Color

American-Arab Anti-Discrimination Committee
Anti-Defamation League
Asian Americans Advancing Justice
Asian-American Legal Defense and Education Fund
Association on Indian American Affairs
Black Lives Matter
Constitutional Law Center for Muslims in America
Council on American–Islamic Relations
Mexican American Legal Defense and Education Fund
Muslim Advocates
Muslims for Progressive Values
National Association for the Advancement of Colored People (NAACP)
National Congress of American Indians
National Urban League
Native American Rights Fund
OCA–Asian Pacific American Advocates
Rainbow Push Coalition
Southern Poverty Law Center
UnidosUS

Laws and Policies That Have Caused Harm

The subjugation of marginalized groups was achieved at least in part by policies that were passed and codified into law by local, state, and federal lawmakers, including the executive branch, as well as Supreme Court decisions. It is often assumed that legislation is passed in order to solve a pressing social problem in a positive and constructive way. However, it is important to keep in mind that policies can be racist and that legislation and court decisions can be designed to be harmful to vulnerable groups in society, as the following examples demonstrate:

- **1830**, Indian Removal Act.
- Laws allowing the slavery of Black people.
- **1857**, *Dred Scott* Supreme Court ruling that slaves were not U.S. citizens and were not protected by the U.S. Constitution.
- Women and African Americans legally barred from voting.
- Laws restricting the immigration of certain groups such as the Chinese Exclusion Act (1882).
- **1896**, *Plessy v. Ferguson* Supreme Court ruling that state laws enforcing racial segregation were constitutional.
- **1954**, Operation Wetback, a program of the Immigration and Nationalization Service (INS) to remove undocumented Mexican immigrants from the United States.
- **1860s–1960s,** Jim Crow laws in the South that enforced racial segregation.
- The internment of Japanese Americans during World War II.
- Laws making birth control illegal.
- Sodomy laws.
- Laws banning gays/lesbians/transgender individuals from joining the military.
- Laws banning gays/lesbians/transgender individuals from adopting children.
- Laws defining marriage as a union of a man and a woman (e.g., Defense of Marriage Act).
- Transgender bathroom laws that require transgender people to use public restrooms according to their assigned sex at birth.

Laws and Court Cases Outlawing Discrimination

A critical component in creating a just and equal society for all citizens has included the use of the legal system and the passage of legislation in order to outlaw discrimination and to redress the harmful effects of past discrimination. Examples are:

- **1863**, President Lincoln's Emancipation Proclamation.
- **1865**, 13th Amendment to the U.S. Constitution that abolished slavery.
- **1868**, 14th Amendment to the U.S. Constitution that granted citizenship to all persons born or naturalized in the United States, including former slaves recently freed. It also forbids states from denying any person "life, liberty or property, without due process of law" and includes the now famous Equal Protection Clause.
- **1870**, 15th Amendment to the U.S. Constitution that granted African American men the right to vote.
- **1920**, 19th Amendment to the U.S. Constitution that granted women the right to vote.

- **1954**, *Brown v. Board of Education* Supreme Court ruling that separate public schools for Black and White children was unconstitutional.
- **1963,** Equal Pay Act and the Lilly Ledbetter Fair Pay Act (**2009**) that addresses pay equity between men and women.
- **1964**, Civil Rights Act of 1964.
- **1965**, Voting Rights Act of 1965.
- **1965**, *Griswold v. Connecticut* Supreme Court ruling that legalized contraceptive use in all states.
- Affirmative action policies.
- **1967**, Age Discrimination in Employment Act of 1967.
- **1968**, Fair Housing Act of 1968.
- **1972**, Title IX legislation that prohibits discrimination on the basis of sex in any federally funded education program or activity.
- **1973**, *Roe v. Wade* Supreme Court ruling that legalized abortion.
- **1978**, Pregnancy Discrimination Act of 1978.
- **1990**, Americans with Disabilities Act.
- **1994**, Violence Against Women Act.
- **2009**, Matthew Shepard and James Byrd Jr. Hate Crimes Prevention Act.
- **2010**, President Obama repeals "Don't Ask Don't Tell," the military's ban on openly gay service members.
- **2015**, *Obergefell v. Hodges* Supreme Court ruling that legalized same-sex marriage in the United States.
- **2016,** U.S. Defense secretary announces that transgender Americans may serve openly in the military.

Hate Crimes Legislation

The first federal hate crimes legislation was passed into law in 1968, signed by President Lyndon Johnson. Then in 2009, the **Matthew Shepard and James Byrd Jr. Hate Crimes Prevention Act** was passed into law after 10 years of advocacy by organizations such as the Human Rights Campaign and numerous civil rights groups, in order to strengthen hate crimes laws and to protect more vulnerable groups, such as LGBTQ individuals. It was prompted by the hate crimes of two men, both of whom were killed in 1998. Matthew Shepard was a young college student who was tortured and killed by two men in Laramie, Wyoming, for being gay, and James Byrd, Jr. was a black man who was chained to the back of a pick-up truck by three White men and dragged to his death in Jasper, Texas. FBI data shows that hate crimes based on race and ethnicity are the largest category, followed by religion and sexual orientation. Their data also shows that hate crimes in 2019 reached highest level in more than a decade (Balsamo, 2020). It is hard to know the exact reasons for the increase though some have conjectured that one factor was the language and tenor used by President Trump that created an environment where some white supremacy groups felt more comfortable engaging in verbal and physical violence against communities of color and Jewish people. There have been a number of recent very troubling violent acts against Asian-Americans, some possibly motivated by rhetoric used by President Trump and other U.S. lawmakers blaming China for the coronavirus. On March 16, 2021, a White gunman killed eight people, six of whom were Asian women, at three spas in the Atlanta Georgia metropolitan area.

Many groups point out that we need better data on hate crimes because it is significantly underreported. According to a 2020 AP news article, "Advocacy groups, including the Anti-Defamation League, called on Congress and law enforcement agencies across the U.S. to improve data collection and reporting of hate crimes. Critics have long warned that the data may be incomplete, in part because it is based on voluntary reporting by police agencies across the country. Last year, only 2,172 law enforcement agencies out of about 15,000 participating agencies across the country reported hate crime data to the FBI" (Balsamo, 2020).

The Politics of Immigration

Immigration has always been a hot-button issue in the United States, but the issue became even more heated and contentious than usual after the September 11th attacks in 2001 as federal lawmakers were forced to grapple with how to keep the nation safe while still allowing people to immigrate to the United States. Lawmakers from both political parties have been in a political stalemate for decades regarding how to resolve the problem of the roughly 10–11 million undocumented people who are living in the shadows in the United States. President Trump has made statements about immigrants that many Americans have found to be offensive and disturbing. He referred to Mexican immigrants as rapists and criminals and has attempted to ban Muslims from entering the United States because there is "great hatred towards Americans by large segments of the Muslim population." He campaigned on building a wall between the United States and Mexico and said that he would make Mexico pay for it (which did not happen).

The United States has always had an uneasy and somewhat contradictory relationship with immigrants. On the one hand, this country often touts itself as "a nation of immigrants." In 1964, John F. Kennedy published a book by this very name. Indeed, every citizen of the United States is a descendent of immigrants except those who are descended from Native Americans. Many people around the world long to come to the United States for a better life, job opportunities, and in order to pursue the American dream. And some business sectors have taken advantage of the benefit they provide in the form of cheap labor. On the other hand, some Americans fear and resent newly arriving immigrants.

From the beginning of this country's founding, each new generation of immigrants has had to face racism and discrimination and hear complaints that they are taking jobs away from other low-wage earners and keeping wages low, do not share American values, and are a drain on public resources. As soon as they arrive, they are pressured to quickly assimilate and to learn to speak English. According to the Pew Research Center, in 2015 there were 43.2 million immigrants, and this is projected to double by 2065. Twenty-seven percent were from Asia, 27% from Mexico, 27% from Latin American, 13.5% from Europe and/or Canada, and 9% percent from other regions (Lopez & Radford, 2017).

All countries have to deal with the issue of how to handle immigration. Government officials must decide who can come in, in what numbers, and under which circumstances. Some countries are fairly welcoming, while others take great care to preserve their country's homogeneity when it comes to race, religion, and culture. In the United States, the pendulum swings back and forth between immigration policies that restrict immigration (e.g., Chinese Exclusion Act, Emergency Quota Act of 1921, Immigration Act of 1924, Operation Wetback in the 1950s) and policies that ease quota restrictions (e.g., Immigration and Nationality Act of 1965, Refugee Act of 1980, Immigration Act of 1990). People who come to the United States generally fall into one of three categories: (1) migrants, (2) refugees, and (3) asylum seekers. According to the UNHCR (2020), in 2020 there were 80 million forcibly **displaced people** in the world, almost double the number from a decade ago.

In most cases, people can immigrate to the United States in one of two ways: (1) family-based immigration (they have an immediate relative here) or (2) employment-based immigration for high-skilled workers (an employer sponsors them to work here). Approximately 5,000 green cards are available for unskilled workers each year, so it is virtually impossible for low-skilled workers to be admitted. It is not unusual for people to wait many years or even decades to obtain their green card to enter the United States.

Defining Terms: Immigration

- **Migrants:** Migrants are people who leave their home country for a better life for themselves and their family members. They leave their home to get a job or education. Migrants also sometimes come to a new country to join relatives or to escape a natural disaster.
- **Refugees:** Refugees are individuals who have had to flee their country due to human rights violations and their own government either will not or cannot protect them. This can include torture or persecution from an armed conflict. Refugees are sometimes fleeing because they have been targeted for who they are (ethnicity) or what they believe (e.g., religion, political beliefs, etc.).
- **Asylum seekers:** This refers to people who are in the process of seeking international protection from another country, but they have not yet been recognized as a refugee.

One tragic chapter in U.S. history is the treatment of **migrant farmworkers**. Before Mexican laborers were used to support American agriculture, it was the Chinese and then the Japanese who worked as "field hands" in California. Then, the **Bracero Program** was created during World War II in order to import temporary guest workers into the United States from Mexico in order to meet the growing demand for agriculture laborers. Under this program, which operated for over 20 years, more than four million farmworkers from Mexico came to work in U.S. agricultural fields. However, these farmworkers had few rights and were often mistreated and exploited. They were not allowed to unionize or demand fair pay or safe working conditions. When their contracts expired, they were forced to return to Mexico. However, out of this struggle, a famous civil rights activist named **Cesar Chavez** was born. Chavez was a cofounder of the National Farm Workers Association, which later became the United Farm Workers (UFW). He became an inspiration to many around the world because he used nonviolent strategies (e.g., strikes, boycotts such as "no grapes" or "uvas no") and inspirational rhetoric in order to demand basic human rights for farmworkers.

The Politics of Illegal Immigration

It is important to note that the terminology surrounding immigration, particularly **illegal immigration**, is very political. Some use the terms *illegal immigrants*, *illegals*, or *illegal aliens* when referring to those who have entered the United States with no legal status. However, some people find these terms offensive and assert that no human being should be described as illegal. Instead, they prefer to use the term **undocumented or unauthorized**, which describes someone who is in the country with no legal status. Sometimes people refer to undocumented immigrants as criminals, but have they actually committed a crime? It turns out that this is a rather complicated question due to the difference between *unlawful entry* and *unlawful presence*. Improper entry by an immigrant is a misdemeanor crime and it is also a crime to reenter the country after being deported. However, once a person is here, or when someone overstays his or her visa, it is a civil violation (similar to getting a parking ticket), and the penalty would be deportation.

After the September 11th attacks in 2001, the issue of illegal immigration rose to the top of the political agenda as concerns over homeland security were heightened. A number of bills were passed into law to address homeland and border security, such as the controversial **USA PATRIOT Act**, the **Enhanced Border Security and Visa Entry Reform Act of 2002**, the **Homeland Security Act of 2002**, and the **Secure Fence Act of 2006,** which authorized the construction of a 700-mile fence along the southern border. In addition, a new program called Secure Communities was started by President George W. Bush and greatly expanded by the Obama administration.

The **Secure Communities program** requires local and state law enforcement to do an automatic check of immigration status for anyone who has been arrested and to report what they find to Immigration and **Customs Enforcement (ICE)**. The goal of the program is to remove those arrested for serious violent crimes, but the program has come under criticism for deporting undocumented immigrants for minor offenses (some with no criminal record) and separating families. Supporters of the program argue this program is an important tool that has resulted in the deportation of violent criminals. However, a growing number of states and localities have become disenchanted with the program and have passed laws to limit their cooperation with the federal program. Some police chiefs have been critical of the law because it forces them to spend limited resources on nonviolent offenders and makes it less likely for undocumented immigrants to report a crime when they have been a witness or victim.

There is a delicate balance between immigration policy and homeland security policy. For example, lawmakers must find a way to pass laws that keep the country safe while at the same time strive to create sensible immigration policies that allow foreigners to immigrate to the United States. Those on both sides of the political spectrum agree that there is a problem and that the immigration system is in need of reform. According to data from the Pew Research Center (2020), roughly 10.5 million undocumented people were living in the United States in 2017. Just over half were from Mexico, yet the undocumented immigration population from Mexico declined significantly from 2010 to 2016, while it has been increasing from countries in Asia, Central America, and Africa.

Advocates of Comprehensive Immigration Reform

In the United States, a significant divide exists over how to address the problems with U.S. immigration policy. On one side are Democrats and pro-business conservatives who have come together in advocating for **comprehensive immigration reform** that would create a path to citizenship for the roughly 10–11 million undocumented immigrants currently residing in the United States. Most of the legislation that has been proposed outlines a process that would create a path to legalization for undocumented immigrants, and some of the bills include penalties (e.g., pay a fine or back taxes). Many of these bills also include increased border security, verification requirements for employers to ensure they are not hiring undocumented workers, and changing the visa system to bring in more high-skilled workers. Under most comprehensive plans, immigrants would have to pass a background check and prove they can speak or are studying English, among other requirements (Wirzbicki, 2012).

Supporters of comprehensive immigration reform point out that people come to the United States illegally not because they are bad people, but because they are seeking a better life and better opportunities for their family. They explain that those in the country without legal status are living "in the shadows" and are extremely vulnerable to exploitation by employers because they cannot go to law enforcement for help. UnidosUS, a prominent national civil rights organization, argues that the United States has a history of exploiting immigrants for their labor but then not affording them any legal protections. They point out that undocumented workers make significant contributions to the economy, pay more taxes than they receive in benefits, and are less likely to commit crimes than native-born Americans (7 ways immigrants enrich our economy and society, n.d.). In fact, many die each year as they attempt to cross the Mexico–U.S. border. According to immigration experts, the current system is broken, full of bureaucratic obstacles, and is a lengthy, expensive process. The box below provides a list of advocacy organizations that focus on immigration.

However, efforts to pass comprehensive immigration reform have failed in Congress since 2004 when President George W. Bush proposed a program that would provide legal status to undocumented workers under a guest worker program, angering conservatives in his own party who labeled it an amnesty program. Some proposals to address illegal immigration over the years have included the construction of a fence on the border between the United States and Mexico. The *New York Times* published an editorial on March 4, 2008, titled "Border Insecurity," and argued that the fence is a symbol of a conflicted nation's effort to literally wall itself off after being unable to resolve the problem intelligently. President Obama vowed to make immigration reform a priority of his administration, but there was little movement due to the divisive nature of this issue.

Immigration Advocacy Organizations

Dreamactivist.org
Immigration Policy Center
Migration Policy Institute
National Immigrant Justice Center
National Immigration Forum
National Immigration Law Center
National Network for Immigrant and Refugee Rights
United Nations
UnidosUS
United We Dream
Young Center for Immigrant Children's Rights

Opponents of Comprehensive Immigration Reform

The Republican Party has been split on this issue between (1) pro-business conservatives who have joined Democrats in supporting comprehensive immigration and (2) social conservatives who advocate for a policy that would treat undocumented individuals as criminals who have broken the law and should be penalized and deported. They argue that undocumented immigrants keep wages low, are a drain on public resources, engage in criminal behavior, and do not speak English and often fail to assimilate and embrace American culture and values.

Opponents of comprehensive immigration reform believe that creating a path to citizenship for those residing in the United States equates to amnesty and argue that it is unfair to grant legal status to those who came here illegally when others are waiting in line and going through the appropriate legal channels. In this context, **amnesty** means that the government would allow undocumented citizens to become citizens without any form of punishment. The last time this was carried out on any widespread scale by the federal government was under President Ronald Reagan in 1986 when the Immigration Reform and Control Act was passed. This act granted amnesty to roughly three million undocumented immigrants.

Opponents of immigration reform are joined by groups such as the **Minuteman Project** (armed volunteers who patrol the Arizona border), the **Federation for American**

Immigration Reform (FAIR), and **NumbersUSA**, all of which fight passionately to end *illegal* immigration and, in the case of FAIR and Numbers USA, significantly reduce *legal* immigration. Those opposing a comprehensive approach to solving the immigration problem have been able to effectively derail bipartisan legislative efforts to pass comprehensive immigration reform since 2004. Many opponents have been in support of legislation such as that passed in Arizona in 2010, SB 1070. The goal of this bill was to identify, prosecute, and deport illegal immigrants, and the bill gave broad powers to law enforcement to question, and later detain, someone when there is *reasonable suspicion* that they are not in the country legally. It also required immigrants to carry their immigration documentation at all times.

On June 25, 2012, The U.S. Supreme Court struck down several key parts of SB 1070 and agreed with the Obama administration that it is the role of the federal government, not state officials, to make immigration policy. But the Court upheld the most controversial part of SB 1070 (the "show me your papers" provision). However, the law was effectively ended in 2016 when a settlement was reached as part of a lawsuit filed by the ACLU and civil rights organizations. The state of Arizona agreed to pay $1.4 million in legal fees and end its practice of requiring police officers to demand the papers of people suspected of being in the country illegally.

What Is the DREAM Act?

The goal of immigration advocates is to get a comprehensive immigration bill passed into law that would provide a path to citizenship for the roughly 10 to 11 million individuals residing in the United States with no legal status. However, given that this has proven very difficult politically, advocates support legislation such as the Development, Relief, and Education of Alien Minors (DREAM) Act, a policy that would result in incremental change, or a small, yet significant step in the right direction. The **DREAM Act** would provide a path to citizenship to undocumented youth who were brought to the United States as minors by their parents, have grown up here, and consider the United States their home. Proponents of the DREAM Act emphasize that these children did not break the law and should not be penalized as such. These youth have been named "Dreamers" as a result of this legislation. There is precedence for this type of policy since the U.S. Supreme Court ruled in *Plyer v. Doe* in 1982 that K–12 schools cannot deny public education to undocumented students.

Because undocumented youth do not have "papers," they cannot obtain a driver's license, get a job, or qualify for federal student loans in order to attend college. In the latest Senate version on the DREAM Act (S. 264) introduced in 2021, the requirements in order to qualify for the DREAM Act are as follows:

- Must have entered the United States as a minor;
- Must have been present in the United States for at least 4 consecutive years prior to enactment of the bill;
- Has not been convicted of certain crimes;

- Has been admitted to an institution of higher education, has graduated high school or obtained a GED, or is currently enrolled in secondary school or a program assisting students to obtain a diploma or GED.

An individual can apply for lawful permanent resident (LPR) status by satisfying one of the following requirements:

- Maintain continuous residence in the United States;
- Demonstrate an ability to read, write, and speak English and have an understanding of American history and government;
- Pass a government background check, have no misdemeanor or felony convictions, and undergo a biometric and medical exam;
- Pay an application fee.

Additionally, a Dreamer would have to complete one of the following three requirements:

- Education track: Complete at least two years of higher education;
- Military track: Complete at least two years of military service with an honorable discharge; or
- Worker track: Demonstrate employment over a total period of three years.

After maintaining LPR status for five years, an individual can apply to become a U.S. citizen.

Who Supports the DREAM Act?

The DREAM Act has wide support including the following:

- The DREAM act is sponsored by a bi-partisan group of federal lawmakers in the U.S. House and Senate, with primary support and leadership coming from Democratic lawmakers.
- Numerous newspaper editorial boards including the *New York Times*, the *L.A. Times*, and the Washington Post.
- Educators including the National Education Association and over 100 university presidents and higher education associations (e.g., American Association of State Colleges and Universities; American Association of Community Colleges; National PTA).
- Over 100 national organizations and child advocacy groups such as the Children's Defense Fund; National Association of Social Workers; and Voices for America's Children.
- Faith communities (e.g., American Jewish Committee; Episcopal Church; United Methodist Church; U.S. Catholic Conference of Bishops).
- Unions and civil rights organizations (e.g., Service Employees International Union; American Federation of Teachers; AFL-CIO; NAACP Legal Defense Fund).
- Hundreds of businesses such as Microsoft, Wal-Mart, Target, and the U.S. Hispanic Chamber of Commerce.

Who Opposes the DREAM Act?

The same groups that oppose comprehensive immigration reform (such as the Federation for American Immigration Reform) do not support the DREAM Act since they view it as giving amnesty to "illegal aliens." Historically, the DREAM Act has been widely opposed by members of Congress from the Republican Party who believe that anyone who has come to the U.S. illegally is a criminal who has broken the law. However, over the years it has gained the support of some moderate Republicans, such as Senator Lindsey Graham from South Carolina. Former Attorney General Jeff Sessions is an outspoken critic of those in the country illegally and is a proponent of the Trump administration's new zero tolerance policy, which has caused many migrant children to be separated from their parents (covered at the end of this chapter).

Practice Exercise 11.1

1. Visit the websites of the National Immigration Law Center, the Immigration Policy Center, dreamactivist.org, and UnidosUS to read more about these organizations and the information they have posted about the DREAM Act. What are their arguments in support of the DREAM act?

2. Visit the Federation for American Immigration Reform to read their opposition to the DREAM Act. What are their arguments against it?

3. In your view, who makes the more compelling case?

What Strategies Have Been Used to Get the DREAM Act Passed into Law?

A version of the DREAM act was first proposed in 2001; thus advocates have been fighting for this legislation for a very long time. The most fascinating part of this story is that the individuals who have been driving the passage of this bill are the undocumented youth who are directly impacted by this problem. They have become courageous youth activists and have honed their skills in leadership and advocacy.

Framing the issue. Advocates have framed this issue as: "The Dreamers are victims of circumstance since they did not break the law." "They are Americans. They have grown up in our communities, attended public school with our sons and daughters, and this is their home." "In most cases, they have little connection to their country of origin, have never been there, and do not speak the language." "These are students with dreams of having a family, going to college, and having a career."

Direct and grassroots lobbying. In the beginning, advocates engaged in traditional tactics such as lobbying legislators, encouraging supporters to contact legislators to urge passage of the bill, and getting resolutions passed by local government. DREAM Act activists have honed their lobbying skills and are able to tell their story to legislators and legislative staff to try to persuade them to vote "yes" on the DREAM Act. Hundreds of thousands of calls, emails, letters and petitions in support of the DREAM Act have been sent to the U.S. Congress.

Advocacy Reflection

Activities involving **political dissent** can include protests, consumer boycotts, strikes, sit-ins, marches, and civil disobedience (i.e., refusal to obey a law that is immoral or unjust). What is your comfort level with these kinds of political activities? Would you be willing to be arrested for an issue you care deeply about?

Political dissent. Over time, these youth activists began employing tactics used by other famous social movements (e.g., Civil Rights Movement) and engaging in political dissent activities in attempts to garner national and local media attention. They have organized peaceful sit-ins at various federal legislators' offices, which have resulted in the arrest of a number of these youth activists (see the Social Worker Spotlight, for activist Isabel Castillo's story of getting arrested). Some have participated in Hunger strikes, such as a November 2010 hunger strike by students at the University of Texas, San Antonio, who were part of a student organization called DREAM Act Now. Activists have also organized "coming out" events where youth publicly reveal their undocumented status.

Figure 11.3   Isabel Castillo

Social Worker Spotlight: Isabel Castillo, BSW

Isabel Castillo graduated with her BSW from Eastern Mennonite University in Virginia in 2007; however, because she is undocumented, she is not able to secure employment and work as a social worker. She was brought to the United States from Mexico when she was six years old by her parents who went to work in the poultry industry in Virginia. Her parents instilled in her the value of education because they wanted her to have a better life than they had. As a result, Isabel excelled in school and graduated high school with a 4.0 GPA. However, she soon learned that she would not be able to attend college because she did not have a social security number and would not be eligible to apply for federal loans to help her pay for her college education.

She was overjoyed to learn that Eastern Mennonite accepted undocumented students and she graduated three and a half years later with her social work degree, after struggling to pay for her tuition each semester (e.g., by working and getting help from her community). She would like to earn her MSW, but finances are currently a barrier. She has now become a DREAM Act activist because this is her only hope for a viable future and the opportunity to use her degree and work as a social work professional.

Isabel's activism began when she attended a conference in Washington, D.C., where she met other "Dreamers." She immediately realized that she needed to start organizing in her home state of Virginia. In October 2009, she helped found a local organization, Dream Activist Virginia, where they would meet weekly and strategize about how to raise awareness and build support for the DREAM Act. They would write letters and lobby legislators. They were able to get a resolution passed by the Harrisonburg City Council and organized the first immigrant rights rally in Harrisonburg. Isabel regularly shares her story by speaking to churches, schools, and community groups and has been interviewed by radio and newspaper journalists.

Perhaps the most exciting activity she participated in was a peaceful protest outside of Senator Harry Reid's office where she was arrested by Capitol Police after being there for five hours. Though Reid has been a supporter of the DREAM Act, Isabel and her fellow Dreamers were frustrated with him for not providing the leadership needed to really move the act forward. On this same day, other Dreamers were arrested for participating in a peaceful sit-in at Senator John McCain's office. The judge and prosecutor were very sympathetic to their stories; yet they were still found guilty of "unlawful entry" with a punishment of one year on probation and a $50.00 fine.

When asked whether she is scared that her activism will result in her deportation, Isabel states, "This is not about me anymore, it's about thousands of students. I am part of a movement." She goes on to explain, "This is home to me. I have grown up here. I am American in every sense of the word except on paper."

In May 2011, Isabel received an honorary doctorate from the University of San Francisco.

Visibility. DREAM Act activists have organized political rallies and marches in support of their cause in cities across the nation, including Washington, D.C. At some of these events, the Dreamers wear caps and gowns and perform a mock graduation ceremony.

Coalition building. Part of this advocacy effort has included sign-on letters demonstrating how many national/state/ and local organizations support the DREAM Act. They work in partnership with organizations such as the Immigrant Legal Resource Center and the National Immigration Law Center. They have built relationships with organizations across the country in order to build a more powerful coalition; for example, Dreamactivist. org, United We Dream Network, Immigrant Youth Justice League, New York State Youth Leadership Council, MEChA, Orange County Dream Team, Students Working for Equal Rights (SWER), The Dream Is Coming, National Council of La Raza (now named UnidosUS), Campus Progress (part of the Center for American Progress), the United States Student Association (USSA), and a number of faith-based organizations and labor rights groups such as SEIU. This list is not exhaustive because it is not possible to list the countless number of national and local groups that have worked in this coalition across the country. The National Association of Social Workers (NASW) supports the DREAM Act and has issued action alerts to its membership asking members to contact their representatives to explain that social workers support policies that provide children of immigrants with access to higher education and policies that do not punish children for their parents' actions.

Earned media. Advocates have engaged in a number of tactics that are designed to garner media coverage, such as press conferences; working with Spanish language television and radio stations to urge supporters to call their elected officials; and four students from Miami Dade College who walked from Miami to Washington, D.C., and called their campaign the *Trail of Dreams*. Many of these stories have been featured on local and national news stations such as CNN and MSNBC and in newspapers, including the piece in the *New York Times Magazine* titled, *"Coming Out Illegal,"* published on October 21, 2010.

Educational outreach. Advocates have hosted community events in many states across the country to bring greater awareness of the plight of undocumented students and the need for the DREAM Act. Screenings of the documentary film *Papers* were held in every state in various communities across the country (more on this film in a separate section).

Social media. This movement has also been built with the help of the Internet and social media such as Facebook and Twitter, which has allowed these youth from all over the country to connect with each other and organize their political activities. Youth activists have used YouTube to tell their stories and have started websites such as **Dreamactivist. org** in order to communicate with each other and to educate the public about this issue.

Advocacy Tip

For the DREAM Act activists, **social media** (e.g., Facebook and Twitter) was an important organizing tool. It was crucial in helping them to share information with each other, mobilize support, and to plan and organize their events.

Tactics Used to Get the DREAM Act Passed into Law

- ☒ Coalition building
- ☒ Direct lobbying (in-person lobby visits, sometimes by a professional lobbyist)
- ☒ Earned media (letters to the editor, actions that lead to media coverage)
- ☒ Grassroots lobbying (e.g., urging people to call, write, email legislators)
- ☐ Paid media (paying for TV/radio ads)
- ☒ Educational outreach (town halls, house parties, community forums)
- ☒ Visibility (rallies, marches)
- ☒ Online advocacy (using social media)
- ☒ Political dissent (e.g., civil disobedience, protest)
- ☐ Paid communication (paid staff who call voters, materials mailed out)
- ☐ Providing testimony in a legislative committee hearing
- ☐ Fundraising activities

Papers, Stories of Undocumented Youth (the Movie)

This story is unique because two dedicated advocates/allies/filmmakers embarked on the making of a documentary film about the DREAM Act to enable undocumented youth to tell their stories and to help build support for the legislation. *Papers: Stories of Undocumented Youth* is a 90-minute film that was directed by Anne Galisky and produced by Rebecca Shine, both of Graham Street Productions. Galisky has a master's degree in history and has conducted research on the Japanese internment during World War II. Shine has a lot of experience working with nonprofit organizations, schools, and public agencies in the areas of economic development, social services, mentoring, and youth leadership. Both have a passion for advocacy and issues of social and economic justice.

However, perhaps the most interesting part of this movie is that filmmakers Galisky and Shine decided to train and engage a youth crew who would collaborate with them in the making of this film. Galisky explains,

> While Rebecca and I were certainly leaders in putting the film together, it would not be the same film without the intensive participation of the youth crew. Their involvement is what makes this film different, both the production and the distribution of it. It is not just a film about undocumented youth, it was made with undocumented youth. I am convinced that this is what makes the film fresh and honest why it appeals to young people. I see our role as facilitating the youth telling their own stories. We could have not have made this film without them.
>
> *(Personal communication, n.d.)*

Shine and Galisky knew the value of including the youth who were affected by this issue in every phase of the filmmaking process, including preproduction, fundraising, filming, marketing, and distribution. Their first planning meeting with youth occurred in January 2008, and just over a year and a half later the film premiered in September 2009. After working with many of these youth activists, the filmmakers have witnessed firsthand the youths' growth and development as they have gained valuable skills in advocacy, public policy, and community organizing. In the view of Galisky and Shine, these young adults have learned what it means to be part of a movement that is larger than themselves, and many of them will become the future leaders of tomorrow.

Papers has been screened in every U.S. state, including a screening on Capitol Hill. Five main characters are profiled in the film to show the diversity of their experiences and backgrounds despite the common problem they all share. Two are Mexican American, one is Guatemalan American, one is Korean American, and one is Jamaican American (e.g., Juan Carlos, Monica, Yo Sub, Simone, and Jorge). Elected officials and leaders from various human rights organizations are also interviewed in their film, which puts the DREAM Act into the larger context of the historic struggle for immigrant rights in the United States.

Practice Exercise 11.2

If your university library has a copy of *Papers*, watch this film in order to critique how well it (1) informs people about the issue and (2) whether it is a good vehicle to get others to act. The DREAM Act is an example of a policy where those who are directly impacted by the issue are among those lobbying for the change. Sometimes social workers advocate for others in the legislative arena, but it is often much more powerful when we can help others tell their own stories in this environment. Think about your own interest in social work—how might you empower your clients to advocate for themselves politically?

Interview with Papers Director Anne Galisky and Producer Rebecca Shine

September 2010

Q: What first drew you to this story?

A: About six years ago, we both began tutoring and mentoring immigrant youth who were at risk of dropping out of high school in Portland, Oregon. Even though we knew a lot about challenges facing at-risk youth, we were dismayed by the extra obstacles that stood in the way of some of these young people because of their lack of "papers." That in turn made us painfully aware of the bigger picture: how much our nation is losing by keeping laws in place that bar millions of children from pursuing their dreams and realizing their potential.

Most of all, we grew to love each of these young people and began wondering how we could help them fight the injustice of their circumstances. We came to believe that making a film would be a great way to help other people meet these extraordinary youth, understand their stories, and hopefully begin to relate to them in a new way. As the idea grew, our group of willing participants grew and evolved into a crew that came to be called El Grupo Juvenil, young people from across the US who wanted to help undocumented youth tell their own stories to a national audience.

Then, in the fall of 2007, two things happened. First, the DREAM Act failed to overcome a filibuster in the Senate. Second, Oregon's Governor, Ted Kulongoski issued an Executive Order changing state law to require that all applicants for state IDs or driver's licenses have Social Security numbers. Both of these events took a terrible toll on the immigrant youth we worked with, and gave us the impetus to start the production of "Papers."

Q: Why don't you show the other side of the debate?

A: We spend the first three minutes of the film, without dialogue, showing images from both pro-immigrant and anti-immigrant marches and rallies to remind audiences of the extremely polarized and vitriolic debate that surrounds these young people every day. We also interviewed over 150 people from across the country who were both in favor of and against immigration reform, and conducted many interviews at the Democratic and Republican National Conventions in the summer of 2008.

However, as we continued to film, we realized how rare it is to hear directly from undocumented students and how common it is to hear anti-immigrant and anti-immigration-reform voices, so we decided to emphasize the students' stories first and foremost. There's no arguing with someone's personal experience and this is the story that is so often overlooked—how do undocumented immigrant youth feel and what do they think about their situation? Politicians, teachers, and community leaders provide the historical, cultural, and political context to the youths' stories.

Q: How did you find the students? Isn't it dangerous for them to appear in the film?

A: We interviewed dozens of undocumented youth across the country. Some we already knew from our work as mentors and advocates, and others were introduced to us as we traveled. Still others heard about the project and contacted us to share their stories. Over the course of a year we identified the five main characters, each of whom was willing to sacrifice anonymity to appear on film, had come from different countries under widely varying circumstances, and who had unique personalities, dreams and struggles.

Each of the main characters: Monica, Yo Sub, Juan Carlos, Simone, and Jorge, had the awareness that telling their stories would encourage other people to become more public about who they are. And we have seen that this is in fact true: at many screenings of the film across the country, young people are "stepping out of the shadows" and, sometimes for the first time, declaring their immigration status openly.

And yes, it does pose risks to publicly declare your undocumented status, so we were very careful to respect each of the students' choices about their level of exposure. Simone, for example, made the choice to only show her eyes in order to protect her safety and privacy. Her choice demonstrates the fear that millions of kids currently live with every day, and emphasizes the huge risk a handful of them are taking by telling their stories.

Despite a recent NY Times article about the Obama administration not prioritizing the deportation of undocumented students, no one knows when the political winds could shift and each of the students is still legally at risk of arrest, detention and deportation at any time.

Q: What is happening in the lives of your main characters today?

A: Jorge recently completed a 14-day hunger strike in front of Sen. Diane Feinstein's Los Angeles office, the latest step in his overall choice to be more public about his immigration status. His personal hope is to convince a filibuster-proof majority in the Senate to support the DREAM Act and then he will move on to pursue a graduate degree in African American literature.

Monica lives with her husband and works in elder care. Her family remains split between the U.S and Guatemala while her father's 19-year-long asylum case is still pending.

Juan Carlos struggles with his limited choices now that he has graduated from high school. He feels that his dreams are on hold until the DREAM Act passes so he advocates for its passage while continuing to try to be a role model for young people in his community.

Simone finished her Associates Degree and wants desperately to contribute to the country she calls home. She worries about her little brother and tries to keep up his hopes so that he will think that it is worthwhile to stay in school.

Yo Sub is getting ready to start his second year of college and is majoring in Economics. He loves college life and is thriving academically as could be expected of someone who graduated high school with a 4.5 GPA. What happens after graduation will depend on whether the DREAM Act or comprehensive immigration reform passes by then.

Q: What has changed in the DREAM Act movement since the film's release?

A: The good news is that momentum is building behind the DREAM Act and it is becoming better known and more widely supported. DREAMers have begun to deliberately draw inspiration from the civil rights movement and the gay rights movement, both in terms of messaging and tactics, which has added a historical dimension to their work that not only adds a great deal strategically, but inspires them and others to see themselves in that proud, and ultimately triumphant, historical context.

They are taking some enormous risks like conducting hunger strikes in New York and Los Angeles, walking from Miami to Washington, DC, taking part in civil disobedience actions including staging sit-ins at Congressional offices, and marching on Capitol Hill. Mostly, they are going public and telling their stories and the American people are starting to listen. President Obama is in support of the DREAM Act and Senate Majority leader Harry Reid has expressed a willingness to bring the DREAM Act forward this fall. Even in an era of rare bipartisan cooperation, both Democrats and Republicans are co-sponsors and proponents of this legislation.

Someday soon we hope to look back on this as an extraordinary time in the history of the immigrant rights movement. We are thrilled to have been able to both chronicle the movement and to support its expansion and public support through "Papers."

Q: You make strong connections between the LGBTQ rights movement and the immigration rights movement in the film. Can you explain how they are linked?

A: One of the main characters in "Papers," Jorge, is both undocumented and queer. He likens his experience to living at two borders at the same time. In fact, as we were working on the film, we found that a large proportion of the young people who are leading the movement and going public about their status as undocumented (they call it "coming out") also identify as queer or LGBTQ.

They realize that there is extraordinary power in their stories and in telling the truth. The boldness of it inspires us. By coming out as undocumented, they risk arrest, detention, and deportation. By coming out as queer, they risk being ostracized from their families, their churches, their cultures of origin and their communities. But in talking with these courageous young people, it is obvious that they are not going to stop being public about who they are. In some ways the most vulnerable, they are also the most brave. They, more than anyone, know the power of "coming out" and recognize that going public is the way to change peoples' hearts and minds.

Q: El Grupo Juvenil is mentioned in the film's credits and on your site. Who are they and what role did they play in "Papers"?

A: El Grupo Juvenil is the "Papers" youth crew. This group of young people was integral to every aspect of the film's production and distribution and includes over 750 participants nationwide. These youth come from a wide variety of neighborhoods, races, ethnicities, religions, and abilities, and vary in immigration status and sexual orientation. We wanted to make a film about undocumented youth but also wanted to include as many of them, and other youth who care about them, in every step of creating the film, and El Grupo Juvenil was our answer.

The group began with the youth we were mentoring and tutoring and soon grew like wildfire into a national network that will have lasting value far beyond helping with the film. Participants developed their leadership capacities, learned public policy advocacy, presented at local, regional and national conferences, and designed and led workshops for middle school and high school students. Some of the group's leaders have now appeared on CNN and Univision, on radio and in newspapers. They were honored in May at a Congressional reception at the U.S. Capitol.

Q: Once the DREAM Act becomes law, why should people buy and watch "Papers"?
A: "Papers" is timeless and universal because it is ultimately about overcoming obstacles, especially those that seem insurmountable. No matter who you are, struggle is a major element of the human experience and something we all relate to. Who knows, it might even be more inspiring after DREAM becomes law—everyone loves to see others succeed despite impossible odds because it gives us faith we can do the same This film directly chronicles five incredible young people facing that challenge, but represents 2 million more such stories.

Q: What's next for Graham Street Productions?
A: Well, we are still very busy with "Papers" this year. The film is coming out on DVD on September 14th, just in time for back-to-school—a period that is extremely hopeful and fun for most families, but that means the beginning of a crisis for the 65,000 undocumented high school seniors who will graduate this year—and we are hoping that will kick off another amazing round of screenings and discussions around the nation.

Anne has continued to film the DREAM Act movement and exploring what to do with that additional footage while also looking forward to starting another yet-to-be- announced film project. Rebecca is working closely with El Grupo Juvenil to expand their youth organizing work in 2011.

Source: Papers press materials.

Filmmakers Shine and Galisky believe that documentary films can be a powerful vehicle for social and political change because of the power they have to move people, touch the audience on an emotional level, and raise consciousness. In their view, people would prefer to learn about an issue by seeing a movie or piece of art. They made a film that was not meant for people to watch alone. It was important for them to make a film that did not make people feel depressed afterward, but rather empowered to act since their film profiles a problem that has a straightforward solution. After the film was made, the film was purchased by individuals and local grassroots organizations across the country where screenings of the film were planned and organized. The majority of the screenings were organized by high school students, college students, and educators. The typical format was as follows:

- Organize screenings in the community so that community members can watch the film together.
- Invite community leaders and elected officials to attend.
- After the film, include a Q&A session and engage the audience in a conversation.
- It was fairly common for the groups that hosted the screening to give action items to audience members after the film, based on what they wanted to mobilize people to do.
- After the screening, people were often moved to act since the stories of these youth are so compelling.

What Is the Current Status of the DREAM Act?

Recall that the first version of the DREAM Act was introduced in 2001, so this has been a long and hard-fought battle, with heartbreaking results for the youth who continue to live in the United States with huge barriers to attending college and/or working legally. The closest the bill came to passage was in 2010 when the bill had 134 cosponsors in the House and 40 cosponsors in the Senate. However, it fell five votes short of the 60 votes needed to overcome a Republican-led filibuster in the Senate. The vote was largely along party lines, although three Republicans went against their party and voted to advance the legislation, while five Democrats went against their party and voted no. For DREAM act activists, it was a heartbreaking defeat. Afterward, President Obama, who supported the bill, expressed his disappointment over the defeat of this legislation.

The most recent version of the DREAM Act (S. 264) was introduced in 2021 in the Senate by Senators Lindsay Graham (R-South Carolina) and Dick Durbin (D-Illinois). A version of the Dream Act was also incorporated into a larger bill called the Dream and Promise Act of 2021 (H.R. 6). Advocates are hoping that the changing political landscape in 2021 will lead to the bill's passage. However, it is important to keep in mind that not all young people will be eligible for the DREAM Act, so for these youth a comprehensive immigration bill that provides a path to citizenship for all undocumented immigrants will be necessary.

The Advent of the Deferred Action for Childhood Arrivals (DACA) Program

An interesting development occurred on June 15, 2012, when President Obama announced a major policy change (via a presidential executive order) with regard to young immigrant youth residing in the United States. Making the announcement to reporters in the Rose Garden, Obama explained, "They are Americans in their heart, in their minds, in every single way but one: on paper" (Preston & Cushman, 2012). White House officials explained that the timing for the policy shift coincided with the 30th anniversary of the *Pyler v. Doe* Supreme Court decision. The program would be named, **DACA**, or Deferred Action for Childhood Arrivals.

As a result of this executive order, the Department of Homeland Security would not have the authority to deport undocumented immigrants who arrived in the United States before age 16, have resided in the United States for at least five years, and are either in school, are high school graduates, or have served in the military (Preston and Cushman, 2012). They must be under age 30 and have no criminal record. However, it is important to note that DACA is a temporary measure and is not a path to permanent citizenship as laid out in the DREAM Act legislation. For immigrants who come forward and qualify, Homeland Security officials have the authority to grant deferred action, a reprieve that has to be renewed every two years. They will then be able to obtain work permits so they can work legally as well as obtain a driver's license.

Reactions to the new policy varied, with many Republicans angered that the president circumvented Congress, while many of the affected youth were elated. "People are just breaking down and crying for joy when they find out what the president did," said Lorella Praeli, a leader of the United We Dream Network, the largest coalition of undocumented immigrant students (Preston & Cushman, 2012). President Obama received praise from many Democratic lawmakers and immigrant rights and civil rights organizations, many of whom pointed out, however, that this is not a long-term solution, and Congress will ultimately need to act. Even Obama acknowledged this in his remarks when he stated, "This is not a path to citizenship. It is not a permanent fix" (Preston & Cushman, 2012). According to U.S. Citizenship and Immigration Services, by the end of 2017 the DACA program has shielded nearly 800,000 undocumented immigrants from deportation since the program's inception.

Immigration Policy Under President Trump ("Zero Tolerance")

When President Trump became president, the immigration landscape changed pretty dramatically. He appointed Jeff Sessions, a known hard-liner on immigration, to be his Attorney General and has implemented a ban on immigration for people from certain Muslim nations. He also announced an end to the DACA program, which has left the lives of hundreds of thousands of young immigrant youth hanging in the balance. However, two federal judges blocked Trump's decision to end the program until the legal challenges could be resolved in court. And on June 18, 2020, the U.S. Supreme Court ruled against the President in a 5–4 decision thereby blocking the Trump administration from dismantling the DACA program. When Joe Biden became president, he issued an executive order stating that the DACA program shall be preserved according to the Obama administration's 2012 guidance.

In an effort to deter people from crossing the Mexican border, in 2018 the Trump administration started enforcing a new **zero-tolerance policy** to prosecute any migrants attempting to cross the border into the United States. In May 2018, Attorney General Jeff Sessions announced, "If you smuggle illegal aliens across our border, then we will prosecute you. If you are smuggling a child, then we will prosecute you and that child will be separated from you as required by law." "So if you're going to come to this country, come here legally. Don't come here illegally" (Barajas, 2018). According to the *LA Times*, "Under the policy, migrants who enter the United States illegally face misdemeanor charges in federal criminal court, felony charges if they have crossed illegally before; parents are sent to federal detention, their children to shelters. In the past, such cases were often handled administratively, not in criminal court" (Hennessy-Fiske, 2018).

As a result of this new policy, according to the ACLU, roughly 5400 children were separated from their parents and held in detention shelters run by the Office of Refugee Resettlement, part of the Department of Health and Human Services (as of October 2019). This policy was widely condemned by human rights and children's rights organizations, including the National Association of Social Workers, which called this policy malicious and unconscionable. After facing immense criticism from Democratic and Republican lawmakers, the general public, and some religious leaders, President Trump announced an end to the practice of separating children from their parents and signed an executive order to this effect. And at the end of June, a federal judge in San Diego ordered that all children separated from their parents be reunited within 30 days. However, this has proven very challenging for children whose parents were deported, children who were placed in a shelter far away from their parents, and children who are too young to identify who their parents are. Additionally, the government had inadequate tracking systems. A 2019 report from the U.S. Department of Health and Human Services Office of Inspector General (OIG) detailed the trauma that children experienced who were impacted by this family separation policy (Alvarez, 2020).

President Trump continued to face criticism for prosecuting and deporting undocumented immigrants and asylum seekers without providing them due process. On June 30, 2018, approximately 700 marches took place across the United States ("Families Belong Together") in protest against the Trump administration's zero-tolerance immigration policy. Meanwhile, the U.S. Congress has been unable to find a compromise on a comprehensive immigration bill, with liberals and moderate Republicans fighting for a path to legalization and conservative Republicans fighting for immigration enforcement, enhanced border security, and against any bill that is viewed as granting amnesty. The task now falls to President Biden to find a federal solution to fix a broken immigration system, which he has vowed to do. And millions of undocumented immigrants continue to live in the shadows and wait.

REFERENCES

Alexander, M. (2010). *The new Jim Crow: Mass incarceration in the age of colorblindness*. New York, NY: New Press.

Alvarez, P. (2020). US government watchdog details trauma experienced by separated migrant children. CNN. Retrieved from https://www.cnn.com/2019/09/04/politics/family-separation-inspector-general-report/index.html

American Immigration Council (2017). The Dream Act, DACA, and Other Policies Designed to Protect Dreamers. Retrieved from https://www.americanimmigrationcouncil.org/research/dream-act

Balsamo, M. (2020, November 16). Hate crimes in US reach highest level in more than a decade. Retrieved from https://apnews.com/article/hate-crimes-rise-FBI-data-ebbcadca8458aba96575da905650120d

Barajas, J. (2018, June 14). How Trump's family separation policy has become what it is today. PBS. Retrieved from https://www.pbs.org/newshour/nation/how-trumps-family-separation-policy-has-become-what-it-is-today

Beirich, H., & Buchanan, S. (2018). 2017: The year in hate and extremism. Southern Poverty Law Center. Retrieved from https://www.splcenter.org/fighting-hate/intelligence-report/2018/2017-year-hate-and-extremism

Black Lives Matter. (n.d.). Herstory. Retrieved from https://blacklivesmatter.com/herstory/

"Border insecurity." (2008 March 4,). *New York Times*. Retrieved from http://www.nytimes. com/2008/03/04/opinion/04tue1.html

Galisky, A. (n.d.). Personal communication.

Hennessy-Fiske, M. (2018, May 18). New zero-tolerance policy immigration crackdown fills border courts. *LA Times*. Retrieved from http://www.latimes.com/nation/la-na-border-migrant-courts-20180518-story.html

Krogstad, J. M. (2017). DACA has shielded nearly 790,000 young unauthorized immigrants from deportation. Pew Research Center. Retrieved from http://www.pewresearch.org/fact-tank/2017/09/01/unauthorized-immigrants-covered-by-daca-face-uncertain-future/

Lopez, G., & Radford, J. (2017). Facts on U.S. Immigrants 2015. Statistical portrait of the foreign-born population in the United States. Retrieved from http://www.pewhispanic.org/2017/05/03/facts-on-u-s-immigrants/

National Park Service, U.S. Department of the Interior. (n.d.). Jim Crow laws. Retrieved from www.nps.gov/malu/forteachers/jim_crow_laws.htm

Norton, M. I., & Sommers, S. R. (2011). Whites see racism as a zero sum game that they are now losing. *Perspectives on Psychological Science*, 6(3), 215–218. Retrieved from http://www.people. hbs.edu/mnorton/norton%20sommers.pdf

Pew Research Center. (2020). Facts on U.S. immigrants, 2018. Retrieved from https://www.pewresearch.org/hispanic/2020/08/20/facts-on-u-s-immigrants/#fb-key-charts-unauthorized

Preston, J., & Cushman, J. H. (2012, June 15). Obama to permit young migrants to remain in U.S. *New York Times*. Retrieved from https://www.nytimes.com/2012/06/16/us/us-to-stop-deporting-some-illegal-immigrants.html

UNHCR. (n.d.). Refugee Data Finder. Retrieved from https://www.unhcr.org/refugee-statistics/

UnidosUS. (n.d.). Seven ways immigrants enrich our economy and society. Retrieved from https://www.unidosus.org/issues/immigration/resources/facts

Wirzbicki, A. (November 11, 2012). Immigration reform could be on new Congress' agenda. Retrieved from https://www.boston.com/news/politics/2012/11/11/immigration-reform-could-be-on-new-congress-agenda

CHAPTER 12   Advocacy for Gender Equality and LGBTQ Rights

"A feminist is anyone who recognizes the equality and full humanity of women and men."

~ *Gloria Steinem, feminist*

"Women's rights are human rights and human rights are women's rights."

~*Hillary Rodham Clinton*

"Love is love is love is love."

~ *Lin Manuel Miranda, playwright/actor/singer*

Figure 12.1   Suffragettes

CHAPTER SUMMARY

The previous chapter focused on the politics of race and immigration; this chapter provides an overview of the politics of gender and sexual orientation. Historically, both women and LGBTQ individuals have been treated as second-class citizens and have faced tremendous barriers to equality in U.S. society. For much of human history, the predominant view has been that females are not as smart and competent as males and that their place is in the home. Women were socialized to be caretakers for their husbands and children and were not allowed to have an identity separate from this. Gay men and lesbians have had to face degrading stereotypes and societal attitudes (some rooted in religious beliefs) that view gay people as abnormal and/or deviant. In 1973, the American Psychiatric Association removed homosexuality from its list of mental disorders. Both females and LGBTQ individuals are vulnerable to intimidation, violence, and hate crimes. However, society began to change with the women's liberation movement and gay rights movement when women and gay people began fighting for dignity, respect, and equal rights in all realms of society, private and public. The progress that has been made, due to these social movements, has been substantial and has resulted in an array of expanded opportunities and social advancement for females and gay Americans. Chapter 12 highlights how advocates waged a successful campaign to legalize same-sex marriage. Finally, this chapter summarizes both the achievements of these movements as well as the challenges that remain.

STUDENT LEARNING OBJECTIVES

- Students will be able to summarize social problems that females have experienced historically and currently.

- Students will be able to summarize social problems that LGBTQ individuals have experienced historically and currently.

- Students will be able to list and describe legislation that has advanced social justice for women.

- Students will be able to list and describe legislation that has advanced social justice for LGBTQ individuals.

- Students will be able to evaluate the political advocacy strategies of advocates who worked for same-sex marriage in the United States.

- Students will become familiar with famous advocates and advocacy groups in the United States that advocate for women and LGBTQ individuals.

Advocacy for Gender Equality in the United States

Women earned the right to vote in 1920 as a result of the **19th Amendment to the U.S. Constitution**, thanks to the women's suffrage movement made up of suffragettes such as Sojourner Truth, Susan B. Anthony, Alice Paul, Ida B. Wells, and Elizabeth Cady Stanton, who fought tirelessly and courageously for this basic human right. These early feminists employed a variety of tactics to win the vote for women, such as distributing campaign literature, writing newspaper and magazine articles, lobbying legislators, making speeches, and participating in protests and demonstrations, including picketing the White House. Many of these early suffragettes were arrested and some suffered physical abuse and neglect while imprisoned. For example, when some suffragettes went on a hunger strike in jail, they were brutally force-fed.

In the 1960s and 1970s, the focus of the feminist movement shifted to larger issues of equality within the workplace and the home and reproductive rights, and this led to a number of important legislative wins. The **Equal Pay Act** (1963), signed into law by President John F. Kennedy, was groundbreaking legislation that made it illegal to offer women a lower salary than their male coworkers for jobs of equal skill, effort, and responsibility. In 1965, the U.S. Supreme Court ruled in *Griswold v. Connecticut* that laws that criminalize contraceptive use were unconstitutional because they violate the right to privacy, and eight years later abortion was legalized by the U.S. Supreme Court via *Roe v. Wade*.

In 1972, a historic policy was passed, **Title IX**, to prohibit gender discrimination in schools and educational institutions that receive federal funding, including colleges and universities. Title IX protects females from sexual harassment and prohibits discrimination in the areas of recruitment, admissions, financial assistance, athletics, pregnancy, and employment. Pregnancy discrimination in the workplace was outlawed in 1978 by the **Pregnancy Discrimination Act**. This law prevents employers from refusing to hire a woman because she is pregnant as long as she can perform the essential functions of the job.

The **Violence Against Women Act (VAWA),** passed in 1994, was the first federal legislation that was designed to improve the way that law enforcement and the courts responded to violence against women, such as sexual assault and domestic violence, and to treat it as a crime instead of a private matter. Then-Senator Joe Biden was a champion of this historic legislation. One of the major goals of VAWA was to increase the availability of services to victims, recognizing that domestic and sexual violence requires a coordinated community response beyond the confines of the criminal justice system. VAWA has to be reauthorized every five years, and each time it gets strengthened and improved (e.g., adding dating violence and stalking; protections for immigrants and Native Americans; enhancing services for LGBTQ victims and victims with disabilities). The original act created the Office on Violence Against Women to administer VAWA, and since 1994 it has awarded billions of dollars to communities to prevent and address violence against women. However, despite this tremendous social and legislative progress for women, many challenges remain. A sampling of advocacy groups for women can be seen in the Women's Advocacy Spotlight.

Women's Advocacy Spotlight

Emily's List
End Rape on Campus

ERA Coalition
Feminist Majority
Feminist Majority Foundation
National Abortion Rights Action League (NARAL)
National Alliance to End Sexual Violence
National Organization for Women (NOW)
National Women's Law Center
National Task Force to End Sexual and Domestic Violence
Planned Parenthood
Rape, Abuse, & Incest National Network (RAINN)
Supermajority
Time's Up Legal Defense Fund
Vday.org
Women's Campaign Fund

The Equal Rights Amendment (ERA) and CEDAW

The overwhelming majority of constitutions around the world (more than 80%) guarantee gender equality, but the United States is not one of them. Feminist activists worked for decades to get the ERA added to the U.S. Constitution, but they failed to secure the required number of state ratifications, and it died in 1982. The amendment, which Congress approved in March 1972, mandates that "Equality of rights under the law shall not be denied or abridged by the United States or by any state on account of sex." However, there has been a renewed effort to pass the ERA spearheaded by the Equal Rights Coalition (www.eracoalition.org). In 2020, Virginia became the 38th state to ratify the ERA, enough to reach the 38—or three-quarters of the states—needed to ratify a constitutional amendment. Advocates are now working to get legislation passed in the U.S. Congress to move this forward. Thus, this story is still unfolding.

The United States in also outlier with regard to the **UN Convention on the Elimination of All Forms of Discrimination Against Women (CEDAW).** The United States is one of only six nations, along with Iran, Sudan, Somalia, Palau, and Tonga, that has not ratified CEDAW, a United Nations treaty that focuses on women's rights and women's issues worldwide. It has been informally dubbed the International Women's Bill of Rights. Opposition in the United States has come primarily from some conservative political and religious leaders who oppose reproductive rights and support traditional gender roles between men and women according to their Christian beliefs. In 2010 during the Obama administration, an effort was made by the Senate Judiciary Committee to move CEDAW ratification forward, but it stalled due to the political polarization between Democrats and Republicans. The full text of CEDAW can be found at http://www.un.org/womenwatch/daw/cedaw/text/econvention.htm.

Sexual Harassment and Sexual Violence (#MeToo)

One of the more important political moments for women in recent years has been the #MeToo movement, which has been very successful in focusing the nation's attention on sexual harassment and sexual violence. This movement has given women a platform to share their experience with these issues. Millions of women and men across the country, and around the globe, attended the Women's March on January 21, 2017 (the day after President Trump was inaugurated) in almost every major U.S. city, including a massive one in the nation's capital, to protest his election, which was dominated by allegations of sexual misconduct in the aftermath of a now infamous videotape of Trump telling a journalist (off camera) that "When you're a star … you can do anything … Grab 'em by the [expletive]." A number of women later came forward and alleged that Trump had engaged in groping behavior against their consent. The Women's March was a sea of handcrafted pink hats that came to symbolize Trump's vulgar remark and also unified activists across the country on issues such as reproductive rights, civil rights, and immigration.

The #MeToo movement was coined in 2006 by Tarana Burke, a victim of sexual assault herself, who was working with young women and girls of color who had also experienced sexual violence. However, the #MeToo became a national phenomenon when it was used by the actress Alyssa Milano in the aftermath of the Harvey Weinstein scandal in Hollywood. At the 2018 Golden Globes ceremony in January 2018, female actresses protested by wearing all black to the ceremony and spoke out about the issue of sexual harassment on the red carpet using the phrase "Time's Up." A handful of actresses brought activists with them to the ceremony, including Tarana Burke, who was the guest of actress Michelle Williams. Oprah Winfrey, who was receiving an award at the ceremony, gave a rousing speech that galvanized the audience with an impassioned plea for addressing sexual violence and believing women who come forward. The #MeToo movement has sparked a national conversation on sexual harassment and sexual violence against women and men in the workplace. A number of accused high-profile men in Hollywood, journalism, and corporate America have lost their jobs or status as a result, some of whom are facing prosecution (e.g., actor Bill Cosby; movie producer Harvey Weinstein; Today Show host Matt Lauer; president of CBS Les Moonves; comedian Louis CK). In September 2018, Bill Cosby was sentenced to 3–10 years for drugging and sexually assaulting a woman 14 years previously. Cosby is now classified as a sexually violent predator and will be required to be on the sex offender registry for the rest of his life. Harvey Weinstein was sentenced to 23 years in prison for rape and sexual abuse in March 2020.

On September 27, 2018, the nation was riveted to the television to watch the Supreme Court hearings for Judge Brett Kavanaugh, whom President Trump had nominated to the U.S. Supreme Court. Judge Kavanaugh had been accused by Dr. Christine Blasey Ford of sexually assaulting her when they were in high school, accusations that he vehemently denied. Dr. Ford testified before the Senate Judiciary Committee and recounted what happened to her when she was at a party in high school. She alleged that Judge Kavanaugh attempted to rape her in a bedroom while a friend of his observed. Judge Kavanaugh passionately denied the allegations when he testified and stated that he does not have any recollection of being at this party. He accused Democrats of a left-wing conspiracy to keep him off the court. Americans appeared divided as people debated whether an event of wrong-doing that occurred in high school should keep someone off of the Supreme Court. Democrats and Republicans were similarly divided as Republicans defended and believed Judge Kavanaugh while Democrats defended and believed Dr. Ford. Since the Republicans control the U.S. Senate, they had the votes to confirm Judge Kavanaugh, but in an interesting late-breaking development, Republican Senator Jeff Flake of Arizona asked the Judiciary Committee to agree to an FBI investigation that could only take one week so that Dr. Ford's allegations could be investigated. They agreed, and President Trump ordered the investigation.

However, on October 6, 2018, Judge Kavanaugh was confirmed by the U.S. Senate by one of the slimmest margins in American history, a vote of 50–48. The senators voted almost entirely along party lines; Senator Joe Manchin of West Virginia was the only Democrat to vote "yes."

There is an important lesson here because there are many existing laws on the books to protect women (and men) from sexual harassment and sexual violence, yet these unwanted behaviors and crimes continue to occur. According to data from the Centers for Disease Control and Prevention (CDC), nearly 1 in 5 women (estimated 25.5 million women) in the United States reported completed or attempted rape at some time in their lives. About 1 in 14 men (nearly 7.9 million men) in the U.S. was made to penetrate someone else (attempted or completed) at some point in their lifetime. Using a more expansive definition of sexual violence, the CDC reports that 43.6% of women and roughly 25% of men in the United States have experienced some form of contact sexual violence (e.g., rape, sexual coercion, unwanted sexual contact) in the 12 months preceding the survey (Smith et al., 2018).

Thus advocates have to be vigilant in holding employers and law enforcement officials accountable for enforcing laws that are already in effect. It is a serious problem when a group of people in society stays quiet because they do not trust those in charge to enforce the laws that are designed to protect them. Sexual violence on college campuses and in the military has been highlighted in recent years, and there have been legislative efforts to combat this (e.g., Military Justice Improvement Act, Campus Accountability and Safety Act). New York Senator Kirsten Gillibrand has been a leading voice on these issues in the U.S. Senate.

Advocacy Spotlight: The Brock Turner Sexual Assault Case (California)

Sometimes a horrible event can help advocates propel a neglected issue onto the political agenda and make significant progress. One recent case that received national attention is the court case of Stanford University student athlete Brock Turner, whom witnesses observed sexually assaulting a 23-year-old woman, who was unconscious, behind a dumpster. The victim read a 12-page letter to the offender during the court proceedings, which described in vivid detail the trauma she experienced, and this letter went viral on the Internet. However, much of the nation was outraged when the California judge in the case, Aaron Persky, gave Brock Turner a six-month sentence for three counts of felony sexual assault (Brock ended up serving three months, plus three years of probation). Months after the ruling, state legislators in California passed two new bills to try to prevent this from happening again, and Governor Jerry Brown signed them into law. The new legislation expanded California's definition of rape and added mandatory minimum sentences for sexual assaults.

After the court case, a recall effort was begun by Stanford University law professor Michele Dauber in order to remove Judge Persky from the bench. Dauber and a dedicated crew of volunteers started a website (www.recallaaronpersky.com) and set out to gather the signatures required that would allow voters to recall him. They gathered more than 90,000 signatures, far more than the 58,634 that were required. They then set out to persuade voters in Santa Clara County that Judge Persky did not deserve to keep his position as judge due to his bad judgment on this case. Some of these advocates believe that Judge Persky overidentified with Brock Turner, since, like Mr. Turner, Judge Persky is a White male and a former athlete from Stanford.

Professor Dauber and her volunteers engaged in get-out-the-vote activities such as getting supporters to put signs in their yards ("Recall Judge Persky!") and calling voters to encourage them to get to the polls on Election Day. Two years later (in 2018), it was a clear victory for these advocates when voters in Santa Clara voted to oust Judge Persky from office. There was mixed reaction to this since some felt this outcome was completely justified, while others felt it is a dangerous precedent to remove a judge from the bench for an unpopular decision.

The Gender Wage Gap and Glass Ceiling

Equal pay between men and women is still a problem in U.S. society. The **glass ceiling** refers to the fact that women still face significant barriers in advancing to the highest-level positions in the organizations where they work (e.g., president; executive director; chief executive officer, or CEO). According to recent data from the U.S. Census Bureau, in 2018 women were paid 82% of what men were paid; this was up from 60% in 1980 (Bleiweis, 2020). And the gap is much larger for women of color. A number of factors explain the gender wage gap—men and women tend to work in different occupations, and women tend to work in occupations that are lower paid; women take on more of the caregiving responsibilities and are more likely to work reduced hours and take parental leave; and gender discrimination. In 2009, President Obama signed the **Lilly Ledbetter Fair Pay Act,** which extended the statute of limitations on filing a claim of gender discrimination in pay. It was named for Lilly Ledbetter, a woman who worked at Goodyear as a supervisor and learned that for years she had been paid less than her male peers for the same work. There are current efforts to update the Equal Pay Act with a new piece of legislation, the **Paycheck Fairness Act** (yet to be passed by the U.S. Congress). This bill would require employers to prove that pay disparities between women and men exist for legitimate, job-related reasons.

Government Representation by Women

In the United States, as of 2020, only about 23% of the 535 members of the U.S. Congress were women. And although more than 70 nations have been led by women, the United States has never had a female president. According to data from the Inter-Parliamentary Union, in 2017 the United States ranked 104th in the world when it came to women's representation in government. Women who wish to hold public office must overcome stereotypes that being a politician is a "man's job." Many Americans were hopeful that this glass ceiling would be broken with the election of Democratic presidential candidate Hillary Clinton, but in a surprise upset she was defeated by Donald Trump. However, a major barrier was broken in November 2020 when Senator Kamala Harris was elected Vice President of the United States, the first time a woman has held this crucial position. It is also important to note that one of the most important lawmakers on Capitol Hill is Democratic Speaker of the House Nancy Pelosi. She will likely go down in history as one of the most effective members of Congress to serve in this role. A number of organizations have the sole purpose of supporting women in running for office and getting elected, such as Emily's List, the National Women's Political Caucus, and the Women's Campaign Fund.

Reproductive Rights and Family Planning

In 1973, the U.S. Supreme Court delivered a historic decision when it ruled that a woman's right to choose an abortion was protected by the privacy rights guaranteed by the Fourteenth Amendment to the U.S. Constitution. However, this decision has not deterred pro-life Americans and politicians from working to dismantle abortion rights, and more than 40 years later it continues to be an area of intense political debate in the United States. A few years after *Roe v. Wade*, the U.S. Congress passed the **Hyde Amendment**, which prevents federal funds (e.g., Medicaid) from being used to pay for abortion; however, there are exceptions for rape, incest, or if the pregnancy is determined to endanger the woman's life. Women's advocates argue that this law creates barriers for low-income women seeking abortion.

Organizations such as Planned Parenthood and the National Abortion Rights Action League (NARAL) continue to fight for policies that advance access to sexual and reproductive health care and safe and legal abortion. Over the last decade, they have fought the efforts of social and religious conservatives who have attempted to restrict abortion rights at both the state and federal levels. Examples of legislation that has been introduced in a number of state legislatures include: forced counseling before an abortion; a mandatory waiting period before an abortion; placing onerous restrictions on abortion providers in efforts to shut them down; requiring a woman to have an ultrasound before an abortion; reducing the number of weeks when an abortion is allowed to occur; and personhood laws, which recognize fetuses, embryos, and fertilized eggs as persons that are separate from the mothers who carry them. In recent years, social conservatives have made numerous attempts to eliminate federal funding for Planned Parenthood because it provides abortion services, though this is a very small part of its overall services. Planned Parenthood provides a wide range of preventative health care and sexual health services to low-income women, such as STD and HIV testing, cancer screenings, and contraceptives.

On June 29, 2020, the U.S. Supreme Court handed down a major ruling on abortion. In a 5–4 decision, the Court struck down a Louisiana law that required physicians performing abortions to have admitting privileges at nearby hospitals. This law could have left Louisiana with just one clinic performing abortions. Women's advocates were thrilled, and conservatives were surprised to see Chief Justice John Roberts join the court's four liberal judges in this ruling. The hope of many social and religious conservatives is to see the highest court eventually overturn *Roe v. Wade*.

Paid Family and Medical Leave

Paid family leave is another important area of public policy for women. These laws help both men and women balance their work and caregiving responsibilities. They allow parents to bond with their child after the birth or adoption of a child and care for a sick child or other family member without fear that they will lose their job. Many are shocked to learn that the United States is the only industrialized nation whose government does not provide *paid* family and medical leave. The United States is a real outlier in this regard. In 1993, President Bill Clinton signed the **Family and Medical Leave Act (FMLA)** into law, which allows up to 12 weeks of *unpaid*, job-protected leave to workers when they need to recover from a serious medical illness, care for a seriously ill family member, or care for a new child by way of birth or adoption. According to Glynn (2013), "The FMLA remains to this day the only piece of federal legislation specifically focused on helping workers manage their dual responsibilities in the workplace and in the home."

The FMLA was a good first step because it guarantees that a parent cannot be fired from his or her job after taking family leave, but it does not guarantee *paid* family leave, and many employees work for employers where paid leave is not offered (e.g., minimum wage workers; contract workers). However, the story is very different for women in other advanced nations, such as the 34 Organisation for Economic Co-Operation and Development (OECD) nations (e.g., France, Germany, Japan, United Kingdom, Sweden). According to the OECD (2017), "In 1970, on average across OECD countries, mothers had access to just 17 weeks of paid leave. By 1990 this had increased to about 40 weeks, and by 2016 to just over one year (52.5)." A handful of U.S. states have passed paid family leave laws, but advocates continue to fight for a strong federal law.

Figure 12.2   Stonewall Inn

Advocacy for LGBTQ Rights

Many regard the 1969 Stonewall Riots as the catalyst for the modern **gay rights movement** in the United States. The riots ensued after New York City police raided a gay club called the Stonewall Inn in Greenwich Village, which led to six days of protests and violent clashes with law enforcement. Roughly 40 years later, the United States witnessed incredible progress with regard to LGBTQ rights in the United States with regard to same-sex marriage, hate crimes, and the right to openly serve in the military, though full equality for LGBTQ people has yet to be achieved. Much of this progress is due to the tireless efforts of activists and advocacy organizations such as the **Human Rights Campaign.**

The rainbow flag became the symbol of this movement, and annual Gay Pride parades have become commonplace in most major U.S. cities across the country. Hollywood and popular culture were ahead of lawmakers as gay characters became commonplace in television and movies in the 1990s and the new millennium (e.g., *Ellen*, *Will and Grace*, *Brokeback Mountain*, *Modern Family*, *Moonlight*, *Glee*, *Grey's Anatomy*). A number of advocacy groups in the United States work tirelessly on behalf of LGBTQ rights (see LGBTQ Rights Advocacy Spotlight).

LGBTQ Rights Advocacy Spotlight

GLAAD

Human Rights Campaign (HRC)

It Gets Better Project

Lambda Legal

LGBTQ Freedom Fund

Matthew Shepard Foundation

National Center for Lesbian Rights

National Center for Transgender Equality

National LGBTQ Task Force

PFLAG

The Transgender Law Center

The Trevor Project

Sodomy Laws

Sodomy laws were passed in many U.S. states to regulate the sexual behavior of unmarried people. Some state sodomy laws applied equally to both heterosexuals and homosexuals, whereas others applied only to gay people. In 1961, Illinois became the first state to get rid of its sodomy law, and many states followed their lead in the ensuing years. In 1986, the U.S. Supreme Court upheld the constitutionality of a Georgia State sodomy law (in *Bowers v Hardwick*), but that ruling was overturned 17 years later in ***Lawrence v. Texas*** (2003) when it ruled that the Texas sodomy law was unconstitutional and that gay men and lesbians have the same right to sexual privacy and intimacy afforded to heterosexual people. The court case was prompted by a case involving two gay men who were found having sex when police barged into one of their homes due to a false weapons disturbance report. The two men were arrested and convicted of violating the state sodomy law in Texas. The 2003 *Lawrence v. Texas* ruling effectively invalidated all sodomy laws in the nation.

Gays in the Military ("Don't Ask, Don't Tell")

Historically, gay people have been barred from serving openly in the military, and this has been an issue that advocates have fought for many years. When Bill Clinton was running for president, he promised to end this ban, and advocates were disappointed when he compromised with conservatives to pass a law that has come to be known as **"Don't Ask, Don't Tell" (DADT)**. DADT, passed in 1993, allowed closeted gay people to serve in the military but prohibited gay service members from serving openly. At the time, President Clinton felt it was a step forward, but he later said that he regretted signing it into law. Over the years, major political pressure grew as advocates argued for an end to DADT. In 2011, President Obama repealed the ban on LGBTQ people serving in the military stating, "Service members will no longer be forced to hide who they are in order to serve our country" (Bumiller, 2011).

LGBTQ Government Representation

In the past, if a person running for political office were to admit that he or she were gay, it would have been political suicide. However, this has changed a lot in recent years as Americans have become more accepting of having a lawmaker who is openly LBGTQ. In 2012, Tammy Baldwin became the first openly gay person to win a seat in the U.S. Senate. In 2016, Kate Brown was the first openly gay person to be elected governor of a state, and two years later a gay man, Jared Polis, was elected governor of Colorado. In the 2020 elections, 334 LGBTQ candidates were elected to public office, including congressional seats, state senate seats, and local government offices. The vast majority were from the Democratic Party, though seven were Republicans. In New York, Democrats Ritchie Torres and Mondaire Jones became the first two gay Black candidates elected to Congress. With the election of Torres and Jones, the U.S. Congress now has 11 openly gay members, the most in U.S. history.

Advocacy Spotlight: Harvey Milk

Harvey Milk made history when he became one of the country's first openly gay elected officials. Before he ran for office, he was a gay rights activist in San Francisco and made a name for himself in the city. He was later elected to the board of supervisors in San Francisco. Unfortunately, a year later, he was shot and killed by Dan White, one of his former colleagues on the board. Mayor George Moscone was also murdered by Dan White. In May 1979 when the jury sentenced Dan White to less than eight years in prison for these murders, outraged protesters stormed city hall and set police cars on fire. The San Francisco Police Department responded by beating up patrons and vandalizing gay bars. Approximately 120 people, including around 60 policemen, were injured in this riot. Harvey Milk's story was so compelling that two films have been made about his life, a documentary titled *The Times of Harvey Milk* and *Milk*, starring Sean Penn, who won an Academy Award for best actor for his portrayal of Harvey.

Laws Banning Conversion Therapy

As of January 2021, 20 states and the District of Columbia have passed state laws to **ban conversion therapy** (i.e., therapy designed to convert an individual's sexual orientation from homosexual to heterosexual) for minors (Movement Advancement Project, n.d.). This type of therapy is also referred to as *reparative therapy*. This therapy is based on the idea that an individual can change his or her sexual orientation through prayer or the help of a practitioner using this type of therapy. All of the nation's leading professional medical and mental health associations, such as the National Association of Social Workers and the American Psychological Association, state that conversion therapy is unethical and dangerous and condemn this practice. California has been considering a bill to ban conversion therapy outright in the state, and some religious groups are working hard to oppose passage. An important historical milestone occurred in 1973 when the American Psychiatric Association removed homosexuality from its list of mental disorders.

Hate Crimes Legislation

In 2009, the **Matthew Shepard and James Byrd Jr. Hate Crimes Prevention Act** was passed into law after 10 years of advocacy by organizations such as the Human Rights Campaign and the mother of Matthew Shepard, Judy Shepard. The bill sought to expand hate crime laws to include gender, sexual orientation, gender identity, and disability and was prompted by the hate crimes of two men, both of whom were killed in 1998. Matthew Shepard was a young college student who was tortured and killed in Laramie, Wyoming, for being gay, and James Byrd, Jr. was a black man who was chained to the back of a pick-up truck by three White men and dragged to his death in Jasper, Texas. The story of Matthew Shepard has been made into a famous play called *The Laramie Project,* and a documentary film titled *Two Towns of Jasper* profiles the tragic story of James Byrd, Jr. FBI data shows that hate crimes based on sexual orientation are the third largest category after race and religion. And a new study by the Williams Institute at the UCLA School of Law analyzed data from the 2017 National Crime Victimization Survey and found that "LGBT people are nearly four times more likely than non-LGBT people to experience violent victimization, including rape, sexual assault, and aggravated or simple assault. In addition, LGBT people are more likely to experience violence both by someone well-known to the victim and at the hands of a stranger" (2020).

Advocacy Spotlight: Judy Shepard

The story of Judy Shepard, and her efforts to pass the Matthew Shepard and James Byrd, Jr. Hate Crimes Prevention Act on behalf of her son, is very inspiring and demonstrates that ordinary people can make a difference politically. Shortly after her son, University of Wyoming student Matthew Shepard, died after being beaten by two men for being gay in October 1998, Judy Shepard became a gay rights activist and made it her mission to expand federal hate crimes legislation to include sexual orientation. She and her husband

Dennis founded the Matthew Shepard Foundation, and Judy became the foundation's executive director. For the next 11 years, Judy worked alongside the Human Rights Campaign to get a bill passed into law by lobbying legislators and participating in marches and rallies in Washington, D.C.

The bill stalled in Congress until 2009 when momentum started to build. Judy met with President Obama in May 2009, and he promised to help her pass the act. The bill finally passed in the 111th Congress by a vote of 249 to 175 in the House and 63 to 28 in the Senate, when it was attached to a Department of Defense authorization bill. The new law expanded hate crimes legislation to include gender, sexual orientation, gender identity, and disability. The Matthew Shepard and James Byrd, Jr. Hate Crimes Prevention Act was signed into law by President Obama on October 28, 2009.

LGBTQ Workplace Discrimination

For many years LGBTQ advocacy organizations have been working on a number of policy issues to help gay and transgender people achieve full equality, including ending **workplace discrimination**. Today, according to federal law, it is illegal to discriminate against individuals in the workplace based on race, religion, sex, national origin, age, or disability; however, until very recently, these federal protections did not include sexual orientation or gender identity (though 23 states have these protections as of January 2021). This means that LGBTQ individuals could be fired, or not hired, due to their sexual orientation, unless they lived in a state with these protections. Since the mid-1970s, advocates have been working to pass legislation that would prohibit workplace discrimination against gay people, but conservative federal lawmakers have not supported these efforts. The latest legislative effort was titled the **Equality Act of 2017**, which would have amended the Civil Rights Act of 1964 to protect Americans from discrimination based on sexual orientation and gender identity in employment, housing, credit, federally funded programs (including education), and federal jury service.

However, a very important development occurred in June 2020 when the U.S. Supreme Court, in a 6–3 decision, ruled that employment discrimination based on sexual orientation or gender identity is illegal under Title VII of the federal Civil Rights Act, which prohibits discrimination based on sex in employment. This was a historic win for the LGBTQ community and a major loss for the Trump administration, which did not support this decision. The National Association of Social Workers (NASW) supported the decision and even participated in an amicus brief led by the Southern Poverty Resource Center. Angelo McClain, chief executive officer of the NASW, stated, "Freedom from workplace discrimination is a fundamental civil right that for too long has not been provided to all people, regardless of their sexual orientation or gender identity. With this historic decision, the Supreme Court is recognizing the worth and dignity of all workers" (NASW, 2020).

The Battle Over Same-Sex Marriage

Marriage equality has been a major hot-button political issue in the United States for many years. Gay rights advocates view the right to marry as a civil rights and human rights issue, whereas many religious conservatives believe it goes against the traditional view of marriage between one man and one woman. In 2015, the U.S. Supreme Court ruled that **same-sex marriage** is legal in the United States. This was a historic change with regard to social justice for LGBTQ Americans. However, the story of marriage equality for same-sex couples has been a long and winding road full of twists and turns that has included battles at the ballot box and the courthouse.

Timeline of Same-Sex Marriage Advocacy

- **1973**, Maryland becomes the first U.S. state to pass a law that defines marriage as a union between a man and woman.
- **1989**, the San Francisco Board of Supervisors passes an ordinance that allows same sex couples and unmarried heterosexual couples to register for **domestic partnerships**; the District of Columbia passes a similar law three years later.
- **1993**, the highest court in Hawaii rules that a ban on same-sex marriage may violate that state constitution's Equal Protection Clause—a first for a U.S. state.
- **1996**, the U.S. Congress passes the Defense of Marriage Act (DOMA), which denies federal marriage benefits to same-sex couples (e.g., social security benefits; federal income taxes, etc.). President Bill Clinton signs it into law. A few months later, Hawaii Judge Kevin S. C. Chang orders the state to stop denying licenses to same-sex couples
- **1998**, Hawaii voters approve a constitutional amendment banning same-sex marriage in the state.
- **2000**, Vermont becomes the first state to legalize **civil unions**, a legal status that provides some state-level marriage benefits to same-sex couples.
- **2003**, the Massachusetts Supreme Court rules that same-sex couples have the right to marry; Massachusetts begins issuing same-sex marriage licenses in May 2004.
- **2004–2006**, 19 U.S. states ban same-sex marriage.
- By the end of the decade, same-sex marriage becomes legal in the District of Columbia and a number of U.S. states through either court rulings or legislation.
- **2008**, the California Supreme Court strikes down a 1977 state law banning same-sex marriage, but a few months later voters approve Proposition 8, which again restricts marriage to heterosexual couples. Prop 8 is later ruled to be unconstitutional. See "The Fight for Same-Sex Marriage in California" for more on the winding road to same-sex marriage in California.
- **2012**, history is made when voters, rather than judges or legislators, in Maine, Maryland, and Washington approve Constitutional amendments permitting same-sex marriage.
- **2011**, the Obama administration announces it will no longer defend DOMA.
- **2013**, the U.S. Supreme Court rules in *United States v. Windsor* that section 3 of DOMA, which defines marriage as a union between one man and one woman, is unconstitutional. This ruling means that the U.S. government can no longer deny

federal benefits to married same-sex couples, yet other parts of DOMA remain in effect. For example, section 2 of DOMA still allows states and territories to refuse to recognize the marriages of same-sex couples from other states.

- **2015**, the U.S. Supreme Court rules in *Obergefell v. Hodges* that laws banning same sex-marriage violate the Equal Protection Clause and Due Process Clause of the Fourteenth Amendment, thus legalizing same-sex marriage in the United States. By this time, 37 U.S. states and the District of Columbia had legalized same-sex marriage, as well as 20 other nations, beginning with the Netherlands in 2001.
- **2016**, public opinion in the U.S. had shifted as well, with the majority of Americans supporting same-sex marriage.

The Fight for Same Sex Marriage in California (Proposition 8)

California is a good example of how advocates must sometimes contend with a series of ups and downs when battling political opponents. California made national news on May 15, 2008, when the California State Supreme Court ruled in *In Re Marriage Cases* that limiting marriage to opposite-sex couples violates the state constitutional rights of same sex-couples and cannot be used to prevent same-sex couples from marrying. This ruling struck down a ballot initiative passed in 2000 (Proposition 22) in which a majority of Californians voted to change California statute so that only marriages between a man and a woman would be recognized. Various organizations and individuals filed 30 amicus briefs urging the court to reject state laws denying marriage equality to same-sex couples. The National Association of Social Workers filed an 87-page brief along with the American Psychological Association, California Psychological Association, and American Psychiatric Association (see the Summary of Argument). Approximately 18,000 same-sex couples were married in California after this court ruling.

Summary of Argument (In Re Marriage Cases)

Submitted by: The National Association of Social Workers, American Psychological Association, California Psychological Association, and American Psychiatric Association

Brief filed: September 2007

Amici, the nation's and state's leading associations of mental health professionals and behavioral scientists present this brief to provide the Court with a comprehensive and balanced review of the scientific and professional literature pertinent to the issues before the Court. In preparing this brief, amici have been guided solely by criteria relating to the scientific rigor and reliability of studies and literature, not by whether a given study supports or undermines a particular conclusion.

Homosexuality is neither a disorder, nor a disease, but rather a normal variant of human sexual orientation. The vast majority of gay and lesbian individuals lead happy, healthy, well-adjusted, and productive lives.

Many gay and lesbian people are in a committed same-sex relationship. In their essential, psychological respects, these relationships are equivalent to heterosexual relationships.

The institution of marriage affords individuals a variety of benefits that have a favorable impact on their physical and psychological well-being.

A large number of children are currently being raised by lesbians and gay men, both in same-sex couples and as single parents. Empirical research has consistently shown that lesbian and gay parents do not differ from heterosexuals in their parenting skills, and their children do not show any deficits compared to children raised by heterosexual parents.

State policies that bar same-sex couples from marrying are based solely on sexual orientation. As such, they are both a consequence of the stigma historically attached to homosexuality, and a structural manifestation of that stigma. By allowing same-sex couples to marry, the Court would end the anti-gay stigma imposed by the State of California through its ban on marriage rights for same-sex couples. In addition, allowing same-sex couples to marry would give them access to the social support that already facilitates and strengthens heterosexual marriages, with all of the psychological and physical health benefits associated with that support. In addition, if their parents are allowed to marry, the children of same-sex couples will benefit not only from the legal stability and other familial benefits that marriage provides, but also from elimination of state-sponsored stigmatization of their families.

Source: Retrieved from http://www.socialworkers.org/assets/secured/documents/ldf/briefDocuments/In%20 re%20Marriage%20Cases%20California.pdf

---

Well before the May 2008 California Supreme Court ruling, opponents of marriage equality were already planning to get Proposition 8 (Prop 8) on the California ballot. The last time they had an initiative on the ballot (Proposition 22) the California statute was amended, but this time they wanted a ballot measure that would amend the state constitution, a tougher standard making it more difficult to overturn in the future and ineligible for a state-based constitutional challenge. Proposition 8, officially titled, "Eliminates Right of Same-Sex Couples to Marry" would amend the California state constitution so that only marriage between a man and a woman would be valid or recognized in the state of California. Supporters of Proposition 8 gathered roughly 1.1 million signatures, far more than the 694,354 valid signatures needed to qualify the measure for the ballot.

The contest over Proposition 8 was extremely heated. Supporters and donors of Prop 8 included the Knights of Columbus (Catholic organization), National Organization for Marriage, Focus on the Family, Mormon Church leaders, evangelical minister Rick Warren, and presidential candidate John McCain. Opponents of Prop 8 included a number of gay rights organizations including the Human Rights Campaign and Equality California, California Teachers Association, presidential candidate Barack Obama, and a host of Hollywood celebrities. On November 4, 2008, Prop 8 passed by 52% of California voters, making same-sex marriage illegal in California once again. Protests erupted around the country and the battle returned once again to the courts.

In *Strauss v Horton* (a consolidation of three lawsuits), the California State Supreme Court ruled that Prop 8 was constitutional but that the 18,000 marriages performed before it went into effect would remain legal. However, supporters of marriage for same-sex couples were not surprised by this ruling and quickly went to the next level and filed a lawsuit (*Perry v. Schwarzenegger*) in federal court challenging the constitutionality of Prop 8. The Prop 8 challenge was financed by the American Foundation for Equal Rights, a recently established nonprofit advocacy group. The two high-profile attorneys who were hired to argue the case, David Boies and Theodore B. Olson, were previous opponents of each other in *Bush v. Gore*, which ruled in favor of George W. Bush over the results of the 2000 presidential election. However, these former foes (one a well-known conservative) would team up to argue that Proposition 8 violates the constitutional guarantee of equal protection and due process.

After a trial that lasted two and a half weeks, Attorney Boies said testimony from the plaintiffs had established three major points: "That marriage is a fundamental right, that depriving gay people of that right caused harm, and that there was no societal benefit to denying gays and lesbians the right to marry" (McKinley, 2010). The other side argued that Californians have the right to establish marriage as between a man and a woman, and they did so when they approved Prop 8.

California made national news again on August 4, 2010, when federal judge Vaughn R. Walker overturned the ban on marriage for same-sex couples saying it discriminates against gay men and women. In his written opinion that was 136 pages long, Judge Walker wrote that Proposition 8 "fails to advance any rational basis in singling out gay men and lesbians for denial of a marriage license" and "does nothing more than enshrine in the California Constitution the notion that opposite-sex couples are superior to same-sex couples" (CNN, 2010). The case next advanced to the Ninth Circuit Court of Appeals. and on February 7, 2012, this three-member panel upheld the lower court's ruling that Proposition 8 violated the constitutional rights of gay men and women in California.

In the decision, Judge Stephen R. Reinhardt wrote, "Although the Constitution permits communities to enact most laws they believe to be desirable, it requires that there be at least a legitimate reason for the passage of a law that treats different classes of people differently." He added, "Proposition 8 serves no purpose, and has no effect, other than to lessen the status and human dignity of gay men and lesbians in California" (Nagourney, 2012). This court case was pivotal in the fight for marriage equality in the United States, and created a legal precedent for a later ruling by the U.S. Supreme Court (*Obergefell v. Hodges*) that same-sex marriage should be legalized.

How the Battle for Same-Sex Marriage Was Won

Many current social movements are awed by the movement for same sex-marriage because advocates were able to create dramatic social change in a relatively short amount of time. How did they do this exactly? According to Marc Solomon, the national campaign director for Freedom to Marry, there were a few key strategies that led to their success (Ball, 2015b):

I. **Building a coordinated coalition**. One problem that was identified was the lack of a well-organized political campaign: "Multiple groups were trying multiple approaches with no centralized strategy, fundraising, or message. To figure out what needed to change, eight organizations, led by Freedom to Marry, formed a secret collaboration that they called the Marriage Research Consortium. They pooled their resources and held a monthly teleconference to share polling, insights, and ideas in real time" (Ball, 2015a).

II. **Using lawsuits and state-level political victories to reinforce one another**. "The marriage campaign's major innovation was fusing litigation with a political campaign, using lawsuits and state-level political victories to reinforce one another. The combination worked to create **an impression of momentum** even as the tide of public opinion gradually turned" (Ball, 2015b). Unlike other issue campaigns, Congress was not their ultimate target. According to Solomon, an important lesson for advocates is to "use state and local politics to put points on the board" (Ball, 2015b).

III. **Framing the issue.** Another major factor was that advocates changed their messaging so that it would resonate more with voters. They went "from an argument about the rights and benefits of marriage to one about the fundamental human desire for love and commitment." This is another lesson Solomon believes other movements could learn: "**Make an emotional argument based on positive values**" (Ball, 2015b). They learned that in order to change people's hearts and minds, they needed to frame the issue in personal terms in a way that would allow voters to see the humanity of gay people. They also needed to convince voters that gay people wanted to join the institution of marriage, not change it (Ball, 2015a). The new ads "featured straight people talking about their gay relatives: the mother or sister or grandfather of a gay person, talking about their loved one's commitment to a partner. A Republican Navy doctor talking about how he wished he could marry his partner." When gay people were featured, it was older lesbians who they found to be the best messengers (Ball, 2015a).

IV. **Persuasion campaign**. They also used a "sophisticated persuasion campaign" in efforts to change people's mind about the issue. For example, paid volunteers and workers would have in-depth personal conversations with voters about family and faith and would use prompts such as, "What does marriage mean to you?" The campaign also asked hundreds of gay couples who had gotten married to talk to their legislator to share their personal story (Ball, 2015b). Additionally, "They saw to it that every single legislator who voted their way got reelected, while some who didn't were targeted and ousted" (Ball, 2015b).

V. **In Sum.** The overall lesson from the success of this movement is that a combination of state-level wins and a laser focus on changing public opinion led to a sea change in American society that allowed the Supreme Court to support it.

Transgender Rights and Protections

A newer area of social policy is focused on **transgender rights and protections**. Our society has grown more accepting of people who are transgender, and this cause has been helped by celebrities such as Caitlyn Jenner (formerly Bruce Jenner), actress Laverne Cox, and actor Elliott Page (formerly Ellen Page), who have talked openly about their experience. In 2016, the U.S. Secretary of Defense announced that transgender Americans would be allowed to serve openly in the military. However, President Trump overturned this decision in 2017 and announced a ban on transgender people serving in the military. Then when Joe Biden became President, he reversed the ban so that transgender people can serve openly once again. Advocates have a long list of priorities that includes: overturning transgender bathroom laws; passing antidiscrimination laws, laws that permit transgender individuals to change the gender listed on legal identification documents, and laws that ensure access to healthcare services, including gender reassignment surgery; preventing violence against transgender individuals; and affirming the rights of transgender students in schools. A major win for transgender people came when the U.S. Supreme Court ruled that employment discrimination based on sexual orientation or gender identity is illegal under Title VII of the federal Civil Rights Act.

Like many social issues in the United States, citizens and lawmakers have been divided over the issue of **transgender rights with regard to bathroom laws**. In 2012, cities such as Austin and Seattle were among the first to pass laws requiring single-user all-gender restrooms. And in 2016, California became the first state to pass legislation requiring all single-toilet bathrooms to be gender neutral. On the other end of the spectrum, North Carolina made national news in March 2016 when it passed a bill that barred transgender people from bathrooms and locker rooms that did not match their biological sex. The state later received a huge backlash from the world of athletics (e.g., NBA, NCAA), entertainment, and business, and a number of sporting events and concerts were cancelled as a result of this new law. The law was repealed one year later. Governor Roy Cooper stated, "For over a year now, House Bill 2 has been a dark cloud hanging over our great state. It has stained our reputation. It has discriminated against our people and it has caused great economic harm in many of our communities" (Hanna, Park, & McLaughlin, 2017).

In February 2017, President Trump rescinded protections for transgender students that were instituted by the Obama administration that had allowed them to use bathrooms corresponding with their gender identity. A month later, the U.S. Supreme Court announced that it would not hear a case of a transgender boy in Virginia, Gavin Grimm, who was not allowed to use the boy's bathroom at his high school. However, in May 2018, a federal judge in Virginia ruled in favor of Mr. Grimm. Federal Judge Wright Allen found that Mr. Grimm's treatment resulted in sex discrimination and that the school could have found another solution in lieu of barring him from the boy's restroom.

The Debate over Religious Freedom

Another issue that has been hotly contested in the United States in recent years is whether people have religious freedom in denying services to LGBTQ persons if this goes against their religious beliefs. Proponents of religious exemption laws argue that they allow people to practice their faith; others disagree and contend that they are a license to discriminate against gay people. For example, should service providers such as healthcare and mental health providers be allowed to refuse services to an LGBTQ individual because it goes against their religion? Should businesses be allowed to refuse services for the same reason? The most famous high-profile example of this occurred in Colorado when a bakery refused to make a cake for a gay people due to their religious beliefs. The U.S. Supreme Court heard this case and issued a decision in June 2018. In a 7–2 decision, the Court ruled in favor of the baker. Reactions to the ruling varied with some legal analysts stating that this was a dangerous precedent that will encourage businesses to discriminate against LGBTQ individuals while others reported that this was a narrow legal decision based on factors that were unique to this specific case.

This case has some similarities to the Hobby Lobby U.S. Supreme Court case (*Burwell v Hobby Lobby Stores*) where the Court ruled (in a 5–4 decision) that owners of profit-making corporations cannot be forced under the Affordable Care Act to provide their employees with certain kinds of contraceptives that offend their religious beliefs. These court decisions focused on religious freedom follow other recent Supreme Court rulings that have found that corporations have some of the same rights as individuals, referred to as corporate personhood. Religious freedom laws will likely continue to be debated in the coming years as states and the federal government grapple with how to balance the rights of women and LGBTQ individuals with the rights of those with conservative religious convictions.

In Closing

The progress that has been made by the women's movement and gay rights movement has been substantial and has resulted in an array of expanded opportunities and social advancement for women and gay Americans. As this chapter shows, social movements often have to experience one step forward and two steps back before they realize their ultimate goal. They have to keep moving forward even when things appear bleak. Social justice issues need legislative champions, but they also need strong social movements and skilled advocates to create the pressure that is needed to motivate lawmakers to support their cause. This chapter highlighted remarkable achievements with regard to women's rights and LGBTQ rights as well as the challenges that remain.

REFERENCES

Ball, M. (2015a, July 1). How gay marriage became a constitutional right. *The Atlantic*. Retrieved from https://www.theatlantic.com/politics/archive/2015/07/gay-marriage-supreme-court-politics-activism/397052/

Ball, M. (2015b, July 14). What other activists can learn from the fight for gay marriage. *The Atlantic*. Retrieved from https://www.theatlantic.com/politics/archive/2015/07/what-other-activists-can-learn-from-the-fight-for-gay-marriage/398417/

Bleiweis, R. (March 24, 2020). Quick facts about the gender wage gap. Center for American Progress. Retrieved from https://www.americanprogress.org/issues/women/reports/2020/03/24/482141/quick-facts-gender-wage-gap/

Bumiller, E. (2011, July 22). Obama ends 'Don't ask, don't tell' policy. *New York Times*. Retrieved from https://www.nytimes.com/2011/07/23/us/23military.html

CNN. (2010, August 18). Activists vow to fight on after court puts same-sex marriages on hold. Retrieved from http://www.cnn.com/2010/US/08/17/same.sex.marriage/index.html?hpt=T1

Glynn, S. J. (2013). The Family and Medical Leave Act at 20: Still necessary, still not enough. *The Atlantic*. Retrieved from https://www.theatlantic.com/sexes/archive/2013/02/the-family-and-medical-leave-act-at-20-still-necessary-still-not-enough/272605/

Hanna, J., Park, M., & McLaughlin, E. C. (2017, March 30). North Carolina repeals bathroom bill. CNN Politics. Retrieved from https://www.cnn.com/2017/03/30/politics/north-carolina-hb2-agreement/index.html

Inter-Parliamentary Union. (2017). Women in national parliaments. Retrieved from http://archive.ipu.org/wmn-e/arc/classif010117.htm

McKinley, J. (January 27, 2010). Proposition 8 trial pauses, but not for ruling. *New York Times*. Retrieved from http://www.nytimes.com/2010/01/28/us/28prop.html?fta=y

Movement Advancement Project (n.d.). Conversion therapy laws. Retrieved from http://www.lgbtmap.org/equality-maps/conversion_therapy

Nagourney, A. (2012, February 7). Court strikes down ban on gay marriage in California. *New York Times*. Retrieved from https://www.nytimes.com/2012/02/08/us/marriage-ban-violates-constitution-court-rules.html

NASW (June 17, 2020). NASW applauds U.S. Supreme Court ruling that protects LGBTQ from discrimination. Retrieved from https://www.socialworkers.org/News/News-Releases/ID/2195/NASW-applauds-US-Supreme-Court-ruling-that-protects-LGBTQ-from-discrimination

OECD Family Database (2017). *Trends in parental leave policies since 1970*. Retrieved from http://www.oecd.org/els/family/PF2_5_Trends_in_leave_entitlements_around_childbirth.pdf

Smith, S. G., Zhang, X., Basile, K. C., Merrick, M. T., Wang, J., Kresnow, M., & Chen, J. (2018). The National Intimate Partner and sexual violence survey (NISVS): 2015 data brief – updated release. Atlanta, GA: National Center for Injury Prevention and Control, Centers for Disease Control and Prevention. Retrieved from https://www.cdc.gov/violenceprevention/pdf/2015data-brief508.pdf

Williams Institute, UCLA School of Law. (October 2, 2020). LGBT people nearly four times more likely than non-LGBT people to be victims of violent crime. Retrieved from https://williamsinstitute.law.ucla.edu/press/ncvs-lgbt-violence-press-release/

CHAPTER 13　A Look to the Future

"First they ignore you. Then they laugh at you. Then they fight you. Then you win."

~*Gandhi*

CHAPTER SUMMARY

Social workers often feel overwhelmed and disillusioned when thinking about being a change agent in the legislative and/or political arena. It is normal to ask: "Can I really make a difference politically?" After four years of the Trump presidency, Americans feel more divided than ever before and talking about politics with others feels like a daunting activity. Countless books and articles have been written to describe the rise in the number of Americans who feel alienated from the government and the political process. Research from the American National Election Studies shows that the public's trust in government has waned significantly since the 1960s. Many Americans have come to believe that politicians are corrupt and only cater to powerful, special interests. These feelings are understandable. However, it is crucial to consider the fact that if social workers remove themselves from the political process in anger, frustration, and disgust, it is typically people at the margins who end up suffering the most. Despite the fact that there are some actual and perceived barriers to social workers' political participation on behalf of vulnerable groups, it is imperative that social workers use political advocacy as one of the many tools in their toolkit when seeking change at the macro level. Social workers have an ethical duty and a moral obligation to share their experience, expertise, and research with legislators so they have the information they need to make good decisions in the area of social welfare policy. In the coming years, the United States will be confronted with a number of critical issues that pertain to its many vulnerable populations, such as immigration, the aging population, LGBTQ rights, the welfare of children, returning veterans, environmental justice, racial justice, and poverty and income inequality.

This chapter ends by providing an overview of challenges faced by the social work profession and potential policy solutions, such as the Social Work Reinvestment Act (SWRA). The heart of the problem centers on the fact that social workers provide an important and necessary role in American society, and although there is a large demand for their services, there are barriers that make social work a challenging career choice for many people. Because of low starting salaries, high levels of student loan debt, and safety concerns, the profession has a difficult time recruiting and retaining talented, highly qualified people. The NASW advocates on behalf of the social work profession and works to educate lawmakers about the challenges that social workers face, as well as the value they bring to our communities and society.

STUDENT LEARNING OBJECTIVES

- Students will be able to list and summarize the major themes of this book based on stories of policy change efforts from Chapters 7–12.

- Students will be able to describe the hot-button political issues of interest for social work in the coming years.

- Students will be able to explain the major challenges faced by the social work profession in the United States.

- Students will be able to analyze current policy efforts to address these challenges.

- Students will be able to evaluate for themselves whether all social work is political.

Social workers often feel overwhelmed and disillusioned when thinking about being a change agent in the legislative and/or political arena. It is normal to ask: "Can I really make a difference politically?" After four years of the Trump presidency, Americans feel more divided than ever before and talking about politics with others feels like a daunting activity. Countless books and articles have been written to report and analyze the trend of increasing numbers of Americans who feel alienated from their government and the political process. Research from the American National Election Studies shows that the public's trust in government has waned significantly since the 1960s (see Chapter 6 for more on this). Many Americans have come to believe that politicians are corrupt and only cater to powerful, special interests. These feelings are understandable. However, it is crucial to consider the fact that if social workers remove themselves from the political process in anger, frustration, and disgust, it is typically those at the margins who end up suffering the most.

This book should provide some hope that **meaningful policy change is possible**. Dramatic policy changes on behalf of vulnerable populations occurred during the FDR administration when the Social Security Act of 1935 was passed into law; during the LBJ administration when historic civil rights legislation was passed and many important social programs were created through legislative action such as Head Start, Medicare, and Medicaid; and during the Obama administration when same-sex marriage was legalized and the Affordable Care Act was passed, which enabled 20 million previously uninsured Americans to obtain health insurance. Despite the fact that there are some actual and perceived barriers to social workers' political participation on behalf of vulnerable groups in society, it is imperative that social workers use political advocacy as one of the many tools in their toolkit when seeking macro-level change on behalf of individuals, families, groups, communities, and society at large.

Themes from This Book About Policy Change

Social workers have an **ethical duty** and a moral obligation to share their experience, expertise, and research with legislators so that they have the information they need to make good decisions in the area of social welfare policy. The Code of Ethics of the National Association of Social Workers (NASW) explicitly states that social workers have an ethical duty to engage in social and political action and to advocate for policies that advance social justice. It does not tell social workers *how much* they need to be involved in social and political action, but it implies that they are not fulfilling their ethical duty as a social worker if they are absent from the political process. Some social workers will engage in policy practice as a career, while others will get involved politically on issues that are connected to their field of social work practice (e.g., mental health, work with immigrants and refugees, child welfare, etc.) or other social justice issues that they are passionate about.

There are many examples throughout history of legislation that has made a dramatic difference in people's lives. It is not helpful when the profession enters into a false debate over whether the profession should emphasize micro-level social work or macro-level social work. The beauty of social work, and what sets it apart from most other professions, is that it includes both. In the words of social work professor Don Schweitzer of Pacific University Oregon, "There is no such thing as a micro social worker or a macro social worker—you are a social worker!" (Personal communication, n.d.).

This book is about how social workers can shape social welfare policy through a social justice lens, which has been termed **social work policy practice.** Most people are aware that social workers engage in direct practice, group practice, and community practice, but few understand that social workers also engage in policy practice in the legislative arena. Social workers affect policy change by (1) getting involved in electoral politics so that those with social justice values get elected and (2) affecting legislation at the local, state, national, or international level. Social workers work to support legislation that will be helpful to vulnerable populations and defeat policies that would cause harm. Chapter 11 included a number of examples of policies that have caused harm to certain groups in our society. On the positive side, policies can improve people's lives for the better, and there are many examples of this in this book. Policies have the power to create new social programs, increase funding levels for existing social programs, provide protections to vulnerable populations, and advance human rights and social justice.

In order to be successful, **social workers must understand politics and the political process,** because decisions that get made are often rooted in power dynamics, relationship building, and the art of compromise and deal-making. For some social workers, this is a reason to avoid getting involved in the political arena. However, social workers have many skills that are incredibly useful in this environment. Social workers are highly trained in ethics and values, diversity and cultural competence, communication skills, problem-solving skills, mediation, and skills in research and analysis. The knowledge base and skillset that social workers develop during their social work education and practice can be directly applied to working in the political realm.

Chapter 3 focuses on the role of **values and ideology** in the policy-making process. This book argues that for many people, views on political issues are rooted in one's personal values and beliefs. This means that when advocates are trying to convince others to support their policy position, they have to speak to people's hearts as much as to their head. The task of a good advocate is to demonstrate to people that the policy he or she is trying to help pass is aligned with voters' personal values and societal values. Even though advocates should use research and data to back up their policy proposal, they also need to help people connect to the issue on an emotional level.

Framing an issue successfully is key to any successful policy effort. This is also referred to as **messaging**. Chapters 7–12 told multiple stories of groups of advocates who set out to create a policy change, and in each of these stories details were provided on how they chose to frame their issue. Skilled advocates understand how to frame their issue by creating a narrative or story because people respond to stories. Advocates who worked to pass the Mental Health Parity and Addiction Equality Act of 2008 framed the issue as one of discrimination against those with mental illness (see Chapter 8). They argued that it was wrong for insurance companies to provide people with generous healthcare coverage and skimpy mental health coverage. Then advocates allowed people who had experienced this to tell their stories about how being unable to access mental health treatment negatively impacted their life. Framing an issue well takes significant time, and sometimes advocates must refine their messaging when it is not working. The advocates working for same-sex marriage did exactly that, as was explained in Chapter 12.

Those who are most effective in working for policy change know that **there are six stages of the policy change process**—problem definition, agenda setting, policy formulation, passage of the policy, implementation, and evaluation. Advocates cannot formulate an effective policy until they have a good grasp of the problem, including the causes of the problem. They must also figure out the best mechanism for the policy change—ballot measure, court decision, legislation at the state level, legislation at the federal level, or executive order (**problem definition stage**). Then they must be able to get their issue onto the political agenda and secure at least one legislator who will agree to champion their bill (**agenda-setting**

stage). Once those two phases have been successful, then advocates must work to get their legislative proposal translated into actual bill language or bill form (**policy formulation stage**). Passage of the policy refers to the "how a bill becomes a law" stage. This is when advocates work diligently to move the bill through the legislative process which includes lobbying lawmakers, testifying in legislative hearings, and working to get a bill voted out of committee (**passage of the policy stage**). Then when advocates are lucky enough to get their bill passed into law, they must then focus on ensuring that the legislation gets properly implemented (**implementation stage**). Finally, advocates should work to ensure that there is a plan to evaluate the impact of the policy. There are three potential outcomes after a bill is passed into law: the policy helped the problem and improved the situation, the policy had no impact on the problem at all, or the policy had unintended consequences and/or made the problem worse (**evaluation stage**).

Another important lesson that can be learned from the stories in this book concerns the importance of **employing a variety of different tactics in order to win** and the increasing reliance on **social media** in order to connect with people, educate the public, and mobilize people for action. When advocates set out to pass a piece of legislation, they meet together to strategize about which tactics will likely lead to their success, and of course they have to consider what is feasible based on their financial and human resources. In each of the stories told in this book, a combination of the following tactics were employed with the goal of achieving a legislative win.

Advocacy Tactics

- ☐ Coalition building
- ☐ Direct lobbying
- ☐ Earned media
- ☐ Grassroots lobbying
- ☐ Paid media
- ☐ Educational outreach
- ☐ Visibility
- ☐ Online advocacy/social media
- ☐ Political dissent
- ☐ Paid communication
- ☐ Providing testimony
- ☐ Fundraising activities

In this book, a number of stories were told of advocates and organizations that attempted to get a piece of legislation passed into law. Though each story is unique, an important theme is that most of the change that comes about in the legislative arena is a result of **many committed individuals and groups working together,** also referred to as **working**

in coalition. Chapter 8 tells the story of how the Paul Wellstone and Pete Domenici Mental Health Parity and Addiction Equality Act of 2008 was passed into law by committed individuals, organizations, and lawmakers who worked together to make it illegal for insurance companies to discriminate against those suffering with mental health disorders. Political and social change requires resources and this includes time, people, and money; thus, the more "people" resources you have at the table, the better. Even though there is some truth to the adage, "One person can make a difference," the real story seems to be, "**Groups of individuals working together really makes the difference**."

Working for change as part of a group is more fun and provides advocates with the support they need when things get tough and they feel dispirited. Perhaps social workers will be encouraged by the results of a study published in the journal *Political Psychology* by Tim Kasser and Malte Klar (2009) that found positive benefits for those who engage in political activism. Coauthor Tim Kasser explains, "There is something about activism itself that is beneficial for well-being. We found that activists were feeling more autonomy and more personal growth. They also felt they had better relationships, more purpose in life, and they liked themselves better" (as cited in Petre, 2010).

Another theme is that when organizations are able to hire **paid, professional staff with expertise in lobbying and running an effective political campaign,** their chance of success increases. The success of the Death with Dignity campaign in Washington State is a great example of this because advocates were able to raise enough money to hire professionals with expertise in running an effective media campaign. Their opponents were very well financed, so it was helpful for them to have financial resources in order to do things like run television ads. Professional lobbyists and campaign workers have the knowledge and expertise that is required to mobilize volunteers, build relationships with legislators and other important decision makers, raise money, and develop professional advocacy materials. It is important to know what work can be done by volunteers and where professional people are needed. This is often vital because in political battles where one side has a strong social justice focus, the opposition is usually better financed.

Finally, perhaps the biggest lesson we can learn from most stories involving social and political change is that **those seeking policy change must be persistent and patient** because success does not usually happen overnight. Most stories of social and political change involve a number of ups and downs, two steps forward and one step back, until a win is achieved. Initially, many social work students operate from the fallacy that micro-level change is easier to achieve than macro-level change. However, after getting some experience at the micro level, new social workers soon discover that helping individuals and families make changes is equally challenging and that change at the micro level can also be frustrating and slow-moving. In both cases, it is important to set small achievable markers of success along the way until the win is achieved.

A few of the stories in this book involve advocates who have yet to achieve their "big win" such as the DREAM Act youth activists, the Mad As Hell doctors, and those working to get the United States to ratify the UN Convention on the Rights of the Child. However, they can each point to progress that has been made along the way such as the number of people who have been educated about the issue, the growth of their organization (e.g., development of a website, growing number of supporters/volunteers, more groups in their coalition), and the skill development of the participating individuals who are part of their movement or cause.

In sum, though some legislative change efforts involve sweeping, monumental, or landmark changes, **most policy change happens incrementally.** Chapter 7 told the story of how the Affordable Care Act (Obamacare) was passed into law. While some progressives were thrilled with this new law, because, in their view, it was a significant step in the right direction, other progressives were dismayed that the legislation was not as far-reaching as it could have been because the goal of universal health care was not achieved. It is good to keep in mind that many policies in the United States were improved over time, such as the Social Security Act, the Violence Against Women Act, and hate crimes legislation. Thus advocates are constantly working to amend and improve existing laws over time.

"Hot-Button" Political Issues on the Horizon of Interest to Social Work

In the coming years, there are a number of critical issues that the United States will be confronted with that pertain to vulnerable populations.

Racial Justice

The social work profession has long been an ally and an advocate for racial justice given that it has a mission of social justice for marginalized populations. However, the events of the past few years with regard to police brutality against Black citizens and the resulting Black Lives Matter movement has brought this issue to the forefront of the social work profession. This includes calls for the social work profession to look within as it seeks to have a more diverse workforce that educates social workers to recognize their own biases so they can engage in anti-oppressive social work practice. The National Association of Social Workers (NASW) has been vocal in their support of this most recent movement for racial justice and equity. The NASW has joined with the American Psychological Association and the American Psychiatric Association in calling on the U.S. Congress to declare systemic racism a public health crisis. Excerpts from two recent press releases from the NASW follow:

> The National Association of Social Workers (NASW) applauds the U.S. House of Representatives for passing the George Floyd Justice in Policing Act of 2020 (H.R. 7120) on June 25. This legislation, which was introduced by social worker Rep. Karen Bass (D-CA), chair of the Congressional Black Caucus, is a crucial step forward in police reform and dismantling the structural inequality left from legacies of discrimination and white supremacy — the root cause of aggressive, brutal, and unaccountable policing.

It is vital that the Senate follow the House's lead by crafting and passing similar legislation that includes strong provisions to reconceptualize and transform public safety and disrupt and dismantle racist policies and practices in policing.

"Racism is real and must be eliminated. Police brutality is real and must be eliminated. Oppressive policing is real and must be eliminated. NASW stands against racism, police brutality and oppressive policing," said Angelo McClain, PhD, LICSW, Chief Executive Officer of NASW.

NASW also implores Congress, state, county, and local governments to reallocate and reinvest resources from law enforcement into mental health, living wage jobs, affordable housing, and alternatives for anti-racist public safety services. These investments will lead to decriminalization of poverty, homelessness, and emergency mental health and help dismantle discriminatory and oppressive police practices that perpetuate white supremacist ideologies.

As the fight for racial justice expands in our nation, NASW will continue to boldly stand for racial equity and work to end multiple injustices facing African-Americans, Latinx, and Indigenous people today: not just police brutality, but also mass incarceration, poverty, unemployment, voter suppression, educational and health disparities and more. Social workers can help by urging their elected officials to support these critical issues.

(NASW, 2020a)

[To read this statement in full, please visit: https://www.socialworkers.org/News/News-Releases/ID/2205/NASW-Seeks-to-Dismantle-Racist-Policing]

While the national conversation remains focused on ending police brutality, racism persists in many other institutions. The child welfare system has often more rigorously regulated and castigated Black, Brown, and Indigenous families. Medical racism, which has origins in slavery and eugenics, has led to modern-day health disparities and inequities in health care access and treatment. The oppressive collateral consequences resulting from mass incarceration, the War on Drugs, and the school-to-prison pipeline have exacerbated economic inequalities in Black, Brown, and Indigenous communities.

Social workers have had roles in perpetuating these harmful social systems, and this history cannot be ignored.

Social work also has a major role to play in creating an antiracist society. As many professions and organizations are doing, we must pause to look inward and use that knowledge to propel us toward action for meaningful social change. We must build upon the good social workers have done in the fight for civil rights, health care access, child protection, the War on Poverty and marriage equality by working more intentionally to elevate Black, Brown, and Indigenous lives in the communities we serve.

We have certainly made mistakes, but we are also a group of professionals committed to helping, lifting up, and advocating for oppressed and marginalized groups of people and fighting injustice in society. Social workers have an ethical duty to dismantle racism, both personally and professionally, and to demonstrate what it means to be antiracist.

Directly confronting racism at the individual, agency, and institutional levels is the antiracist mandate we all must embrace. By using the NASW Code of Ethics as a guidepost, social workers can help dismantle systems of oppression, take action against white supremacy culture, and be leaders in the movement for racial justice.

(NASW, 2020b)

[To read this statement in full, please visit https://www.socialworkers.org/News/ News-Releases/ID/2219/Social-Workers-Must-Help-Dismantle-Systems-of-Oppression-and-Fight-Racism-Within-Social-Work-Profession]

Immigration

Immigration will continue to be an important issue politically because people from both sides of the political spectrum agree that the immigration system is broken and in need of reform. Congress has been divided between those who want to punish and/or deport those who are here with no legal status and those who advocate a path to citizenship for the roughly 11 million undocumented immigrants residing in the United States. There are plenty of innocent people caught in the crosshairs of this debate, such as those who were brought here by their parents when they were children (see Chapter 11 on the DREAM Act) who now want the opportunity to go to college and work in the country that is their home. The DREAM Act has not been passed by Congress since 2001. Social workers serve immigrants (both documented and undocumented) in many settings and should be part of the discussion and solution. NASW (2018) has gone on record as supporting the DREAM Act and has the following policy position supporting a comprehensive immigration bill that would provide a path to citizenship for those who are undocumented:

It would be incredibly challenging, if not impossible, to completely seal our borders and equally impossible to deport the millions of undocumented individuals already here, as well as make up for the economic contributions to the U.S. economy. Therefore, the issue of passing a comprehensive immigration reform bill that would provide policies and procedures that clarify and redefine the immigration status of currently undocumented residents is integral to the social and economic health of our country. Recent steps taken by the executive branch to ban immigrants and refugees from certain countries is both legally questionable and antithetical to the principles of our Constitution and the social work profession, and indicates a rise in anti-immigrant sentiment on the populist level.

(p. 187)

Older Adults and Aging

Many social workers are concerned about whether the United States will be sufficiently prepared for the "graying of America" in the coming years as a result of decreasing fertility rates, increasing life expectancy, and the millions of baby boomers who will be retiring from the U.S. workforce. Many questions will need to be addressed by our policymakers, such as: How do we ensure that older adults do not experience income, housing, and food insecurity and elder abuse? How can we combat social isolation among aging adults? Will the Social Security and Medicare systems continue to be financially sound? Will the government support and fund home healthcare programs that will allow older adults to receive care at home when feasible and appropriate instead of being automatically placed into expensive institutionalized care? How will we support adults who are caregivers for their aging relatives?

And can we have rational conversations about policies focused on end-of-life care without it devolving into political diatribes against "death panels"? NASW's (2018) position on end-of life care includes the following statement:

> Within the social work profession, a variety of opinions exist regarding the legalization of physician aid in dying (PAD). Mindful of this diversity, and recognizing that decisions governing PAD occur at the state level, NASW has not adopted a national position either in support of or in opposition to legalization of PAD. In states in which PAD is legal, however, NASW affirms both the right of individuals to choose this option and the responsibility of health care systems and practitioners to honor client's choices.
>
> *(p. 108)*

The NASW's (2018) policy position on aging more generally is as follows:

> Integral to the well-being of society is how it perceives and responds to aging, including how society supports the contributions and well-being of older adults. Moreover, social determinants of health have a profound influence on each person's aging process and support network. Accordingly NASW supports age-friendly environments, including the provision of coordinated, person-centered, culturally and linguistically competent services to older adults across settings. NASW also supports legislation, policies, programs, research, and funding that promotes late-life wellness.
>
> *(p. 23)*

Equal Rights for LGBTQ Individuals

Some have characterized rights for LGBTQ individuals as the civil rights issue of our time. In the coming years, America will continue to debate equal rights for those who are lesbian, gay, bisexual, and transgender in many areas such as marriage, parenting, and workplace discrimination. Violence against LGBTQ individuals has been a huge concern as the country has witnessed high-profile cases of students in colleges and public schools who have taken their own life as a result of bullying and intimidation by their classmates. One major step forward was the passage of the Matthew Shepard and James Byrd, Jr. Hate Crimes Prevention Act in 2009 that gives federal officials the power to investigate and prosecute crimes of violence when the victim was targeted because of his or her actual or perceived race, color, religion, national origin, gender, sexual orientation, gender identity, or disability.

Luckily, due to a 2020 Supreme Court ruling, it is now illegal to discriminate in the workplace on the basis of sexual orientation and gender identity or expression. Prior to this, advocates had been working for decades to get legislation passed in the U.S. Congress with no luck. The Human Rights Campaign is the premiere advocacy group in the nation for LGBTQ individuals, and LGBTQ advocacy groups can be found at the local level in most states. NASW's (2018) policy position on lesbian, gay, and bisexual issues and transgender and gender nonconforming people is as follows:

> NASW supports the adoption of local, state, federal, and international policies and legislation that ban all forms of discrimination based on sexual orientation. LGB people must be granted all rights, privileges, and responsibilities that are granted to heterosexual people, including, but not limited to, inheritance rights, insurance, marriage, child custody and visitation, employment, credit, housing, and immigration.
>
> *(p. 215)*

> NASW supports the full human rights and the end to all public and private discrimination on the basis of gender identity and gender expression, whether actual or perceived, and regardless of assigned sex at birth, including denial of access to employment, housing, public accommodations, education, appropriate treatment in segregated faculties matching self-identification, familial status, appropriate medical care and mental health care coverage and appropriate identity documents.
>
> *(p. 327)*

Services for Veterans

You may be surprised to learn that the Department of Veterans Affairs (VA) is the largest employer of social workers with master's degrees in the United States. In recent years, social workers have worked to support veterans returning from Iraq and Afghanistan. Combat veterans face a variety of challenges after returning home, which can include posttraumatic stress disorder (PTSD) and traumatic brain disorder, unstable housing and/or homelessness, suicidal ideation, mental health disorders, help recovering from a physical injury, being faced with a permanent physical disability, addictions, and a range of difficulties adjusting to civilian life. Social workers who work with veterans are in the position to advocate for them to ensure that they, and their families, have the resources and support that they need. NASW (2018) supports "federal investment allocated based on need, towards resources that have been proven to help veterans become or remain stably housed," including HUD-VA Supportive Housing, which supports chronically homeless veterans (p. 165). Social workers often assist veterans with finding and maintaining employment in the civilian world. The social work profession must also grapple with issues concerning the morality of war and when it is necessary and right for the United States to enter into war with other nations. They should also engage in conversations about military spending levels in comparison to spending on public welfare and spending for the public good.

Poverty and Income Inequality

Poverty and income inequality are rarely seriously addressed by our leaders and policy-makers at the local and national levels. This is despite the fact that according to the U.S. Census Bureau, 10.5% of Americans (34 million) were living in poverty in 2019, and it was worse for other vulnerable groups. In 2019, 18.8% of Black Americans were poor, 15.7% of Hispanics, and 14.4% of children (U.S. Census Bureau, 2020). According to a 2017 report from the Federal Reserve, the richest 1% of Americans owned almost 39% of the nation's wealth in 2016, nearly twice as much as the bottom 90%. The bottom 90% of families owned just 22.8% of the wealth, down from about one-third in 1989 (Federal Reserve, 2017). Couple this with recent data from the Economic Policy Institute, which found that in 2016 CEOs of major U.S. corporations averaged 271 times the average compensation of American workers (ratio of 271 to 1); in 1965, the ratio was 20 to 1 (Mishel & Schieder, 2017).

A number of national organizations advocate for low-income individuals, such as the Coalition on Human Needs, the Half in Ten Campaign, the National Alliance to End Homelessness, the Alliance to End Hunger, the Center for American Progress' Task Force on Poverty, and the National Urban League. There are also poverty research centers located at Columbia University, the University of Kentucky, the University of Michigan, the University of Washington, and the University of Wisconsin–Madison.

Various strategies to help move people out of poverty that advocates point to include raising the minimum wage; living wage ordinances; promoting unionization; investing in improving education at all levels (including early childhood education); asset building strategies, such as the use of individual development accounts (IDAs); microcredit programs to help spur entrepreneurship among the poor; expanding the earned income tax credit and child credit; affordable housing programs; and experimental programs that are showing promise such as the Harlem Children's Zone. The NASW (2018) policy position on economic justice follows:

> NASW has been a champion of economic justice and equity since its inception. The social work profession was founded on the notion that those living in poverty are often politically marginalized and in need of advocates to help mitigate their

plight. We reject any suggestions that the United States cannot achieve economic reforms that lead to economic justice and end economic disparities based on race, ethnicity, and gender. Priorities include promoting just policies that build a universal system of support, promote financial security, and provide an adequate safety net for those in need

(pp. 84, 87)

The Welfare of Children

Chapter 9 outlined the many challenges facing children and youth in this country. The NASW (2018) recommends that the United States ratify the UN Convention on the Rights of the Child. However, it is a little known fact that children get the short end of the stick when it comes to federal spending. The bulk of U.S. federal spending goes to defense, Social Security, and Medicare. Children are not a budget priority despite decades of solid research showing the importance of investing in children ages 0 to 5 years, because these are critical years for brain development. According to a 2016 report from the Urban Institute, per capita spending on the elderly is significantly higher than per capita spending on children. In 2015, the federal government spent $6 on the elderly for every $1 spent on children (Edelstein et al., 2016). According to Edelstein and colleagues (2016):

> The combined spending of federal, state, and local governments on the elderly ($29,308 per capita) was 2.3 times their combined spending on children ($12,816 per capita) in 2013. Health care expenses are a significant portion of public expenditures on the elderly—roughly $11,800 per person, compared to about $1,900 per child in 2013—but per capita spending on the elderly remains considerably higher than per capita spending on children even when health spending is excluded.

(p. 18)

In 2015, adults over age 65 were 14.9% of the population while children came in at 24.2%. Spending on older adults is higher due to the expensive social programs that are devoted to serving them, such as Social Security and Medicare, and because of the growing aging population. However, children are just as vulnerable as older adults and require strong social programs to ensure that their developmental, health, and mental health needs are addressed, particularly in the first five years of life when their brains are developing. They also need to be protected from abuse, neglect, and exploitation.

The NASW (2018) recommends that a BSW degree should be the minimum requirement for staff in child protective services and that sexual abuse and physical abuse prevention programs should be mandated in all schools from kindergarten to high school. Unfortunately, states and the federal government underspend on child protection, making a tough job for child protection caseworkers even harder. It is hard to know whether this spending imbalance is due to societal attitudes that devalue children, the fact that senior citizens are a strong and mobilized voting bloc, or both.

Advocacy for Environmental Justice

Some social work academics, activists, and leaders have been calling on the social work profession to get more involved in issues of **environmental justice and sustainability**. Climate change has been a huge political issue in recent years, but many social workers have viewed it as outside of the social work profession's scope and expertise. However, the NASW (2018) states in their policy statement on environmental policy, "Social work, with its focus on political advocacy, can be an important force in addressing environmental issues. Social workers can engage in strategizing to organize and confront environmental justice through grassroots organizing, political action, and collaboration with communities, including indigenous leaders" (pp. 115–116). Some argue that environment degradation (e.g., contamination of our water, land, and soil with chemicals and toxic waste) is a social justice issue because it disproportionately affects low-income and minority communities. For example, sewage treatment plants, landfills, and hazardous waste sites are typically located in areas where poor people live. Social workers need to be at the forefront and working in collaboration with others on issues of **environmental injustice** and **environmental racism**. According to an expert on environmental justice, Dr. Robert Bullard (2016), from Texas Southern University:

> We reviewed 80 years of disaster responses, from the 1927 Mississippi River flood to Hurricane Katrina in 2005 and the BP oil spill in 2010. What we found was that government is disproportionately slower to respond to disasters when communities of color are involved. Unequal protection is a reality. The right to clean air, clean water and safe places for kids to play is something that affluent communities take for granted. But many low-income and minority communities don't get parks, or street lights, or housing code enforcement, or safe drinking water. The cumulative environmental stresses in these neighborhoods create a toxic stew. And then government agencies don't respond when people complain. The government's nonresponse to Flint's water crisis is on the scale of the federal nonresponse to Hurricane Katrina.

Reforming Government So That It Operates in the Interest of the People

Many Americans choose not to get involved in politics because they believe it is an unfair system that only works in the interests of political elites. A number of organizations are working to reform the political process in the United States in order to remove corruption and the influence of powerful special interests and to help create a system of government that protects the interests of average Americans. Having people disillusioned, uninformed, and disengaged works well for those in power. If our systems of government were more fair and accessible to average Americans, we would likely see more people involved in the affairs of their community and government at all levels, which is a sign of a healthy democracy. In 2021, one of the biggest news stories was the restrictive voting law passed by the state legislature in the state of Georgia. Conservative lawmakers there argued that they were trying to reduce voter fraud and protect the integrity of elections. Democrats, on the other hand, argued that there is no evidence of widespread voter fraud and that this was a political strategy to make it harder for low-income and communities of color to vote. Individuals and organizations are working to reform our government in the following areas, and anyone can join these efforts:

- Abolishing the Electoral College and electing the president by national popular vote (visit www.nationalpopularvote.com);
- Moving to a system of publicly financed campaigns in order to get big money out of politics and curtail the influence of lobbyists and special interests (visit www.commoncause.org);
- Instituting term limits for those who serve in the U.S. Congress so that those in Congress are less motivated by getting reelected and ending the practice of career politicians who are next to impossible to unseat (visit termlimits.com);
- Getting rid of the filibuster rule in the U.S. Senate that requires 60 votes to end debate and move to a vote (on some legislation) instead of a simple majority vote;
- Having more political parties to end the dominance of the two-party system;
- Eliminating voter suppression and barriers to voting and allowing citizens to vote by mail (visit www.commoncause.org and www.fairfight.com);
- Electing people to office from historically underrepresented groups (women, racial/ethnic minorities, younger people, and LGBTQ individuals) (visit the websites for Emily's List; LGBTQ Victory Fund; New American Leaders Project; Latino Victory; Higher Heights; Collective PAC; APAICS);
- Addressing the problem of gerrymandering where one political party is able to redraw the boundaries of districts to ensure that their party will win;
- Improving media coverage of politics to ensure fair and truthful journalism;
- Increasing civic engagement knowledge and skills of citizens, particularly for those who tend to be less active politically.

Advocacy for the Social Work Profession

Most policy change efforts by social workers address a wide variety of social problems that are experienced by the populations they serve. Most of the time, these legislative efforts focus on issues of social and economic justice, and social workers view their role as advocating for children, aging adults, those suffering from mental disorders, groups facing discrimination, and families living below the poverty line, just to provide a few examples. Indeed the bulk of this book is devoted to these issues.

However, there are times when the focus of the policy change effort is the social work profession itself, and social workers are in the position of advocating for themselves. Workforce issues, such as **the need to recruit and retain high-quality social workers**, are a continuing challenge faced by the social work profession. Other helping professions have been successful in increasing the status of their profession by unionizing and educating lawmakers about the challenges they face and the value of the services they provide. For example, nurses have made great strides in raising awareness about the crisis the profession is facing in terms of having a shortage of nurses in the United States in order to meet the need. Social workers are facing this same type of crisis in the coming years, yet the public is largely unaware. One interesting development is the **Congressional Social Work Caucus** that was created in the 111th Congress by social workers and Congressman Ed Towns (D-NY), who has a master's degree in social work. The purpose of the caucus is to educate lawmakers on Capitol Hill about issues of importance to the social work profession (see The Congressional Social Work Congress).

The Congressional Social Work Congress

In March 2011, the Congressional Social Work Congress (CSWC) was launched. The CSWC is made up of members of Congress who either (1) are social workers, or (2) support the social work profession. It is chaired by Congresswoman Barbara Lee (D-CA), who is a professional social worker. As of July 2018, there were approximately 60 members in the Congress.

Mission statement: The Congressional Social Work Caucus was launched on March 15, 2011. It was founded by Congressman Edolphus Towns, representative of New York's 10 District. The purpose of the CSWC is to create a platform on the Hill representing the interests of over 600,000 social workers throughout the United States who positively impact the lives of the elderly, the disadvantaged, children, veterans, or other individuals in need of guidance and direction in their lives. Every day social workers help people find solutions to poverty, divorce, addiction, emotional distress, and other psychological and social issues, yet they often face a host of workforce challenges such as low salaries, high educational debt, and safety concerns. The Congressional Social Work Caucus will put a spotlight on the dedicated work of social workers in child welfare agencies, health clinics and outpatient healthcare settings, mental health clinics, schools, government agencies, social service agencies, private practice, criminal justice environments, and many more arenas in the public and private sectors.

Source: https://www.crispinc.org/social-work-caucus/

However, when social workers focus too much on efforts to promote or protect the profession, they can be criticized for serving their own interests at the expense of their clients. Others argue, however, that the profession cannot effectively serve its clients if it fails to recruit and retain social workers because they are overburdened by student loan debt and/ or leave the profession due to poor working conditions and poor compensation. They point to other professions, such as teaching and nursing, that have done a much better job of advocating for better salaries and working conditions. This has enabled them to recruit more attractive candidates to their fields. After all, a highly trained and highly qualified workforce is better for service recipients. But this debate raises an important question: When state and federal resources for social welfare programs are scarce, should they fight for funding that supports the social work workforce? Or, does this take away from their primary mission of service to others?

What Are the Biggest Problems Facing the Social Work Profession?

The heart of the problem for the social work profession centers on the notion that social workers provide an important and necessary role in our society, and there is a large demand for their service, yet there are barriers that make social work a challenging career choice for many people. Because of low starting salaries, high levels of student loan debt, and difficult working conditions (e.g., unreasonably high workloads), it can be challenging to recruit and retain talented, highly qualified people to the field of social work.

Low Compensation and High Levels of Student Loan Debt: The Need for Student Loan Forgiveness

According to the Bureau of Labor Statistics (n.d.), the employment of social workers is expected to increase by 13% from 2019 to 2029, which is faster than average for all occupations. Employment of child, family, and school social workers is expected to grow by 12%; mental health and substance abuse social workers by 17%; and healthcare social workers by 14%. Much of this demand is fueled by the growing aging population. However, due to the barriers described in this chapter that make it difficult for people to enter the field of social work, and because retiring social workers need to be replaced, the NASW is projecting a shortage of social work professionals to meet the need for social work services in the coming years.

Despite this demand for their services, many students do not consider a career in social work due to low starting salaries and fears that they will be unable to pay off their student loans.

The Council on Social Work Education (CSWE) reports that in 2019, 73% of BSW graduates and 76% of MSW graduates had student loan debt. The average loan debt was $28,323 for BSW gradates and $46,951 for MSW graduates (CSWE, 2020). The median pay for social workers in 2019, according to the Bureau of Labor Statistics (n.d.), was $50,470 a year. The NASW advocates for social workers to receive adequate pay and reimbursement that is comparable to other similar helping professions.

The NASW has made **student loan forgiveness** one of their main advocacy priorities due to the challenges that social workers face in paying off their student loans. The argument is an easy one to make because social workers have chosen a career of service that provides tangible benefits to society, yet lawmakers have been slow to vote for a solution that would represent significant change for social workers. There are a couple of loan forgiveness programs in existence (e.g., Public Service Loan Forgiveness Program, National Health Service Corps Loan Repayment Program), but the scope of these programs is limited. The NASW is asking federal lawmakers to provide dedicated funding to social workers for loan forgiveness.

Title Protection for Social Workers

Many states have passed legislation that protects the title of "social worker" to help ensure that consumers are being treated by someone who is qualified, has the appropriate degree and training, and must abide by an ethical code. Social workers get miffed when a child protection caseworker is taken to task in the media and referred to as a "social worker," when in reality they do not have a degree in social work (e.g., they are a child protection caseworker with a degree in sociology). Many journalists and members of the general public do not understand that just because someone is working in social services, does not mean that he or she is a social worker. Unfortunately, some workplaces refer to their employees as "social workers" when in reality they do not have a bachelors or master's degree in social work. Title protection laws make it illegal for anyone to use the title of professional social worker unless they have a degree in social work.

Many social workers feel this is an important issue because, in the same way that medical professionals must have medical training and be licensed by the state, social workers in the United States need to be valued and recognized for their social work education and training. Social workers graduate from social work programs that are accredited by the Council on Social Work Education and have attained competencies in how to carry out a planned change process, research methods, human behavior in the social environment, social welfare policy and practice, cultural competency, and ethics, just to name a few. Title protection laws also protect consumers since they have the right to know whether the professional treating them is an actual social worker with the requisite degree and training.

Safety Concerns for Social Workers

The NASW also includes the issue of safety for social workers as one of their advocacy efforts. According to NASW, some social workers work in settings where their safety can be at risk, and they believe that federal resources are needed to help social workers have the training and resources that they need to do their jobs safely. There have been cases of social workers who have been harmed, and even killed, as they were carrying out their job. The NASW is working to pass the **Protecting Social Workers and Health Professionals from Workplace Violence Act of 2019**, which will:

- Establish a Social Worker Safety Grant Program within the Department of Health and Human Services to fund State's efforts to improve safety measures for social workers.
- Allow these grants to be used to deploy safety equipment (such as security cameras and GPS locators), make facility improvements, implement safety training programs, and provide support services for professionals who have been victims of violence. The bill provides $10,000,000 per year, to be awarded over 5 years (NASW, n.d.)

Overview of the Social Work Reinvestment Act (SWRA)

The National Association of Social Workers (NASW) is the organization most devoted to advocating for social workers in the U.S. For many years, NASW has been lobbying for passage of the **Social Work Reinvestment Act**, a federal piece of legislation that is asking the U.S. Congress to "invest" in social work and recognize the value of the profession in serving those in society who are most vulnerable. The Social Work Reinvestment Act is legislation that addresses the social work profession's workforce challenges for the 713,000 social workers in the United States by securing federal and state investments to support recruitment, retention, recognition, and adequate reimbursement of professional social workers. In order to ensure that the social work profession can be effective, social workers need to be compensated fairly, have reasonable workloads, and work in programs with adequate resources.

The Social Work Reinvestment Act is named after two pioneers of social justice, Dorothy I. Height and Whitney M. Young Jr., who were both active leaders in the civil rights movement in the United States. The act was introduced once again in the 116th Congress by Congresswoman Barbara Lee (D-CA), who is also a social worker. The language of the bill was crafted with input from various social work organizations, such as NASW and the CSWE. The Social Work Reinvestment Act asks the federal government to "invest" in the profession of social work and to address the impending shortage of social workers in the coming years. Below is the bill summary (Congress.Gov, n.d.):

> This bill directs the Department of Health and Human Services (HHS) to (1) establish the Social Work Reinvestment Commission to advise on social work policy issues, (2) award specified grants to support social work activities, and (3) develop public service announcements to promote the social work profession.
>
> HHS shall award grants to (1) certain entities that employ social workers to carry out workplace improvement programs to address concerns related to the social work profession; (2) institutions of higher education to support social work students and faculty; (3) eligible state or local government entities or nonprofits to test and replicate effective social work interventions; and (4) postdoctoral researchers in social work.

The Social Work Reinvestment Act is being championed by members of the U.S. Congress who are social workers. NASW has been working to get the Social Work Reinvestment Act passed into law by lobbying federal lawmakers, providing information on the act on their website and via social media, testifying at legislative hearings, and sending action alerts to NASW members asking social workers to contact their legislators to ask them to support this legislation. It can be an effective strategy, for example, for social workers to contact their legislator (in writing, by phone, or in person) to tell their personal story of how challenging it is to work as a social worker with a low salary while trying to pay off high levels of student loan debt.

All Social Work Is Political

The first chapter of this book proposed the question, "Is all social work political?" This question is certainly up for debate, but the author of this book would argue in the affirmative. It is almost impossible to identify any realm of social work practice that is not impacted by politics and the legislative process. For example, social workers in most states must abide by laws that require them to be licensed by the state they work in and to get continued training, many work in organizations that receive government funding, and most social workers are impacted by various laws and regulations that affect how they carry out their practice with individuals, families, and communities.

Maryann Mahaffey (1925–2006) is recognized by NASW as a "social work pioneer." She had a distinguished career as a social worker that included working as a social work professor at Wayne State University; publishing a book titled *Practical Politics: Social Work and Political Responsibility*; and serving as the first female president of NASW and as a member of the Detroit City Council for 31 years, including 11 years as its president. She was passionate about social workers being involved in the political process, and the following quote is from her book that was published in 1981:

> A social worker brings to the political process something that's unique, that no one else has. Anyone else can learn how to play games, you know power games. Anybody else can learn to negotiate. Anybody can learn to do the power manipulations. Those are techniques and skills that can be learned fairly easy. What the social worker brings is a value system that, if implemented, along with the skills, makes the difference.
>
> *(cited in Haynes and Mickelson, 2006, p. 6)*

One of the strengths of social work is the broadness of the profession, yet this strength can also be a weakness because it can be quite challenging to unify social workers who work in silos in diverse fields of social work practice (e.g., health care, mental health, child welfare, school social work, etc.). The critical challenge for social workers is to figure out how to unite in order to become a visible and strong political force in the U.S. and a powerful voice for social and economic justice.

REFERENCES

Bullard, R. D. (2016). Flint's water crisis is a blatant example of environmental injustice. The Conversation. Retrieved from https://theconversation.com/flints-water-crisis-is-a-blatant-example-of-environmental-injustice-53553

Bureau of Labor Statistics, U.S. Department of Labor (n.d.). *Occupational outlook handbook*. Retrieved from https://www.bls.gov/ooh/community-and-social-service/social-workers.htm

Congress.gov. (n.d.). H.R.1289—Dorothy I. Height and Whitney M. Young, Jr., Social Work Reinvestment Act. Retrieved from https://www.congress.gov/bill/116th-congress/house-bill/1532?q=%7B%-22search%22%3A%5B%22social+work+reinvestment+act%22%5D%7D&s=2&r=1

Council on Social Work Education. (2020). 2019 statistics on social work education in the United States. Retrieved from https://cswe.org/getattachment/Research-Statistics/2019-Annual-Statistics-on-Social-Work-Education-in-the-United-States-Final-(1).pdf.aspx

Edelstein, S., Hahn, H., Isaacs, J., Steele, E., & Steuerle, C. E. (2016). Kids' share 2016: Federal expenditures on children through 2015 and future projections. Retrieved from https://firstfocus.org/wp-content/uploads/2016/10/Kids-Share-2016.pdf

Federal Reserve. (2017). Changes in U.S. family finances from 2013 to 2016: Evidence from the Survey of Consumer Finances. Retrieved from https://www.federalreserve.gov/publications/files/scf17.pdf

Haynes, K. S. & Mickelson, J. S. (2006). *Affecting Change: Social workers in the political arena* (6th ed.). Boston: Pearson.

Klar, M., & Kasser, T. (2009). Some Benefits of Being an Activist: Measuring Activism and Its Role in Psychological Well-Being. *Political Psychology*, 30(5), 755–777.

Mahaffey, M. (1981). *Practical politics: Social work and political responsibility*. Washington, D.C.: NASW Press.

Mishel, L. & Scheider, J. (2017). CEO pay remains high relative to the pay of typical workers and high-wage earners. Economic Policy Institute. Retrieved from https://www.epi.org/files/pdf/130354.pdf

National Association of Social Workers. (2018). *Social work speaks* (11th ed.). Washington, D.C.: NASW Press.

National Association of Social Workers (July 14, 2020a). NASW seeks to dismantle racist policing. Retrieved from https://www.socialworkers.org/News/News-Releases/ID/2205/NASW-Seeks-to-Dismantle-Racist-Policing

National Association of Social Workers (August 21, 2020b). Social workers must help dismantle systems of oppression and fight racism within social work profession. Retrieved from https://www.socialworkers.org/News/News-Releases/ID/2219/Social-Workers-Must-Help-Dismantle-Systems-of-Oppression-and-Fight-Racism-Within-Social-Work-Profession

National Association of Social Workers. (n.d.). Social worker safety. Retrieved from https://www.socialworkers.org/Advocacy/Policy-Issues/Social-Worker-Safety

Petre, R. (2010). Smile, you're an activist! In These Times. Retrieved from http://www.inthesetimes.com/article/5955/smile_youre_an_activist

U.S. Census Bureau. (2020). Income and poverty in the United States: 2019. Retrieved from https://www.census.gov/library/publications/2020/demo/p60-270.html#:~:text=The%20official%20poverty%20rate%20in,and%20Table%20B%2D5)

Index

Printed in the USA
CPSIA information can be obtained
at www.ICGtesting.com
LVHW081427120124
768789LV00001B/16